NEVER COMING
TO A THEATER NEAR YOU

NEVER COMING
TO A THEATER NEAR YOU

A

CELEBRATION

OF A

CERTAIN

KIND

OF MOVIE

KENNETH TURAN

PublicAffairs
New York

Published in the United States by PublicAffairs™,
a member of the Perseus Books Group.

Book design by Jane Raese
Text set in Bulmer

Library of Congress Cataloging-in-Publication Data
Turan, Kenneth.
Never coming to a theater near you: a celebration of a certain kind of movie /
Kenneth Turan.—1st ed.
p. cm.
Includes indexes.
ISBN 1-58648-231-9
1. Motion pictures—Reviews. I. Title
PN1995.T788   2004
791.43'75—dc22
2004050512

3 5 7 9 10 8 6 4 2

To those who watch and dream,
and to B, always

CONTENTS

CONTENTS

2

FOREIGN LANGUAGE FILMS

CONTENTS

3

DOCUMENTARIES

CONTENTS

4
CLASSICS

INTRODUCTION

IN WAYS THAT MIGHT NOT BE SUSPECTED, being a film critic can be like having a career in the legendary sewers of Paris. This has little to do with working conditions or even the quality of the product to be dealt with, though at moments of weakness I'm tempted to think it does. Rather, it's that with both occupations, civilians invariably have a line of questions about exactly what the job is like.

A key part of these conversations, whether they're with friends or strangers, is the quest for recommendations about what's worth seeing. Unless you're a teenager, a night at the movies is a not inconsiderable investment of time, money, and psychic energy, and no one wants to waste any of that on motion picture territory best left unexplored.

Over the dozen years I've been a critic at the *Los Angeles Times,* I've noticed an increasing disconnect between the films I recommend person-to-person because they've meant the most to me and the ones most people have managed to see. The pressures to experience the blockbusters of the moment are too great and the time that smaller films remain on screens is so finite (the good really do die young in this business) that most people, even with the best intentions, find that the production they really meant to go to is no longer in theaters by the time they carve out the leisure to see it.

In theory, the wide reach of videos and DVDs makes it possible for viewers to catch up on the films they've missed, but in practical terms, faced with an intimidating vastness of rental choices, most people blank out on the names of features they've been meaning to see and reach for whatever's handiest. Which is where this book is meant to come in.

Just as every working critic took a different path to his or her job, every critic has a different reason for wanting to do it. For me, helping viewers to duplicate the great and wonderful highs I've experienced in front of a screen and avoid the excruciating lows, being, so to speak, a guide for the perplexed, has always been a key motivation.

Just as the apostles wanted to spread the gospel, literally the "good news" about Jesus, I want to spread the gospel about the films that have meant the most to me.

I've envisioned this book as a resource for anyone wishing to discover—or rediscover—films. Use it to first read up on and then catch up on the great but less-than-omnipresent films that you never got around to seeing, or, as the title indicates, that never quite made it to a theater near you in the first place. So, though I've valued major Hollywood films such as *L.A. Confidential* and *Lord of the Rings,* those reviews aren't here because most people don't need to be reminded of their existence.

Since God doesn't tell me (or likely anyone else) what a good film is, this selection is a reflection of my taste, of what I've found especially satisfying over the past decade and more. I hope and believe it represents the kind of sophisticated, mature, always entertaining films people tell me they are hungering for and really value.

This knowledge has not been easy to come by. The 150 or so revised and updated reviews included here represent something like 5 percent of my viewing life, and anyone who thinks that only the studios make bad films has not endured the wave after wave of woebegone independent and foreign language productions it is a critic's lot to experience and pass judgment on.

Yet despite all that unsatisfactory time and effort, I have to say that the opportunity to see the films I've chosen to include here has made my professional life richly rewarding and well worthwhile. These are motion pictures I likely would not have experienced—and possibly not even have heard of—if reviewing weren't my job, and there isn't one of them I wouldn't rush to see again in a New York minute. For a critic, that's saying a lot.

Finally, to paraphrase Raymond Chandler, if there were more films like these, the world would be a better place to live in, and yet not too dull to be worth living in. Individually and en masse, these are the films that have enriched my life beyond measure. With any kind of luck, they will enrich yours as well.

part one

ENGLISH LANGUAGE FILMS

Introduction

It may not be immediately visible, but the benign shadow of the American independent film movement looms over this section like the cinematic version of Caspar the Friendly Ghost.

That's not apparent at first because close to half of these films are not from the United States at all. More than twenty come from either Great Britain or Ireland, another bunch began in Australia and New Zealand, and there is even one motion picture, the singular *Thirty Two Short Films about Glenn Gould,* that managed to make it in from Canada.

More than that, unexpected though it may be from a book on films that got away, more than a few of these motion pictures were originally released by a Hollywood studio, albeit a studio that had no idea how to sell what it found on its hands. That's why the most powerful marketing force in the world was no help when it came to iconoclastic works such as *Devil in a Blue Dress, Election, The Iron Giant, Out of Sight,* and *Wonder Boys.*

Even the independent films I've chosen don't necessarily fit into preconceived categories. There are familiar directors in unfamiliar guises (John Sayles as children's filmmaker with *The Secret of Roan Inish*) and celebrated actors in unexpected roles (Nicole Kidman as a Russian mail-order bride in *Birthday Girl*). There are films everyone liked (*Whale Rider, You Can Count on Me*) and films that seemed to work only for me (*Next Stop Wonderland, A Soldier's Daughter Never Cries*).

Most poignant of all is that the relevance of some films has only increased since they were released. What *Last Resort* said about refugees, *My Son the Fanatic* about Islamic fundamentalism, *Safe* about environmental dangers, and *Wag the Dog* about war conducted for political reasons seems almost frighteningly to the point today.

Yet no matter where they came from or who released them, all of the films in this section are imbued with the spirit of the American independent movement, made in the belief that being smart, thoughtful, and adult isn't necessarily a barrier to reaching an audience.

Although film journalists and critics like to periodically moan that the independent world isn't all it could be, that having companies such as Miramax and New Line owned by major studios (in this case, Disney and Time Warner, respectively) has fatally compromised the kinds of films out there, the reality is that this is a glass much more half full than half empty.

Absent a thriving independent film movement, many of the exceptional films presented in this section, whether British, Canadian, Australian, or American in origin, would not have been made, or, if made, may not have found a way into distribution. Yes, things could no doubt be better, but they could also be a great deal worse. And a world without these marvelous films is not one any of us wants to contemplate. Least of all me.

The Adventures of Priscilla, Queen of the Desert
1994

"Drag is the Drug," the posters at Cannes promoting *The Adventures of Priscilla, Queen of the Desert* announced, not without reason. The comic pizzazz and bawdy dazzle of this film's vision of gaudy drag performers trekking across the Australian outback certainly has a boisterous, addictive way about it.

But like any self-respecting drug, *Priscilla* comes with its own built-in hangover. Sharing screen space with the film's raunchy humor and outrageous musical numbers is a strain of conventional sentimentality that would not be inappropriate on the Disney Channel. It doesn't ruin the fun, but it certainly takes the edge off it.

One of the reasons writer-director Stephan Elliott has given for making *Priscilla* was a desire to bring back the vintage Hollywood musical, and, like the old MGM classics, this film is definitely at its best when its trio of actors are performing with a lip-synced song in their hearts.

Whether it's Mitzi (Hugo Weaving) opening the movie with a torchy rendition of "I've Been to Paradise but I've Never Been to Me" or Felicia (Guy Pearce) belting out a Verdi aria in a silver lamé gown on top of a moving bus, or the two of them plus Bernadette (Terence Stamp) launching into synchronized versions of "I Will Survive," "Shake Your Groove Thing," or almost anything by ABBA, all in outfits that beggar description, the musical numbers are surefire and irresistible.

While Mitzi and Felicia are more conventional (if that is the right word) drag queens who also answer to the names Tick and Adam, respectively, Bernadette is a hormone-ingesting transsexual who goes ballistic whenever her former given name, Ralph, crosses anyone's lips.

Despite having made a career out of being what Elliott calls "a heterosexual icon," Stamp is the movie's major surprise, gracefully convincing as Bernadette, a woman no longer trapped in a man's body. Elegant and dignified with enough hauteur for an entire royal family, the resilient Bernadette is a creature of haunted and exquisite gestures, and Stamp doesn't allow you to feel that even the smallest of them is false.

Though this performance is *Priscilla*'s most fully realized, the other two leads are also expertly done, partly because Elliott has written them with a well-adjusted liveliness and specificity that gives the actors a good deal to work with.

Tick is the most solid and stable of the three, an established performer and the catalyst for the trip as well. (Weaving, incidentally, was memorable in a completely different role as the angry blind photographer in Jocelyn Moorhouse's *Proof*.)

Unknown to his pals, Tick was married before he became a fixture of Sydney's gay scene, and unexpectedly he gets a phone call from his ex, who manages a resort in middle-of-nowhere Alice Springs and is desperate for entertainers. Can he make the trip, and, more important, dare he tell his friends who asked him to perform?

Bernadette, grieving for a recently dead husband, is persuaded to come along for a change of scene. Adam, an amusingly malicious party animal, is always up for something new and even produces the money for the group's bus, christened Priscilla. Besides, he confesses, he's always wanted to travel to the outback and "climb Kings Canyon as a queen," decked out in a Gautier gown, heels, and a tiara.

The trio's alcohol-drenched trip through the desert (which caused French critics to call the film *Florence d'Arabie*) takes up most of *Priscilla*. The best part of that is the ribald interaction among the three performers, all of whom, especially "cesspool mouth" Adam, have rude and dangerous tongues that can flay the flesh off the unwary.

Less unsettling, in fact regrettably predictable, are most of the adventures that these three run into on their pilgrimage. Not surprisingly, their appearance completely flummoxes the uncomprehending and often angry straight people at each of their stops, and the homophobic scrapes that result have a tendency to feel contrived.

And with the exception of auto mechanic Bob (veteran all-purpose Australian actor Bill Hunter), those met on the road who are not hostile, such as Tick's wife, are as unconvincingly cheerful and saccharine as Adam is blistering. Their glibness and compassion make an odd contrast with the bitchy talk on the bus, but, to its credit, whenever things get too treacly, *Priscilla* knows enough to break out those frocks and get the show in gear. That is entertainment for sure.

*Both Guy Pearce (*L.A. Confidential*) and Hugo Weaving (*The Matrix trilogy*) may have gone on to bigger budget films, but they've never been more fun on screen than they are here.*

Bhaji on the Beach
1994

Bhaji on the Beach is one of those small but remarkable pictures that smiles at the supposed difficulties of moviemaking. Warm and charming while sacrificing neither its integrity nor its point of view, it covers considerable personal and political territory without overreaching or condescending. And it never forgets to have fun.

The debut film of director and co–story writer Gurinder Chadha, apparently the first Indian woman living in Britain to direct a film in that country, *Bhaji* is further evidence that Britain's supposedly moribund film industry is turning into cinema's most celebrated invalid. Though economic difficulties have seriously curtailed output, those British films that do get made are invariably models of strength and compassion.

The seriocomic story of a day trip to the seaside resort of Blackpool by several generations of women, *Bhaji* has points in common with work by other socially conscious British directors, particularly the pioneering Ken Loach, whom Chadha views as a mentor, and Mike Leigh, from whom she has borrowed ideas on using extensive rehearsals to define character.

Yet as indicated by the *bhaji* of the title, an only-in-England snack derived from a traditional Indian dish, this is very much its own film, flavored by the distinctive sensibility of the Indian community that it depicts.

Although *Bhaji*'s key protagonists may sound just like the English they live among, they are separated from them not only by skin color but also by the difficulties of being a transitional generation, with one foot in the clannish, fearful society of their immigrant parents and the other in the modern Western world in which their futures will take place.

Bhaji begins in Birmingham, an industrial city in the Midlands, and its almost too-rapid introduction of characters gives audiences a sense of the crowded, hectic conditions of the Indian community there. Married children still live with their parents, and the whole business is overseen by a network of vaguely related, invariably censorious older women known collectively (as they were in the similarly themed *The Joy Luck Club*) as "aunties."

But by the time a bus holding a cross-section of women sets out for a day of "female fun" at Blackpool under the tutelage of the feminist Simi (Shaheen Khan), two of the passengers, each with her own romantic catastrophe, have come into focus as the film's parallel protagonists.

Ginder (Kim Vithana) has precipitated a crisis in the close-knit community by leaving her husband, Ranjit (Jimmi Harkishin), and moving into a women's shelter with her young son. And Hashida

(Sarita Khajuria), a college graduate about to enter medical school, knows she will cause even more of a sensation if word gets out that (a) she is pregnant though unmarried and (b) the father, Oliver, is a young black man of Caribbean descent (Mo Sesay).

When the bus arrives at Blackpool, the city itself, with its gaudy, Coney Islandish air of down-at-the-heels frivolity, takes its place as a character in the film. A setting like this by definition encourages a loosening of bonds, allowing everyone from teenage sisters Ladhu and Madhu to decorous Auntie Asha (Lalita Ahmed) to engage in amusing flirtations. And with both Ranjit and Oliver headed toward Blackpool to try to resolve their difficulties, more serious events are likely to occur as well.

It is this ability to move with grace and ease between comedy and drama that is *Bhaji*'s particular accomplishment. For though Meera Syal's script deals with provocative issues, from racism to the place of women in society and the often injurious power of custom and tradition, both she and director Chadha employ a fluid touch that allows points to be made with welcome subtlety.

Critical to this accomplishment is the fondness and empathy for its characters that marks the film's every scene. The chance to put situations close to their own experience onto the screen must have meant a great deal to everyone involved, and the sense of vivid life that results has made *Bhaji on the Beach* into a film that manages to be as pleasant as it is pointed.

Nearly a decade later, filmmaker Chadha returned to the same Anglo-Indian milieu and turned Bend It Like Beckham *into a major international success.*

Birthday Girl
2002

Birthday Girl is something rather different, both for star Nicole Kidman and for us. It's an adventurous, unsettling, heedlessly implausible film, equal parts comedy, romance, excitement, and raw emotion. In a fierce black farce, *Birthday Girl*'s remixing of traditional genre elements tells you from frame one that a distinctive film sensibility is at work.

That sensibility belongs to British director Jez Butterworth, who wrote the film with brother Tom and recruited brother Steve to work as producer. Jez also wrote his directing debut, *Mojo* (1997), which won numerous British theater awards as a play, and he is nothing if not fearless in his casting. For Nadia, a Vampirella-in-spiked-boots Russian mail-order bride, Butterworth went with Australian Kidman. And he picked two young stalwarts of the French film industry, actor Vincent Cassel and actor-director Mathieu Kassovitz, for the film's other pair of Russian characters. It's a tribute to how intriguing all three performers found the project that everyone learned to speak the language convincingly enough to get their parts.

Despite this international flavor, *Birthday Girl* is set in the very English Hertfordshire town of St. Albans, where young John Buckingham (Ben Chaplin of *The Truth about Cats and Dogs*) works long and tedious hours as a bank teller. A sad-eyed, timid soul whose biggest problem is an ant infestation in his tidy home, John despairs of finding a mate in the neighborhood. So, in an act he considers "quite brave," he sends a video off to the endless steppes of Russia in search of a mail-order bride. "Someone you can really talk to" is what he's looking for. After all, "communication is the key."

When dark-haired Nadia shows up at the local airport, she is definitely not what John bargained for. Resembling a man-eating spiderwoman and not speaking a word of English, Nadia dresses a bit like a hooker and considers the Russian-English dictionary John helpfully provides as useful only for squashing those wayward ants.

Terrified of what he's gotten into, John tries to return Nadia like an unsatisfactory Fortnum & Mason's fruitcake. That proves tricky, especially after Nadia discovers and caters to his kinky sexual preferences. Alternately frightened, bewildered, and delighted, John can't decide if he's fallen in love or just found a flesh-and-blood sex toy. And that's just the start of his confusion.

When a besotted John plans a birthday party for Nadia, who should show up—and ask to stay a while—but her long-lost cousin

Yuri (Kassovitz) and Yuri's obstreperous new friend Alexei (Cassel). John, who doesn't want to share Nadia with anyone, is aghast at the invasion of two feckless louts whose motto is "Plans are for architects." "Boisterous" is a mild word for this pair's shenanigans, but the moment John finally feels he's had enough is the point at which *Birthday Girl's* plot really begins.

For, complex though it may sound, the above is merely a prelude to *Birthday Girl's* main action. That surprising series of constantly changing events moves so fast—and so enjoyably—that it's hard to notice or really care that it doesn't necessarily make a whole lot of sense.

Keeping us involved are the uniformly fine performances of this polyglot cast, starting with the convincingly Slavic and always entertaining Kidman, who has considerable fun as the strong-minded, intrepid woman no man can resist.

As for the men, Chaplin is adept as the buttoned-down, follow-the-rules functionary who's gotten himself into something wild, while Kassovitz and Cassel, friends in real life, add a believable touch of bizarre comradeship to their portrayal of stereotypical Russians on the make.

Though *Birthday Girl* is probably too unnerving and at times savage a relationship comedy to be a universal taste, its success on its own terms says a lot for the gifts of director-writer Butterworth. He guides us through the world of chaos and romantic confusion he's created as if it's the most natural place in the world. After a while, we actually believe it is.

Bloody Sunday
2002

Bloody Sunday was, as a character says, a moment of truth and a moment of shame. It was a savage blow delivered decades ago that the Northern Irish city of Derry has yet to put behind it. It caused a national furor so long-lived that the British government was recently forced to reopen its investigation into the event. And it has inspired first a classic song by U2 and now an exceptional film, a compelling, gut-clutching piece of advocacy cinema that carries you along in a torrent of emotion as it explores the awful complications of one terrifying day.

Bloody Sunday, which shared the Golden Bear award at the 2002 Berlin Film Festival, shows the power of real events dramatically conveyed. Made by writer-director Paul Greengrass out of a sense of communal outrage that has not gone away, this film never wavers, never loses its focus or its conviction. It takes us from dawn to dusk on January 30, 1972, a day in which British troops opened fire on unarmed civil rights marchers. Twenty-seven people were hit, at least five shot in the back; fourteen died.

Though he's made some dramatic features, Greengrass is best known for his ten years of doing documentaries for a top British TV series. Starting from the painstaking book *Eyewitness Bloody Sunday,* by Don Mullan, which led to the reopening of the case, and taking Gillo Pontecorvo's landmark *Battle of Algiers* as a model, Greengrass and his team (production designer John Paul Kelly, editor Clare Douglas, and director of photography Ivan Stasburg) have re-created the events of that day with such potency you feel you are there with the marchers, personally experiencing the awful inevitability of history gone terribly wrong.

Cinematographer Stasburg deserves special mention for the way his expressive, jittery, hand-held cinema verité camera work, lurking around corners and eavesdropping on conversations, creates the immediacy of newsreel footage. *Bloody Sunday* plays like it's the work of a documentary crew with great instincts and total access. It manages the difficult trick of conveying chaos while allowing us to recognize the patterns in the madness. It's both spontaneous enough to resemble reality captured on the fly and focused enough to be intensely dramatic.

Bloody Sunday's narrative device retains its potency throughout the film: Everything is structured around cutting back and forth between two of Northern Ireland's perennial antagonists, the beleaguered British Army and the province's restive Catholic minority.

The Catholics, ironically led by their Protestant member of Parliament Ivan Cooper (an outstanding James Nesbitt), are holding a press conference restating their determination, as believers in peaceful protest in the Martin Luther King Jr. tradition, to march the next day for civil rights and against the British practice of internment without trial.

At the same time, the British Army, personified by the ultra-confident Major General Robert Ford (the impeccable Tim Piggott-Smith), is holding a press conference of its own, reiterating that marches are banned and that people "organizing such events are liable to immediate arrest. Any responsibility for violence must rest on their shoulders."

Though both sides speak the same King's English, genuine communication is nonexistent. Fortified by internal logic and vocal supporters, the army and the Catholics are equally sure they are in the right, a situation that leads to a fatal end.

Bloody Sunday focuses on a quartet of protagonists, two on each side, representing a kind of "Upstairs/Downstairs" look at the day's events as they unfold. The youngest character is seventeen-year-old Gerry Donaghy (Declan Duddy, himself the nephew of a seventeen-year-old who died on that day). A Catholic boy just three weeks out of prison for throwing stones, he needs to stay out of trouble but doesn't want to miss the excitement. The youngest person on the other side is Soldier 027 (Mike Edwards), one of the hated, red beret–wearing British paratroopers who've been secretly brought into the city to snatch up the march ringleaders and stamp out stray hooligans. Authentically played by ex–military men, the paras perfectly convey cogs in a military machine whose programmed eagerness to get out and do what they were trained to do proves catastrophic.

The commander of British troops in the city, Brigadier Patrick MacLellan (Nicholas Farrell), also feels hamstrung, caught between local leaders who want peace and the obdurate General Ford, determined to teach the Catholics a lesson about exactly who is in charge.

Far from being a hothead, Ivan Cooper, the man in charge on the other side, feels exceptionally responsible for the marchers' safety. He even convinces his colleagues to change the route so as to lessen the chance of hostilities. "We just want a peaceful march," he says. "This is our day."

Yet what happened turned out to be beyond anyone's control. Emotions on both sides proved impossible to contain, and *Bloody Sunday* conveys to an almost unbearable extent the chaos that resulted.

Though it's clear where its sympathies lie, the film has been careful not to treat even the British as anything other than fallible individuals operating under hellacious pressures. Once positions hardened, tragedy was all but inevitable, and *Bloody Sunday* does the spirit of that awful day full and unforgettable justice.

Bottle Rocket
1996

Bottle Rocket has just what its characters lack: an exact sense of itself. A confident, eccentric debut about a trio of shambling and guileless friends who become the Candides of crime, *Rocket* feels particularly refreshing because it never compromises its delicate deadpan sensibility. Unlike most lost generation tales, this one never loses its way.

Bottle Rocket is especially exciting because it was put together by a core group of under-thirties, all of whom are new to features. Director Wes Anderson co-wrote the script with his friend Owen Wilson, who, in very much of a family affair, co-stars with his brothers Luke and Andrew.

Bottle Rocket is likewise a story of the limits and strengths of friendship and other relationships. It generously invites us into the dim-bulb world of a gang that can't think straight, where daft self-delusion can always find a home, and reality has only a limited appeal. A world whose always-in-earnest characters would be shocked to find out how funny they are.

Anthony (Luke Wilson) and Dignan (Owen Wilson) are best friends in their twenties who are searching for a handle on life, though searching may be too strenuous a word for how they go about things. Anthony, the quieter, more apologetic of the two, is a wistful romantic who's just been hospitalized for what is euphemistically called "exhaustion." His younger sister is hardly fooled. "You haven't worked a day in your life," she points out. "How can you be exhausted?"

Nominally more directed but in truth just as clueless is Dignan, who has as much juice as the Energizer bunny but no real idea of what to do with it. A high-intensity motormouth given to writing out plans for the next seventy-five years of his life, Dignan is desperate to be the head of a crack criminal team.

The only trouble is, the only people he has to work with are himself and his goofball friends. Terribly sincere and insecure, always concerned about whose feelings have been hurt, these earnest misfits are not the most promising material for a life outside the law.

Anthony and Dignan hook up with the equally disaffected Bob (Robert Musgrave), a timid soul abandoned by his wealthy parents and terrorized by his older brother, Futureman (Andrew Wilson). Bob gets to join the gang because he's the only one they know who has access to the essential getaway car.

The kind of team the word "misadventure" was invented for, the boys are to serious criminals what bottle rockets (cheap, unimpressive fireworks) are to real explosives. After pulling a few desultory jobs, they flee to an isolated motel to "lie low until the heat cools down." There they meet one of the only people in the film to have a true sense of direction.

Her name is Inez (*Like Water for Chocolate*'s Lumi Cavazos), and she's an immigrant from Paraguay who works as one of the motel's housekeepers. Though Inez speaks no English, Anthony instantly falls wholly in love ("It's just so unexpected," he marvels), to the point where he's helping Inez make beds while a threatened Dignan grouses about his friend's flabby commitment to a life of crime.

Also forceful is the man Dignan idolizes, the enigmatic, all-knowing Mr. Henry (James Caan). Head of a grounds-keeping organization called the Lawn Wranglers by day, Mr. Henry runs an erratic crew of career criminals by night, and being accepted as one of his cohorts is Dignan's ultimate fantasy.

With these two versions of purposeful reality to choose from, the question is not only which one Anthony will select, but whether he can bring himself to choose anything. "You're like paper," Inez accurately tells him through the good offices of a dishwasher/translator, "flying here and there."

Though *Bottle Rocket* is wryly amusing from beginning to end, the hard edges of the real world are never too far from its surface. And it is the particular grace of the film that though all its characters end up with something like what they're looking for, it's not exactly how they'd imagined it would be. And getting it doesn't prevent them from staying delusional to the end.

A cracked coming-of-age movie merged with a comic caper, the kind of flip side to *Heat* that the Italian *Big Deal on Madonna Street* was to *Rififi*, *Bottle Rocket* at times seems reminiscent of any number of things, including Donald Westlake's wonderful Dortmunder mystery novels *Bank Shot* and *The Hot Rock*.

But what is finally special about this film is its singularity, the ways in which it does not seem quite like anything else. Starting life as a short film that was accepted at Sundance, *Bottle Rocket* found a patron in executive producer James L. Brooks, who recognized in this gentle comedy of alienation and its cures a unique cinematic voice. Here's hoping there are others out there this fresh and this bright.

Both Wilson brothers went on to serious Hollywood careers, and Anderson's subsequent films, Rushmore *and* The Royal Tannenbaums, *made him a star of the independent world, but this remains their most completely satisfying work.*

The Commitments
1991

Try as you might, there's no resisting *The Commitments*. Yes, it's sporadically slick, surfacy, and manipulative (it is directed by Alan Parker, after all), but those are just words, and words don't have a chance against the supple power of some of the most melodic, euphoric music ever written, a sound so potent it could probably liberate the world.

We're talking, to borrow a phrase from the late Sam Cooke, about "that sweet soul music," an entire Stax-Volt and Atlantic catalog of classics such as "Try a Little Tenderness," "Mr. Pitiful," "Chain of Fools," and "Mustang Sally." Join those tunes to an energetic and photogenic group of youthful performers and a fantasy plot decked out to look like reality, and you have an astute formula for high-spir-ited, infectious entertainment that *The Commitments* executes with a brisk and breathless brio.

Taken from a novel by Roddy Doyle (who wrote the script along with veteran Brits Dick Clement and Ian La Frenais), *The Commit-ments* begins with a young man with a dream in a town without pity. Jimmy Rabbitte (Robert Arkins) is Dublin, Ireland, born and bred, and music has always been his passion. The first in the neighborhood to have a Frankie Goes to Hollywood tape, his musical credentials are impeccable, and two friends, tired of playing retreads at local celebra-tions, ask him to help them form a new band.

Jimmy agrees, but only a soul ensemble will do for him. "The Irish are the blacks of Europe, Dubliners the blacks of Ireland, and North-siders the blacks of Dublin," he explains to his dubious pals. "And we would be working class if there was any work." After rejecting names such as "A Flock of Budgies," "The Commitments" is settled on be-cause "all the good '60s bands were 'The Somethings.'"

Placing an ad in the newspaper stating his intentions, Jimmy, very much like the protagonist in *Seven Samurai,* goes about gathering his band of outsiders. He finds a lead singer in Deco (Andrew Strong), a tram conductor with an attitude prone to performing drunk at wed-dings. An aging "born-again" trumpet player, Joey (The Lips) Fagan (Johnny Murphy), shows up on a bike with credentials that run from Elvis to Otis and announces, "The Lord sent me." And three of the comeliest of local girls are recruited as Commitment-ettes, the backup group no soul aggregation can be without.

Interestingly enough, director Parker instigated a parallel search when it came to casting this film. Shrewdly intent on a non-star en-semble, he organized an open casting call in Dublin that drew more than 1,500. Finally, of the dozen principal roles, only two were filled by professional actors, the other ten by musicians (including sixteen-year-old Strong, with a raucous voice easily twice his age). And though many of them talk with fairly thick Irish accents, the context, if not always the exact words, is never less than clear.

A director known for bringing not the lightest of hands to some very heavy scenarios (*Midnight Express* and *Mississippi Burning,* for example), Parker has loosened up quite a bit here, not forcing the action as much as he did in the similar *Fame* and bringing a surprisingly loony touch to characters such as Jimmy's Elvis-obsessed father. No doubt complicit in this good humor is Parker's cast, whose first-timer enthusiasm fills the film with the kind of cheerful, pulsating vitality it is impossible to fake and wonderful to share in.

Not only lively, these kids can play, and one of the most captivating things about *The Commitments* is watching their inevitable jelling into a group to be reckoned with. Much of the film, in fact, comes to feel like MTV-with-a-plot, as Parker alternates video-like presentations of their songs with the inevitable tension, dissension, romance, and rivalries that no self-respecting movie band lacks.

Fortunately, each aspect reinforces the other: We care about the singers because of what we know of their lives, and the strength of their performances help us forgive the clichéd nature of their difficulties and the sketchiness of some of the characterizations.

For though the gritty locale of Dublin is a relatively unused setting for a film, the story *The Commitments* tells is hardly a new one, and one of the problems the film has is that its arc is awfully familiar. Also, Parker, ever the preacher, can't resist imbuing Jimmy with a Bible-seller's fervor about the benefits of soul music, which he imparts in brief, overly earnest pep talks.

But whenever *The Commitments* threatens to get bogged down in its own problems, Parker is savvy enough to pull it back with more of that invigorating music on the soundtrack. When that band starts to sing, the screen fills with genuine life, and that is too rare a commodity for anyone to second-guess for long.

Croupier
2000

Intense, hypnotic, assured, *Croupier* mesmerizes from its opening image of a roulette ball on the move. A taut journey inside the world of professional gambling, this enigmatic, beautifully made film crosses the traditions of film noir with a distinctly modern anomie, with results as ice cold and potent as the vodka its protagonist keeps in his freezer.

It's been nearly twenty years since *Croupier*'s director, Mike Hodges, made *Get Carter,* arguably the most influential of British gangster movies, described by one disapproving critic as "a bottle of neat gin swallowed before breakfast." And it's been almost twenty-five since writer Paul Mayersberg wrote the haunting, David Bowie–starring *The Man Who Fell to Earth.* Collaborating for the first time, Hodges and Mayersberg have fashioned an elegant jewel, hard and bright, where the austerity of Robert Bresson meets the laconic toughness of Raymond Chandler.

Our guide is Jack, a tyro writer with dyed blond hair compellingly played by Clive Owen. Jack's detached habit of referring to himself in the third person in *Croupier*'s extensive voice-over gives him a distant, uninvolved air, but don't confuse his coldness with complete amorality. Jack's lack of surface emotion masks passions he's had to bury because in his world, no moment of humanity or warmth goes unpunished.

Jack is no more than half in love with Marion (Gina McKee), the London policewoman turned store detective he lives with. "You're an enigma, you are," she says fondly, to which Jack accurately responds, in the voice-over only the audience hears, "Not an enigma, a contradiction." His unspoken credo is "Hang on tightly, let go lightly."

Jack is trying to be a writer, but the only editor he knows is not exactly encouraging: "Celebrity is what sells books," the man tells him. "We can always find someone to do the writing." So when Jack's estranged, amoral father calls and says he's lined up a job for his boy at London's Golden Lion casino, he's more receptive to the offer than he might have been.

Jack, as it turns out, has had enough casino experience in South Africa to make him wary of returning to the pit. But the lure of regular income persuades him to take his hair back to its original, more sepulchral, jet black and accept a job as croupier, the person who rakes in the chips and pays the winners on games of chance from roulette to blackjack.

Though we never learn exactly why, Jack categorically refuses to gamble and has near-contempt for those who do. Still, when he enters the mirror-walled Golden Lion for the first time, his needling voice-over insists, "Welcome back, Jack, to the house of addiction." Later, Jack elaborates in the usual third person: "A wave of elation came over him. He was hooked again, watching people lose."

Photographed by Mark Garfath and edited by Les Healey, *Croupier* beautifully captures the tactile quality of the gaming world: the inviting spin of the roulette wheel, the click of the chips, the whoosh of cards turning over on felt. The film, smartly acted across the board, also allows audiences to feel how and why all this becomes addictive, to experience the rush inside that airless world rather than simply have it described.

Being a croupier demands the nerves and skill of a close-up magician, and though Jack likes to behave like a detached voyeur, much given to ironic comments, in fact the pressure is so unbearable he literally shakes for hours after his shift. Ever the writer, Jack quotes Ernest Hemingway from *A Farewell to Arms* about his own situation: "The world breaks everyone and afterward many are strong at the broken places. But those that will not break it kills."

Despite his attachment to Marion, Jack is drawn to two very different women whom he meets through the casino. One, Bella (Kate Hardie), is a mousy fellow dealer he glances at and concludes, "She looks like trouble." The other, Jani de Villiers (*ER*'s Alex Kingston), is a glamorous gambler who's also spent time in South Africa. Mayersberg's intricate, carefully structured plot involves them all as they try their best to survive in a "bent world" where no one can be trusted, yourself least of all.

Dead Man Walking
1995

It is happenstance as much as anything else that gets Sister Helen Prejean (Susan Sarandon) to death row. On impulse she answers a letter from an inmate at the Louisiana State Penitentiary at Angola, and now she's in the chaplain's office, listening politely as he tells her that condemned prisoners are without exception manipulative and barbaric. "Do you know," he asks her evenly, "what you're getting into?"

She doesn't, of course, but more to the point, neither do we. For *Dead Man Walking,* written and directed by Tim Robbins from Sister Prejean's highly praised book on her death-row experiences, is neither easy nor conventional. Unusual in both its subject matter and its approach, this film guides us on a pair of intertwined paths that American movies rarely venture down.

Taking the death penalty as its subject, *Dead Man Walking* is, first of all, an example of the cinema of ideas. Robbins, an accomplished actor whose directorial debut was the political satire *Bob Roberts,* is a careful and forceful filmmaker whose movies have something to say. His thrust here is not so much polemical as exploratory: He wants to examine capital punishment with as much dispassion as possible, trusting the power of events to engage us without the aid of over-dramatization.

But because Sister Prejean is its protagonist, *Dead Man Walking* has another aim as well. Her involvement with convicted murderer Matthew Poncelet (Sean Penn) has to do with saving his soul, with helping him to take responsibility for his acts so he can die in peace and grace. So, with something like the austere gravity more usually associated with the films of French director Robert Bresson, *Dead Man* takes us on the reluctant, difficult, essentially spiritual journey these two unlikely people make together.

For this kind of straight-ahead movie to work, the acting must be strong without even a breath of theatricality, and Penn and Sarandon are performers capable of making that happen.

Though it's hardly a stretch for Penn to be playing a bad boy, he brings a renewed conviction and a skewered intensity to this part that

makes his performance fresh and overpowering. Everything about Poncelet is unsettling and slightly off-center, from his helmet-like, lacquered pompadour to the disturbing restraint with which he talks. Cold around the eyes and as mesmerizing as a snake, Poncelet is disturbing as only hard-core evil can be, yet Penn also has the ability to make the character's emotional turmoil believable.

Since complete goodness is harder to make convincing on screen than unblinking evil is, Sarandon's part is by definition more challenging. Though her portrayal finally breaks through and gives the film much of its power, it is not as clear-cut or straightforward a success as Penn's work is.

Easy and secure in her belief, with a resilient smile and an unflappable temperament, Sister Helen works at Hope House in a particularly hopeless corner of New Orleans. When she answers Poncelet's letter, goes to meet him on death row, and helps interest attorney Hilton Barber (Robert Prosky) in his appeal, she sees her aim of saving a human life as simple and self-evident.

It doesn't remain that way for long. Though Poncelet (a composite of two real-life inmates) maintains his innocence, Sister Helen is disturbed by the horrific nature of the crime he and an associate were convicted of, the brutal murder of a pair of teenage lovers. She is disgusted by his unalloyed prejudice and finds that as her involvement with his case gets into the papers, her friends and family are increasingly unsympathetic to what she's doing. "A full heart," her mother warns her, "shouldn't follow an empty head."

In fact, *Dead Man Walking* is weakest in not expanding on Sister Helen's reasons for persevering with a case that is causing difficulty with almost everyone close to her. She simply shrugs, smiles, and soldiers on, which, combined with Robbins's occasional coldness as a director, makes her seem not as believably human as she needs to be.

One thing that is explored in provocative detail is the strongest jolt Sister Helen receives, the hostility of the murder victims' parents. Their agony at a wound that can never be healed, their challenge to the sister to comfort them as well as the condemned man, are compassionately explored, and their emotional stories are likely to tear up audiences as much as they do Sister Helen.

But though one of the parents tells the sister she must choose sides—that she can't have it both ways—Sister Helen disagrees. She is determined to minister to the parents if they'll let her, but also to be Poncelet's designated spiritual adviser, to be with him in the final week before his execution, trying to break through his reserve and save him. Although *Dead Man*'s conclusion has its doubtful moments, by the time it arrives Sarandon has demonstrated the strength and resolve of Sister Prejean, the sheer forcefulness of her will to goodness.

Though it is not hard to guess which side Robbins is on in all of this, *Dead Man Walking* is not an anti–capital punishment pamphlet. By giving a full hearing to several aspects of this complex issue, the director wants audiences to do what the sister does, to see both Poncelet and the parents as people first and symbols second, to find the human places in this acrimonious and often impersonal debate.

Deconstructing Harry
1997

People are going to be furious at this Woody Allen film, and it's not difficult to see why. Writer Harry Block, played by Allen himself, is petty, spiteful, and vindictive, and his self-absorbed, misogynistic antics are painful to experience.

But *Deconstructing Harry* is also bracingly funny, and from a dramatic and psychological point of view, it is compelling viewing. A bravura act of self-revelation, its vivid portrait of one man's fears, fantasies, and neuroses uses a mixture of reality, imagination, and comedy to create one of the writer-director's most involving films.

What makes *Harry* especially fascinating is the way it counterpoints recent Allen films such as *Mighty Aphrodite* and *Everyone Says I Love You.* There, too, he played an unlikely Lothario who always manages off-putting romantic scenes with young and attractive actresses. But while those films have been unhappy masquerades, trying without success to pass off their smarmy aspects as light entertainment, Allen here drops the mask.

So though Harry Block's actions are familiar, no attempt is made to paint them as charming. Allen, in fact, originally wanted to title his film *The Worst Man in the World,* and the jazz standard "Twisted," with lyrics such as "My analyst told me I was out of my head," runs over the opening credits. Spiritually bankrupt and sexually obsessed, Harry is uncompromisingly presented as an unsavory scoundrel, albeit one with a sense of humor. Told that his life is all about nihilism, sarcasm, and orgasm, Harry shoots back, "In France, I could run on that ticket and win."

Not necessarily a mea culpa, *Harry* feels, despite pro forma disclaimers to the contrary, like the most nakedly autobiographical of Allen's recent works, complete with the usual references to baseball, Chinese food, therapy, and Manhattan's Upper West Side. In this, his twenty-eighth theatrical feature, the director has come closest to the lacerating and defiant self-revelation of one of his idols, Ingmar Bergman, though it goes without saying that Allen's soul is both funnier and considerably more Jewish than Scandinavian.

Twenty-eight is a lot of features, and while some have a tossed-off, who-cares feeling about them, *Harry* is the opposite. Its intricate and carefully worked out structure would defeat a less experienced director, and Allen, collaborating once again with cinematographer Carlo DiPalma and editor Susan E. Morse, has worked more substance into his 95 minutes than studio behemoths have managed at twice that length.

Harry's opening sequences give an indication of Allen's method. Lucy (Judy Davis) is shown furiously exiting a Manhattan cab on a rainy night not once but some half a dozen times, the repetition emphasizing the extent of her rage. Then comes a vacation-home scene where a writer named Ken (Richard Benjamin) is seen having farcical sex with his sister-in-law Leslie (Julia Louis-Dreyfus).

Next it's back to Lucy, who has come to Harry's house with the intent of murdering him because his last novel caused the breakup of Lucy's marriage and created a rift between Lucy and her sister Jane (Amy Irving), Harry's third wife. The farcical sex scene we've just seen turns out to be a dramatization of Harry's novel, and Lucy is the real-life sister-in-law who's had to face the effects of Harry's callous use of personal experience in his fiction. "You take everyone's suffering and turn it into gold," Lucy hisses at him as only Judy Davis can. "I want to kill the black magician."

Lucy may be hysterical, but she is dead-on correct. Harry has always heedlessly exploited the people closest to him for his work and been indifferent about the consequences. And among this film's cleverer aspects are dramatizations of Harry's earlier fiction, including a deft Kafkaesque story about an actor named Mel (Robin Williams) who discovers that he's literally gone out of focus. Harry even meets one of his fictional doppelgängers outside the Red Apple Rest, a venerable New Jersey roadside restaurant, and has a conversation with the double about the kind of person he's become.

Deconstructing Harry also exposes us to the contorted personal side of a blocked writer who drinks too much, swallows pills to counteract depression, is ambivalent (at best) about being Jewish, and complains to his latest analyst about the way his compulsive sexual fantasies have wreaked havoc with his life. "Did Raoul Wallenberg," he muses, "want to bang every cocktail waitress in Europe?"

After being simultaneously involved with wife Jane and sister Lucy, Harry left both of them to carry on with the inevitably younger and more attractive Fay (Elisabeth Shue). And the writer's selfish attempts to manipulate her life for his own short-term benefit is one of the film's major strands.

In the midst of all this, Harry learns he's to get an award from Adair, the college that expelled him once upon a time. Not surprisingly, given his repellent personality, no one wants to go with him to the presentation, and the group he ends up with—including his young son, his old friend Richard (Bob Balaban), and a hooker named Cookie (Hazelle Goodman)—leads to absurdist scenarios that are comical and devastating.

Allen has helped make the film's problematic scenario involving by assembling his usual command-performance cast and utilizing them in unexpected ways. Who else would have Eric Bogosian as a religious zealot or even think of casting Demi Moore as an Orthodox wife fervently reciting blessings in Hebrew? And Allen's sense of humor, with its irresistible zest for the dark side ("To evil," a toast runs, "it keeps things humming"), is as sharp as ever.

But what feels like *Deconstructing Harry*'s almost compulsive honesty is its strongest lure. When Harry says, "I'm no good at life, but I write well," it's a fitting coda to a scathing look at one man's disastrous experiences with marriage, adultery, and the literary life. Self-flagellating and fearless, *Deconstructing Harry* does a lot of things, but holding back because of what an audience might find objectionable is not one of them.

The Deep End
2001

The Deep End is melodrama dressed up in its Sunday best. Exquisitely made with a mesmerizing sense of style, it shows the wonderful things that can happen when traditional material is both handled with care and adroitly updated.

Writer-directors Scott McGehee and David Siegel understand the terrible power of melodrama. They not only know how compelling the noir staples of homicide and blackmail can be when transferred to the bright sunlight of middle-class America, they also know how to make these impossible dilemmas gripping and convincing.

Based on *The Blank Wall*, a 1940s novel by Elisabeth Sanxay Holding, the rare tale of suspense that writer Raymond Chandler approved of, *The Deep End*'s theatrical story of self-sacrifice and spoken and unspoken love revolves around a completely unlikely thriller heroine.

Margaret Hall is the mother of three, a couldn't-be-more-traditional Navy wife who lives with her children and her borderline doddering father-in-law on the shores of Lake Tahoe while her husband spends months away at sea. She may be someone whose idea of a crisis is a glitch in carpool scheduling, but Margaret is a mother above all else, and when danger looms, there turns out to be little she can't or won't do to protect her child.

To play this most conventional woman, *The Deep End* subversively cast a most unconventional actress, the remarkable Tilda Swinton. Though she's starred in films for fifteen years, the Scottish-born Swinton is largely unknown to American audiences because much of her excellent work has been for art-house directors such as Derek Jarman (*Caravaggio*) and Sally Potter (*Orlando*). Her performance here is quietly astonishing, a triumph of demure urgency and controlled desperation.

Margaret's dilemma not only sounds like the plot of a 1940s Hollywood film, it was one. *The Blank Wall* was filmed once before, with Joan Bennett and James Mason starring in 1949 for director Max Ophuls in the equally persuasive *The Reckless Moment.* The plot similarities between the two are naturally numerous, but the new film has shrewdly changed and updated a key story point.

While the 1949 film has Joan Bennett's mother protective about the lecherous advances of an unscrupulous older man toward her innocent young daughter, Margaret has to contend with the more disturbing notion—for her—of an unscrupulous older man getting into a romantic relationship with her teenage son.

Reno club owner Darby Reese (Josh Lucas), the picture of bemused, rakish seductiveness, is the man in question. In addition to its metaphysical implications, *The Deep End* is the name of his establishment, and the film opens with Margaret knocking on its door on a hot Nevada morning, oblivious to how out of place she and her SUV look in front of it even in broad daylight, determined to get the oily Reese to stay away from her son.

That would be seventeen-year-old Beau (Jonathan Tucker), a high school senior and promising musician who gets all whiny and adolescent with his mother when she brings up the liaison, insisting she's blowing it all out of proportion. Reese, however, knows better. "She's a mother," he tells the boy at a rendezvous at the family boathouse, "not a moron."

Reese is more right than he's ever going to know. A web of coincidence, circumstance, and accident leads to a very bad thing happening at that boathouse and leaving Margaret all alone with the task of trying to prevent something almost as bad from happening to her son, all alone coping with crises she can see and those that completely blindside her.

Alek Spera (*ER*'s Goran Visnjic) is one of the latter. Dark, intense, with deep, piercing eyes, he appears at her door and announces, "I came to talk about Darby Reese and your son." As it did for James Mason, who played the part in 1949, his slight foreign accent makes what he says a bit more unnerving. Yet while his activities may be criminal, Alek is not a thug. Rather, he's that rare hard guy who is also capable of moral ambivalence, and his interplay with the increasingly frantic Margaret is *The Deep End* at its most effective.

Filmmakers McGehee and Siegel, who debuted with the less successful *Suture,* have here turned out something coolly confident and exquisitely controlled. They've understood how stylized restraint complements excessive material, and, working with editor Lauren Zuckerman, they display an exact grasp of what to keep, what to emphasize, and what to discard.

Peter Nashel's deliberate, unsettling score is essential to setting the mood, but the biggest advantage in this regard is *The Deep End*'s visual sense. Faultlessly lit, composed, and shot by director of photography Giles Nuttgens (whose other credits run the considerable gamut from Deepa Mehta's *Fire* to *Battlefield Earth*), *The Deep End* has a beautifully modulated color scheme (Kelly McGehee and Christopher Tandon do the superb production design) and the ability to utilize a wide variety of water imagery without overdoing the notion.

Finally, however, actress Swinton is this film's greatest asset. By temperament and by necessity, Margaret is a woman who has learned to keep everything, especially her voice, under tight control. So Swinton's performance, simultaneously emotionless and emotion-laden, uses an extraordinary range of facial expressions to benchmark the transformations her character undergoes. If you're going to reinvent melodrama for modern times, there's no one you'd rather have on your side.

Devil in a Blue Dress
1995

Hard-boiled fiction is a been-around genre about done-that individuals, so the pleasant air of newness and excitement that *Devil in a Blue Dress* gives off isn't due to its familiar find-the-girl plot. Rather, it's the film's glowing visual qualities, a striking performance by Denzel Washington, and the elegant control that Carl Franklin has over it all that create the most exotic crime entertainment of the season.

There's an irony about *Devil*'s exoticism, because its setting isn't some remote overseas locale but right in Los Angeles, the circa 1948 streets surrounding a vibrant Central Avenue. It says quite a bit about the nature of Hollywood and the history of American race relations that that time and place are as remote as Burkina Faso as far as mainstream movie audiences are concerned.

For writer-director Franklin, adapting the first of Walter Mosley's popular series of Ezekiel (Easy) Rawlins detective novels for a major studio also had its exotic aspects. Franklin's previous film was the acclaimed and accomplished low-budget thriller *One False Move,* and carrying off the transition to larger budgets without the loss of creative edge could have presented a problem.

Instead, *Devil in a Blue Dress* turns out to be a major accomplishment, a fluid, persuasive piece of moviemaking graced with the considerable visual sophistication of Tak Fujimoto, executive producer Jonathan Demme's favorite cinematographer. Starting with its mood-setting credit sequence—a slow pan over a gorgeous Archibald Motley Jr. painting of *Bronzeville at Night* while a T-Bone Walker blues piece plays on the soundtrack—this is a film in smooth control of its ways and means.

Also in complete charge of his resources is Denzel Washington, who establishes himself once again as a superb leading man. Coolly handsome, able to project sly humor and measurable sexuality as well as dignity and strength, Washington can also play confusion and uncertainty when the story demands it. And no one since Marlon Brando's *A Streetcar Named Desire* days has looked better in a tight T-shirt.

Washington also has the sensitivity to play Easy Rawlins as a man of his era, a 1940s Negro who must out of necessity leaven his heroic qualities with the kind of circumspect behavior demanded by those more overtly racist times, when it was risky for black men to venture north of Wilshire Boulevard at night, and even the Ambassador Hotel was segregated by color.

Devil opens with Easy in trouble. Fired from his job at a defense plant, he has an overdue house payment and a lack of prospects. Then a bartender introduces him to the mysterious Dewitt Albright (Tom Sizemore), whose living consists of "doing favors for friends." He asks Easy to help him find a white woman named Daphne Monet (Jennifer Beals), the fiancee of one of the city's most powerful men, who fancies jazz and likes to hang out around Central Avenue. It sounds too easy, which, of course, it is.

With its frequent twists and references to corruption at the highest levels of Los Angeles's power elite, *Devil* owes a good deal to Robert Towne's script for Roman Polanski's classic *Chinatown.* To no one's surprise but his own, Easy is soon in way over his head in the usual world of murder, blackmail, and betrayal, where all his attempts to do the right thing only get him into more and more trouble.

Fortunately for Easy, Mouse, a pal from his past who would truly as soon kill someone as look at them, shows up and helps out. Played with a picture-stealing bravado by Don Cheadle, Mouse is a more comic character here than in Mosley's book, but that change, like the others Franklin has made to the novel, turns out to be an audience-friendly alteration.

Though *Devil*'s plot is a standard one, the same is not true of its setting. Production designer Gary Frutkoff and his team have superbly re-created not only Central Avenue but also the interiors of loud bars, smoky jazz clubs, and all the rest of Rawlins's milieu. To watch this film is to feel like a privileged visitor in an unfamiliar world that ought to be gone but, *Brigadoon*-like, unexpectedly lives again.

Carl Franklin makes *Devil*'s world worth visiting. It's a brutal place, but Franklin, as *One False Move* showed, knows how to make on-screen violence effective without overdoing things. It is also rife with prejudice, and Franklin refuses to shortchange that while insisting on his characters' dignity and humanity. If there were more films like this, movie houses would be safer places to visit without becoming too boring to bother with.

Dirty Pretty Things
2003

Nigerian-born Okwe, an immigrant cabdriver hustling for customers at a London airport, knows just how to chat up potential fares abandoned by their car services. "I am here," he says with elegance and precision, "to rescue those who have been let down by the system."

It is, however, one of the many ironies of the exceptional *Dirty Pretty Things* and its gripping examination of dislocation and uncertainty among that city's refugees that no one is more let down by the system than Okwe himself.

Vividly, unexpectedly, convincingly, *Dirty Pretty Things* thrusts us into Okwe's unsettling world of clandestine, quasi-legal foreigners, "the people you do not see," where the stability, security, and accountability many people take for granted are close to unreachable.

It's a world where the most savage things happen to the best people, where fearful underdogs search for an angle to lift them off the bottom, where attempts at morality can seem foolish, even inhuman. An upside-down world where "there is nothing so dangerous as a virtuous man," and falling in love is the riskiest thing you can ever do.

Disturbing and intriguing, *Dirty Pretty Things* fits a great deal into its 94 quicksilver minutes. Directed by Stephen Frears from a remarkable script by Steven Knight, this is a film that insinuates itself deeply into our awareness. It's that rare pulp story with something on its mind, an unnerving, socially conscious thriller with a killer sense of narrative drive.

Those qualities flow from Knight's persuasive screenplay, the first theatrical feature from an experienced television writer who was also an unlikely creator of *Who Wants to Be a Millionaire.*

With its real feeling for language and the way it is spoken by individuals as well as different immigrant groups, Knight's writing places us in the center of these uncertain lives. He also has a gift for unexpected plotting, for adding a touch of the indefinable to create a story that feels not quite like those we've seen before.

For his part, director Frears is a complete filmmaker, attracted to intelligent language as well as memorable images. Although he's had his share of misfires, Frears is indisputably one of Britain's top directors, and when he gets hold of superior material, as he has in films as varied as *My Beautiful Laundrette, The Grifters,* and *High Fidelity,* he knows it. Working with top-of-the-line cinematographer Chris Menges and veteran editor Mick Audsley, Frears creates a moody, tawdry atmosphere, a London that is anonymous, uncaring, even threatening.

Desperate to survive as he faces ever-increasing obstacles is Okwe (Chiwetel Ejiofor), for whom being a cabdriver is only one of two full-time jobs. Chewing on a medicinal root to stay awake, he also works as night-shift clerk at a questionable hotel, a bizarre mini-U.N. where the doorman is Russian, the hookers multinational. Here, his accurately named Spanish boss, Sneaky (Sergi Lopez), explains the film's title. "Strangers come to hotels to do dirty things," he tells Okwe. "In the morning it's our job to make things pretty again."

That homily is Sneaky's way of responding to Okwe's baffling discovery of a vital organ blocking the toilet in one of the hotel rooms. Although he's guarded about his personal history, Okwe is a former doctor, and while his innate sense of decency pushes him to investigate and to try to help, his questionable status and something dark in his past ("It is an African story" is all he'll say) limit what he feels he can safely do.

A similar dynamic animates Okwe's relationship with Senay (French actress Audrey Tautou), a Turkish immigrant and fellow hotel worker whose couch he chastely sleeps on. Although Okwe has something of a crush on her, Senay, timid and terrified of seeming promiscuous, tries her best to not so much as talk to him.

This tenterhooks relationship becomes even more complex when British immigration enters the picture and Okwe looks deeper into what goes on in the hotel after hours.

With its combination of familiar and unfamiliar actors, the film's excellent cast facilitates our bonding with the characters. A British actor whose Nigerian parents helped him with his accent, Ejiofor uses stillness and interior strength to give a powerful presentation, while Lopez, memorable in the French film *With a Friend Like Harry,* brings oily panache to his role as the ultimate fixer. As for Tautou, she delivers a major emotional performance in a role that is the complete opposite of her breakthrough work in *Amelie.*

The protective coloration of immigrant communities provides a welcome anonymity that these characters count on, but that's not always a reliable strategy.

In a film that takes no one's happiness for granted, it is not at all sure that there is room for both love and survival. What does it mean finally to attempt to do good in this kind of a corrupt, compromised society? When a character demands of Okwe, "Stop acting like you've got a choice," it's a measure of the integrity and individuality of *Dirty Pretty Things* that it is far from clear whether he does.

Election
1999

They get all the movies—or at least it seems that way. They control an impressive share of America's free time and disposable income. And most everyone covets their youthful good looks. You've always suspected it, and *Election,* a sharp and merciless comedy, tells you it's true: Teenagers rule.

The best and brightest high school adventure since the groundbreaking *Heathers* (1989), *Election* posits a devastatingly funny world where fumbling adults are powerless when confronted by determined young people motivated by the devil of self-interest. Co-written and directed by Alexander Payne (*Citizen Ruth*) and powered by expert performances by Reese Witherspoon and Matthew Broderick, this is a fierce teen satire that adults will have no difficulty cherishing.

One reason high school has proved to be such an effective incubator of blackly humorous films is that it's the adult world writ small. Anyone looking, as Payne surely is, to skewer the ways self-centered behavior is camouflaged and rationalized by ambitious minds couldn't feel more at home than among the mainstream kids at Omaha's mythical George Washington Carver High.

Adapted by Payne and his *Ruth* co-writer, Jim Taylor, from a novel by Tom Perrotta, *Election* is both funnier than *Ruth* and subtler in its choice of targets. Helped by being adroitly cast down to its tiniest roles (Lisa Beach was the casting director), this is a nearly flawless little film, a cheerful nightmare that knows just where it wants to go and uses precisely calibrated comic effects to get there.

Payne and Taylor get some of their best results by employing multiple voice-overs. Each of the film's major characters has his or her shot at providing after-the-fact commentary on events as they unfold, competing in a very adversarial way to get his or her personal version of what we see happening onto the official record.

In an alternate universe, Jim McCallister and Tracy Flick could have been allies, even friends. Both care enormously, almost unreasonably, about what happens at Carver High. But destiny pulls them apart, and as Tracy puts it with typical off-kilter bluntness, "you can't interfere with destiny. That's why it's destiny."

Broderick, in a role that is a near-perfect fit, plays the slightly lost, slightly woebegone but awfully sincere McCallister, the kind of educator everyone calls Mr. M. He's been named teacher of the year three times at Carver, a school record. Mr. M means it when he says, "I got involved, I made a difference."

Tracy (a completely delightful Witherspoon) also got involved, and with a vengeance. Bright-eyed, chipper, and determined, she's everywhere at Carver, playing Hodel in *Fiddler on the Roof,* working on the yearbook, and thinking nothing of customizing 480 cupcakes should the need arise. Mr. M views Tracy as the most ambitious student he's ever seen. And, for a variety of reasons, he can't stand her.

So when Tracy decides to run for student council president, Mr. M encourages star athlete Paul Metzler (a telling debut for Chris Klein) to run against her. The most popular as well as the densest man on campus, Paul is the kind of guy who seeks serious spiritual guidance from *The Celestine Prophecy* and then falls asleep trying to read it.

Naturally, Tracy takes competition as a personal affront; "the weak," she squeaks in her purposeful little voice, "are always trying to sabotage the strong." The battle that ensues, which eventually involves Tammy Metzler (Jessica Campbell), Paul's sexually confused sister ("I'm not a lesbian but I'm only attracted to women"), and even Mr. M's wife Diane (Molly Hagan), leaves few people or institutions unscathed.

Election's humor comes not just from its farcical situations but its dead-on, deeply tongue-in-cheek dialogue. And Payne, who enjoys periodically jolting the audience with either a bit of particularly raw sexual dialogue or an unexpected visual point of view, directs it with a great sense of dark comic style.

Election takes particular glee in demonstrating the obtuseness of adults (such as gee-whiz principal Walt Hendricks, played by Phil Reeves) and showing how conniving students can be when they're consumed by their jealousies, rivalries, and relationships. *Election* enjoys making the audience complicit in all these wicked schemes; making us feel good about people being bad is one of this film's most satisfying triumphs.

Flirting with Disaster
1996

Flirting with Disaster doesn't just begin, it irrepressibly erupts, like champagne too impatient to stay in the glass. A beautifully balanced, frenetic comedy about searching for love in too many places, *Flirting* thrusts you into a sexy, giddy maelstrom of confusion, mischance, and misadventure that gets funnier and funnier as it goes along.

Written and directed by David O. Russell, whose debut film was the completely different *Spanking the Monkey*, *Flirting* brings to mind sturdy clichés such as "inspired lunacy" that haven't fit anything for years. A light-on-its-feet, catch-the-jokes-on-the-fly adventure, this is the hardest kind of comedy to do well, but you wouldn't know that from the casual ease with which Russell handles the material.

He also knows his way around actors, unexpectedly but adroitly combining youngsters Ben Stiller, Patricia Arquette, and Tea Leoni with wise old heads Mary Tyler Moore, George Segal, Alan Alda, and Lily Tomlin, all of whom blend as though this was meant to be.

Flirting's success also comes from how seamlessly it combines two quite different comic traditions into one harum-scarum whole, tying it all up with a clever title that encapsulates the anarchy of the proceedings.

One strand, the tightly wound Woody Allen neurotic on the loose, is concentrated in indecisive, uncertain entomologist Mel Coplin (Stiller). Married to the warm and loving Nancy (Arquette doing the best work of her career) and the father of a four-month-old son, Mel should be glowing, but instead he's so stressed out that he and his wife have been unable to decide on the baby's name.

The adopted son of awesomely maladjusted New Yorkers (Moore and Segal), Mel feels his troubles would vanish if he could locate his birth parents. No problemo, says the Maidstone Adoption Agency, adding grandly that "the mystery of your unknown self is about to unfold."

It's not quite that simple.

First off, the agency saddles Mel and Nancy with elegant, about-to-be-divorced psychology graduate student Tina Kalb, assigned to videotape the reunion. Played by Leoni, Tina amusingly combines an ex-dancer's body with the bottomless psychobabble of an earnest academic. As the senior Mrs. Coplin says, "This woman strikes me as very dangerous."

Undeterred, not to say obsessed, Mel, Nancy, and Tina head off on what becomes a genetic wild goose chase that has the trio hopscotching all over the country, meeting a cracked collection of eccentrics, as their lives are thrown into the most delicious confusion.

It's during this manic journey that *Flirting*'s adroit juggling of multiple characters brings to mind a different strain of American comedy, the satiric screwball farces of the 1930s and '40s, especially *The Lady Eve* and *The Palm Beach Story*, which were written and directed by the master of the form, Preston Sturges.

Russell is no Sturges yet, but he does do a number of things remarkably well for a young director. He creates moments of physical comedy that are intrinsic to the story while being unexpected and wildly funny. And he is so gifted at moving his plot along at a break-neck pace that there's never time to draw breath, let alone wonder what makes sense and what doesn't.

All of this, as well as Russell's facility for mocking such American institutions as bed and breakfasts and white Taurus rental cars, puts *Flirting with Disaster* into a category of its own.

In fact, this film is such a deft juggling of so many balls it may turn out to be a one-of-a-kind performance, difficult to duplicate even by its creator. But such worries should not be allowed to dilute the pleasure of this bustling comedy.

Russell's next film turned out to be the equally idiosyncratic and well made but more serious Three Kings.

Fly Away Home
1996

First came the horse. Then the wolf. And now the geese. When direc-tor Carroll Ballard makes a strong connection with the animal king-dom, a special kind of film results.

Ballard, whose previous credits include *The Black Stallion* and *Never Cry Wolf,* knows how to be both caring and restrained, mini-mizing a movie's saccharine content while maximizing the sense of wonder. His *Fly Away Home* is a pleasant and high-spirited affair, one of the rare films that manages to be irresistible without resorting to emotional blackmail.

Like those previous Ballard pictures, *Fly Away Home* features char-acters intent on impossible tasks. For father Thomas Alden (Jeff Daniels) and his estranged thirteen-year-old daughter Amy (Anna Paquin), the problems are twofold.

Thrown together at Thomas's southern Ontario farm by a family tragedy after a decade apart, father and daughter have so little in com-mon that the forging of any kind of relationship seems out of the question.

A Gyro Gearlose–type of eccentric inventor-sculptor with a chaotic lifestyle and hobbies such as early-morning hang gliding, Thomas is not ideal father material. This kind of straight-arrow-with-a-twist role has become second nature to Daniels, who lends conviction and believability to the part.

After her Oscar-winning role in *The Piano,* it's also no surprise to see Anna Paquin artfully playing a prickly, forthright young woman, suspicious of her father's new girlfriend (Dana Delany) and having a hard time shaking the air of watchful sadness that clings to her.

Enter the geese. Thomas's land is near a breeding ground for Canada geese, and when rampaging developers tear up the area, Amy rescues an abandoned nest of eggs. She takes it home, keeps a careful watch, and widens her eyes in appropriate astonishment as sixteen tiny beaks break through their shells and come out to play.

In truth, there is no resisting these fluffy individuals, either as fuzzballs or when they get older and, viewing Amy as their mother, impetuously follow her everywhere in response to her chirpy "come on, geese" commands. Both father and daughter inevitably get attached to their charges, which begins to solve the bonding problem but leads to the second dilemma: What to do when the birds begin to fly?

Insisting it's illegal for domestically raised geese to take flight, a local wildlife officer is determined to literally clip their wings. And since geese are taught how and where to migrate by their parents, how was Amy's orphan flock going to find the threatened wetlands in North Carolina that were eager for their arrival?

The solution, based on successful real-life experiments carried out by a Canadian artist named Bill Lishman, makes use of both the father's fascination with ultra-light aircraft and the way the geese have imprinted on the daughter. Fly away home, indeed.

Of course this scenario is sentimental, but that is balanced by the magic created by seeing the gang in flight through Caleb Deschanel's clear and luminous cinematography. Aside from a few computer-generated sequences (a flight through city streets is the most obvious one), the flying is done by real geese, and the soft, discreet touch director Ballard uses throughout works especially well here. By refusing to be cheap or insincere, *Fly Away Home* allows us to enjoy our emotions without feeling we've been criminally manipulated. Even seeing pigs flying would not be so rare a treat as that.

Groundhog Day
1993

Groundhog Day may not be the funniest collaboration between Bill Murray and director Harold Ramis, and it never had a chance of being the most financially successful. Yet this gentle, small-scale effort is easily the most endearing film of both men's careers, a sweet and amusing surprise package.

Though endearing is not an adjective often associated with the deadpan, ruefully misanthropic style of humor Murray is known for, it is his comic hostility that makes *Groundhog Day* as agreeable as it is. Taking the bitter with the sweet is not only a venerable cliché, it's also a recipe for making sentimentality palatable on screen.

Much of the credit for this charm ought to go to first-time screenwriter Danny Rubin, who came up with the original idea (and shares script credit with Ramis). There is a romantic innocence about his concept that survives the overreliance on Hollywood shtick that weighs down the film's first part and makes us believers by the close.

Murray stars as Phil Connors, a Pittsburgh TV weatherman who is so self-involved he's convinced he doesn't just report the weather, he creates it. Jaded and cynical, Connors hates nothing more than having to journey to rural Punxsutawney, Pennsylvania, once a year and participate in the unsophisticated shenanigans centering on whether a certain groundhog does or does not see his shadow.

But on this particular February 2, some things turn out to be different for Phil. For openers, he has a new producer, the cheerful, good-natured Rita Hanson (Andie MacDowell). For another, Phil discovers that, much as he dislikes it, February 2 is a day he just can't escape. Ever.

Upon awakening in Punxsutawney on what should be February 3, Phil gradually realizes that everything about this day, from the clock radio playing "I Got You Babe" at precisely 6 A.M. to the chitchat of total strangers, is exactly the same as it was on February 2. But while everyone else is living this day for the first time, Phil is not only repeating it, he seems destined to repeat it again and again and again until the end of time.

What would you do if there were truly no tomorrow, if you knew everything that was going to happen on a given day and nothing you did ever had even a hint of consequences? As he comes to understand, if not accept, his situation (which, like all fairy tales, is offered blessedly free of explanation), Murray's Phil quickly disposes of the obvious choices. He pigs out on pastries, drives with abandon, seduces women, and flouts the law. Does any of this make him happy? No, it does not.

Then, almost in desperation, Phil remembers Rita, and he decides, for want of something better to do, to seduce her using the knowledge he gradually accumulates as he keeps reliving Groundhog Day. It is a clever conceit, and one that has life-changing consequences that even Phil can't begin to imagine.

A lot of things can go wrong when repetition is the essence of a film, not the least of which is that seeing the same situation over and over sounds like a considerable bore. And, in the opening stages of *Day,* when moments such as stepping into a puddle of ice water are given more than their due, it looks as if Murray and company won't be able to escape that trap.

But Rubin's story has more warmth than you might anticipate, as well as its own kind of resilience, and having the gruff Murray (rather than some more fuzzy and cuddly actor) endure a change of heart makes the softer emotions easier to accept. With MacDowell as the pleasant foil, Murray turns *Groundhog Day* into a funny little valentine of a film. It won't overwhelm you or change your life, but after all the more obvious laughter is over, it may just make you smile.

Heavenly Creatures
1994

Heavenly Creatures is what Pauline Parker and Juliet Hulme called each other, but those are just words, and words, no matter how passionate and adoring, can only hint at the intensity of the attachment these two teenage girls felt.

Inseparable real-life schoolmates and soul mates in Christchurch, New Zealand, in 1952, Pauline and Juliet inhabited a symbiotic world that was giddy, euphoric, and chilling. Frightfully self-absorbed, their conduct unnerved the adult world and led, with horrible inevitability, to what is still considered the most celebrated criminal case in New Zealand history.

New Zealand director Peter Jackson, best known for the cult fright favorite *Dead Alive,* has nervily translated the Parker-Hulme case into film terms, and an adventurous, accomplished piece of business, burning with cinematic energy, it turns out to be.

Utilizing a thoughtful, thoroughly researched script that he co-wrote with Frances Walsh, Jackson directs in a way that is both tightly controlled and highly emotional. Photographed by Alun Bollinger, *Creatures* has a witty, overwrought visual style that the girls themselves would probably favor, and it makes good dramatic use of state-of-the-art special effects.

Related in voice-over taken from a diary kept by Pauline, *Creatures* begins with a newsreel of Christchurch, the kind of quaint, bucolic, boring place that scandal isn't supposed to touch. The city takes especial pride in the Christchurch Girls High School, a classically prim establishment that insists on proper uniforms and sensible shoes.

Pauline (Melanie Lynskey), her sullen face framed by dark curly ringlets, is a bright but quietly resentful ninth-grade student who comes from undeniably lower-class stock. Her feckless father, Bert (Simon O'Connor), is prone to silly sight gags involving fish, and her hardworking mother, Honora (Sarah Peirse), has to take in boarders to pay the family expenses.

All this ceases to matter to Pauline the day Juliet (Kate Winslet) arrives from dreamy England. Totally upper class, knowing more about the intricacies of the French subjunctive than her teachers, and not shy about proving it, Juliet may be outwardly glamorous and confident, but she is as high strung and emotionally needy as Pauline. Almost immediately, they bond with a fierceness that no one knows quite what to make of.

Starting with a shared passion for Mario Lanza, "only the world's greatest tenor," Pauline and Juliet progress to creating elaborate candle-lit shrines to their idols. Determined to either go to Hollywood ("It's better than heaven; no Christians") or have a novel published in New York, they begin to jointly work on a project.

Realizing "how hard it is for other people to appreciate our genius," the girls retreat more and more to an imaginary place they call "the Fourth World," which includes a medieval kingdom named Borovnia. With fine use of up-to-the-minute effects, *Creatures* makes it possible for audiences to physically enter these worlds with Pauline and Juliet and to experience the surrender to fantasy as completely as they do.

This ability to get us inside hysteria and obsession, to make us feel sensations as intensely as the film's protagonists, is what makes *Creatures* memorable.

Helped by remarkable performances by its young actresses (Winslet had worked in theater and TV in England, Lynskey was pretty much an absolute beginner), *Creatures* insidiously encourages us to side with these two young women. Clearly they are so much fresher, more radiant, and energetic than their elders, who begin to dully suspect that something as mundane as sexual attraction is holding these two together.

So when Pauline and Juliet teeter at the edge of sanity, when their infatuation becomes uncontrollable, their willfulness frightening, we go over the top with them, horrified co-conspirators almost to the end. *Heavenly Creatures* does not romanticize or excuse, it merely presents the inevitable and leaves us to shake our heads in wonder.

The gift for character and psychology he displayed here was Peter Jackson's secret weapon when he went on to direct the Lord of the Rings *trilogy.*

High Fidelity
2000

"What came first," Rob Gordon (John Cusack) desperately wants to know, "the music or the misery?"

Overstimulated by the sounds coming out of his outsize headphones, morose Rob is seizing the moment of his breakup with Laura (Iben Hjejle) to reflect on "the thousands of hours of heartache, rejection, pain, misery, and loss" he experienced while exposing himself to wave after wave of popular music. "Did I listen because I was miserable," he wonders, "or was I miserable because I listened?"

Further proof of how funny we can be when we're at our most despondent, *High Fidelity* is a sharp and satisfying romantic comedy about the difficulty of commitment that utilizes Stephen Frears's incisive direction and some very knowing and sophisticated writing to give actor Cusack one of the best roles of his career.

That is saying something, because Cusack, talented as well as shrewd about what he gets himself into, doesn't go in for weak material. Rob Gordon, a part Cusack had a hand in writing, is specifically tailored to his everyman persona, to his gift for intimacy with the audience and his ability to humanize characters who are difficult and potentially off-putting.

The last time out for Cusack and writing partners D.V. DeVincentis and Steve Pink was *Grosse Point Blank,* in which the actor played a hit man with a career crisis; *High Fidelity* presents them with a character who faces a less lethal kind of challenge. (Scott Rosenberg of the glib *Things to Do in Denver When You're Dead* and *Con Air* also gets a writing credit.)

The Cusack pack had the advantage of starting from Nick Hornby's fine novel, a delightful book that is very savvy about the vagaries of relationships, especially from the male point of view. It's Rob, using either voice-over or direct talk to the camera, who preserves the book's first-person quality as well as chunks of its dialogue. *High Fidelity* presents him as someone who is his own worst enemy, a tortured and grumpy eternal adolescent who doesn't have to hide his weakness for being a real jerk to gain our sympathy.

Given his opening rant about the pernicious effect of lyrics, it's not a surprise that Rob's life is pop music. He owns Championship Vinyl, a Chicago establishment (smoothly moved from the novel's London) that's a shrine to old-fashioned phonograph records and a mecca to obsessive geeks who "spend a disproportionate amount of their time looking for deleted Smiths singles and 'ORIGINAL NOT RERELEASED' underlined Frank Zappa albums."

This universe's two biggest geeks, Dick and Barry, a.k.a. "the musical moron twins," just happen to work for Rob, and as played by Todd Louiso and Jack Black are the comic center of the film. Dick is the sensitive flower while Barry is rowdy, abrasive, and downright hilarious. They join Rob in insulting the customers, making abstruse jokes about the Beta Band and Ryuichi Sakamoto, and constructing an endless number of all-time Top 5 lists, from Top 5 dream jobs to Top 5 songs about death ("Leader of the Pack," "Dead Man's Curve," "Tell Laura I Love Her," etc.).

Though the Championship Vinyl store (magnificently created for the film by a crew that includes production designers David Chapman and Therese DePrez, art director Nicholas Lund, set decorator Larry P. Lundy, and property master Timothy W. Tiedje) is real enough to be a character in its own right, it's not the best place for empathy, and that's what Rob needs after his break with Laura. Initially he faces the split with bravado, yelling at her that she doesn't even make his all-time Top 5 list of memorable split-ups (yes, he has one), but that fighting spirit is not fated to last.

As the pain of Laura's absence (and her possible connection with someone else) sinks in, Rob is forced, for perhaps the first time, to think about his life and confront his difficulty with romance and commitment. "What's wrong with me? Why am I doomed to be left?" he wonders plaintively. In an attempt to find out, he thinks back on that list of all-time memorable ruptures, amusingly reconsidering liaisons with Catherine Zeta-Jones, Lili Taylor, and others.

Director Frears, who is noticeably good with realistic relationships that have a touch of comedy in them (*The Snapper, My Beautiful Laundrette*), knows his way around this scenario. Under his guidance, Cusack's painful but funny reexamination leads to a getting of wisdom that is no less welcome for coming years after it should have.

Cusack, with his ability to project glowering desperation and a sense of aggrieved entitlement, is perfect for this role. As Laura, the woman he can't live with or without, Danish actress Hjejle (the prostitute-turned-housekeeper in that country's *Mifune*) displays both faultless English and a formidable sense of integrity that allows her to more than hold her own in fairly heady company.

For it's a tribute to how well *High Fidelity* has been written (and to the respect other performers have for Cusack and Frears) that the film employs quite a number of excellent actors in small roles. In addition to Taylor and Zeta-Jones, there are parts for Tim Robbins, Joan Cusack, Lisa Bonet, Sara Gilbert, and Natasha Gregson Wagner.

The film's music (more than fifty songs are listed in the credits, with artists ranging from Aretha Franklin to Stereolab) is expertly chosen, and there's even a cameo by Bruce Springsteen, giving sage romantic advice. Of course, Rob needs it, but whether he can take it is, obviously, quite another story.

Hilary and Jackie
1998

It takes two to be sisters, two to have a rivalry, and two exceptional actresses to turn *Hilary and Jackie* into a compelling look at the most intimate and troubling of family dynamics. An assured take on the nature of sibling bonds, *Hilary and Jackie* also provides an unorthodox examination of the burden that being gifted places on all concerned— the one with the talent as well as those in the emotional vicinity.

Hilary and Jackie is based on *A Genius in the Family,* a book by Hilary and Piers Du Pré about their celebrated sister, Jacqueline Du Pré, the brilliant young English cellist who died in 1987 at age forty-two after being stricken by multiple sclerosis sixteen years earlier at the height of her career.

One of the great musicians of her generation, celebrated for her interpretation of the Elgar cello concerto, and half of a golden couple with conductor and pianist-husband Daniel Barenboim (who once described her as having "the gift of making you feel she was actually composing the music she was playing"), Du Pré is very much a revered figure in Britain.

So her siblings' book and its revelations about what life with Jackie could be like caused a tremendous ruckus, with one critic proclaiming he could do without Du Pré being turned into "Du Praved, the sexual predator."

As a result, *Hilary and Jackie* ends its credits with the most detailed disclaimer in memory, admitting in part that "composite characters, representative incidents, adjusted chronology and context, constructed dialogue and other fictionalized elements have been used for dramatic purposes. . . . No implication should be drawn that any of the persons depicted have authorized or approved this production."

While this fuss is intriguing, it's largely beside the point. In fact, viewers in this country, where Du Pré is hardly a household word, are likely in a better position to appreciate what should be viewed as something inspired by reality instead of the exact real thing. Screenwriter Frank Cottrell Boyce (*Welcome to Sarajevo*) and first-time feature director Anand Tucker have created an absorbing human story and have told it with an unexpected structure and a determination to be evenhanded with all its conflicting parties.

Tucker, whose BBC background is in documentaries, shows off his strong storytelling sense and visual assurance with an opening dream sequence, the meaning of which doesn't become completely clear until later in the film. In a scene that is both fun and somehow sad, he introduces two little girls playing by the shore, bright girls with vivid imaginations, and sisters for sure.

These would be young Hilary (Keely Flanders) and younger Jackie (Auriole Evans). Their mother, Iris (Celia Imrie), is determined to give them a strong musical education, under which they both thrive. It is Hilary, two years older, who excels first on the flute, with Jackie's flowering as a prodigy on the cello shown to be inspired by their mother's edict, "If you want to be together, you have to play as well as Hilary."

These two child actresses do a remarkable job of underlining the poignancy of young girls working ever so hard on their adult music. Once Hilary and Jackie grow up, the parts are taken even further by two of the best actresses working today, Rachel Griffiths and Emily Watson.

The Australian Griffiths, best known for her role in *Muriel's Wedding*, brings a keen mixture of melancholy and resilience to the part of Hilary, who feels the separation that Jackie's sudden success brings with it and whose own life as a musician becomes reduced to answering the question, "And how is your marvelous sister?"

As Jackie Du Pré, British actress Watson more than fulfills the promise of her celebrated Oscar-nominated work in *Breaking the Waves*. She completely inhabits the role of the troubled young cellist, living it as much as acting it. As Jackie appears to gradually turn into a kind of beautiful monster, selfish and needy in a way that feels directly proportional to her amazing gift, Watson knows how to create involvement without special pleading on her part.

Once Hilary and Jackie become adults, the narrative splits in two. In a device reminiscent of Akira Kurosawa's celebrated *Rashomon*, the story of their troubled but powerful interaction is told first from Hilary's point of view, and then, about 45 minutes later (and announced by a large "Jackie" on the screen) from her sister's.

It's a mark of how evenhanded *Hilary and Jackie* manages to be that this technique works as well as it does, forcing us to recognize the honest subjectivity and selective memory that makes up each woman's view of reality. As a general rule, Hilary tends to feel abandoned by her soul mate, while Jackie finds herself lonely and even desperate, trapped by her talent in a bizarre life. Even as simple an act as Jackie's sending her dirty laundry home to England during her first European tour is depicted from a pair of radically different perspectives.

Though loving, the two sisters are always competitive, even where men are concerned. Hilary gets involved first, marrying Christopher (Kiffer) Finzi (David Morrissey), the son of composer Gerald Finzi, whose brash persona is a breath of fresh air for her after her cloistered life at home. Not one to be overshadowed, Jackie snags the celebrated young musician Barenboim (James Frain). As Jackie gets more insecure and voracious, the personal lives of the sisters get even more intimately intertwined—an agony that worsens when Hilary's MS is diagnosed.

There is, inevitably, something of *Shine* about this story of music and emotional torment, but *Hilary and Jackie* feels completely its own picture. The powerful yet delicate ties of sisterhood it illuminates are so intricate and mysterious, and so superbly acted, that this exploration feels like a revelation.

The Iron Giant
1999

Straight-arrow and subversive, made with simplicity as well as sophistication, *The Iron Giant* does things differently. It remembers the wonder of being a child and understands how to convey that in a media-savvy age. Both a step back and a step forward from the trends of modern animation, it feels like a classic even though it's just out of the box.

Directed by Brad Bird, *The Iron Giant* is loosely based on something Ted Hughes, Britain's poet laureate, wrote for his children after the death of their mother, Sylvia Plath. It's a simple, straightforward tale of a small boy and his oversized, otherworldly friend, and Bird has wisely chosen both traditional and modern ways of visualizing it.

In a decision that fits well with the film's 1957 setting, Bird has utilized old-fashioned, flat, two-dimensional animation to tell most of his story. That makes sense for creating the Norman Rockwell–inspired town of Rockwell, Maine, and also makes for frames that look more like carefully drawn storybook illustrations than much of modern animation is interested in.

When it comes to animating the 50-foot metal behemoth that gives the film its name, however, Bird and company went to computer-generated images to underline the creature's differentness and to give this giant metal object a kind of grace and personality it might not otherwise have had.

The key dramatically to *Iron Giant*'s success is a parallel ability to adroitly blend competing sensibilities. Written by Tim McCanlies from a screen story by Bird, the film has the same honest warmheartedness that marked the writer's previous *Dancer, Texas Pop. 81.* But though it's got heart, *Iron Giant* is far from square, exhibiting a dryly humorous Rocky and Bullwinkle–influenced antiestablishment sense of humor fueled by one of its main characters, an espresso-drinking hipster named Dean McCoppin (perfectly voiced by Harry Connick Jr.) who wears shades and listens to cool jazz far into the night.

Dean's character is not the only good use *Iron Giant* makes of its 1957 setting. Various amusing segments remind us that this was an era characterized by science-fiction films about alien invaders as well as the intertwined fears of the Communist menace and the atomic bomb. Maybe people didn't lock their doors, but there was considerable fear in the air.

Nine-year-old Hogarth Hughes (Eli Marienthal), by contrast, is completely unafraid, a feisty and independent tyke who lives with his hardworking waitress mother Annie Hughes (Jennifer Aniston) and is always game for adventure.

When Hogarth hears a local fisherman talk of sighting an enormous metal monster, he's all ears. And when he hears suspicious noises outside his house one night, naturally Hogarth investigates. What he finds, to his complete shock, is a classic 1950s-type metal-eating robot, 50 feet tall, which the film's opening shots have shown arriving from outer space.

Because Hogarth, in an "Androcles and the Lion" maneuver, helps the giant out of some difficulty, and because the iron man is something of a big kid itself, the two become friends. And though his voice (courtesy of Vin Diesel) sounds like a garbage disposal attempting to speak, the giant even learns to express himself in appealing English.

Some of *Iron Giant*'s most pleasing moments convey the pure glee Hogarth feels at having this completely delightful playmate. "My own giant robot," he says, genially puffed up with pride. "I am the luckiest kid in America."

But happy though he is, Hogarth is smart enough to know he has to hide the giant from the rest of Rockwell. "People just aren't ready for you," he says before choosing the junkyard run by hipster (and would-be sculptor) Dean as the most likely refuge.

A refuge proves especially necessary when officious government agent Kent Mansley (Christopher McDonald), a 1950s version of an *X-Files* investigator, starts snooping around town, trying to get on Hogarth's good side by calling him "chief," "scout," "sport," "skipper," and any other bogus appellation he can think of.

The Iron Giant takes special glee in poking fun at the pipe-smoking, trenchcoat-wearing Mansley, the epitome of wrongheaded, xenophobic authority whose thoughts about the giant boil down to, "We didn't build it, that's reason enough to blow it to kingdom come."

While it does turn out that the giant is not always a benign figure, the lessons this film wants to teach are of the gentle variety. It is against guns, against killing, against nuclear weapons (which make a scary cameo appearance), and for the existence of souls and personal self-determination: Both Hogarth and the giant learn that "you are what you choose to be."

In addition to calling the boy Hogarth after the eighteenth-century British artist, the makers of *Iron Giant* pay specific tribute to other comic illustrators, from the makers of Superman to Will Eisner, creator of the cult-favorite Spirit. The film also echoes earlier efforts, such as *King Kong, Frankenstein,* and *E.T.,* but with a refreshing spirit of bemused, nonaggressive hipness that is completely, and delightfully, its own.

Jesus' Son
2000

In an age of known quantities, *Jesus' Son* is almost indefinable. In a sea of one-note symphonies, this touching feature is bleak and comic, heartbreaking and affirmative, romantic and tragic, gimlet-eyed and sympathetic, all at the same time. It's the sweetest, most punishing of lowlife serenades, a crawl through the wreckage created by, protagonist FH informs, "people just like us, only unluckier."

Jesus' Son is true to the off-center vision of Denis Johnson, a poet of the feckless and dispossessed whose celebrated literary collection is its source. Those linked short stories set in the 1970s took their title from a line in the Velvet Underground drug anthem "Heroin," so it's not a shock that FH doesn't stand for "Fat Head." Not quite.

FH, frankly, earned his name by his penchant for screwing up. But to see him only as an addict and a sneak thief, while accurate enough, is to miss what director Alison Maclean and her trio of writers (Elizabeth Cuthrell, David Urrutia, Oren Moverman) intuitively understand. With his shambling, shuffling walk and radiant smile, FH is a kind of holy innocent who never loses his childlike thirst for life, no matter how much it confuses and betrays him.

The notion of a befuddled junkie saint is not a new one, but it's almost never played with the kind of grace, humor, and wistful vulnerability that Billy Crudup (*Without Limits, Waking the Dead*) manages. An actor of enormous, unforced likability, Crudup carries us with him as perhaps no one else could on FH's erratic journey around America, trying to do more than just stay afloat on life's roughest seas.

Jesus' Son is also a major success for director Maclean, who hasn't managed a feature since *Crush,* her acclaimed 1992 New Zealand debut. Maclean's feel for the American heartland in the 1970s is exact down to the music on the soundtrack. She gets disciplined, on-point performances from the excellent supporting cast (Samantha Morton, Holly Hunter, Dennis Hopper, Denis Leary, Will Patton, and Jack Black, among others), and, most important, she is able to cherish these people without sacrificing the ability to see them and their killing imperfections with complete clarity.

FH tells his own story, but his voice-over, like that of a man telling an elaborate tale from a barstool, is meandering, even circular. He starts in the middle then jumps back to the beginning before reaching the end. At the center, always, is Michelle (a compelling Morton, Oscar-nominated as Sean Penn's mute foil in *Sweet and Lowdown*), the woman of his feverish dreams.

FH meets Michelle in Iowa City in 1971 at a druggy party at an outlying farmhouse. They don't get together until a year later, and their love-among-the-ruins romance, complicated by a mutual dependence on heroin, pills, and whatever else is handy, is the film's core.

"There was something wrong with us," FH says distractedly at one point, "and we didn't know what to do about it."

When it's not following this relationship, *Jesus' Son* trails FH and his peculiar acquaintances on the kind of strange, almost defiantly comic escapades (like working in a hospital emergency room when someone comes in with a hunting knife sticking out of his head) that only junkies seem to have. These exploits rarely play well on the screen (or on the page, for that matter), but the combination of Maclean's direction, Johnson's original vision, and the gifts of the trio of screenwriters makes a considerable difference here.

Maclean strikes the right matter-of-fact tone with the hallucinatory aspects of FH's story—like the time he saw a nude woman floating by on a parachute. More critically, the film has the feel of being told from the inside, by an articulate survivor. "There is a price to be paid for dreaming," FH says at one point, and *Jesus' Son* is always aware of what that means.

Land and Freedom
1996

As self-contradictory as the concept of "a good war" has to sound, Spain in 1936 comes close to fitting the description.

After fascist conservative forces led by Francisco Franco rose against an elected left-of-center government, believers from all over the world, including young novelists Ernest Hemingway and George Orwell, made their way to Spain to fight for democracy and progressive reform. Ragged and rebellious, they were heroes with dirty faces, naive and idealistic child crusaders in adult bodies, and *Land and Freedom* pays moving and thoughtful tribute to their thwarted romanticism.

Winner of the International Critics' Prize at Cannes and the Felix Award for the year's best European film, *Land and Freedom* is remarkable for its naturalistic treatment of human truths, its point-blank refusal to shortchange passion and emotion while dramatizing a political situation that its protagonist aptly characterizes as "dead complicated."

Given that *Land and Freedom*'s director is Ken Loach, this is not unexpected. Loach is the bedrock of the British independent movement, a role model for directors such as Neil Jordan, Stephen Frears, and Mike Leigh because of his ability to do honest and heartfelt work for more than thirty years while refusing to compromise his political and aesthetic beliefs.

But while Loach's best-known films, from *Cathy Come Home* and *Poor Cow* in the 1960s through *Riff-Raff* and *Raining Stones* decades later, have all been small-scale, kitchen-sink dramas, *Land and Freedom* is the opposite. It's an epic, a working-class *Lawrence of Arabia* that enlarges Loach's scope while losing none of the qualities for which he has become celebrated.

As written by veteran Loach collaborator Jim Allen, *Land and Freedom* makes use of a framing story, a death in a working-class flat in today's Liverpool that leaves a young woman named Kim without her grandfather. Going through her grandfather's things, Kim comes across a small suitcase crammed with letters, photos, and newspaper clippings, as well as a red bandanna filled with earth. Spanish earth.

It's now 1936, and an intense working-class young man named David (Ian Hart, who played John Lennon in both *Back Beat* and *The Hours and the Times*) decides to go to Spain and fight for the Republic.

Though a member of the Communist Party, David (like George Orwell) ends up in a militia unit on the Aragon front run by a socialist organization called POUM. It's an international affair, with Spanish fighters such as the fiery Blanca (Rosana Pastor) shouldering arms with the American Lawrence (Tom Gilroy) and an ex-IRA man named Coogan (Eoin McCarthy). "It's a real people's army," David writes home with proud excitement.

Inevitably, the story of *Land and Freedom* is the story of this young man's often painful journey from innocence to experience. Involved in a love affair, witness to chaos and wretchedness on the battlefield, David goes through a process of personal maturation that actor Hart finely conveys.

The film also details a political coming of age, as David increasingly has to deal with troublesome actions by his beloved Communist Party. For *Land and Freedom* says quite forcefully that the tragedy of Spain was the betrayal of the principles of the revolution by the rigid ideology of party regulars who were moved around like so many chess pieces by Joseph Stalin and his Soviet hierarchy.

Loach, as usual, precisely calibrates his emotional effects, avoiding overdramatization and telling his story simply but with conviction. And while Hart and Pastor are clearly the stars here, Loach cast the sixteen-person militia unit as a whole, and the film excels at showing the camaraderie, the fellow feeling that made these people risk their lives for an ideal.

A passionate film, *Land and Freedom* takes its tone from the high spirits of those convinced that pure belief could make a difference. Change that to can make a difference, Loach and Allen would say, which is why they use granddaughter Kim to stress the continuity of the progressive tradition. And if there is a statement of David's this film would leave you with, it's his belief that "revolutions are contagious. Had we succeeded, we would have changed the world." Having revolutionized film in Britain, Ken Loach is still looking for that next frontier.

Last Orders
2001

Michael Caine. Tom Courtenay. David Hemmings. Bob Hoskins. Helen Mirren. Ray Winstone. It's an exceptional cast, a gathering of some of the most impressive names in British acting, but it's part of the grace of *Last Orders* that it's not immediately clear what attracted them all to this particular project.

For *Last Orders,* feelingly directed by Fred Schepisi from Graham Swift's resonant Booker Prize–winning novel, is deceptive in the best sense. Gathering its forces slowly, this careful, thoughtful film, quietly but deeply moving, is dramatic without seeming to be.

A story of the involving secrets behind ordinary lives, *Last Orders* touches on memory and regrets, dreams and disappointments, what tears people apart and what holds them together—all the things that show how complex simple lives can be if we but have the time and wisdom to look.

The film's celebrated, experienced cast is a considerable asset in this, and not just because its members give the natural, subdued performances the material requires. It's also because regular moviegoers will have vivid memories of these people when they were younger, of Courtenay, for instance, in *Doctor Zhivago* and *Billy Liar,* and Hemmings in *Blowup.* And growing older, and just maybe, if you're lucky, getting a little bit wiser, is very much what this film is about.

Last Orders begins quietly and unobtrusively, as four men of a certain age come together in their local London pub, the Coach and Horses. One of their number, Jack Dodds (Caine), the group's guiding force, has died, and they are here to fulfill his surprise last request.

When the bartender says things won't be the same, one of the men cracks, "You ain't seen the last of Jack yet." He means it as a joke, because Jack's cremated ashes are about to appear on the scene, but the comment turns out to have a larger relevance as well. For Jack's "last order" becomes an opportunity for all these men to examine their lives, the impetus for a journey that is fraught with emotion and surprise.

What Jack has asked is that his ashes be scattered off the pier at the seaside town of Margate. Even with a direct itinerary, the auto trip would not be short, but the route of "four geezers and a box" turns out to be anything but straightforward. Unexpected detours are made, unfinished emotional business gets examined, and we gradually come to know the entirety of these very human, very fallible lives.

The driver of the car, a Mercedes to suit the occasion, is Jack's son Vince, a car dealer familiarly known as Big Boy and exactly played by Winstone (Ben Kingsley's prey in *Sexy Beast*) as someone who manages to be simultaneously brutish and sensitive.

The most serene of Vince's passengers is Vic (Courtenay), an undertaker as dignified as his job would indicate. Not serene at all is the blustery Lenny (Hemmings), a former boxer who still holds a variety of grudges. And then there is Ray (Hoskins), known as Lucky because of his gift for the horses, who's had the longest and most complex relationship with Jack.

One person who might be expected to be in the car but isn't is Jack's widow, Amy (Mirren), who has a different kind of family business to take care of. Though she is not on the trip, Amy's story is central to *Last Orders,* and Mirren, allowing herself to look almost unrecognizably pinched and severe, gives a beautiful performance as a woman trying to hold her own in an indifferent world.

As adapted by director Schepisi, *Last Orders* mirrors the book's intricate structure, easily switching both time periods and points of view. We see all the characters, including the now departed Jack, at several points in their lives, some so early that other, younger actors are required to play the scenes. One of the pleasant paradoxes of *Last Orders* is that though Schepisi is an Australian filmmaker some of whose best work (*The Chant of Jimmie Blacksmith, A Cry in the Dark*) is set in that country, he has done an impeccable job of bringing to life an intensely English story. This is an especially subtle film where, as Winstone has said, "it's all about how you look in the rearview mirror during the dialogue in the car. The camera does a lot of the talking for you." It's hard not to be moved by what it has to say.

Last Resort
2001

Last Resort is an intimate chamber piece about love, hope, and despair, not necessarily in that order. Spare yet unsparing, emotionally affecting without even a hint of excess, it's an honest, haunting look at the connection between a pair of lonely people who wonder where they belong.

Written and directed in English by Pawel Pawlikowski, a Pole who works largely in Britain, *Last Resort* was a consistent award winner at festivals throughout Europe. Using a neo-documentary style as well as a Mike Leigh–influenced workshop method that allows the actors to have a hand in developing their own dialogue, *Last Resort* combines Leigh's concern for truth with Ken Loach's social realism and Pawlikowski's own involving visual point of view.

Last Resort is also striking because it has chosen the world of political refugees searching for asylum as its milieu. Powerless outsiders whose existence we prefer not to acknowledge, people used to being looked at without being seen, these are truly lost souls, strangers in a land with a particular strangeness they never anticipated.

Tanya (Russian actress Dina Korzun) calls herself "a refugee by accident." We meet her at London's Heathrow Airport, newly arrived from the old country with her ten-year-old son, Artiom (Artiom Strelnikov), who reads to his mother from guidebooks sunnily promising "In Britain, friendly people start conversations by talking about the weather."

Actually getting into Britain, however, proves more difficult. Tanya and her son have arrived with only $85 and no visible means of support. She tells the immigration authorities she's supposed to be met by her fiance, but he doesn't show up. Increasingly distraught to the point of panic, not really knowing what she's getting into, Tanya suddenly decides to apply for political asylum for herself and her son.

What she's asked for is a one-way ticket to a bleak, crowded seaside high-rise that serves as a holding area for asylum seekers. It's a lonely, isolated tower, surrounded by fences and even barbed wire, located next to a distressed amusement park with a brazen "Dreamland Welcomes You" sign that mocks them with its unconvincing courtesy.

Only gradually does Tanya realize the kind of Kafkaesque situation she's involved herself in. She's trapped in a bureaucratic maze, unable to go anywhere until her case is decided, a process that could take twelve to sixteen months. "You're joking," she tells the official who gives her this piece of news. He's not.

Unlike Tanya, Alfie (Paddy Considine of *A Room for Romeo Brass*) is in the Dreamland vicinity by choice, not necessity. A former boxer who manages an amusement arcade by day and calls bingo by night, Alfie has exiled himself to what he calls "the armpit of the universe" because, in its own way, his life was not working out any better than Tanya's.

An all-or-nothing romantic who is addicted, her son says, to loving men who make her cry, Tanya doesn't know what to make of Alfie, whose decency seems genuine and whose trustworthiness soon makes a friend of young Artiom. Increasingly distraught and emotional, she catches the eye of the slimy Les (Lindsey Honey), who dangles the possibility of sexually explicit modeling on the Internet as an ultimate kind of safe—and potentially lucrative—sex.

Perhaps because they helped create their roles, both the expressive, vulnerable Korzun and the matey Considine are quietly compelling, as is Honey, described in the press material as something of a pornographer in real life as well.

Though it is only 75 minutes long, *Last Resort,* metaphorical title and all, is a quite impressive film. Pawlikowski (working with cinematographer Ryszard Lenczewski and co-writer Rowan Joffe) has the restraint necessary to hit all his notes just right. This is the best class of poetic realism, the kind you can believe in without a trace of hesitation.

Lawless Heart
2003

Lawless Heart is a charming, disarming, and in some ways humbling film. It is so adroit in its structure, so insightful in how it explores its vivid characters, that it forces us to acknowledge not only how complicated all lives are but also how easy it is to be self-centered and miss those complications in everyone else.

A thoughtful, funny, and melancholic meditation on the notion that all hearts are lawless and out of control when under emotional stress, this British independent film is a pleasure on several fronts, including its high level of acting and how much it gives us to chew on in its mere 87 minutes.

Also, given its specific sensibility and idiosyncratic cast of characters, it is a shock to find that *Lawless* was written and directed by two people, Neil Hunter and Tom Hunsinger. But the biggest surprise of all is how effective the film's simple but unexpected twist on a *Rashomon* structure turns out to be.

That 1950 Japanese film added a new concept to the language by offering four contradictory versions of the same incident. What *Lawless* does is show not one finite event but a longer period of several days' duration from the contrasting points of view of three characters, each of whom gets his own half-hour in the sun.

The notion here is not that people remember the same things differently, but rather, that by the nature of their lives they see different parts of the same whole and are privy to different experiences. What's peripheral to one individual is central to another, what looks puzzling from one set of eyes is easily explained through someone else's. Each successive story fills in gaps left by the previous ones, gradually providing key additional information and motivations earlier tellings have been oblivious to.

Though we end up with a complex, almost omniscient overview of these characters' lives, initially we're thrown so cold into the story that we are not sure who anyone is and who is worth paying attention to. We are intentionally made to feel late to the party, a beat behind the plot, but *Lawless*'s people are so involving, it's worth the wait to understand them better.

Set in England in Maldon, Essex (where filmmaker Hunter grew up), *Lawless Heart* starts with a funeral for a young man named Stuart. Though we never see him (except for old home-movie footage), Stuart was a major influence on the lives of all the film's characters. "Stuart," says Tim (Douglas Henshall), "was half the fun in this town." A carefree hippie just returned to town after a walkabout of eight years, Tim is introduced early on, but the first character whose shoes we walk in is Dan (the veteran Bill Nighy).

A dour farmer who looks as if he's wandered in from an Ingmar Bergman film, Dan is married to Judy (Ellie Haddington), the dead man's sister. Since Stuart died without a will, she's inherited his money and has to decide whether to keep it for the family farm or give it to Stuart's bereft lover, Nick (Tom Hollander).

None of this is immediately on Dan's mind at the funeral because he finds himself engaged in an unexpected flirtation with the town's seductive French florist, Corinne (Clementine Celarie looking like a young Jeanne Moreau).

Talking to this virtual stranger, Dan finds himself being candid and, incidentally, expressing many of the film's themes. How is it, he wonders, that possibilities that once seemed great have narrowed? Was he now not living his life but, rather, watching it, like a comedy? The life you have, Corinne asks, is it the life you want?

Once Dan has grappled with this interlude's possibilities, the film's focus shifts to Nick, for whom Stuart's unexpected death has been a special disaster. Waiting for Judy to decide about the money, he lets the feckless Tim move in with him and soon regrets it. Then he meets Charlie (Sukie Smith), an impulsive young woman, as good-hearted as she is bubble-headed, whose unceasing good cheer draws him in.

The last person we hear from is, of all people, Tim, who finds himself attracted to a young woman named Leah (Josephine Butler). It's in the third part of *Lawless* that the strength of the film's structure really takes hold: Tim's actions looked at from his own point of view turn out to be very different from what we've seen before.

Believability is finally one of the keys to the success of *Lawless Heart,* along with its insights, its humor, and its compassionate ability to discern that all of us, even the unlikeliest, have our great passions and our secret sorrows. And it understands that people barely visible in the periphery of our lives have things to teach us.

Laws of Gravity
1992

Laws of Gravity is a black diamond of a film, hard-edged and compelling, a remarkably accomplished piece of work that knows exactly what it wants to do and then goes out and does it. Volatile, verbal, and streetwise, it neither complains nor explains. It simply puts a world on display and dares you to be indifferent to it.

Set among the petty hoodlums and junior-grade hard guys of Brooklyn's Greenpoint section, *Laws of Gravity* is American independent filmmaking the way it ought to be done. It is a first feature not only for its twenty-nine-year-old writer-director, Nick Gomez, but also for most of its cast, and its $38,000 budget is threadbare by any standard. Yet its ability to convey emotion and experience couldn't be improved no matter what the cost.

The center of *Gravity* is Jimmy (Peter Green), a lean, goateed, small-time street outlaw who earns whatever living he can by lifting goods off of unguarded vans and selling the loot to a convenient fence. Married to Denise (Edie Falco), a waitress at the neighborhood bar, Jimmy, while horrified at the thought of actual work, is stable by local standards, content to stay in the mildly criminal grooves his life has marked out for him so far.

Jon (Adam Trese) is another story. The original hothead, with a temper that is always a wink away from erupting, he is a natural-born troublemaker who explodes first and thinks about it later, if he thinks about it at all. Almost no one can stand Jonny Boy for long, including his off-again, on-again girlfriend, Celia (Arabella Field). No one, that is, except Jimmy, who improbably considers Jon his protégé and junior partner in misbehavior.

Into this unstable friendship comes the amiably sinister Frankie (Paul Schulze), an old friend who fled to Florida to escape a stretch on Riker's Island. Now he's back, traveling in a stolen car with a bag full of illegal firearms in the trunk. Selling them on the street and making a sweet profit soon becomes the focus of everyone's attention, and the catalyst for *Gravity*'s climactic action.

Though its plot is certainly sufficient, *Laws of Gravity* is episodic by nature, and its real success is in the way it replicates the texture of this low-rent criminal environment, where "ratting someone out" is the ultimate sin and it's okay to smack your old lady around if you do it at home and keep the agony off the streets.

Gomez's script and the improvisations his tuned-in actors have worked off it capture the sense of these violent, haphazard lives. Not only does the often funny, always in-your-face dialogue ring brutally true, but the film understands from the inside the strutting cockiness of its characters, as well as how haunted their lives are under all that bravado.

Though the actors all perform beautifully, an argument could be made that the real star of this film is the exceptional cinema verité camera work of Jean de Segonzac, a veteran documentary cinematographer whose credits include the Oscar-winning *Common Threads: Stories from the Quilt.*

Darting in and out of groups, elegantly eavesdropping on private conversations, de Segonzac's camera manages to be unobtrusive and pivotal at the same time. It underlines the immediacy that is one of this film's strongest virtues and is critical in making *Laws of Gravity*, despite its downbeat situations, into an intense cinematic experience.

A gripping performance by Edie Falco years before The Sopranos *was a gleam in anyone's eye.*

Living in Oblivion
1995

Living in Oblivion is a crooked valentine to the independent film world, a bemused and caustic billet-doux to the boys and girls who don't quite have the clout to figure in *The Player* but end up addicted to the business anyhow.

As the cinematographer of Jim Jarmusch's *Stranger Than Paradise* and the director of the Brad Pitt–starring *Johnny Suede,* writer-director Tom DiCillo has certainly been there. And he has turned his experience into a consistently funny inside-movies comedy, a witty revenge against the dream factory, low-budget division, that won the Waldo Salt Screenwriting Award at the Sundance Film Festival.

Starring some of the best actors in the independent world, including Steve Buscemi, James LeGros, and Dermot Mulroney, *Oblivion* is an intricately constructed film-within-a-film, gathering in one small place every problem, both conceivable and otherwise, a struggling film might encounter.

Originally concocted as a half-hour short to showcase actress Catherine Keener (the co-star of *Suede* and Mulroney's wife), *Oblivion* has a quirky three-part structure in which film, reality, and fantasy double back on one another. Each section involves a single scene that put-upon director Nick Reve (Buscemi), the kind of intense young cineaste who has a poster for Fritz Lang's *M* on his bedroom wall, is trying desperately to commit to film.

The first section, which approximates the half-hour short, is the most ingeniously structured, with color (for the film-within-a-film, also called *Living in Oblivion*) alternating with black-and-white. As take succeeds take, with problems piling up like cordwood, we meet the movie gang, in many ways more compelling than the material they're struggling with.

Nicole (Keener), whose big scene is being shot, wants to be taken seriously as an actress but is universally known as the girl who had a celebrated shower scene with Richard Gere. And her confidence isn't helped by overhearing crew members ripping her to bits.

Not initially prone to doubt is Wolf (Mulroney), the self-absorbed director of photography who lives with forceful assistant director Wanda (Danielle Von Zerneck) and, as his leather vest, beret, and eventual eye-patch indicate, fancies himself the artist on the set.

The funniest member of this team, though he doesn't know it, is Nicole's co-star, Chad Palomino (LeGros), who appears in the second section. A Hollywood player set to star next as "the sexy serial killer Winona Ryder shacks up with," Palomino is a fatuous oaf slumming in the indie world who drives everyone crazy with his womanizing, his improvisations ("Just stop me if I'm out of line"), and his scattershot flattery. "I want to learn from you," he tells Nick earnestly. "You're the genius." This is easily the most pointed portrait in the film, as well as the most humorous, fueling speculation at Sundance that DiCillo had drawn just a bit on his previous experience with Brad Pitt.

Oblivion's third section has poor Nick trying to shoot a dream sequence while coping with a troublesome dwarf and a rambunctious smoke machine. It's not quite up to the standard set by the first two, but it does provide an opportunity to nicely wrap things up.

Though *Living in Oblivion* may sound like a one-joke movie, the pleasure of the endeavor is that it has no trouble holding your interest without feeling repetitive. Mark it down to the excellence of the acting, including the smallest roles, and the amusing and accurate way the ambience of bargain-basement filmmaking is captured.

This realism extends from the physical look of the production to movie terminology to, most important, the psychology of the business. Everyone in the production, from the gaffer to the director, is to varying degrees ambitious, egocentric, rife with insecurities, in constant need of reassurance, and eager to push his or her own agenda. But, hey, it's only a movie. Isn't it?

Peter Dinklage, the actor who plays the troublesome dwarf, went on to star in the Sundance award–winning The Station Agent.

Love and Death on Long Island
1998

As the determined enemy of all things modern, British cult novelist and "erstwhile fogy" Giles De'Ath (it's pronounced "day-ath," thank you very much) is not a person one expects to find in a movie theater. In fact, if he hadn't accidentally locked himself out of his London flat on a rainy afternoon, he wouldn't be there at all.

Expecting to see a refined E.M. Forster adaptation, Giles accidentally wanders into *Hotpants College II.* Suitably horrified, he's about to leave when he catches a glimpse, just a glimpse, of a face on the screen. It's mega-dreamboat Ronnie Bostock, "one of Hollywood's most snoggable fellows," and against all logic, reason, and expectation, Giles is overwhelmed and a magnificent obsession is born.

Starring John Hurt in one of the great performances of his career as the transfixed writer, and *Beverly Hills, 90210*'s Jason Priestley as teen idol Bostock, *Love and Death on Long Island* is sharp, sophisticated, and completely delicious, a purposeful comedy that focuses on the power of screen images to uproot lives and the poignancy of *amour fou,* totally mad love.

Love and Death (taken from Gilbert Adair's novel of the same name) is also the impressive feature debut of British TV's writer-director Richard Kwietniowski. Wildly unlikely yet completely believable, droll enough to practically define the word, this film uses exactly calibrated bursts of dry wit and killing dialogue to uncover mania where others wouldn't even dare to look.

What gives *Love and Death* a special grace is the exquisite, nuanced performance of veteran actor Hurt, Oscar-nominated for his work in *Midnight Express* and *The Elephant Man*. Hurt's grasp of the role couldn't be surer—who, after all, is in the actor's league when it comes to the quizzically raised eyebrow?—and his ability to squeeze all possible humor out of lines such as "I've never really approved of the pre-Raphaelites" is unquestioned. There is an entire universe in Hurt's face, a world of bemusement, bafflement, comic hauteur, and disdain that is intoxicating to observe.

At first, Giles's fascination with Ronnie Bostock takes a conventional route. He scours fan magazines for color photos, pasting them in an album grandly titled *Bostockiana*. And, not caring that *Sight & Sound* has called them "puerile romps without a single redeeming feature," he tries to catch up on *Skidmarks* and *Tex-Mex*, earlier items from the Bostock oeuvre. It's a difficult proposition when (a) you don't realize VCRs have to be connected to TV sets, and (b) you can't tell a TV from a microwave.

Then the madness goes up a notch. Giles imagines himself on a TV quiz show where the category is Bostock; he visualizes his new hero as the subject of the Tate Gallery's classic painting *The Death of Chatterton*; he even starts constructing a new novel around "the discovery of beauty where no one thought to look for it."

Inevitably, Giles decides to track this beauty to its source—and this from a man who hates to so much as leave his apartment. He makes a pilgrimage to the small Long Island town where Ronnie lives with a model named Audrey (Fiona Loewi) and puts his own considerable personal charm at the service of worming his way into the young man's life.

Under Kwietniowski's completely controlled direction, this film delights in exploring the clash of cultures that's inevitable when De'Ath hits Long Island and discovers places like a diner called Chez d'Irv. When the writer ignores a "Thank You for Not Smoking" sign and informs the astonished cabdriver, "As I am, I don't expect to be thanked," it's a moment of such heedless and hilarious urbanity you want to stand and cheer.

When the oblivious actor (nicely played by Priestley, tweaking his own teen idol image) and the conniving writer—two people who speak the same language only in theory—finally meet, it's an irresistible case of worlds colliding. Yet it's a mark of the skill with which *Love and Death* has been made that as his mania plays itself out, Giles never becomes ridiculous, never turns into a melancholy version of *Lolita*'s Humbert Humbert.

The combination of Hurt's magnificent presence and Kwietniowski's uncompromising writing and direction give the lovelorn writer a dignity and an emotional heft he never loses. Not even when he's in the throes of the desperation born of what even De'Ath knows enough to call "the most irrational desire of all mankind, the desire to fall in love."

Lovely & Amazing
2002

Lovely & Amazing is all but indescribable, and what a good thing that is. Like the best of personal, independent cinema—terms that too often provide cover for a multitude of sins—it is both marvelously observed and completely individual. There is no film like this film, and that is something you don't hear every day.

Lovely & Amazing is a product of the distinctive sensibility of writer-director Nicole Holofcener, whose debut film, *Walking and Talking,* provided a similar experience. She has an exact eye and ear for the way things are, a rueful sensitivity to how quietly ridiculous our twenty-first-century existence can be. Sort of savage but in a quiet, unassuming way, this is a funny and charming film about some painful situations.

Lovely & Amazing is set in today's Los Angeles, and, like Doug Liman's *Swingers,* it's so accurate about how people attempt meaningful emotional connections in an uncaring world of self-involvement, obtuseness, and free-floating insecurity that it ought to be put in a time capsule. But while *Swingers* focused on men, *Lovely & Amazing* introduces us to a family of women doing the best they can to get along.

The group's matriarch, Jane Marks (Brenda Blethyn), is concerned enough about doing good in the world to have adopted an eight-year-old African American girl named Annie (Raven Goodwin), whose birth mother was a crack addict.

But Jane is also someone who can spend an inordinate amount of time and money covering her bed with so many designer pillows that there's no room to sleep. Her main preoccupation these days is impending liposuction, a cosmetic procedure she seems to want at least in part because she has a crush on the handsome Dr. Crane (Michael Nouri).

Jane has a pair of birth daughters, self-absorbed in different ways; between the two of them, they seem to have cornered the market on neuroses. Elizabeth (Emily Mortimer) is introduced first, an actress so insecure about her body that it's fitting we meet her in agonies of awkwardness posing for a picture in *Vogue* in a very revealing designer dress. "I don't feel quite like myself," she says, to which the photographer replies, "Who does?"

Elizabeth, it turns out, is not getting much help in the support department. Her agent's idea of personal service is giving her second-hand presents (she calls it "re-gifting"), and her boyfriend, Paul (James LeGros), is a nature journalist with the personality of a bump on a log. It's not a surprise to discover that Elizabeth is such an aggressive rescuer of stray dogs that her place resembles an animal shelter.

Given all this, one of the surprises of *Lovely & Amazing* is that Elizabeth is considerably more empathetic than her sister Michelle (a letter-perfect Catherine Keener), a former homecoming queen with an exaggerated sense of her own importance.

Keener, who starred in *Living in Oblivion* and Holofcener's *Walking and Talking,* has often played hard-edged individuals, but they're hardly ever as exactly observed as Michelle, a provocative character who mainlines so much aggrieved entitlement that she has only a dim sense of how hollow and futile her life has become.

Introduced trying to sell her homemade miniature chairs to a crafts store, Michelle is shocked to find that a former junior high classmate is now a pediatrician. When the woman reminds her that, after all, "we are thirty-six," Michelle's response—"we're not thirty-six thirty-six"—is telling.

Although she is the mother of a little girl, Michelle in her own mind won't grow up, won't deal with her abysmal marriage to an uncaring personal sound engineer ("he buys stereos for rich people"), won't—or can't—differentiate between taking charge of a situation and being hostile and bossy. Even the relationship she has with young Annie, who shows signs of developing the same insecurities as her sisters, plays like sibling rivalry despite their difference in age and situation.

Each woman faces difficulties during *Lovely & Amazing,* from Michelle's experimenting with the working world to Elizabeth's need to participate in a "chemistry read" with a major movie star (Dermot Mulroney) to answer the burning question "Are you hot together?" An immediate change in anyone's outlook is not this film's style, but the potential for future corrections is there in a gentle, wistful way.

With a cast that includes some of the top actors working in independent film, *Lovely & Amazing* involves us because it is so incisive, so bleakly amusing in showing the way we go about our lives. Many of these characters are people we almost hate to love, but by illuminating their humanity, this film doesn't give us a choice.

Love Serenade
1997

Love Serenade offers as precise and merciless a comic vision as anyone could want. A wickedly funny examination of obsessive romantic behavior, its satiric vision of women in love and men on the make was devastating enough to earn writer-director Shirley Barrett the prized Camera d'Or at Cannes, given to the best first film both in and out of competition.

Barrett is Australian, one in a slew of filmmakers adept at creating bizarre psychological landscapes where comic delusion is the rule.

Love Serenade's producer, Jan Chapman, has worked with both Jane Campion and Gillian Armstrong, and though this is Barrett's debut, she gives every evidence of belonging in their company.

A smartly acted four-character drama, *Love Serenade* is set in the completely parched hamlet of Sunray, where time has not so much stood still as been baked in its tracks. The local radio station, 101.4 on your FM dial, is so bedraggled it's never so much as seen a compact disc, and no one has broadcast from there for months.

Into the studio and the surrounding lunar landscape comes a refugee from the wider world. Ken Sherry (veteran Australian actor George Shevtsov), once the Drivetime King of Brisbane radio, arrives in town complete with aviator sunglasses, reptilian smile, and lounge lizard manner.

An aging hipster who favors shirts open to mid-chest level, Ken Sherry has a seductive voice that drowns its listeners in waves of ennui. He has a taste for rambling personal monologues and the funkadelic sounds of Barry White, and the whole package has a devastating effect on a pair of unwary twentysomething sisters whom fate has placed in the house next door to this self-proclaimed "fool where women are concerned."

Vicki-Ann (Rebecca Frith) is the oldest, a prim beautician who may be the only person in town to have heard of Ken Sherry. She casts covetous eyes on the new arrival from the big city, bombarding him with a baffling string of homemade casseroles and perky smiles.

Vicki-Ann, it develops, sees the world exclusively in glowing romance-magazine terms. "Ken Sherry," she earnestly informs her mopey sister Dimity, "has come to Sunray to heal. Slowly, bit by bit, he may learn to love again."

Dimity (Miranda Otto, winner of an Australian Oscar for Armstrong's *The Last Days of Chez Nous*) is not so sure about any of this. Awkward, ill at ease, but more scheming than her fog-bound psyche would indicate, Dimity (who works at the local Chinese restaurant) doesn't see why uneaten casseroles need be the only route to a man's heart.

Never mind that Ken Sherry is a pig in a poke, a dissipated Barry Manilow wannabe addicted to fake intimacy. To Dimity and Vicki-

Ann, he is closer to Prince Charming than they ever expected to get, and, mutually and madly infatuated, they engage in a peevish rivalry for his wandering affection.

Drawn into this battle from time to time is Albert Lee (John Alansu), Dimity's boss, a man of almost regal formality and comic diction who has always admired Vicki-Ann from a distance. A stern moralist and spare-time nudist, Albert takes a strong dislike to Ken Sherry when he rashly questions the freshness of the establishment's prawns, and little happens to make him change his mind.

Beautifully consistent in tone from its waspish beginning to a savage, surreal ending, *Love Serenade* is one of those films that shows how essential it can be for writers to direct their own work. No one but Barrett could understand the bizarre nuances of this arch and heavily ironic comedy of obliviousness, with its subtext of men and women being completely different species, or guide its actors so expertly toward understanding characters who have no insight themselves.

This is a pitiless kind of comedy, and it works especially well against the backdrop of the sullen romantic ballads of Barry White, including "Never Gonna Give You Up," "I'm Gonna Love You Just a Little Bit More Baby," and the song that gives the film its name. In this cracked, hot-house world, those throaty extravaganzas begin to sound as if they're making sense. "We're all odd," Ken Sherry says, and this film is not about to argue the point.

The Madness of King George
1994

Late in 1788, in the twenty-eighth year of the reign of England's King George III, something extraordinary happened: As one historian tactfully put it, "The king's mind broke down." A bizarre kind of dementia overtook the monarch who had already lost the American colonies, and everyone who was anyone in the country's ruling circles was faced with a crisis beyond all imagining.

As if to prove that the unlikeliest material can make for the best films, *The Madness of King George,* directed by Nicholas Hytner from

Alan Bennett's prizewinning play, has taken this footnote to history and transformed it into a tale that's potent, engrossing, and even thrilling to experience.

This is due in great measure to Nigel Hawthorne's work as the deranged monarch, a heroic performance that enlarges our understanding of what acting can accomplish. The sixty-five-year-old Hawthorne swept his country's major theatrical awards when he played the part on the London stage. And Hytner, who directed that version as well, has ensured that his interpretation was transferred to the screen with its intensity intact.

Although not as celebrated here as he is back home, writer Bennett (who has a brief cameo as a mild member of Parliament) is one of Britain's most respected men of letters. Discerning folk will remember him as the screenwriter for the Joe Orton biography, *Prick Up Your Ears,* and the Alan Bates–starring *An Englishman Abroad,* as well as for being one of the nonpareil quartet (along with Peter Cook, Dudley Moore, and Jonathan Miller) that made the Beyond the Fringe satirical troupe so brilliant.

What Bennett has done in *Madness* is to powerfully re-imagine the atmosphere of George's royal court, giving the dialogue a modern twist while keeping it from sounding anachronistic. The pleasure he takes in the spoken word, his ability to etch characters in both acid and compassion, to write such lines of dialogue as "The state of monarchy and the state of lunacy share a frontier," set this film well apart.

Confessing, in the play's introduction, that he has "always had a soft spot for George III," Bennett introduces the monarch at the height of his powers. A genially choleric man, bluff, gruff, and plain-spoken, he is proud of his popularity with the common folk but is a trial to his fifteen children, especially his bored-to-death heir, the Prince of Wales (Rupert Everett).

Setting a hectic pace and ending most sentences with a speedy "What, what?" the king's energy looks even greater than it is because he is surrounded by effete whiners and smooth careerists. Except for Greville (Rupert Graves), his loyal equerry, all of them, including ice-cold Prime Minister William Pitt (Julian Wadham), are both irritated and comforted by the knowledge that they are more sophisticated than their ruler.

George's most heartening and moving relationship is with his Queen, Charlotte, beautifully played—albeit with welcome dramatic license (the real queen was said to be "as dull as she was ugly")—by Helen Mirren. Never apart for so much as a day in their twenty-eight years of marriage, they call each other "Mr. King" and "Mrs. King" in private and still seem very much in love.

Then, with almost no warning, the madness begins, difficult to detect at first because, as one character asks, "Who can say what is normal to a king?" But after bouts of waking everyone up at 4 A.M. with screaming fits about nonexistent floods and zealous sexual attacks on the attractive Lady Pembroke (Amanda Donohoe), one of the queen's attendants, there can no longer be any doubt that the monarch is not himself.

When the king's condition becomes known, the political maneuvering begins in earnest. For if Parliament declares George unfit to rule and the noxious Prince of Wales is installed as regent, Pitt will be out and the hungry opposition, led by the troublesome Charles James Fox (Jim Carter), will take power.

In the meantime, George's condition is made worse by the barbaric treatments, verging on medieval torture, that his crackpot Three Stooges medical team inflict on him. Finally, as a last resort, he is put in the hands of Willis (Ian Holm), a former clergyman with unusual ideas about the treatment of the mentally ill.

It is a measure of Hawthorne's performance in the title role that, like King Lear (who is pointedly referred to), the worse his condition becomes, the more he inspires our sorrow and pity. His madness adds to his moral stature by making him increasingly human, and we root for him to recover his wits with a surprising passion. Meanwhile, the looks of confused horror and self-loathing that flit across his ravaged face express torment as heartbreakingly as acting is able to.

Director Hytner, known for his stage work on *Miss Saigon* and *Carousel,* is so at home with film that it is difficult to believe this is his feature debut. Working with cinematographer Andrew Dunn and Oscar-winning production designer Ken Adam (*Barry Lyndon*), he has faultlessly opened up the play and made a distant world seem physically real. Down to its final footnote on modern theories about the cause of the royal illness, every aspect of *The Madness of King George* keeps us amused, surprised, and delighted. Who wouldn't wish long life to a film as worthy as this?

Manny & Lo
1996

Even at the bare-bones level, film is such a cumbersome art, so dependent on mechanics, logistics, and throngs of people, that it's a surprise and a pleasure to discover a new writer-director capable of almost casually bending it all to his or her will.

Lisa Krueger is that kind of a filmmaker. Her *Manny & Lo* is an unapologetically small but wholly original movie, warmhearted but not precious, and possessed of a gently wacky sensibility. Without seeming to be trying, Krueger insists we see the world in her plucky and caring way.

Basically a three-character drama, *Manny & Lo* begins with the sisters of the title. Sent to separate foster homes after their mother's death, they've run away and reunited for a tenuous life on the road.

"The No. 1 rule is keep moving and you won't get nailed," says sixteen-year-old Laurel (Aleksa Palladino), who goes by "Lo." Surly, mistrustful, quick to take offense, Lo is petulance personified, a not very bright young woman who thinks she's got everything figured out.

Eleven-year-old Amanda, "Manny" for short (Scarlett Johansson), is Lo's opposite number. A wise soul in a young body, she is serious and responsible, watchful where Lo is oblivious. Manny is the one who notices, while Lo tries stubbornly to ignore it, that her older sister is pregnant.

Up to now the two girls have lived on what they could shoplift from convenience stores with the help of a gigantic Cheerios box and slept by breaking into furnished model homes. But Lo's pregnancy changes everything.

First the girls stop roaming and move into a temporarily unoccupied vacation home deep in the woods (one of several touches that give the film something of a fairy-tale feeling). Then, intent on finding a reliable book on pregnancy, they stumble into Connie's Baby Connection and the redoubtable Elaine (Mary Kay Place).

A prim and precise pregnancy know-it-all whose favorite phrase is "I've never been wrong once," Elaine astounds the girls with her extensive knowledge of babies, which encompasses everything from what color sleepwear to clothe them in to the correct way to rock a cradle (head to toe, not side to side, if you must know).

Rather than simply ask questions, these two baby-fat desperadoes decide to kidnap Elaine, nurse's uniform and all, and force her to assist with the coming child. But like the kidnappers in O. Henry's "The Ransom of Red Chief," the girls find Elaine to be more than they bargained for.

Though the film nicely delineates the parallel comradeship and independence of the two sisters, *Manny & Lo* really pulls into focus with Elaine's arrival. As willful as Lo at her worst, proclaiming with wounded pride, "I do not give in to criminals," Elaine, much to the girls' amazement, turns out to be just as off the charts as they are.

And, though everyone is too preoccupied to notice at first, something else unites Manny and Lo and Elaine. Unresolved personal issues, the need to grow up, and the thwarted desire to be part of a family unit all combine to put these three into eccentric comic situations that not one of them could have imagined on her own.

Best known for her Emmy-winning work on TV's *Mary Hartman, Mary Hartman,* Place has numerous feature credits, but her gift for mock-dignified comedy has rarely been so well used. As the only adult with major screen time, her role is critical, and she handles it adroitly and with a terrific amount of style.

Writer-director Krueger's gift is for the unexpected, for creating people and situations just a notch off normal, and it's often visible in the film's details. When we watch Manny spray her bed with Right Guard because it reminds her of her mother, or see Lo practicing for her dream job of stewardess by walking on her sister's back while holding a tray, we know we are seeing a movie nobody else could have come up with, and that is a wonderful thing.

Actress Johansson has gone from strength to strength, including starring roles in both Lost in Translation *and* Girl with a Pearl Earring.

Muriel's Wedding
1995

Her own wedding is the event Muriel wants so much to happen but fears never will. How is she to feel otherwise when her frightful best friends insist she surrender a bridal bouquet she's just caught? "Give it back, give it back," they yap at her like well-dressed terriers. "Nobody's ever going to marry you."

That scene, which opens P.J. Hogan's marvelous debut film, sets the tone for what is to come. Wickedly mocking but empathetic, able to laugh at its characters while paying attention to their sorrows, this subversive comedy about self-esteem resists the notion that films have to timidly remain within tidy genre rules.

Winner of four Australian Academy Awards, including best picture, *Muriel's Wedding* is one of a series of brash and rowdy comedies from that country that includes *Strictly Ballroom* and *The Adventures of Priscilla, Queen of the Desert.* Made with energy, raucous good humor, and noticeable wit, its ability to recognize the poignancy in its situations makes it special even in that uninhibited group.

Played with take-no-prisoners comic enthusiasm by Toni Collette, twenty-two-year-old Muriel Heslop is the kind of hapless young woman who wears a shoplifted leopard-skin dress to a wedding—and gets caught by the store detective. Overweight, with bad skin, a braying laugh, and a frighteningly wide grin, aggressively unattractive Muriel is known locally in Porpoise Spit for saying and doing the wrong things. Even her taste in music, her devotion to ABBA's bubbly but outmoded melodies, makes her nominal friends wince.

And when it comes to matrimony, Muriel is so in love with the idea of being married that she is on intimate terms with every frame of Princess Di's wedding tape. Glassy-eyed and obsessive on the subject, Muriel looks on a marriage license as a membership card in the human race that will prove to everyone, herself most of all, that she has finally become a worthwhile person.

Muriel comes by her insecurities the way most people do, through her dysfunctional blood relatives. Father Bill Heslop (veteran Australian actor Bill Hunter), known as "Bill the Battler" to his intimates, is a politician and influence-peddler whose hobby is running down everyone in his family, from his catatonic wife Betty (Jeanie Drynan) to his horde of professional couch-potato children.

Muriel takes her fair share of abuse, but she has something rare, and that is spirit. Though it tends to come out in unhelpful ways, such as in her weakness for telling strings of lies, that quality makes Muriel believe that some day things will go her way. "I know I'm not normal," she says earnestly, "but I can change."

That passion also makes Muriel defy logic and seriously bend some rules to accompany her horrified trio of harpy girlfriends when they take a Club Med–type vacation on Hibiscus Island. There Muriel meets Rhonda (Rachel Griffiths), a full-bore party animal who truthfully says, "My whole life is one last fling after another."

Unexpectedly, Rhonda responds to the free spirit in Muriel, and the validation of that friendship proves liberating. It starts Muriel on a wild and chaotic journey of self-discovery, filled with wacky and eccentric plot turns, that will gradually cause her to rethink almost all her most cherished ideas.

Clearly, *Muriel's Wedding* would be much less than it is without the right stars, and Collette, who has the courage not to shortchange Muriel's more off-putting qualities, and Griffiths, who looks like a mature Juliette Lewis and makes Rhonda's character believable, were both remarkable enough to win Australian Academy Awards. And the rest of the cast, even the old warhorse Bill Hunter, completely catches the spirit of the piece as its members join forces to form a gifted ensemble.

The credit for this has to go to writer-director Hogan and a production team led by co-producers Lynda House and Jocelyn Moorhouse (who directed the memorable *Proof* and is Hogan's wife). They've come up with a slashing guerrilla attack on accepted notions of marriage, family, and self-improvement that never allows us to forget the doubt that makes its characters human. Though it is consistently funny, *Muriel's Wedding* is savvy enough not to play things just for laughs.

Both Collette and Griffiths went on to major international careers, and director Hogan directed the Julia Roberts–starring My Best Friend's Wedding *as well as* Peter Pan.

My Son the Fanatic
1999

My Son the Fanatic opens with what should be a high point in the life of Parvez (Om Puri), born in Pakistan, but for the past twenty-five years a cabdriver in the northern English city of Bradford.

Parvez and his wife are having a celebratory tea with their son's presumptive future in-laws, the Fingerhuts. Farid (Akbar Kurtha) is engaged to the daughter of one of the town's top officials. "This boy of ours, I can assure you he's all-around type going whole hog," Parvez says in his charmingly mangled immigrant's English, so delighted he doesn't notice the cross-cultural discomfort everyone else in the room is feeling.

Best known for *My Beautiful Laundrette,* writer Hanif Kureishi calls his latest work "a romantic film with ideological edges," and what makes it exceptional is how much subtlety and compassion Kureishi and director Udayan Prasad bring to both halves of that equation.

Effortlessly well-written, with nuanced characters that easily come to life on the screen, *My Son the Fanatic* does justice to the unlikely love story it uncovers as well as the troubling underlying reality of adapting to a new country and a new culture. Intelligent, poignant, and witty, it involves us in real issues without stinting on their complexity and without forgetting to be caring toward people caught in the undertow of forces they cannot begin to control.

Even without this impending marriage, Parvez initially feels content. He still loves his wife, Minoo (Gopi Desai), though over the years their relationship has grown distant and pro forma. He doesn't even envy the success that his best friend Fizzy (Harish Patel) has had in the restaurant business. Then, like an emotional pincers attack, three factors combine to bring his life to a crisis.

Most devastating is the change in Parvez's only child. Once a boy who loved clothes and considered modeling, Farid is now intent on getting rid of all his worldly possessions, including his music and even his cherished guitar. "You always said there were more important things than 'Stairway to Heaven,'" he tells his baffled father, "and you were so right."

Parvez initially suspects drugs, but the truth is even more devastating. In a reverse twist on the usual scenario of traditional parents and modern children, it is the searching son who embraces the Muslim fundamentalism the father rejected. "Our cultures cannot be mixed," Farid insists, and flays modern Britain for being "a society soaked in sex."

As if to underline that point, Parvez becomes the regular driver for a visiting German (Stellan Skarsgard), an amoral businessman, more obtuse than anything dangerous, who lives only for pleasures of the flesh and says things like "Don't you love the sound of silk on skin?"

That last remark is inspired by Bettina (Rachel Griffiths, Oscar-nominated for *Hilary and Jackie*), a local prostitute who uses Parvez's taxi for late-night service. Almost without knowing it, this pair of societal outsiders begin to depend on each other for the honesty and quiet decency they can obtain nowhere else. With all his moorings gone, desperate for tenderness, Parvez finds himself emotionally drawn to Bettina even as he realizes how impossible their situation would be.

Celebrated Indian actor Puri, a veteran of dozens of films, from *Gandhi* to the works of Satyajit Ray, gives a moving, captivating performance as the capsized Parvez, struggling to believe that the truths he's always held are still valid. Griffiths is also outstanding as a woman who knows what reality is but also knows what she wants and needs.

Director Prasad (a British TV regular whose feature debut was *Brothers in Trouble*), always sensitive and empathetic, is impressive in the way he honors the script's determination to give all aspects of this complex situation their due.

For though *My Son the Fanatic* is at times bemused at Farid's zealotry, it leaves no doubt that the racism and lack of respect he decries in British society is both real and pervasive. And while Parvez is equally convinced that the rigidity of fundamentalism and its insistence on purity and conformity is not a solution to anything, he has difficulty formulating an alternative that has any meaning for his son.

My Son the Fanatic is too subtle and thoughtful to offer simple solutions—Parvez's declaration that "there are many ways of being a good man" may be as close as it gets to a summing up—and Kureishi and Prasad have given this story a nuanced, bittersweet ending that has more staying power than a more conventional finale would. For if the answers to these pervasive problems were simpler, if the tangled emotions these peoples' lives call forth were easier to sort out, *My Son the Fanatic* wouldn't be half the film it turns out to be.

Naked
1993

When we talk about unforgettable characters, often they are characters we'd give almost anything to forget, savage malcontents who leave pain and anguish in their wake. Characters, at first glance, much like Johnny, the sour and dissatisfied protagonist of Mike Leigh's remarkable, unnerving *Naked*.

A refugee from Manchester who in the film's opening minutes flees to London in a stolen car after committing a rape, Johnny is a raging nightmare. A red-haired beanpole with a ragged beard and a hacking cough, he is a vicious misogynist who beats women physically and verbally assaults anyone within striking distance of his blistering, abrasive tongue.

In conventional movie terms, Johnny is far enough over the edge of acceptable behavior to make him a very tough centerpiece for a film.

But nothing British writer-director Mike Leigh has ever done is conventional, and *Naked,* which won best director at Cannes and best actor for star David Thewlis's searing performance, is a departure even for Leigh.

Leigh's unusual films are not improvised, though they often give that impression, but neither are they conventionally scripted. Rather, Leigh and his cast participate in an extensive rehearsal period (twelve weeks for *Naked*) during which roles are, in effect, grown from the ground up.

The result, as recent films such as *High Hopes* and *Life Is Sweet* testify, is work that cuts deeper and goes further in terms of character development while providing more opportunities for actors to astonish than anything else on the screen today.

While those two examples have a partially whimsical tone, Leigh's earlier work, including theatrical pieces and the TV films *Bleak Moments, Grown Ups,* and *Meantime,* had much more of a downbeat thrust. Still, *Naked* is the most extreme, intense, and daring work that Leigh has yet attempted.

When he gets to London, Johnny heads for the flat of ex-girlfriend Louise (Lesley Sharp). She's at work, but Sophie (Katrin Cartlidge), her stoned waif roommate, is on the premises, and, out of a combination of boredom and spite, Johnny seduces her just to pass the time.

Smarter than most of the people with whom he comes into contact, Johnny is facile with words. Both with Sophie and with Louise, when she shows up, he delights in verbal humiliation, in being showily cynical, letting his scathing fury at the world and everyone in it spray people like an acid bath. "You might already have had the happiest moment in your life," he snarls at Sophie in one of his milder outbursts, "and got nothing to look forward to but sickness and death."

Too antsy to stay at the flat, this sullen drifter heads out into a London as bleak as anything Charles Dickens ever described. *Naked* records Johnny's two hellish nights on those bitter streets, detailing the people he meets along the way, the eccentrics and dead-enders with nowhere else to go but at each other's throats.

Initially, however, it doesn't seem that bleak, as the first people encountered are Scottish street folk Archie (Ewen Bremner) and Maggie (Susan Vidler), a pair so horrifyingly daft even Johnny can't help but be gently amused.

Then, in one of *Naked*'s most extended sequences, Johnny runs across Brian (Peter Wight), a night watchman guarding an empty building, who shares Johnny's autodidactic state of mind. Discussions about the philosophical nature of the past, the present, and the future ensue, with Johnny insisting, his gorge rising, that "nobody has a future. The party's over, it's all breaking up."

Though that statement can be accurately read as an expression of Johnny's core nihilism, one of the things that makes *Naked* so provocative is the thread of unspoken social consciousness that lies beneath the surface. For Johnny's anger is more than personal; it inevitably expresses the frustration of Britain's on-the-dole underclass. Their talents wasted, these people are left out in the cold both literally and metaphorically as the go-goers of the Margaret Thatcher years (here represented by Greg Cruttwell's odious Jeremy) continue to rake in the spoils.

More than anything, though, *Naked* is a mesmerizing character study, an attempt to stretch the emotional boundaries of truth on film as far as they will go. Leigh's film is like an etching by M.C. Escher: Once we think we've seen as much of Johnny as we can take, we start to see something else, a glimpse of another person easily missed.

Just slipping through the cracks of Johnny's mask of savage anger can be noticed a haunted, hunted look, flashes of empathy and even self-knowledge. His intelligence begins to register, and we discover he is a ferocious reader.

What Leigh and his collaborators are after here is hardly a whitewashing of Johnny, a simplistic excusing of the more wretched of his qualities. On the contrary, *Naked* is determined never to let Johnny off the hook, excuse him, forgive him, or think him less of a monster than he is.

What *Naked* is after instead is an illumination of the intricacies of life, an elaboration of the obvious truth, rarely this passionately explored, that people are more though not necessarily better than they seem, that their qualities feed off each other, the good inseparable from the bad. The Johnny at the close feels intangibly but totally different from the one we experienced at the opening, and a film that allows us to view reality through that kind of double lens is impressive indeed.

Next Stop Wonderland
1998

Next Stop Wonderland is a romance, but not just any romance. Smart and beguiling, it manages the impressive feat of believing wholeheartedly in the power of love without checking its mind at the door. Discriminating romantics will not believe their good fortune.

Though its plot echoes other films (including Claude Lelouch's *And Now My Love* and Krzysztof Kieslowski's *Red*), *Wonderland*'s bemused, delicately ironic sensibility, supplied by co-writer, editor, and director Brad Anderson, is strictly its own.

Helping to set that tone is the subtle yet sensual bossa nova music that dominates the soundtrack: classic Brazilian works by artists including Antonio Carlos Jobim and Astrud Gilberto. In fact, Anderson has said, it's the Brazilian concept of *saudade*, a kind of happiness and sadness at the same time, that helped inspire this film.

In Hope Davis, one of the independent world's most appealing performers, Anderson has found the classic personification of this notion. It's unusual for a young actress to have the opportunity to carry an entire picture, and rarer still does one succeed with the aplomb Davis displays here.

Set in Boston, where Wonderland is, in fact, a train station close to the airport, *Next Stop* introduces both its droll sensibility and Davis's Erin Castleton at a low point in her life.

Walking home from her night-shift job as a registered nurse, Erin is confronted by her live-in boyfriend Sean (the dead-on amusing Philip Seymour Hoffman) frantically trying to move out before she returns. A gung-ho political activist, he's off to help a needy Native American tribe, leaving her with a cat named Fidel and a tape postulating "Six Reasons Why Our Relationship Is Doomed."

Understandably hurt and angry, Erin is, as it turns out, a self-sufficient woman perfectly content to be on her own and quite capable of turning a tart tongue on those who don't believe that, especially her social butterfly mother, Piper (Holland Taylor).

Though she can appear dismissive and judgmental, Erin, we come to realize, partly as we experience her love of poetry, acts that way to protect a good and caring heart. She may proclaim to her friends that she doesn't believe in "the unseen hand leading to the garden path," but part of her would be delighted if the right man came her way down that very path.

Piper Castleton, however, is not one who waits for fate. Without her daughter's permission, she places a personal ad for Erin in a Boston alternative paper. Erin is furious at first, but when she checks in on her responses, she's astonished to discover there are sixty-four of them.

Partly out of boredom, partly out of curiosity, Erin decides to meet some of her suitors, and the scenes that follow, with their deft skewering of male ego and vanity, are irresistible. The zealot who sells small rubber parts (played by Robert Stanton) is a standout, but look also for the putative divinity student who talks about God being "a big subject"—it's the film's co-screenwriter, Lyn Vaus.

Paralleling Erin's life is that of another Boston resident, Alan Monteiro (Alan Gelfant), who's beset by a different set of problems. A third-generation plumber who works part time at the Boston Aquarium while studying to become a marine biologist, Alan is a mature, hardworking young man who spends a lot of his life taking evasive action.

In school, Alan tries to avoid Julie (Cara Buono), an attractive fellow student with a crush on him, and at work he tries to avoid Frank (Victor Argo), the loan shark he owes money to, as well as Frank's boss Arty Lesser (Robert Klein), a mortuary kingpin locked in a battle with the aquarium.

Though Erin and Alan live lives that seem completely separate, *Next Stop Wonderland* adroitly insinuates that maybe, just maybe, they are meant for each other.

It starts with a simple shot that frames them together: he in a subway car and she seated on the platform seen through a window behind him. As the film progresses, we see, though neither one of them does, just how intertwined their lives have become even though they have never actually met. Again and again, in the same room, even on the same telephone line, they just miss connecting.

This is a very delicate balance for a director to maintain, keeping audiences honestly on edge as to whether two people will finally mesh or not, and filmmaker Anderson, in only his second film (the first was the Sundance entry *Darien Gap*), keeps his footing beautifully.

Wonderland succeeds because it shares a sensibility with its heroine: Despite its clever dialogue, it's an empathetic vehicle at heart, a work whose well-developed characters, even the sillier ones, insist we care, even as they're making us laugh.

Because we're concerned about Erin and Alan, and because there is just enough sadness in this film for us to know that things don't have to work out, we feel terribly protective of these two. And as their individual romantic lives get more complicated, we worry desperately about their vulnerability, and ours. Much as we'd like to, this is one outcome we can't predict with complete assurance, and few things are more delicious than that.

Out of Sight
1998

Hollywood has been doing business with Elmore Leonard for decades, and the novelist has quite a store of amusing stories about the unmitigated fiascoes the studios have made out of his novels. Like the time Patrick McGoohan came up to him on the set of *The Moonshine War* and said, "What's it like to hear your lines all fouled up?" Only he didn't exactly say "fouled."

Those tales, however, have begun to show their age. Recently, in the kind of Hollywood ending reality rarely provides, the movies in general, and screenwriter Scott Frank in particular, have figured Leonard out. A quartet of diverting movies has been made from his books, including Quentin Tarantino's *Jackie Brown* and Paul Schrader's *Touch*. Frank, however, has written the best two: First came *Get Shorty*, directed by Barry Sonnenfeld, and now, its engaging and consummately entertaining successor, *Out of Sight*.

Like a benevolent character in a fairy tale, Leonard has been good to those who've treated him right. His work is a key inspiration behind Tarantino's accomplishments; he gave Schrader an unlooked-for sense of humor and boosted John Travolta's career with *Get Shorty*. Similarly, *Out of Sight,* a wised-up, insouciant love story between a deputy U.S. marshal and the veteran bank robber she's trying to incarcerate, was a boon to all concerned.

As Jack Foley, whose 200-plus bank robberies place him at the top of the FBI computer, George Clooney is suave and debonair in a role that silences doubts about his movie-star status. And Jennifer Lopez, an actress who can be convincingly tough and devastatingly erotic, uses the part of a law-enforcement agent who only gets emotional about her Sig Sauer .38 to solidify her position as a woman you can confidently build a film around.

Helped even more is director Steven Soderbergh, whose erratic career after *sex, lies, and videotape* has included self-indulgent misadventures such as the unwatchable *Schizopolis*. His work in *Out of Sight,* however, turns out to be impeccable. He has brought together a diverse and exciting supporting cast (Ving Rhames, Don Cheadle, Dennis Farina, Albert Brooks, Nancy Allen, Catherine Keener, Isaiah Washington, Steve Zahn, Luis Guzman, newcomer Keith Loneker, and Michael Keaton in an unbilled cameo) and well understands that a level of criminal reality in Leonard is the key to setting up the comedy.

For what makes the novelist irresistible, aside from his unmatched gift for playful language, is his pleasure in finding it in unlikely places. Leonard's books are Oscar Wilde behind bars, drawing-room comedies set amid the bemused venality of a harsh criminal world. Serious bad guys and almost-competent cons crowd his pages as both heroes and villains, and a pleasing combination of tension and humor is one of his trademarks.

Frank has proven himself expert at presenting and framing Leonard's bemused wackiness on screen. Large chunks of the novelist's dialogue get the call, but Frank has also adroitly juggled the book's characters and plot elements and polished a tone that's more romantic than the book's elegiac, somewhat bittersweet mood.

After a prologue that shows how he got there, we hook up with Foley in Florida's medium-security Glades Correctional Institution. With the help of his ex-wife and magician's assistant Adele (Keener) and pals Buddy and Glenn (Rhames, Zahn) from an earlier incarceration at Lompoc, the shrewd Foley is about to piggyback onto someone else's escape attempt.

Karen Sisco (Lopez) is up at Glades, too, delivering some paperwork. She stumbles into the escape and ends up, in a seriously bizarre first date, sharing the trunk of a getaway car with an apologetic Foley, comparing thoughts on movies and life with the unwashed desperado as casually as if they were flirting over a pair of cappuccinos.

All first dates have to end, even ones in car trunks, but, cynical as they are, both Foley and Sisco have the odd feeling they'd like to see each other again, something which neither her father (Farina) nor his friend Buddy can quite understand. "Why," Buddy asks, far from unreasonably, "would you want to have cocktails with a woman who wants to shoot you?"

Making this second date more amusingly difficult to pull off is Sisco's determination to rearrest Foley and his eagerness to reach Detroit and get to work on a potentially big score involving the homicidal Maurice "Snoopy" Miller (Cheadle) and a wealthy white-collar criminal (a charming Brooks) everyone knows from Lompoc.

As always with the best of Leonard, it's the journey, not the destination, that counts, and director Soderbergh lets it unfold with great skill. Making adroit use of complex flashbacks, freeze frames, and other stylistic flourishes, he's managed to put his personal stamp on the film while staying faithful to the irreplaceable spirit of the original. Both he and Frank have learned the main lesson of Elmore Goes to Hollywood: What becomes a legend most is, quite simply, respect.

Persuasion
1995

Jane Austen never married, possibly never received so much as a passionate kiss, and formed her closest emotional bonds with her spinster older sister. Yet, in one of the enduring mysteries of genius, few writers have had a more acute sense of romantic psychology or had more piercing insights into the relationships of people in love. No place in the human heart was unknown to her, which is why her popularity not only endures, but increases. Especially in Hollywood.

Persuasion is the first (except for the *Emma*-based *Clueless*) of a projected series of Austen adaptations, and it is going to be difficult to improve upon. Literate, sophisticated, bitingly funny, it's a Cinderella romance so delicious you want it never to end.

The film's source is Austen's last completed novel, published posthumously in 1818. Though not as well known as *Pride and Prejudice* or *Sense and Sensibility*, *Persuasion* is a favorite among readers for several reasons.

Its heroine, Anne Elliot, is twenty-seven, no longer young by the standards of Regency England. Its lovers are more emotionally experienced than is usual with Austen, probably because by this time she was more knowing herself, and its story has a poignancy that director Roger Michell and screenwriter Nick Dear (both veterans of the Royal Shakespeare Company) effectively blend into the usual Austen mix of courtship and clever satire.

Persuasion starts with a brisk dose of Austen fun, a scathing look at Sir Walter Elliot of Kellynch Hall (superbly played by Corin Redgrave, Lynn's and Vanessa's brother), an obtuse monument to snobbishness and pretension, who is at the moment having to face the unpleasant reality of a lack of funds.

Though he despises the navy (calling it, in one of Austen's typically bracing lines, "the means of bringing persons of obscure birth into undue distinction"), Sir Walter is convinced by his neighbor Lady Russell (Susan Fleetwood) to move to Bath and rent the hall to one Admiral Croft and his wife (John Woodvine and Fiona Shaw). Sir Walter and his entourage depart at once, but daughter Anne

(Amanda Root) is left behind to tend to all the tedious details of moving.

The good, sensible, sympathetic daughter, Anne is used to this kind of treatment, but as she goes about her duties, including visiting her married sister Mary (Sophie Thompson), a thoroughly imaginary invalid, one thing troubles her. Now that Mrs. Croft is established in the neighborhood, her brother, Frederick Wentworth, is sure to make an appearance, and there is more than a little history between these two.

Eight years earlier, Anne was engaged to Wentworth, at the time a spirited young man with no prospects. Under the persuasive influence of Lady Russell, she was convinced to break off the match, and now her former beau is returning as a wealthy, supremely eligible naval captain, and Anne, who can barely say his name, is terrified they will meet.

Naturally, they not only meet, but circumstances also throw them together a good deal. Though the captain (played with enviable posture and self-possession by Ciaran Hinds) tells friends that he finds Anne "so altered, he would not have known her," it's impossible not to wonder how much of a spark remains between them. The business of *Persuasion* is to answer that question, and to show how both Anne and Wentworth deal with the obstacles society (and the appearance of possible new matches for each of them) throws in their way.

Making this story difficult for filmmakers is that Austen's world was not known for frank speech or dramatic action. Fortunately, director Michell and screenwriter Dear, working with cinematographer John Daly and a splendid troupe of actors, are up to doing what's needed. Which is capturing a nuanced society of looks and smiles, where more is implied than spoken and the subtle pressure of a hand helping a woman into a carriage can be as dramatic as a slap across the face.

And though fine period re-creations are not scarce, a telling effort has been made to make the physical atmosphere as real as possible. The actors wear little makeup, the costumes and furnishings all seem lived in, not merely worn, and no face, no matter how minor, has been anything but carefully chosen. Dear has succeeded in his stated aim of trying to marry the wit of Austen to some of the psychological reality of Ingmar Bergman.

Because the nature of Regency society was such that Anne can't do very much on her own, can't be the mistress of her fate, an actress with the skill to win over an audience via quiet persuasiveness was necessary, and Amanda Root, another Royal Shakespeare Company veteran with great, deep, soulful eyes and a delicately expressive face, does that beautifully.

Director Michell, in his debut theatrical feature, does a superior job of marshaling all these resources and enforcing a uniformly engaging tone. Both for veteran Janeites and those new to the religion, *Persuasion* is a most persuasive place to be.

Pipe Dream
2002

Don't get David Kulovic wrong. It's not that he's unhappy in his work, but the kind of attractive, available women he'd like to meet aren't interested in, well, plumbers. But movie directors, that's a different story. Or so David thinks.

Pipe Dream, a smart, sweet, playful romantic comedy starring Martin Donovan and Mary-Louise Parker, shows what happens when David gets to live out his (and a lot of other people's) fantasies and pretend he's ace New York director David Copelberg (named after the only two filmmakers whose work he knows).

Set in Manhattan's independent film scene, *Pipe Dream* takes wry pleasure in poking fun at the mores of a business in which no one would even think of telling the truth, and in which rumor, evasion, and small lies are the order of the day. And that's not the plumbing business either.

Pipe Dream was directed and co-written (with Cynthia Kaplan) by John C. Walsh, who made a small splash with his completely charming 1996 Sundance film *Ed's Next Move.* The two films share Walsh's unmistakable sensibility, a gentle and unforced way of examining the vagaries of human behavior that is as sure-handed and insightful as it is understated.

Casting is key in films like this, and both Donovan, last seen in

Christopher Nolan's *Insomnia,* and the Tony Award–winning Parker are just what's needed for their respective roles. Parker's intelligent, confident performance is especially noteworthy because she gave it during the day while appearing on Broadway in *Proof* at night.

Parker plays Toni Edelman, an aspiring screenwriter who lives in the same building as the handsome plumber. They connect for a single night, but her chagrin at actually getting involved with someone so plebeian stings him so much that he decides to take corrective action and leave the invisible serving class behind.

With the help of RJ (Kevin Carroll), a casting director friend who owes him money, and some script pages that he purloins from an unsuspecting Toni, David sets himself up as a director looking for actors and promptly develops a crush on tyro actress Marliss Funt (Rebecca Gayheart). Against all reason, and partly fueled by the rumor that Robert Redford is a silent producer, David's movie (also called *Pipe Dream*) becomes quite the hot property, as does David, even though he's such a naif that he thinks questions about representation have to do with whose congressional district he lives in. Naturally, Toni gets wind of all this, and no end of complications ensue.

Pipe Dream manages to be funny about numerous aspects of moviemaking, from agentry to craft services, without losing track of its core notion that it's who you are as a person, not your position in the pecking order, that finally counts. Even glamorous directors could do worse than take that to heart.

Pollock
2000

Jackson Pollock, one of the key figures in Abstract Expressionism and America's first postwar art star, was a man destined to be consumed by his own internal fires. As insecure as he was gifted, a full-blown alcoholic prone to frightening rages, he was often on the edge of agony, a prisoner of demons he could no more identify than control.

Putting a figure like this on film, someone so close to the stereotypical Hollywood view of the artist as tormented and self-destructive, is a chancy enterprise. Though it's taken him nearly a decade of involvement to make it happen, Ed Harris, working as star and producer as well as first-time director, managed to bring it off successfully.

It's not that *Pollock* doesn't have its share of standard, conventional elements—it does. But the intensity of Harris's performance—the best of his career, and that's saying a lot—and his gift for guiding co-star Marcia Gay Harden and cameo performers such as Amy Madigan to an equally high level make everything else less important.

More than that, *Pollock* stands out among creative biographies for an ability to show art being made in a way that's as realistic and exciting as it can be on screen. To watch Lisa Rinzler's expressive shots of Harris-as-Pollock create his paintings, especially the famously acrobatic drip canvases, to Jeff Beal's Aaron Copland–influenced music is little short of thrilling.

Harris was first attracted to Pollock when his father pointed out how much he looked like the artist, but the actor hasn't stopped with a physical resemblance that is in truth uncanny. Harris has invested himself completely in the part, even changing his cigarette brand and building a studio behind his house so he could throw himself into practicing action painting, finally inhabiting Pollock with an intensity and force of life that is almost frightening.

Going along with this integrity, the film's solidly built albeit old-fashioned script by Barbara Turner and Susan J. Emshwiller doesn't try to explain how Pollock got the way he was. Aside from a brief reference to the artist being classified "4F" for being "too neurotic," it takes an *ecce homo* approach to his torments, refreshingly avoiding the kind of psychological theorizing that tends to be facile and simplistic.

Harris's Pollock is a complicated man, wary, restless, and almost bursting with so much physicality and controlled energy that he's as happy breaking a door down as unlocking it. Pollock also radiates the kind of fragility that can be terrifying, displaying enough congenital desperation to cause one character to say, "You remind me of a trapped animal."

That look confronts us in the film's opening sequence, set in 1950 at a packed Manhattan gallery opening at the height of Pollock's fame, after *Life* magazine had anointed him America's premier artist and every canvas sold as soon as he touched it. Yet the artist has the face of a man who's seen a ghost, and, we soon learn, the ghost was quite likely himself.

Pollock then flashes back nine years, to the artist as a mentally unstable alcoholic living in Greenwich Village with his brother and his brother's disapproving wife. Everything changes for him when a knock on his door reveals fellow painter Lee Krasner (Harden in easily the strongest performance of her career), cheekily introducing herself, as she puts it, to the only Abstract Expressionist in New York she hasn't met.

Raised in Brooklyn, from a Russian Jewish background, Krasner is in many ways Pollock's opposite: She's verbal and self-assured and faces the world with confidence. Both parties immediately sense the possibility of a relationship, but there is a tension as well as a complicity between them, the intuitive knowledge that whatever transpires will be as dangerous as it will be life-changing.

Once they are together, Krasner becomes Pollock's tireless advocate and propagandist. She encourages him in his work, does the best she can with his alcoholic binges, even masterminds his introduction to the eccentric but influential collector Peggy Guggenheim (a dark-haired Madigan in a superb cameo). And she is the driving force in the couple's move to Long Island, where Pollock does his best and most influential work.

Though the film has no shortage of dramatic confrontations or cameos of celebrated people (Val Kilmer, the man of a thousand accents, plays Willem De Kooning; Jeffrey Tambor is influential critic Clement Greenberg; Jennifer Connelly is the beautiful and willing Ruth Kligman), it is to the painting that it always and most successfully returns. Even occasional on-the-nose lines, such as "You've done it, Jackson, you've cracked it wide open," can't hurt that focus.

Whether it's Harris warily sizing up an enormous blank canvas, looking at it for weeks before picking up a brush, or the moment when he discovers drip painting and then uses it in a way that the film emphasizes is anything but casual and accidental, *Pollock* has an innate feeling for the process of painting that its subject would appreciate. Even in his darkest moments, when success would mock him as even failure never had, Pollock always respected the work, and Ed Harris's film is as successful as it is because it passionately follows the artist's lead.

Marcia Gay Harden won the Oscar for best supporting actress for this performance.

Proof
1992

Proof is a pleasantly twisted little picture that has the kind of off-center impact money can't buy. A sharp and self-confident debut for Australian writer-director Jocelyn Moorhouse, it takes an unlikely protagonist and involves him in curious, darkly comic situations leading to a graceful conclusion. Not at all bad for a film that came in well under a million dollars.

Blind since birth but a passionate photographer, Martin (Hugo Weaving) is an abrupt, angry man with a deep-seated grudge against the world. He wields his cane as if it were an attack weapon, and when a waitress ignores him in a restaurant, he empties a bottle of wine on the table to get her attention. Definitely not a happy camper.

Martin's sole human contact appears to be the acerbic Celia (Genevieve Picot). Nominally his housekeeper, she is also his merciless partner in an endless series of mutually tormenting and humiliating mind games that revolve around the attraction she feels for him that he apparently is not interested in returning.

Quite by accident, Martin meets Andy (Russell Crowe), a cheerful dishwasher who appears to be everything the blind man is not: easygoing, guileless, always ready to have some fun. They tentatively become friends and even go on some adventures together, a wild and anarchic night at the local drive-in being an especially funny example.

Martin has been taking pictures since, as a boy, he began to suspect that his mother was lying to him about the world. It's an occupation that baffles Andy, to whom Martin explains that the photographs serve as proof, "proof that what I sensed is what you saw through your eyes—the truth." Ever suspicious, Martin is dependent on people whom he can trust to describe the photos to him, and, a bit uncertain at first, Andy agrees to take on the job.

Not surprisingly, this does not sit well with Celia, and the working out of the Martin-Celia-Andy triangle is what *Proof* is all about. Writer-director Moorhouse, who shares a cheerful bleakness of attitude with fellow Australian Jane Campion, has written a distinctive script that has the carefully thought-out tightness of a top-drawer short story as well as something more.

Proof also creates characters who have the capacity to surprise, because Moorhouse wouldn't dream of limiting the range of emotional connections open to them. The understated but exceptional acting she has coaxed out of her cast is indispensable to the film's success, as is Martin McGrath's super-bright photography and an unnerving score from the celebrated Australian group Not Drowning, Waving.

But despite its modest dimensions, what makes *Proof* a memorable enough film to have won seven Australian Film Institute Awards is the number of themes it pointedly touches upon. A film about trust, love, and control, about the differences between truth and reality and the risks you run when you leave yourself open to intimacy, *Proof* aims to unsettle—and unsettle it definitely does.

The Quiet American
2002

Graham Greene's spirit hovers over *The Quiet American,* the film version of his prescient 1955 novel, like a shrewd and dispassionate ghost. Star Michael Caine, who gives one of the great, inescapably moving performances in a career filled with them, based his character on personal impressions of the late author. And Greene's lifelong concern with moral ambiguity gives this film a texture and complexity that movies don't usually achieve.

No one today is writing books quite like those by Greene, the author of *The Third Man, The Comedians, Our Man in Havana,* and two dozen more, novels known for their elegant writing and their deft, almost casual mixture of dramatically compelling plots and profound issues.

Set in Vietnam circa 1952, at a time when the French were the embattled colonial power we later became, *The Quiet American* is about the corruptibility, not the more typical transcendence, of the human spirit; about how easy it is to become tainted and complicit; about how even a cynic has innocence to lose, and even an innocent can do terrible harm.

Australian director Phillip Noyce, best known for major Hollywood action thrillers (*Patriot Games, Clear and Present Danger*), has returned to the tone of his earlier, more human-scale works, *Heatwave* and *Newsfront*. *The Quiet American* is a graceful, contemplative film that gradually and artfully draws us into a world where the personal and the political get fatally intertwined.

Noyce and his cast—Caine as skeptical British journalist Thomas Fowler, Brendan Fraser as the dangerously idealistic American of the title, and Do Thi Hai Yen as the stunning Vietnamese woman they both love—are helped by a script that was touched by many hands but ended up elegantly written and very much in the Greene spirit.

Credited to Christopher Hampton and Robert Schenkkan, *The Quiet American* performs numerous nips and tucks to the novel's plot, but none that seriously affect the thrust of the piece. It's safe to say that Greene, who was said to be furious at the way the 1958 Audie Murphy and Michael Redgrave version (written and directed by Joseph L. Mankiewicz) distorted the book's unhappiness with Americans, would be much more pleased with this effort.

Though it is set in Vietnam before the United States got involved on an earthshaking scale, Greene's novel is extremely discerning about what it is in the American character—the messianic zeal, the sureness of being right—that made what came later inevitable. Its message (characterized by the novel's opening Lord Byron quote about an "age of new inventions/For killing bodies, and for saving souls,/All propagated with the best intentions") couldn't be more relevant in today's world.

Should this sound too serious, don't forget that it was Greene's gift, shared by the film, to clothe these concerns in compelling drama.

It also helps to have the fluid Christopher Doyle, the cinematographer of choice for many Asian directors (most notably Wong Kar Wai for *In the Mood for Love*), behind the camera. Doyle is adept at capturing both the chaos of Saigon street life and the country's parallel mystery and delicate beauty.

The man with the best intentions is a bright and idealistic thirty-two-year-old American economic aid worker, Alden Pyle (Fraser). He's described in the novel as someone "determined to do good, not to any individual person but to a country, a continent, a world," with the narrator waspishly adding, "God save us always from the innocent and the good."

That skeptical narrator is seen-it-all British journalist Fowler (Caine), an old Vietnam hand who prides himself on his dispassion. "I don't get involved," he tells Pyle, who cultivates the older man's friendship to get to know the lay of the land. "I just report what I see."

Fowler is not so old that he doesn't have a beautiful Vietnamese mistress, Phuong, played by Do Thi Hai Yen, with whom Pyle falls in love literally at first sight. As Fowler's graceful voice-over puts it, "Saving a country and saving a woman would be the same thing to him."

Fowler is at a disadvantage in this contest because he has a wife in England who won't divorce him, and Phuong has an unromantic, avaricious sister who sees Pyle as a prime catch. As the relationship drama plays out, the American gets increasingly involved with what he calls a "third force," a putatively democratic alternative to both communism and colonialism headed by the mysterious General The.

It is the nature of Greene's plots that people are not as they seem and the world stands revealed as a more complex place than anyone anticipated. It's not just, as the novel has Fowler say of Pyle, that "I never knew a man who had better motives for all the trouble he caused," it's that everyone's motives and actions get called into question.

This is a story about the mutability of acting well and acting badly, about how easy it is to cross that line, a story that underlines the impossibility of staying neutral and the inevitability of taking sides.

Both Fraser, cast to type as the square-shouldered American with a felled-ox quality, and the quietly enigmatic Do, seen in Tran Anh

Hung's lovely *The Vertical Ray of the Sun,* do impeccable supporting work here, but finally this film succeeds as well as it does because of Caine.

A veteran of more than 100 TV dramas and some 80 theatrical films, Caine gives the kind of seemingly effortless performance an actor needs an entire career to prepare for. With a face that has known a thousand compromises, and a world of regret in his every gesture, Caine's Fowler, open to tears, to rage, to disappointment as well as love, seems actually to have the character's life. Caine's performance is intricate without seeming to be, a nuanced marvel of the actor's craft.

Ratcatcher
2000

Bleak childhoods make for the best cinema, and *Ratcatcher* stands at the head of the class.

From acknowledged favorites such as François Truffaut's *The 400 Blows* to underappreciated works such as Robert De Niro and Leonardo DiCaprio's *This Boy's Life* and Jean-Claude Lauzon's French-Canadian *Leolo,* films that let us into the push and pull of difficult young lives have a power to create emotion like almost nothing else. Even in that company, Scottish writer-director Lynne Ramsay's exquisite feature debut is something special.

A knockout in its premiere at Cannes (where Ramsay had previously won two Prix du Jury for her short films), *Ratcatcher* is not only made with unhurried artistry and unblinking assurance, it also combines two very different and usually mutually exclusive kinds of filmmaking.

Hearing that *Ratcatcher* is set in one of Glasgow's poorest neighborhoods during a 1973 sanitation strike that led to massive garbage pileups and a major rodent explosion, it would be simple to assume that it's wholly in the tradition of socially conscious directors like Ken Loach, that it can be summed up simply as, in Ramsay's words, "another grim film from up north." Nothing could be less true.

It's not that the writer-director, herself a Glasgow native, doesn't tear at your sympathies with her depiction of this pitiless environment, where tragedies strike quickly and uncaringly, where chances for tenderness are rare and elusive. With her ability to give every moment its correct emotional weight and an unwillingness to trespass on the realities of lower-class life, Ramsay shows the kind of empathy and concern that is heir to Loach's.

But, and this is especially rare for socially conscious directors, Ramsay also has a remarkable visual imagination, a gift for putting vivid, poetic images on the screen. Working with the same creative team (cinematographer Alwin Kuchler, editor Lucia Zucchetti, production designer Jane Morton) she's used since film school, Ramsay creates unexpected, even daring shots of lyrical beauty that go right to the heart.

Typical is *Ratcatcher*'s striking opening sequence. It's unsettling and hard to read at first, and then we realize we're watching the slowed-down sight of a boy completely enveloped by and twirling around in his mother's curtains. The background sound is muted, as it would be for a boy in what has to be a sort of dream state, one of the few escapes from a troubling reality open to someone like him.

Out of the curtains comes twelve-year-old James Gillespie (William Eadie, like many of the film's child actors, a nonprofessional). His incongruously large ears bookend what has to be called a tragic face, one that seems to know instinctively the kind of unhappy life fate is planning for him.

It's typical of *Ratcatcher*'s nerve that James's first post-curtains scene not only locates him unmistakably in his environment but also sets a powerfully disconcerting tone. No matter what happens to James during the troubling summer vacation that lies before him, what we've seen at the start never leaves our minds, or his. Living with his parents, his older sister Ellen (Michelle Stewart), and his younger sister Anne Marie (Lynne Ramsay Jr., the filmmaker's niece), James feels trapped by his surroundings, his actions, his very life. He's the kid nobody wants around, not his siblings, not the neighborhood gang, not even his hard-pressed parents.

It's indicative of *Ratcatcher*'s sensibility that its character judgments are not schematic. His mother (Mandy Matthews) is overworked, his father (Tommy Flanagan) a problem drinker and a phi-landerer, but the love that once animated their relationship is quite visible when it's not overmatched and exhausted by the extent of their problems. The only hope the family has of escaping suffocation is a potential move to new community-sponsored housing out in the suburbs.

As for James, the only friends he manages to connect with are mis-fits and outcasts like himself. There's Kenny (John Miller), a mentally slow animal lover, and fourteen-year-old Margaret Anne (Leanne Mullen), the neighborhood's abused and victimized sexual mark. The unlikely bond she forms with James answers the need they both have for simple childhood innocence that is available to them nowhere else.

Ramsay's imaginative shot-making gifts make for a sublime result, creating a different sort of magical realism than we're used to seeing. *Ratcatcher* is clearly the work of a natural film artist, and experienc-ing her debut (helped by subtitles that the thick Glasgow accents mandate) is as much a privilege as it is a pleasure.

Richard III
1995

Richard of Gloucester is one of Shakespeare's most magnificent mon-sters, and *Richard III* is a film audacious enough to match his aston-ishing villainy. Made with gusto, daring, and visual brilliance, this stripped-down, jazzed-up *Richard* pulsates with bloody life, a tri-umph of both modernization and popularization.

Shakespeare's plays have been subjected to numerous interpreta-tions, so many that when *The Folger Shakespeare Filmography* was published in 1979, it took 64 pages to list every one. There have been traditional versions, total updates (such as the unlikely *Joe Macbeth* in 1955), even films cleverly disguising their Shakespearean origins (such as the science-fiction classic *Forbidden Planet*, based on *The Tempest*).

But while it's not uncommon on stage, what director Richard Lon-craine and star Ian McKellen (who also collaborated on the screenplay) have done is rare on screen. They've kept to the spirit of Shakespeare's words (though the play is much-abridged here) but switched the setting from the fifteenth century to a unique version of 1930s England. In the process, they've liberated the same kind of energy that Akira Kurosawa did when he moved *Macbeth* to medieval Japan and came up with the magnificent *Throne of Blood*.

McKellen toured extensively with the stage version of this production, but since film is a more realistic medium, he and Loncraine (with splendid help from cinematographer Peter Biziou, production designer Tony Burrough, and costume designer Shuna Harwood) have been able to create a convincing cinematic universe to house it in.

The setting is, in effect, an alternate England, what the country might have looked like in the 1930s if there had been a civil war and if motorcycle-riding, black-shirted fascists (the followers of Sir Oswald Mosley, perhaps) had taken over the government and the monarchy. With inventive use of arresting locations and attention to period details such as ticker tapes, cigarette holders, and big-band music, *Richard* creates an unsettling, crooked copy of those days, not a gimmick, but a breathing, functioning reality.

Employing this eye-catching look has also freed up the filmmakers to creatively re-imagine every aspect of the play's plotline, such as Richard's celebrated wooing of Lady Anne, the woman whose husband he's just killed, which they place in a bloody and claustrophobic hospital morgue.

In addition to splitting Richard's initial "now is the winter of our discontent" speech into two parts, a public address and a private monologue delivered in a men's room, the film brazenly postpones it for 10 minutes, opening things instead with a literally smashing sequence of Richard at war that lets you know at once that this isn't going to be Shakespeare as usual.

Although these pyrotechnics could compensate for a good deal of bad acting, in *Richard III* they don't have to. The title role has always attracted the best of actors (Sir Laurence Olivier did it on film, George C. Scott had his first major New York stage success with the part, and Al Pacino has his own movie version), but even in this group McKellen's delicious version is special.

Insinuator, instigator, a matchless deployer of nets and traps, Mc-Kellen's smirking Richard is a master of oily dissimulation. With his awkward hump and withered arm, he is at once a scuttling apparition that dogs bark at and everyone's concerned false friend, "too childish, foolish for this world."

It's part of McKellen's gift to make it seem that Richard is taking the audience into his confidence via his monologues because his contemporaries are too dense to be appreciative—and he has to share his consummate villainy with someone. Richard first describes and then shows how he'll woo Anne and coolly eliminate anyone who stands between him and the throne, including his two brothers, one of them Edward IV, the current monarch.

Supporting McKellen in this masterly performance are some of Britain's best actors, including Kristin Scott Thomas as the Lady Anne, Nigel Hawthorne and John Wood as Richard's brothers, Maggie Smith as their mother, the Duchess of York, and Jim Broadbent as the duplicitous Buckingham.

Not only are these players in exceptionally good form, they've made a conscious attempt to avoid declaiming, to speak Shakespeare's dialogue as if it were casual and conversational, which successfully makes the words sound as modern as possible.

The one place the casting has gone slightly astray is in using two Americans, Annette Bening and especially Robert Downey Jr., as Edward's Queen Elizabeth and her brother Earl Rivers. Though the filmmakers defend these seemingly commercial choices by saying the original two were outsiders at Edward's court (being members of the rival house of Lancaster), there is something unnecessarily jarring about hearing their domestic accents, though Bening, to her credit, does handle the role with assurance and authority.

Finally, that flaw is barely a blip as far as *Richard III*'s overall impact is concerned. This is Shakespeare exciting enough for even the most dubious, which, after all, is no less than the man deserves.

Ronin
1998

They're tense and intense, been there and been around, world-weary and drop-dead professional. They're five hard men with implacable faces and murky pasts brought together to do a dirty job they don't even pretend to understand. If their story sounds familiar, that turns out to be a very good thing.

Ronin, directed by John Frankenheimer from a script that David Mamet had a noticeable hand in, is an old-fashioned thriller brought efficiently up to date. It's a welcome throwback to the days when the world didn't have to end or tanker trucks explode to get an action audience's attention, and it calls out for traditional adjectives, such as "crisp" and "gripping," that have almost fallen out of fashion in the face of modern bloated fare.

It couldn't be more fitting that a picture this traditional was directed by the sixty-eight-year-old Frankenheimer, whose credits go back to 1954 and live television and include features such as *Birdman of Alcatraz, The Manchurian Candidate,* and *Seven Days in May.*

Working in a lean, laconic style he acknowledges was influenced by French director Jean-Pierre Melville (*Le Samourai*), Frankenheimer brings his experience to bear on a scenario that has been smartly pared down in order to ratchet up the tension, especially in the film's series of heart-stopping car chases.

It was newcomer J.D. Zeik, one of the film's pair of writers, who came up with the idea of doing a contemporary take on the traditional Japanese notion of *ronin,* masterless samurai who are forced into the humiliating position of working for hire for anyone with the means to pay them.

In modern Paris, five of these freelance operatives, unknown to each other, congregate in a small Montmartre bistro and a nearby warehouse. They include Slavic electronics whiz Gregor (Stellan Skarsgard), British weapons specialist Spence (Sean Bean), American wheelman Larry (Skipp Sudduth), and French jack-of-all-trades Vincent (Jean Reno).

Though he's self-effacing enough to say his worst crime is that he "hurt someone's feelings once," it's the fifth man, an American named Sam, who emerges as the group's center. Tautly played by Robert De Niro, an actor who's a natural at being both forceful and impassive, Sam probably doesn't remember his last human emotion, and nothing short of a tactical nuclear weapon landing in his lap would make him blink.

The contact person/employer for this group is an Irish woman named Deirdre (Natascha McElhone), who fills the lads in on their assignment. They're to lift a silver metal briefcase, heavily guarded by parties unknown in the scenic South of France. It's coveted by the Russians, among other parties, and getting it is worth paying each of these men $5,000 a week plus a $20,000 bonus when the deed is done.

If that sounds kind of sketchy, it's going to have to stay that way, because that box and its mysterious contents are a classic McGuffin, a plot device more important for getting *Ronin*'s action juices flowing than for what's actually inside.

Making *Ronin* even harder to figure out is the film's self-consciously clipped and elliptical dialogue, lines such as "Whenever there is any doubt there is no doubt." The other writing credit reads Richard Weisz, but figuring out that it's a pseudonym for David Mamet (who apparently no longer believes in using his name on shared writing credits) wouldn't have been difficult even if the fact hadn't become public knowledge.

Although Mamet's cadences can be an irritant, they make a good fit with this film's fast-paced, cinematic style. Actually, lots of things about *Ronin,* including its implausible coincidences, crosses and double-crosses, and unnamed super-secret organizations, would cross the line into silliness except that Frankenheimer's fast-moving ability to tighten scenes to their maximum tolerance (aided by Elia Cmiral's ominous, percussive score) leaves us little time to ponder anything.

Ronin is especially satisfying in its several impressive car chases, which blast through the old section of Nice and the winding roads of the Côte d'Azur as well as central Paris. Frankenheimer was determined to film these realistically, without digital compositing, and working with stunt coordinator Joe Dunne and car stunt supervisor Jean-Claude Lagniez, he has come up with startling sequences that remind us how exciting the basics of filmmaking can be when skillful people care enough to do them right.

Safe
1995

It starts with a sniffle. Then things get worse. And you think you know what's going to happen on screen. But you don't.

Safe, the elegantly unnerving film by Todd Haynes, is all about uncertainty. A strange illness descends on protagonist Carol White (Julianne Moore), and the insecurity and unease she feels spills over into the audience. Insidious and provocative, *Safe* refuses to lend a hand, avoids taking sides or pointing the way. Everything that happens in this beautifully controlled enigma is open to multiple interpretations, and that extends finally to the title's meaning as well.

A measure of *Safe*'s subversiveness is that it mimics the forms of standard genres only to turn familiar conventions inside out. Its theme, for instance, is apparently a right-thinking one—the dangers of environmental pollution—but the deeper you get into the story, the more uncertain that becomes.

And while its healthy-woman-gets-sick-and-fights-back structure has a shrewd and superficial resemblance to numerous movies of the week, *Safe* finally encourages you to view all the stages of Carol's story as toxic in different ways, and even to think that perhaps her time of greatest illness is the closest she comes to a kind of life.

Set in the San Fernando Valley in 1987, *Safe* opens with a polished tracking shot (typical of the sharp, pristine quality of cinematographer Alex Nepomniaschy's images) that follows a Mercedes down a manicured street and behind the motorized gates of the luxury home where Carol lives with a bland husband (Xander Berkeley) and his son from a previous marriage.

With her tiny voice and passive character, uninvolved during sex and incapable of sweating in aerobics class, Carol has the doll-like existence of an up-to-date Stepford wife. A "total milkaholic" who wears pearls to lunch and spends her days gardening, exercising, and worrying about furniture, Carol is a Nora who never even thinks of slamming the door, who looks around at her elite surroundings and is content.

Julianne Moore does remarkable work in a role she wanted so much she reportedly burst into tears when she got it. Ever so delicately, she animates this detached mouse, allowing us to feel for the kind of passive, emotionally disconnected character whose first thought when illness encroaches is to apologize for the inconvenience she's causing.

As sniffles are succeeded by unexpected tiredness, extended coughing, difficulty breathing, and frightening fits, Carol's physical disintegration gets worse and worse. Her doctors are baffled, her husband frustrated, but it is Carol herself who thinks she's found the answer when she spots a flyer that asks the daunting question, "Do you smell fumes? Are you allergic to the 20th Century?"

What Carol is told she has is a disease you catch from your surroundings, something referred to as "an immune system breakdown based on environmental factors." Just living in the modern world, with its 60,000 chemical substances, is what has made her ill. Now she goes nowhere without a filter mask and an oxygen tank, and when she hears about the Wrenwood Center outside of Albuquerque, a place that offers a chemically free safe haven, she decides that this will be her salvation.

Wrenwood is the final, most ambiguous stage of Carol's journey, and what happens within its walls intensifies the questions that *Safe* encourages us to ask but refuses to answer conclusively. Is the regimen there truly a cure, and at what cost does it come? Is Carol's illness a reaction to her physical environment, or could it be a psychological plea for release from the barren life of a good little girl? And in a world so rife with strange maladies and stranger remedies, how outmoded is the very concept of safeness?

Working with deliberation and controlled precision, writer-director Haynes, whose *Poison* took the Grand Jury Prize at Sundance and became a political cause célèbre, solidifies his reputation as one of the most intellectually challenging of current directors. Helped by composer Ed Tomney's ominous score, he has created not a simple cautionary tale about the air we breathe but a withering portrait of American society, an attack on the sterility and toxicity of modern life and the profound sense of malaise that it can foster. Subtlety is the rarest quality in today's filmmakers, and *Safe* demonstrates why it is valuable as well as scarce.

Searching for Bobby Fischer
1993

The board has sixty-four squares, alternating light and dark. The pieces number sixteen on each side, including king, queen, knights, and (for what is combat without them?) a full complement of pawns. The game is chess, only maybe it isn't really a game but a sport, a science, perhaps an art, but always an obsession. And the quest for mastery of it at the highest levels has driven brilliant men quite literally mad and destroyed human relationships with the finality of an ax.

Searching for Bobby Fischer is set in the world of chess, but it wouldn't be a fraction of the film it is if chess were all it was about. A story of childhood simultaneously exalted and at risk, of the demands of parenthood and the burdens of competition and of genius, it is also the most impressive and promising of directing debuts.

For writer-director Steven Zaillian proves as much of a prodigy as his chess-playing subject, turning out a film that is a beautifully calibrated model of honestly sentimental filmmaking, made with delicacy, restraint, and unmistakable emotional power. The feelings it goes for are almost never the easy or obvious ones, and the levers it presses are all the more effective because of that.

Nominated for an Academy Award for the script of *Awakenings* (a prime example of dishonestly sentimental direction), and the writer who adapted Thomas Keneally's *Schindler's List* for Steven Spielberg, Zaillian once again deals with a true story. *Bobby Fischer* tells what happens when a typical New York City kid with dreams of playing second base for the Yankees discovers that he has so much innate chess ability that he puts people in mind of that celebrated former world champion, as breathtaking a player as ever lived.

Given his abilities as a writer, it might be expected that as a director Zaillian would lean too hard on his own words, so one of the things that is most impressive about *Bobby Fischer* is that the opposite is true. Considerably aided by celebrated director of photography Conrad Hall, Zaillian, determined to tell his story without words whenever possible, has made a conspicuously visual debut.

This nonverbal assurance is most impressive in the film's opening scene. Seven-year-old Josh Waitzkin (Max Pomeranc) is fooling around with some pals in a park when for no particular reason he looks up and sees a group of men playing chess, the pieces and the board curiously reflected in a pair of sunglasses. Not a word is spoken, nothing is heard but James Horner's evocative score, but the subliminal connection Josh makes with the game, the way the lust for it seeps into his blood, is magically visible on the screen.

On the surface Josh remains a regular kid, getting his baseball mitt oiled by his sportswriter father, Fred (Joe Mantegna), and taking walks in Washington Square Park with his mother, Bonnie (Joan Allen). But on his own he has somehow mastered the basics of the game, even constructed his own set of chessmen, and on one of those walks he pulls his uncertain mother over to watch the park's raffish group of regular players go at it.

Soon he starts to play, and his ability catches the eye of Vinnie (Laurence Fishburne), a shaved-head, jive-talking, cigarette-dangling, possibly drug-using master chess hustler who writes Josh's name down on a newspaper, much to his mother's horror. "Hey, the boy used pieces in combination, in attack," Vinnie yells after her as she, uncertain whether to feel pleased or threatened, nervously shepherds the boy toward home.

After Fred Waitzkin is convinced (in a clever, humorous, and again largely visual scene) of Josh's ability, father and son head off to a local chess club to approach somber guru Bruce Pandolfini (Ben Kingsley) about teaching him.

No, Pandolfini says, he doesn't teach anymore. Period. But a glimpse of Josh at the board makes the man doubt his resolve. Then he tries to undermine Fred's resolve to see his son succeed in chess by telling him about what a neurotic-ridden, miserable world it is. Finally, he tells the father the truth. Chess may be an art, but "most players, even the great ones, are forgers. Your son creates. Like Bobby Fischer."

Though this may sound like some kind of happy ending, it is in fact only the beginning of a whole series of painful struggles, initially between Josh's two mentors for control of his mind and his game. The emotional Vinnie believes in attitude and tactics, the conservative Pandolfini in preparation and position. Neither man is above manipulation, and each wishes the other would shrivel up and go away, but one of the graces of *Searching for Bobby Fischer* is how well it understands that to portray them as simply vice and virtue would do an injustice to what is a considerably more intricate reality.

For it turns out that everyone who comes into contact with the enormity of Josh's gift has an agenda, a stake in the boy's success, even his father. Though initially unconcerned and even blasé about his son's accomplishments, Fred Waitzkin soon gets caught up against his will in the blood sport of winning, snapping at an uncomprehending teacher, "My son is better at this than I've been at anything in my life."

At its core, then, *Searching for Bobby Fischer* is about much larger issues. What do you do when your child is a genius, how do you best serve both the gift and the tiny, fragile person who possesses it? Can Josh survive as an individual and still be a champion, or must his decency be beaten out of him if he is to reach his maximum potential? And, hovering over all these questions, evoked in newsreels, interviews, and Josh's voice-over, is the cautionary spirit of Bobby Fischer, a vision of the ultimate boy genius gone painfully astray.

Though its thrust is undeniably sentimental, it can't be overstated how elegantly writer-director Zaillian has put this together. He has gotten all the right notes from veterans Kingsley, Mantegna, and Allen, while Fishburne, who seems to just get better and better, is electric in his small but pivotal role. Most impressive is the performance that comes from Pomeranc, himself a gifted chess player mak-

106

ing his acting debut, whose soulful work as a miniature adult with the most trusting eyes is guilelessly convincing.

In addition to all these adult riches, *Searching for Bobby Fischer* happens to be the family film anyone with a family has been hoping for with increasing desperation. Unwilling to patronize the children in its cast and unable to let its concern for values stand in the way of on-screen excitement, its final message is, "There are only so many things you can teach a child. Finally, they are who they are." Can there be any doubt but that this is a film not only to enjoy but also to cherish?

The Secret of Roan Inish
1995

The problem with most children's films is that they make older folk glad they're all grown up. Yes, we say, this sort of thing is fine for the kids, sweet and decent and good, but fortunately we can count on something a bit more substantial when it's our turn to watch.

The Secret of Roan Inish is not that kind of children's film. Though its protagonist is a ten-year-old girl, it is a crackling good tale with a sense of wonder and mystery strong enough to captivate any age group. A movie that believes in magic but knows enough not to be insistent about it, *Roan Inish* is just the kind of impressive independent work that has become habitual with writer-director John Sayles.

Roan Inish's story of young Fiona Coneelly's determination to penetrate her family's mysterious past, to understand the truth behind the legends she hears of curious appearances and disappearances, of animals with strange and disturbing powers, may not sound like ideal Sayles material, but in many ways it is.

For one thing, Sayles has always been interested in the human qualities of situations that cross the line into the mythic: Both the "Black Sox" World Series scandal depicted in *Eight Men Out* and the West Virginia coal-mine labor violence that was *Matewan*'s backdrop fit that description as nicely as does *Roan Inish*.

And Sayles's habitual, straight-ahead filmmaking style turns out to be well suited to transferring this kind of fable (based on a novella by Rosalie K. Fry) to the screen. Understanding that fantasy needs to be treated with respect but not fawned over, Sayles operates with a matter-of-factness that makes the magic seem all the more plausible and real.

Like many a young heroine, Fiona Coneelly (Jeni Courtney) is introduced with troubles to overcome. The time is just after World War II, her mother has died, and her father, a weary slave to his job in the city, has sent her to live with her grandparents, Hugh (Mick Lally) and Tess (Eileen Colgan), on the isolated west coast of Ireland.

Though they now live on the mainland, the grandparents, in fact Fiona's entire family, used to have houses on the nearby small, mysterious island of Roan Inish, sharing the space with herds of seals. Economics and loneliness drove everyone from it, but life does not seem as sweet to the Coneellys away from their traditional home.

To make the loss less painful, the family lingers over tales of the island and the past, shown in vivid voice-over flashbacks. Grandfather Hugh tells Fiona of the troubling disappearance of her brother, Jamie, an infant who floated out to sea in his cradle and was never seen again. And her cousin Tadhg (John Lynch) recounts the legend of ancestor Liam Coneelly who fell in love with a beautiful *selkie,* a creature half animal, half seal, who can be controlled only if her seal skin is stolen.

As Fiona hears these stories in bits and pieces, she comes to realize, in the best young heroine tradition, that she has a definite role to play. She believes that these are not just silly old rumors but indications of a critical contemporary situation that the adults are too dense to grasp, a situation that has been waiting for her help to resolve.

Though she gets some assistance from her older cousin Eamon (Richard Sheridan), Fiona is a splendidly self-reliant heroine. With the long golden hair of a fairy-tale princess and the feisty spirit of Nancy Drew, Fiona (well played by nonprofessional Courtney) is a fearless creature, determined to do what needs to be done.

Helping to make Fiona's quest believable is the care that has been taken to make the film's setting authentic. Mason Daring's Celtic-themed original music creates an exquisite backdrop, and Sayles's artful script has the feel of the land to it. Also, having actors of the caliber of Lally and Lynch, able to animate lines such as "What the sea will take, the sea must have," is a considerable advantage.

If Sayles has a key confederate, however, it is master cinematographer Haskell Wexler, who also shot *Matewan*. A wizard with light, Wexler has captured the brooding, fog-bound, romantic ambience that *Roan Inish* must have to succeed, and he has done it in a way that refuses to call unnecessary attention to itself.

With its emphasis on what people owe to their physical surroundings, on the ancient kinship between man and the animal world that sometimes gets frayed around the edges, *The Secret of Roan Inish* manages to be both contemporary and timeless. Its enchantments are many, and they fall with happy equality on any age you can name.

Secrets & Lies
1996

Secrets & Lies, winner of the Palme d'Or at Cannes as well as the best actress award for star Brenda Blethyn, both sums up a career and takes it further.

For openers, it ranks with the best of the features that Mike Leigh has written and directed in Britain, including *Life Is Sweet* and *Naked,* during a quarter-century-long creative journey that has brought honors but limited American visibility. More than that, it is a piercingly honest, completely accessible piece of work that will go directly to the hearts of audiences who have never heard of him. If film means anything to you, if emotional truth is a quality you care about, this is an event not to be missed.

Secrets & Lies could in a sense be the subtitle for all of Leigh's films, dealing as they do with the painful yet often ruefully funny complexities of human experience. Here the focus is on the need for understanding, connection, and love, on discovering who and what we are. Though the film's basic plot could be summarized in a sentence or two, Leigh's facility with shadings and nuances creates strong and unforgettable waves of feeling.

At the center of *Secrets & Lies* is Cynthia (Blethyn), one of those needy, sentimental, good-hearted people whose desperation puts off anyone they might look to for love and support. Rarely without a cigarette in her hand or a phrase like "I wouldn't know him if he stood up in me soup" on her lips, Cynthia works in a London box factory and lives in a state of undeclared war with her determinedly surly daughter, Roxanne (Claire Rushbrook). Most strident when she's trying to be useful, Cynthia finds herself repeatedly screeching, "I'm just trying to help," as Roxanne lays into her.

Secrets & Lies focuses on the attempts of two different people to get closer to this plaintive but caring woman. One is her brother Maurice (Leigh veteran Timothy Spall), a portrait and wedding photographer who has made a success of his career and his life with his high-strung, house-proud wife, Monica (Phyllis Logan).

All edges and prone to lash out with little provocation, Monica has contributed to easygoing Maurice's long-standing estrangement from his sister, but now the opportunity to give niece Roxanne a twenty-first birthday party promises to reunite the family, at least temporarily.

Then there is Hortense (Marianne Jean-Baptiste), a tranquil, sophisticated, single black woman who works as an optometrist and seems to have no possible connection to this emotionally impoverished world. But Hortense is adopted, and when her mother dies (it's her funeral that opens the picture), she decides to search out her birth mother. Astonishingly, it turns out to be Cynthia.

Nothing illustrates what Leigh's films accomplish and how they do it better than the scene in which Hortense and Cynthia, after a few rushed and awkward conversations on the telephone, sit down side by side and talk it out in a deserted tea shop.

Cynthia, who gave her daughter up after a teenage pregnancy without looking at her, reacts to Hortense's claims by insisting, "There's someone having a joke on you. I'm ever so sorry, sweetheart." If she'd ever had sex with a black man, she would remember.

Then, in a breathtaking moment daringly presented in a rigorous two-shot unbroken by close-ups, that very memory comes back to Cynthia in a furious rush, flooding her face and bringing on uncontrollable weeping. If there are truer, more powerful moments to be found in modern film, they do not come to mind.

The bulk of *Secrets & Lies* is concerned with watching how these revelations and the needs they spawn reverberate through the characters' lives, culminating in that chaotic birthday-party barbecue for Roxanne. Though in outline the film's situations may sound familiar, seeing them play out emphasizes the essence of Leigh's gift. Like a well that goes deeper to get purer water, *Secrets & Lies* stretches the bounds of psychological truth on film, balancing humor and pain without ever tipping over.

This is largely due to Leigh's celebrated method. Using a process of his own devising, he and his actors work together for months to build the film's script from scratch, using extensive improvisation and rehearsal to, in effect, organically grow the characters and their relationships.

As a result, all of Leigh's people, even the ones glimpsed just for a few seconds in a charming montage of Maurice's photographic clients, have a heft and a texture that other film characters can't equal.

Unforced, confident, and completely involving, with exceptional acting aided by Dick Pope's unobtrusive camera work and John Gregory's telling editing, *Secrets & Lies* is filmmaking to savor. Not just today, but always.

For a British independent film, Secrets & Lies *had a major impact in Hollywood. Though it didn't win, it was nominated for five Oscars, including best picture, director, screenplay, best actress for Blethyn, and best supporting actress for Jean-Baptiste.*

Sexy Beast
2001

You can tell from the opening shot, an overhead view of an overweight man baking in the super-hot Spanish sun, that *Sexy Beast* is going to have style that burns. And it does. But there's more.

The feature debut of Jonathan Glazer, one of Britain's most sought-after young commercial and music-video directors, *Sexy Beast* also has a strong plot (credit the writing team of Louis Mellis and

David Scinto) and a pair of excellent performances, including one by Ben Kingsley as a flesh-and-blood "Terminator" terrifying enough to forever banish all thoughts of *Gandhi* from your mind.

Sexy Beast is one more example of what has become the most reliable of British genres, the unsentimental gangster film. From *Get Carter* and *The Long Good Friday* through *Croupier* and *Lock, Stock and Two Smoking Barrels,* U.K. filmmakers have shown a liking and facility for crime stories featuring hard guys tested by intolerable dilemmas.

As his nickname indicates and his physique emphasizes, Gary "Gal" Dove (Ray Winstone) is not as hard a guy as he once was. He's not even in England anymore but retired to Spain's Costa del Sol, where he's as much in love with his wife DeeDee (Amanda Redman) as with a sybaritic lifestyle where teasing the pool boy and having drinks and dinner with pals Aitch (Cavan Kendall) and Jackie (Julianne White) pass for a day's work.

Vividly shot by Ivan Bird, *Sexy Beast*'s opening sequence of a sunstruck Gal being parboiled by his pool ("I'm sweating, roasting, you can fry an egg on my stomach") does more than announce the jazzy, enveloping, music-heavy visual style Glazer brings to the table. It also introduces actor Winstone, previously bleak as they come in two of the grimmest films ever, Gary Oldman's *Nil by Mouth* and Tim Roth's *The War Zone,* who goes on to give a strong, charismatic performance as someone desperate to hold on to the good life but not sure if he has the strength to manage it.

And, when a rogue boulder rolls down a hillside and narrowly misses Gal, the sequence foreshadows the arrival of Don Logan (Kingsley), Gal's former nemesis from the London underworld and very much an unguided missile himself.

The psychotic Logan is spoken about before he's seen. He has phoned from Britain to say he's coming over, and everyone is terrorized by just the mention of his name—and the fact that he insists Gal reenter the criminal life for one last job. Even the fake bravado of "What's the worst that can happen?" is not calming when referring to a man who knows how to hurt people in every way they can be hurt.

Logan is first seen from behind, walking through a Spanish airport with the pumped-up and purposeful stride of a human projectile. Played by Kingsley with a goatee and shaved head, the forceful Logan is a coiled-spring presence, a soul-eater with an unswerving instinct for exploiting human weakness.

One of the mechanisms of *Sexy Beast* is the psychological duel between the vulnerable Gal and his all-menace, all-the-time tormentor. The film also features the nifty burglary scheme that Logan is recruiting for, a plan with an intriguing back story that we see as Logan relates it to Gal.

The criminal power behind the plan is the cool and menacing Teddy Bass (British TV star Ian McShane), a.k.a. Mr. Black Magic, who uses an orgy to make the acquaintance of the aristocratic Harry (the veteran James Fox). Harry turns out to run Europe's most secure safety-deposit firm, with a security system that's all but impregnable. Teddy thinks it can be had, Don thinks he needs Gal for the job, and as the screws tighten, the man himself ends up having to play a terribly dangerous game to survive.

Though it can overreach for emotional effect and overplay its hand at times, *Sexy Beast* brings considerable virtues to telling this tale, including a great eye for faces as well as director Glazer's palpable excitement at working in the feature medium.

Also a factor, and this is key, was Glazer's willingness, unusual for a commercial director moving to film, to take on a project that's strong on people and laced with pithy language. "I purposefully chose something dialogue-intensive and character-driven," he told *Film Comment.* "I wanted to learn. It felt silly to accept a script with huge visual set-pieces—that seemed dead to me." American commercial directors may pay lip service to caring about the script when they turn to features, but their films show that they're not fooling anyone.

The Snapper
1993

The Snapper is amiability itself. Good-humored and sassy, it is one of those charmingly off-the-cuff films that doesn't let its small scale stand in the way of pleasure. And, filled with Ireland's bawdy and bit-ing wit, it takes a satisfaction in the music of spoken language that is as engaging as it is rare.

That language comes from Irish writer Roddy Doyle. His first book about Barrytown, a working-class Dublin suburb, was the source for Alan Parker's *The Commitments,* and his latest, *Paddy Clark, Ha, Ha, Ha,* won the Booker Prize, Britain's premier literary award.

In between, Doyle wrote *The Snapper,* its title taken from Irish slang for the baby that its comic, chaotic story revolves around. The same crisis-a-minute family returns from the earlier film, though now, for contractual reasons, named the Curleys instead of the Rabbittes. It is still a family in which no one so much as thinks of holding his or her tongue. But the spirit this time is more natural and less grandiose than in *The Commitments,* and for that credit Stephen Frears.

One of the most versatile of British directors, with work ranging from *My Beautiful Laundrette* to *Dangerous Liaisons* and *The Grifters,* Frears knows how to make comedy funny without short-changing the often painful emotions underneath. And it is that realis-tic balance between humor and distress that makes *The Snapper* so vital and appealing.

Certainly nothing seems initially comic about the predicament of eldest daughter Sharon Curley (Tina Kellegher). Just twenty years old, she informs her father, Dessie (Colm Meaney), and her mother, Kay (Ruth McCabe), that she is pregnant. Not only that, she's not telling who the father is.

Nonplussed at first, Dessie's strongest response to the news is his usual, all-purpose, "A man needs a pint after that." And the local pub is, in fact, where Sharon heads as well, gossiping with her lovelorn pals and refusing to reveal anything about the unknown father except that "it wasn't Bart Simpson."

In as small an enclave as Barrytown, however, where your neigh-bors know your business before you do and no one is spared the lash of ironic wit, the question of "who Sharon's having it for" becomes one of ever-increasing fascination. And when hints of a suspect emerge (it isn't Bart Simpson), it plunges the neighborhood into a comic, horrific tizzy that has everyone talking.

At the center of that verbal firestorm is not only Sharon but also her loving, if perplexed, father, both of whom find the crisis changing them in ways neither one expected. And though the film's success wouldn't be possible without the vigorous performance it gets from Kellegher, it is Colm Meaney's exasperated but resilient Dessie that makes the strongest impact.

Meaney, who had the advantage of playing the same character in *The Commitments,* is human, vulnerable, and triumphant as the father of six, a knight in rusty armor whose family is forever threatening to get the best of him. With a mobile face, a command of the language, and a fine repertory of puzzled looks, the Dessie who worries, "I'm only the dad, they'll laugh at me," is a cinematic parent to marvel at and enjoy.

It is characteristic of the way *The Snapper* thrives on the interplay of fine writing and empathetic acting that some of its most memorable moments are in small family scenes that don't advance the plot at all. For we are so caught up in these characters and their lives that nothing they do fails to interest us.

And the feeling *The Snapper* has of just appearing on screen without outside assistance is an indication of what an expertly self-effacing job of directing Stephen Frears has done. Like Alan Parker and Neal Jordan before him, he has refreshed himself in local waters after being parched in Hollywood, and this fiercely alive film is the welcome result.

A Soldier's Daughter Never Cries
1998

The things *A Soldier's Daughter Never Cries* does best are as difficult to describe as to accomplish. Somehow, against considerable obstacles, it has captured something true about families and friendship, creating a texture of believable emotions on screen. To watch this touching story of a young girl's coming of age is to feel that someone felt this, someone cared about it, and someone understood how to translate it into film.

Soldier's Daughter is based on an autobiographical novel by Kaylie Jones that deals with her own experiences growing up in Paris and the United States in the 1960s as the daughter of celebrated novelist James Jones (*From Here to Eternity, The Thin Red Line*).

Behind the scenes is the veteran team of producer Ismail Merchant, director and co-screenwriter James Ivory, and his writing partner, Ruth Prawer Jhabvala, whose team successes include *A Room with a View, Howards End,* and *The Remains of the Day.*

Except for that latter film, the twentieth century has not been the most fertile ground for the respected Merchant-Ivory group, which has stumbled with modern efforts such as *Slaves of New York* and *Surviving Picasso.* But this film is for the most part different, a positive exercise that may have missteps, but not ones fatal to the general spirit of acceptance and love.

The key here may be the personal connection that Ivory, who has also led an expatriate life, apparently felt with several aspects of the material, a linkage that led to a measured empathy that resists excess.

What results is a memory piece with a very loose and fluid form, a series of three sketches from childhood. The main dramatic focus, watching a young girl move uncertainly toward maturity, has been attempted before, and more than once, but *Soldier's Daughter* manages to get under the skin in unpredictable ways.

The film's final success is especially unexpected because *Soldier's Daughter* is the kind of film that starts awkwardly but gains assurance as it goes along. In fact, its first section, "Billy," comes off as its rockiest and most confusing.

For one thing, the introduction of writer Bill Willis (Kris Kristofferson), his passionate wife, Marcella (a spirited Barbara Hershey), and their expatriate life of jazzy parties and lusty poker games feels initially phony and too broadly drawn.

Also, the plot of this first section, involving the decision by the Willises to adopt a small French boy named Benoit, is filled with so many complications it's no wonder that the family's natural daughter, Channe, outright rejects the new addition at first.

But the film shows its integrity in the gradual way Channe comes to accept the boy, who changes his name to Billy and as a young man (Jesse Bradford) becomes especially close to his sister.

The teenage Channe is played by Leelee Sobieski, a remarkably poised young actress. It's not a coincidence that the film gains impact in the final two segments, both named after other pivotal men in Channe's life.

The first of those is called "Francis," after Paul Francis Fortescue (beautifully played by Anthony Roth Costanza), a flamboyant young man whose close teenage friendship with Channe is threatened when she starts to take a romantic interest in other boys. Again, the awkwardness and entanglements of those years is tricky material to handle well, but Ivory, who once said that in creating this character, "I sometimes drew on myself," knows how to make it valid.

"Daddy," the namesake of the final section, figures more in Channe's life when the Willises move back to America, partly because of her father's concern over the onset of hereditary heart disease.

Though the film's title makes it sound as if World War II veteran Bill Willis were a disciplinarian and a hard case, in fact the opposite is true. Firm but kindly and an invariable source of excellent advice, especially where boyfriends are concerned, the senior Willis comes off as the father we'd all like to have had. His daughter's tribute to him, to the rest of her family, and to herself is fond and clear-eyed, and, by all indications here, well-deserved.

State and Main
2000

Contradictory as it sounds, Hollywood is the kind of place you have to despair of to truly love. Where else can a director caught in an untruth say, "It's not a lie, it's a gift for fiction," or a producer insist, "I made $11 million last year, and I don't like to be trifled with"? And where else, for that matter, can a horse be a legitimate candidate for an associate producer credit?

True, these are not real people, or a real horse, but as pungent characters in writer-director David Mamet's completely delicious show-biz satire *State and Main,* they might as well be. An occasional worker in Hollywood for nearly twenty years, Mamet knows where bodies are buried and how to use the corpses to bring a smile to your face. *State and Main* is a quintessentially wised-up insider comedy, ideally cast and filled with sharp writing from start to finish (a line about associate producers at the tail end of the credits is especially worth waiting for).

It may be cynical, but, in another paradox, *State and Main*'s story of what transpires when a major studio movie comes to a small New England town may be the warmest film Mamet has yet made. Someone who once said that complaining about Hollywood is like a boxer coming out of the ring and saying, "That guy hit me." Mamet doesn't moralize, he just records it all with a can-you-believe-this kind of bemused glee.

Like the real-estate-office setting of his Pulitzer Prize–winning *Glengarry Glen Ross,* Hollywood is ideal Mamet territory. Both worlds are filled with people who bend words to their particular uses just as they bend the rules of morality in an attempt to cope with increasingly desperate situations.

In fact, *State and Main* has a lot of Mamet's trademark characteristics, including numerous plot twists, all presented in a looser, more relaxed form than we're used to. Even his clipped, pungent dialogue isn't delivered in quite as rigid a cadence as the director usually insists on. And maybe because the movie business brings its own particular darkness and devilry with it, Mamet has felt freer to make his vision more amiable than it's ever been.

Accentuating the comedic aspects is the terrific farce situation Mamet the screenwriter has come up with. Fast pacing and intricate plotting, with endless complications bringing on recriminations, vendettas, and worst-case scenarios, guarantee that the invention and the energy never flag.

This kind of manic, antic storytelling brings to mind the classic 1940s comedies of Preston Sturges, a writer-director whose influence here Mamet acknowledges. Like Sturges, Mamet has increased the laughter through his adroit casting of a large and expert ensemble. Alec Baldwin, Charles Durning, Clark Gregg, Philip Seymour Hoffman, Patti LuPone, William H. Macy, Sarah Jessica Parker, David Paymer, Rebecca Pidgeon, Ricky Jay, and Julia Stiles, take a bow. You've earned it.

Until the movie business came to town, the only thing the bucolic fictional hamlet of Waterford, Vermont, and its most ambitious politician, Doug MacKenzie (Gregg), ever got worked up over was the new traffic light at that State and Main intersection.

Then the cast and crew of *The Old Mill,* mysteriously ejected from neighboring New Hampshire, enter the picture. First to arrive is director Walt Price, who likes what he sees. Beautifully played by Macy, Price is the pragmatic facilitator with a solution for everything. He's the good cop who could placate an aroused polar bear, who knows what to say to everyone, even sending a few words of atrociously pronounced Yiddish to his killer producer Marty Rossen (Paymer).

An attorney who just happens to travel with the statutes on statutory rape, Rossen is the bad cop, the kind of guy who says, "Don't flinch when I'm talking to you." His mandate is dealing with big problems, such as placating the town's mayor (Durning) and his social-climbing wife (LuPone). And coping with whatever crises his stars will inevitably precipitate.

With female lead Claire Wellesley (Parker), it's a reluctance to take off her shirt. Yes, she signed a contract agreeing to do just that, but without an added $800,000, she's threatening to walk.

Her co-star Bob Barrenger (Baldwin), who shows up with the "I'm just here to do a job" swagger of the world's top box-office attraction, turns out to have a weakness for underage girls. "Everyone," he says by way of shameless explanation, "needs a hobby." Naturally, the presence in town of a fetching and sharp-eyed teenage waitress (Stiles) doesn't escape his notice.

Expected to be creative in the midst of this chaos is the awkward, woebegone writer Joseph Turner White (Hoffman), who starts off on the wrong foot by (a) being the writer, and (b) immediately losing his typewriter.

Fortunately for him and the film, White gets a big break when he makes a connection with local bookstore owner Ann Black (Pidgeon), who's sane, sensible, and smart, with a pithy sense of humor thrown into the mix. Ann is the emotional center of the film, someone who makes the fictional world of Waterford not only a great place to visit, but also someplace we actually might want to live. And that, for a David Mamet setting, is saying a lot.

The Station Agent
2003

People and porcupines, the German philosopher Arthur Schopenhauer famously wrote, are very much alike: They want to stay close to obtain warmth and companionship, but they also insist on a certain distance to avoid pricking one another. The characters in *The Station Agent,* a quite wonderful comic drama, fit that description exactly.

Written and directed by Tom McCarthy, an experienced actor and stage director making his behind-the-camera debut, *The Station Agent* did well at Sundance, taking the audience award, the Waldo Salt Screenwriting Award, and a share of co-star Patricia Clarkson's special prize for outstanding acting. But even that doesn't say enough about the film.

For this sophisticated entertainment made with a true gift for character is more than a Sundance prizewinner. Its charming and delicate story of the unlikely intersection of three highly individual lives is the kind of completely personal yet universal film that the festival and even the entire independent movement came into being to celebrate. And it does it all in 88 surprisingly funny minutes.

Typical of *Station Agent*'s strength is that it makes its optimistic points about community, about how and why we're drawn to each other almost in spite of ourselves, with people who sound in the abstract unlikely to come alive, let alone come together.

But filmmaker McCarthy knew what he was doing. Having met his principals through his Manhattan stage experience, he wrote each part with a specific actor in mind, using his sense of what the actors could accomplish to create a complex tissue of interactions that becomes irresistible.

First among equals is Peter Dinklage, who brings charisma and contained emotion to the role of four-foot-five-inch Fin McBride, someone whose great passion and escape in life is trains. Fin works in a hobby shop for model train buffs by day and spends his nights meeting with fellow enthusiasts and watching films they've taken of, yes, trains.

This zeal notwithstanding, Fin is not an outwardly passionate man. Rather, he's a figure of formidable dignity not in spite of but because of his size. After having endured every joke, every look of disbelief, every nudging reference to Fantasy Island, Fin has made himself as solitary as any cloistered monk, creating a buffer that's given him the distance necessary to survive.

When a sudden death leaves Fin with an inheritance that includes an abandoned train depot in rural Newfoundland, New Jersey, he immediately moves out there, looking not for something but for nothing. He just wants to be left alone. What he does not count on is Joe.

For parked outside Fin's isolated depot is a coffee truck manned by a gregarious young Cuban (Bobby Cannavale) who's been sitting in for his ailing father for six weeks. To call Joe chatty is like calling Fin small: Deprived of his usual level of companionship, the man is desperate for conversation, and he latches on to Fin with the zeal of a fire-and-brimstone minister out to save a soul.

It doesn't matter what Fin says or does, Joe refuses to be discouraged from his desire to hang out. Whether its watching for trains for hours or walking the right-of-way, Joe wants to be there. He is literally impossible to discourage, and it is a mark of the grace of Cannavale's engaging performance that Joe manages to be as ingratiating as he is irritating—someone you have to like even as he's driving you crazy.

The way Fin meets Olivia (Clarkson), a regular customer of Joe's, is too delicious to reveal. A painter separated from her husband, she also doesn't want to talk, but for a more serious reason: She's still in shock from the death of her young son. Clarkson, always effective, gives Olivia the wistful tentativeness of a fragile person just barely holding it together.

Though the relationship between these three is the heart of *The Station Agent,* this film seems to have nothing but memorable characters, including Emily (*Dawson's Creek*'s Michelle Williams), the town's sylph-like librarian, and an inquisitive young person (*Lovely & Amazing*'s Raven Goodwin) who wants to know what grade Fin is in.

In fact, the key accomplishment of writer-director McCarthy and his actors is how finely these characters are drawn. McCarthy has a superb ear and eye for what makes people individual as well as an exact sense of how far he can push things without sacrificing delicacy and believability. He knows how messy other people's lives turn out to be when you get involved with them, and he understands not only the risks to yourself when you do, but the cost to yourself when you don't.

Strictly Ballroom
1993

Strictly Ballroom is close to irresistible. Shamelessly derivative but told with unflagging energy and style, it is so awash in good spirits that audiences hungry for pure entertainment will be nibbling on it for some time to come.

Sly and sure-footed, *Ballroom* was shot in Australia, made its reputation at Cannes, and played successfully from Japan to Iceland. Its heart, though, belongs to the golden age of Hollywood, to those simple days when on-screen wishes always came true and lovers never stayed apart for more than a few reels.

A wised-up homage to the musicals of Fred Astaire and Ginger Rogers, *Ballroom* manages to both update and honor the conventions of the genre. Viewers can wink knowingly at how old-fashioned these traditions have become as well as feel happy at the respect they're given.

This combination of spoof and seriousness extends to the film's exotic setting, the world of competitive ballroom dancing. Though just about unknown in this country, it has adherents on several continents and is quite popular in Australia, where director Baz Luhrmann (who also came up with the story and co-wrote the script with Andrew Bovell) made its acquaintance as a young boy.

Competitive ballroom dancing is like an over-the-top version of

Olympic ice skating, but without the free-style segment. Though the costumes the teams wear are dazzling enough to make Mr. Blackwell blanch (Angus Strathie's exuberant designs apparently exhausted Australia's entire supply of Austrian diamantés), the routines themselves are the picture of rigidity. Points are given for how well you follow the rules, not how much originality you bring, a situation that dancer Scott Hastings (Paul Mercurio) finds increasingly wearing.

Scott is not just any dancer, he was primed, as the mock documentary that starts *Strictly Ballroom* somberly informs the camera, to win the acme of dancing competitions, the mighty Pan Pacific Grand Prix Amateur Championships. And then came that fateful samba.

As explained by Scott's regretful coach, Les Kendall (Peter Whitford), Scott and his bleached blond partner, Liz Holt (Gia Carides), found themselves boxed into a corner by another couple. To escape, Scott daringly attempted "those flashy crowd-pleasing steps" he'd resorted to before. "He forced me into it," a horrified Liz explains, and then all heck broke out.

For in the tight little world of *Strictly Ballroom,* doing things your own way is the road to career suicide. Not only are Les and Liz furious with him, so is his dauntingly cheerful mother, Shirley (Pat Thomson), and the oily impresario of the ballroom world, Barry Fife (Bill Hunter).

Scott, a rebel with a cause, couldn't care less. No matter that he loses Liz as a partner with the Pan Pacifics, yes, only weeks away; no matter that everybody at the local dance studio thinks he's making the mistake of his life; he is sick—do you hear, sick—of dancing somebody else's steps.

As it turns out, not quite everybody is terminally furious at Scott. His lost soul father, Doug (Barry Otto), is too out of touch to express any kind of opinion. And then there is Fran (Tara Morice).

To call this uncertain young woman an ugly duckling would be far too kind. Wearing unflattering glasses and an oversized T-shirt under bad-hair-day hair, so gawky she practically walks into walls and so new at ballroom dancing she still has another girl for a partner, Fran, with the temerity of a frog approaching a prince, tells Scott she believes in his steps and wants to help him dance them.

It is the great pleasure of *Strictly Ballroom* that it turns its absolute predictability into a virtue almost as an act of will. Luhrmann has worked on multiple variations of this story for nearly a decade (starting with a student film that was put on for a budget of $50), and there can be no doubt that he has finally got it right.

Luhrmann and his team, including design collaborators Catherine Martin and Bill Marron, have told this version with visual panache as well as a distinctly modern pace and sensibility, understanding perfectly the necessity of camping up the comedy while leaving the romance charmingly alone.

Because it is kidding on the square, because its parody both of old movie forms and ballroom society is done from the inside and with love, *Strictly Ballroom* offers a surprisingly wide variety of satisfactions.

Between laughing at the stuffed shirts who run the show, gasping at the plot's crises and catastrophes, and rooting for Scott and Fran to beat the odds and show everyone a thing or two, not to mention being diverted by some nifty dancing, audiences will not believe their good fortune. The movie musical may not have been dead after all, just resting up until this lot came around.

Luhrmann went on to Moulin Rouge, *a musical with a much higher profile, but the charms of* Strictly Ballroom *remain undiminished.*

Sweet Sixteen
2003

Ken Loach believes the truth will set you free. A man whose independence, vigor, and passion for naturalism have inspired several generations of British filmmakers, he's been a socially conscious director for nearly forty years. Loach's best films—*Kes, Raining Stones, My Name Is Joe*—play as though he's somehow convinced reality itself to pitch in and make his points for him.

Loach's *Sweet Sixteen* won the best screenplay prize at Cannes as well as the award for the best British independent film. It's one of the most emotional and compelling the filmmaker has ever made. Confident, uncompromising, and blisteringly realistic, *Sweet Sixteen* is a gritty and immediate film, yet it goes right to the emotions. The title may be intentionally ironic—there's little unadulterated sweetness in this snapshot of Scottish urban life—but the volatile, unforgiving nature of the story rings true and moves us more than we might think possible.

Initially, the credit for this goes to screenwriter Paul Laverty, who has collaborated with Loach before, most notably on another Cannes prizewinner, *My Name Is Joe.* Though these films are connected only spiritually, their writer and director consider them to be two parts of a projected Glasgow-area trilogy, a look at life among the city's struggling classes.

Because the setting is Glasgow and because authenticity is prized, *Sweet Sixteen* takes the unusual and very welcome step of using subtitles to make what's being said in heavily accented English—which even people in London have trouble understanding—clear to viewers.

Yet, paradoxically, one of the strengths of *Sixteen* is that, despite the trappings of foreignness, this story of the conflict between decency and expediency, of the limited choices and chances available to people who need them the most if they are to break the familiar cycle of poverty and crime, is completely relevant to any American city.

Another key to the film's success is Martin Compston, the actor who plays young Liam. Loach is especially adept at working with nonprofessionals like Compston and draws a thrilling performance out of his star, who portrays a charismatic but frustrated young man determined to make a better life for his mother.

Liam and his best friend, Pinball (William Ruane), collectively mocked as "Simon and Garfunkel," live lives of small-time juvenile criminality, selling stolen cigarettes for a meager profit. Liam is clearly ambitious and capable, but he's also headstrong, with more nerve than sense, a dangerous combination in the profane, unforgiving world he lives in.

It's characteristic of this world that Jean (Michelle Coulter), the mother whose future Liam cares so much about, is currently behind bars, having taken the rap for her drug-dealing boyfriend, Stan (Gary

McCormack), and her own low-life father (Tommy McKee). Though Liam's sister Chantelle (Annmarie Fulton) has broken off with Jean because she wants a new start for herself and her young son, Liam is determined to give his mother that same start. With the impetuousness of youth, he wants to set it all up by the time his mother gets released, the day before his sixteenth birthday.

The unflinching twist to *Sweet Sixteen*'s plot is that, in this culture, the only thing Liam can think to do, the only viable option that he sees to improve his status in life, is to deal drugs. "An opportunity like this for someone like you comes only once," an established criminal tells him, and the drama and conflict inherent in that statement are the core of the film.

Liam is so real, so naked in his dreams and frustrations, that this scenario doesn't play out as schematically as it may sound like it would. The more Liam succeeds, the more our emotions are divided. Because we care for him and his aims, we desperately want him to do well, but it is difficult to share in his happiness because we fear he is getting in over his head more than he knows in a world that is more complex and pitiless than even he understands.

Played with impeccable honesty and a real feeling for the truth of its characters and their situation, *Sweet Sixteen* brings to mind *The Asphalt Jungle*'s famous dictum that crime is no more than a left-handed form of human endeavor. For not the first time, it is the business of Loach to involve us in a world where, tragically, that hand is the only one offered.

Thirty Two Short Films about Glenn Gould
1994

Everything that is distinctive and irresistible about *Thirty Two Short Films about Glenn Gould*—its audacity, its nervy playfulness, how smart and confident a motion picture it is—comes through in its first scene.

It's a deceptive episode, simple yet exhilarating. The camera is motionless, fixed on a frozen landscape, dazzling and empty. Then a figure appears at the far distance, walking toward us but taking his own time about it. The closer he gets, and it takes nearly 2 minutes (an eternity in film terms) for him to arrive, the more aware we become of the rising music in the background, the liquid, intoxicating piano playing of the man himself, Glenn Gould.

A consummate musician who shocked the concert world by abandoning live performance for recordings when he was only thirty-two, and who'd given layers of new meanings to the concept of the eccentric virtuoso by the time he died from a stroke at age fifty in 1982, Gould was too original a figure to fit into a conventional filmed bio, and Canadian director François Girard, who co-wrote the screenplay with Don McKellar, has not even attempted to give him one.

Instead, Girard has orchestrated (and that really does seem to be the best word) a film infused with its subject's singular spirit. A window into what it might be like to be a genius that is as off-center and uncompromising as the man himself, this is that rare piece of work that not only knows exactly what it wants to do but also just how to go about doing it.

The concept is to assemble a mosaic-like portrait of Gould combining unrelated facets of his life, personality, and career. That there are thirty-two of these is a nod to Bach's "Goldberg Variations," Gould's debut recording and the music behind that opening scene. The episodes range in length from less than a minute to more than 10 minutes, each one self-contained and carefully set off from the others with its own on-screen title.

If this sounds schematic, the reality is the opposite. For after *Lake Simcoe*, which straightforwardly deals with Gould's sheltered youth as a prodigy sure of his future by age five, the filmmakers have been quite thoughtful about the points they want to make about Gould as well as lively and inventive in how they've illustrated them.

To indicate his interests outside of music, for instance, there is a sly comic sequence called "The Tip" showing Gould manipulating the stock market, plus an excerpt from "The Idea of North," a dizzying sound-collage documentary made for radio. To show how others felt about him and his numerous peculiarities, real-life friends are interviewed, and actors playing journalists demonstrate the kind of inanities the man who treasured solitude had to put up with from the press.

First and finally, though, there is always the music, the center of Gould's life. His hypnotic playing of everything from Bach to Schoenberg hovers in the background of about three-quarters of the sequences, and the film casually utilizes an impressive variety of ways to convey the music in visual terms, most memorably in "CD 318," where we are taken inside Gould's favorite instrument to see exactly how its sounds are made.

It is in the showcasing of the passion with which Gould approached music that *Thirty Two Short Films* surpasses itself. In sequences from "Hamburg," where the pianist, loping around a hotel room like Groucho Marx, insists that a chamber maid share his pleasure in his latest recording, to "Passion According to Gould," where he goes into a pure trance at the caress of his own music, the joy of creation is beautifully put on screen in a way that avoids all the usual clichés.

For a film this ambitious to be successful, the execution must match the ideas, and it does. Alain Dostie's measured, eloquent camera work provides crystalline images that are often hypnotic, and the Girard-McKellar script, which makes extensive use of ironic voice-over adapted from Gould's own words, conveys the wry and acerbic sensibility of a man who felt that "the ideal audience-to-artist relationship is a one-to-zero relationship."

Not every actor can pull off a character like Gould, simultaneously self-assured and erratic, and *Thirty Two Short Films* would be difficult to imagine without Colm Feore, a mainstay of Canada's Stratford Shakespeare Festival, in the title role. In addition to a confident and insinuating voice, Feore has the passionate spirit essential to playing Gould, a spectral wraith as transfixed by the sounds he created as the actor is by the opportunity to convey that obsession.

In the end, the great thing about *Thirty Two Short Films about Glenn Gould* is that, rather than creating a desire to meet this formidable individual, it makes you feel as if in some way you actually have. "Gould was inexplicably gifted," biographer Otto Friedrich wrote, "with a phenomenal natural talent for playing the piano." Exactly what that means is what this film is so marvelous at conveying.

This Boy's Life
1993

This Boy's Life is every boy's life, every child's nightmare. Told with unblinking truthfulness and remarkable sensitivity, its true story of one particular and painful coming of age manages to touch us all, underlining the notion that nothing we do in our lives is anywhere near as difficult as just plain growing up.

While maudlin, whiny tales of adolescent difficulties are one of the curses of today's Hollywood, the power and frankness of this exceptional film is something else again. But as much as being based on Tobias Wolff's spare and moving memoir of the same name published in 1989, *This Boy's Life* has the advantage of having fallen into the hands of a creative team that has managed to transfer the reality and emotional heft of the printed page onto the screen.

Cleanly and feelingly written by Robert Getchell (Oscar-nominated for *Alice Doesn't Live Here Anymore* and *Bound for Glory*) and directed with great care by Michael Caton-Jones, *This Boy's Life* is equally fortunate in its acting. The ensemble work of Ellen Barkin, Leonardo DiCaprio, and Robert De Niro is expressive without overdoing it and almost hypnotic in its honesty.

Though eighteen-year-old DiCaprio does finely nuanced work as a teenager trapped in an inner and outer storm, it is De Niro's shattering performance as stepfather Dwight Hansen that is the film's core.

As complex a character as he's ever played, De Niro's Dwight is a taut piece of work that will disturb and fascinate audiences as much as the real Dwight, an enigmatic and frightening figure, shook up those whose lives he dominated.

However, when Toby (DiCaprio) and mother Caroline (Barkin) first appear, scuttling across the 1957 Southwest in a shaky white and yellow Nash as Frank Sinatra sings "Let's Get Away from It All" on the soundtrack, Dwight has yet to make his presence felt.

Instead, Caroline, the type of person who solves problems by leaving them behind, is headed for what she is sure will be a new life among the instant riches of the uranium fields of Utah. Buoyant, high-spirited, and divorced from Toby's father, Caroline (acutely played by Barkin) is also a woman with more courage than common sense.

Worse, she is a woman with abysmal taste in men, and this particular trip was caused by a desire to flee from a boring and mean blue-collar lout named Roy. A similar spur-of-the-moment burst of high hopes then causes her to grab Toby and impulsively head out for Seattle and yet another stab at the good life. Not that the boy minds. "I was caught up," he says in a literate, persuasive voice-over that echoes the book's tone, "in the delight of my mother's freedom."

If Caroline is problematic as a mother, Toby is a disaster as a teenage son. A prankster, liar, and sneak thief who regularly cuts school, cracks wise, and demands that everybody call him the more masculine-sounding "Jack," Toby's rootless scorn is more than anything else a plea for attention from a kid who is afraid of the sensitivity that lies beneath his own bravado. Wanting to change but feeling helpless to do so, Toby is clearly a candidate for a little parental discipline. What he gets instead is Dwight.

Caroline's most persistent Seattle suitor, auto mechanic Dwight is an easy target for the wised-up Toby to mock. With his Bronco Nagurski brushcut, laughably elaborate way of lighting a cigarette, and artificial jack-o'-lantern smile, Dwight appears to be a harmless dope, a comic relief Mr. Square who lives near the nowhere town of Concrete with three children from a previous marriage. What possible lure could this drone have for his dazzling firefly mother?

Part of Dwight's appeal, it turns out, is his belief that he can straighten Toby/Jack out, eliminate his discipline problems root and branch. Her emotional resources exhausted, Caroline is willing to let him try, setting the stage for one of the most wrenching intergenerational confrontations since Raymond Massey turned on James Dean in *East of Eden*.

For while it is clear to everyone except perhaps Caroline that the superpolite Dwight who brings flowers and helps her on with her coat is a facade, no one, least of all Toby, is at all prepared for exactly who he turns out to be.

Humorless, angry, with a formidable "I don't make the rules" self-righteousness, Dwight is a relentless bully and needler who announces the reversal in Toby's fortunes in no uncertain terms. "Don't pull that hotshot stuff on me," he challenges the boy. "You're in for a change, you're in for a whole 'nother ball game. Oh yeah."

Yet to say all this about Dwight is to make him less complex than he is, to fail to understand what makes him so unnerving. Knowingly written by Getchell and brilliantly played by De Niro, Dwight is that all too realistic sadist who thinks he is the one being abused, the warped disciplinarian who truly believes that all the harsh things he is doing are both underappreciated and for Toby's good. The fact that Toby himself begins by feeling that maybe he does need some straightening out only makes the dynamic between them unfold in ways that are that much more twisted and destructive.

The job of integrating all these combustible elements falls in the unlikely lap of director Michael Caton-Jones, whose two previous films (*Memphis Belle* and *Doc Hollywood*) were marked by a sentimentality that would be out of place here.

Yet something in this story appears to have touched Caton-Jones, bringing back the strength of *Scandal,* his directing debut, for he responds beautifully to the challenges of the material. He has made the film all of a piece, making sure that the three lead performances complement rather than overwhelm each other. And he has avoided (despite an emphatic Hollywood ending that departs from the book) either condescending to the situation or downplaying its harrowing aspects. *This Boy's Life* doesn't flinch, and its conflicts will disturb your dreams as they do those of the boy who lived them once upon a time.

To Die For
1995

To Die For isn't afraid of the dark. A smart black comedy that skewers America's fatal fascination with television and celebrity, it employs an unerring nasty touch to parody our omnipresent culture of fame. And it uses a rather unlikely combination of talents to do the job.

Star Nicole Kidman, director Gus Van Sant, and screenwriter

Buck Henry have difficulty fitting into the same sentence, let alone the same film about a creature of the media whose mad passion for the limelight is as addictive as a drug. But, brought together by producer Laura Ziskin, they create a kind of unexpected but very successful synergy.

Though he had an acting role in Van Sant's bloated *Even Cowgirls Get the Blues,* screenwriter Buck Henry, whose credits date to *The Graduate,* does not mimic the director's sensibility. His dialogue is clever and witty, he's at ease with parody, and he knows how to skillfully adapt a novel, in this case pumping up the humor in Joyce Maynard's devilish book, which in turn was suggested by a real-life New England scandal.

Working with a tight, classically structured script is definitely a departure for Van Sant, known for loopy, eccentric films such as *My Own Private Idaho.* But the director was unexpectedly charged by the experience, adding his trademark absurdist sensibility to the mix as well as an empathy for inarticulate, inchoate teenagers that turns out to give this film a good deal of its impact.

Placing Nicole Kidman (who up to this point has been identified with films such as *Days of Thunder* and *Far and Away,* co-starring with husband Tom Cruise) in this company may seem like a stretch, but the opposite turns out to be true. Known as a more adventurous actress in her earlier career in Australia, Kidman's perfectly pitched comic performance, as fearless as it is poisonous, ends up being the kind of nervy knockout the film couldn't succeed without.

Using a dead-on American accent, Kidman plays Suzanne Maretto, formerly Suzanne Stone, who, *To Die For* immediately reveals, has brought an unlooked-for note of scandal to the town of Little Hope, New Hampshire. Her husband, Larry, has been murdered, and America's tabloids, both print and TV, can't get enough of the possibility that Mrs. Maretto had a very particular hand in his death.

Suzanne is introduced doing what she loves best, talking to a camera and telling her version of the events leading up to what she demurely lowers her eyes and calls "my recent tragedy." But, she admits, brightening immediately, the situation is not without benefits for someone who believes, as Suzanne absolutely does, "You're not anybody in America if you're not on TV. What's the point of doing anything worthwhile if nobody's watching?"

Not necessarily agreeing are Suzanne's friends and relatives, whose on-camera reminiscences are intercut with conventional flashbacks and talk-show appearances in *To Die For*'s always involving structure.

Through these multiple viewpoints we get a picture of a cold steel magnolia whose happy-face passion for television celebrity flabbergasts everyone who comes into contact with her, a woman you say no to completely at your own risk.

Most taken with Suzanne, or "Sooze" as he calls her, is her husband, Larry (convincingly played by Matt Dillon), the kind of regular guy who is surprised to realize that artificial plants in the family Italian restaurant will eliminate the need for water. Though his suspicious sister Janice (a breakthrough role for Illeana Douglas) is dubious, Larry sees Suzanne as the kind of delicate golden girl he wants to take care of forever.

Seeing a more relentless side of Suzanne is Ed Grant (Wayne Knight), the station manager at WWEN, the local no-watt cable-access channel that advertised for a gofer and ended up with a zealous self-described "on-air correspondent." Inevitably giving in to Suzanne's tireless pestering, he lets her do the weather, which she treats with the gravity of the Normandy invasion, and then tentatively okays a documentary on local high school kids called "Teens Speak Out."

The teens in question, scuzzy pals Jimmy (Joaquin Phoenix), Lydia (Alison Folland), and Russell (Casey Affleck), are wistful losers who, as Ed Grant rightly comments, "would have a major struggle reciting the days of the week." But Suzanne, bless her, takes them seriously as career advancement fodder. Then, when Larry foolishly takes a stab at derailing her career plans, she realizes they might be useful in other ways as well.

The most accurate assault against the media age since *Network, To Die For*'s killer lines and wicked sensibility are given added poignancy by the off-center, sensitive performance of Joaquin Phoenix, the only person more deluded about Suzanne than she is about herself. Told with a panache that extends from the opening credits to its closing frames, *To Die For* plays its themes for everything they're worth, and, regrettably, they seem to be worth more every day.

A timely showing at the Cannes Film Festival saved this film from oblivion and allowed both audiences and critics to see Nicole Kidman in a new light.

12 Monkeys
1995

A man appears and announces he's a traveler from the future, from a world that has survived, but barely, a viral epidemic that slaughtered 5 billion people and caused those few left alive to abandon the surface of the Earth. He's immediately thrown into a mental hospital, and no wonder. But what if, just possibly, he's telling the truth?

As set up by David Peoples (who had a hand in *Blade Runner* and wrote Clint Eastwood's *Unforgiven*) and Janet Peoples, *12 Monkeys* has the sound of a conventional futuristic science-fiction thriller. But when Terry Gilliam is the director, no project stays conventional for long.

A cheerful, eccentric visionary with a consistently irreverent point of view, Gilliam successfully joined an extravagant visual sense to a playful sensibility in *Time Bandits,* the brilliant *Brazil,* and *The Adventures of Baron Munchausen.* Nothing he touches has a chance of remaining ordinary, and while that is usually a good thing, too much of a good thing can become simply too much.

So on the one hand, *12 Monkeys* is a magical Old Curiosity Shop, filled with strange and wonderful sights and happenings that capture the eye and intrigue the mind. But on the other, Gilliam gets so distracted by these diverting sideshows that he loses his focus and forgets to pay attention to the mechanics of plot, allowing the film to wander into narrative cul-de-sacs it has difficulty finding its way out of.

A more conventional director would have made *12 Monkeys* more streamlined and easier to follow, perhaps even more exciting, but oh the things we would have missed out on along the way.

12 Monkeys is based on one of the classics of French avant-garde filmmaking, Chris Marker's unsettling 1962 short, *La Jetée,* which tells its tale of a man so haunted by a childhood memory that he pursues it into the past entirely with still photographs and voice-over narration.

James Cole (Bruce Willis) is similarly haunted by a chilling vision of a gun going off in an airport; it's the first sequence in *12 Monkeys,* and it recurs periodically in the film, though Cole is certainly not in a dreamy situation.

The year is 2035 and, having abandoned the Earth because of that extra-lethal virus, humanity has reconstructed a kind of civilization underground, from which coerced "volunteers" are periodically sent to the surface to bring back specimens for scientific evaluation.

Cole is one such volunteer, and the deserted city he finds when he surfaces, a skyscraper-filled automobile graveyard where tigers and bears roam at will, is only one of several striking alien environments envisioned by Gilliam and his design collaborators.

Because of his success in this mission, Cole is dragooned into a more critical assignment. Even though what has been done cannot be undone, fuller knowledge of the past can help the ruling elite cope with the awful present, so Cole is shipped back to 1996 to attempt to determine exactly where and how the fatal virus outbreak began. His only clue: the name of a shadowy group called 12 Monkeys.

But, in a touch Gilliam must have delighted in, the clunky time machine sends Cole back to 1990 instead. And as soon as he starts to talk, albeit monosyllabically, about what he is trying to do, the powers that be throw him into a mental institution, where two very different people influence his life.

One is a motor-mouthed fellow inmate, psycho-ward politician Jeffrey Goines (a surprisingly funny Brad Pitt), who has nonstop opinions on everything. The other is Dr. Kathryn Railly, a psychiatrist who specializes in the linkage of madness and prophecy and who, not surprisingly, thinks Cole is completely delusional.

Dr. Railly is played, in a shrewd bit of casting, by Madeleine Stowe, an excellent actress with a grounded, non-flighty persona. The sanity of her presence in a film where everyone else is either mad or might as well be is an essential audience surrogate, a welcome life raft, as the plot of *12 Monkeys* gets crazier and crazier.

An unlikely love story combined with a visionary detective yarn, *12 Monkeys* is baffling and difficult to decipher at times, but it's never a standard brand. Mystifying, intriguing, even infuriating, it shows what happens when an unconventional talent meets straightforward material. Almost against his will, Gilliam finally succeeds in building some dramatic momentum, and when he does, *12 Monkeys* catches hold in a way an ordinary version probably wouldn't. Nobody, Gilliam would probably be happy to tell you, said this was going to be easy.

Ulee's Gold
1997

An unadorned and unexpectedly moving look at personal redemption and the resilience of family, *Ulee's Gold* stands out for its sureness, its quiet emotional force, and writer-director Victor Nunez's ability to find and nurture the mystery and power in the events of an ordinary life.

One of the prime movers of the American independent movement, Nunez, who also serves as his own camera operator and editor, has always made well-regarded but little-seen films, from *Gal Young 'Un* in 1979 through *Ruby in Paradise,* starring Ashley Judd, in 1993. With *Ulee's Gold* he's added a streak of melodrama that, if anything, heightens the intensity of his work.

Set, like Nunez's other films, in northern Florida (he once joked that his camera would break if it crossed the state line), *Ulee's* is built around a compelling performance by Peter Fonda that unmistakably echoes the work of his father, Henry, while serving as the capstone of the son's long career.

Fonda plays Ulee Jackson, a third-generation beekeeper specializing in Tupelo honey, a stubborn and solitary man proud of his self-reliance. A distant, reserved Vietnam veteran who survived the war, when his friends did not, by being both tricky and lucky, Ulee's intrinsic faith in family has been shaken by the actions of his own kin.

His son Jimmy (Tom Wood) is in jail for robbery, and his daughter-in-law Helen (Christine Dunford) has run off and abandoned their daughters, teenage rebel Casey (Jessica Biel) and her soulful younger sister Penny (Vanessa Zima). The girls live with Ulee, who tells Jimmy he keeps them on a short leash because "one round of fools is enough, don't you think?"

Serving as both a counterpoint to this chaos and a solace to Ulee are his bees, and among the most memorable scenes in *Ulee's Gold* are unhurried examinations of the rhythms and rituals of beekeeping. Serene and simply poetic, these sequences have a profound and mesmerizing quality, benefiting from Nunez's lifetime of craft and his belief in the significance of what he's showing.

A phone call from his imprisoned son puts an end to Ulee's removed life. Jimmy's wife, Helen, has turned up in Orlando, strung out on drugs and staying with the criminal lowlifes who took part in her husband's failed robbery. Though Ulee's initial reaction is a forceful "I could care less and you know it," his core belief that "we don't ask outsiders for help" makes it inevitable that he will become involved.

That involvement takes two forms. One is the situational drive—resisted by everyone from Ulee to the initially out-of-control Helen to even her children—to reintegrate her into the family. Helping here is Connie Hope (*Home Improvement*'s Patricia Richardson), a neighbor who works as a nurse, who is leery herself of too much personal contact.

More dangerous is the insistence by Eddie Flowers (Steven Flynn) and Ferris Dooley (Dewey Weber), Jimmy's erstwhile criminal partners, that Jimmy knows more than he's saying about the robbery. Either Ulee helps them get at the truth, or family lives will be sacrificed.

Nunez and his insightful ensemble cast have taken this familiar material and woven it into an affecting drama of surprising complexity and impact, neither overstating the melodrama nor ignoring how difficult it can be to make lasting human connections. Most convincing is Fonda, wearing metal-rimmed glasses that echo his father's, who brings a deliberateness and a weight to Ulee's stillness that say more than pages of dialogue could. His performance holds the film together, and it's one that all generations of Fondas can be proud of.

Not only do these characters have realistic interior lives, but the locale itself, as in all Nunez's films, becomes a palpable presence. As camera operator (working with cinematographer Virgil Mirano) as much as writer-director, Nunez's extensive knowledge of this part of Florida so roots his story in a defined sense of place that it practically grows out of the soil.

Better still, Nunez has over the years mastered the technique of allowing his narrative to seem to tell itself. *Ulee's Gold,* unfolding in its own way and at its own pace, illustrates how much is gained when a filmmaker has the nerve to take his time. There is a quality about this film's deliberation that comes, at times, wonderfully close to magic.

Unstrung Heroes
1995

"A hero," Selma Lidz tells her son Steven, "is anyone who finds his own way through this life." Only twelve, Steven is on the verge of discovering how difficult that task can be. And how much unexpected help he can get from his two fiercely eccentric uncles, the "unstrung heroes" of this lovely film's title.

Written by Richard LaGravenese and based on an autobiographical novel by Franz Lidz, *Unstrung Heroes* is a pivotal moment as well in the directing career of Oscar-winning actress Diane Keaton. Though she has directed TV movies, music videos, and feature documentaries, this is Keaton's first drama for the large screen, and how much she and her team have accomplished is as impressive as how casually they seem to have done it.

For *Unstrung Heroes,* while easy to absorb, is surprisingly rich in the feelings it conveys. It is at once a story of adolescent self-discovery in the face of terrible family crisis, a love note to motherhood, and a passionate tribute to idiosyncratic behavior. And in its unexpected ability to mix slapstick with subtlety, sadness with mad farce, it touches an unusual and especially emotional chord.

Set in Los Angeles in the early 1960s, *Heroes* seems at first to be focusing on Steven's father, Sid Lidz (sharply played by John Tur-

turro). An oddball inventor whose not-ready-for-prime-time projects include a "perpetual-motion baby-jumper" and a "mild-monsoon sprinkler system," Sid talks as fast as a rocket, oblivious to the thoughts of his son (Nathan Watt) and the boy's younger sister, Sandy (Kendra Krull).

"Is Dad from another planet?" a troubled Steven asks his mother, who smiles with the reassuring knowledge that his father is just a bit different. As Selma Lidz, the warm, caring, human element in the Lidz equation, Andie MacDowell simply blossoms, giving an appealing and natural performance, one of her best ever, as the family's unflappable anchor.

Suddenly, that anchor threatens to give way when Selma collapses on the floor, stricken with an obviously serious but unnamed illness that both puzzles and frightens everyone, especially the children, who are told little about it. Sid, frantic for his own reasons and pleading Selma's need for rest, unthinkingly shuts their mother out of Steven's and Sandy's lives. Almost wild with the need for comfort of any kind, Steven takes off one night to visit his father's two brothers in their strange apartment in a run-down residence hotel.

Up to this point, the uncles have been shadowy figures to Steven, known largely through his father's scorn of them as cautionary examples of "what can happen to an undisciplined mind." Now, turning to them in desperation, Steven discovers a kinship with their childlike, comic idiosyncrasies.

Uncle Danny is the more assertive of the two, which is a polite way of saying he is a raging paranoid conspiracy theorist who thinks his pancakes might be bugged and is convinced that "'Idaho' means Jew-hater in Cherokee." *Seinfeld*'s Michael Richards plays Danny with a daring, full-throttle brio, managing to make his character sympathetic as well as manic.

To say Uncle Arthur, exquisitely played by veteran actor Maury Chaykin, is a collector does not hint at the scope of his ambition. Operating on the assumption that "people throw out a lot of things that are good," Arthur has made it his life's work to save all of them. And the brothers' apartment, jammed floor to ceiling with newspapers, rubber balls, wedding cake decorations, and everything in between (all collected over a period of months by set decorator Larry Dias), is as vivid a presence as any of the actors.

Though the film's thematic elements are uniformly strong, it is its treatment of Danny and Arthur that is especially impressive. The uncles are neither condescended to nor treated with gooey reverence, the way eccentrics usually are on film, but embraced, loved, and respected as straight-ahead human beings.

Which, as Selma's illness worsens and Steven is allowed to spend the summer with the brothers, is how they treat their nephew. Positive that "our Steven has a rare gift," convincing him "you're the one to watch" and even deciding to change his name to the less ordinary "Franz," they see possibilities in the young man that neither his parents nor even Steven himself had imagined.

It was Diane Keaton's job to ride herd over this engaging menagerie, and she has done it with the kind of gentle but sure empathy toward all sorts of human behavior that has made all the difference. Moving in a way we are not accustomed to, *Unstrung Heroes* demonstrates that even the saddest stories can be wistful and joyous if the right people are involved in the telling.

Vanya on 42nd Street
1994

Vanya on 42nd Street is an afterthought to be thankful for. A movie version of an exploration of Anton Chekhov's *Uncle Vanya* that was not originally intended for an audience, let alone film, it is that rare melding of cinema and drama that does honor to both disciplines.

If movie stars fantasize about Oscars, theatrical actors dream of playing Chekhov and inhabiting his sensitive and complex characters. The Russian dramatist, who died in 1904 at age forty-four, wrote four remarkable plays in the last decade of his life: *The Sea Gull, The Three Sisters, The Cherry Orchard,* and *Uncle Vanya*.

Theatrical director Andre Gregory (known to film audiences as the title character in *My Dinner with Andre*) decided in 1989 that he wanted to work on a production of the play using a contemporary adaptation by David Mamet.

After gathering his cast, which included *Dinner* co-star Wallace Shawn as Vanya, Gregory and company worked on and off on the piece for four years, first in a New York loft space and then, in 1991, before small invited audiences of twenty or thirty in a decaying movie theater near Times Square.

In 1992, the company's oldest actress, eighty-nine-year-old Ruth Nelson, died, and the performances stopped. Then, a year later, there was an urge to begin again, and, with Nelson's Group Theater colleague Phoebe Brand joining the cast, Louis Malle, the director of *Dinner,* agreed to film it.

In keeping with the spirit of the original workshops, Malle and Gregory reproduced the atmosphere of the invited performances by filming in front of a small audience in the crumbling interior of Times Square's once-glamorous New Amsterdam Theater.

Everyone ambles into the theater, director Gregory and the audience exchange greetings, the actors chat as they gather on the stage, and, unless you've read the text the night before, the opening lines of the play blend so seamlessly with the conversation that it takes a minute or two to realize the action has started.

As with many of Chekhov's plays, *Vanya* concerns an extended family. It is set on the estate of Serybryakov (George Gaynes), a retired professor who gained control of the land when his first wife died.

In the past, Serybryakov has been an absentee landlord, content to live off the revenues, and allowing his daughter, Sonya (Brooke Smith), and his brother-in-law, Vanya (Shawn), to run the place for him. But now, at the play's opening, financial difficulties have forced him to return to the estate, bringing with him his young and alluring second wife, Yelena (Julianne Moore).

The presence of this couple stirs up a lifetime's worth of resentments not only for Vanya, who is in love with Yelena and has begun to fear that his years of toil have been for nothing, but also for the local doctor, Astrov (Larry Pine), whom young Sonya has innocently had her eye on.

To watch this *Vanya* is to marvel, as always with Chekhov, at his insights, at how rigorously and effortlessly nonjudgmental he is, at how much empathy he has for all his characters, for the resentments they feel at being trapped by the frustrations of their idle, often squandered lives.

Under Gregory's and Malle's direction, the actors captivate. Shawn is strong as the prickly, ironically self-deprecating Vanya, but the surprise of the production is Julianne Moore's Yelena.

Moore, who got her role in Robert Altman's *Short Cuts* after the director saw her in one of the *Vanya* run-throughs, shows us that the Raymond Carver adaptation used only a thimbleful of her abilities. Here the actress utilizes all the opportunities this role provides, and her Yelena understandably intoxicates and frustrates every male she encounters.

Malle has used his documentary background to unobtrusively serve and enhance the production. "We all want to talk," Vanya says at one point, and this version of the play underscores once again how sublime it is when Chekhov's characters unburden their souls and do just that.

Wag the Dog
1997

"Why does a dog wag its tail?" Glad you asked. "Because a dog is smarter than its tail. If the tail were smarter, the tail would wag the dog."

With a title taken from that tart bit of pre-credits philosophy, *Wag the Dog* is set in the topsy-turvy times we live in, where illusion means more than reality, and a lie is halfway around the world while truth is still pulling on its boots.

A gloriously cynical black comedy as well as a wicked smart satire on the interlocking worlds of politics and show business, *Wag the Dog* confirms every awful thought you've ever had about media manipulation and the gullibility of the American public. And it has a great deal of fun doing it.

Directed by Barry Levinson and starring Dustin Hoffman, Robert De Niro, and Anne Heche, *Wag* is also that rare major-player production that was made on a sane budget of $15 million. It was shot in such an expeditious manner that the producers include a line in the final credits specifically thanking "the cast and crew for completing principal photography in 29 days!"

The reason people accustomed to a more, shall we say, leisurely pace agreed to work so crisply had to be the lure of *Wag*'s deft script. Written by Hilary Henkin and David Mamet from a novel called *American Hero* by Larry Beinhart, *Wag* is a sharp-edged farce where the lines are hard enough to cut glass and the plot's gleeful twists and complications never flag.

Though *Wag the Dog* focuses on a popular president who is scant days shy of reelection, we never see the man. But we are told of his actions, specifically that he badly misbehaved with an underage Firefly girl in the Oval Office. Now the *Washington Post* has the story, and the disloyal opposition, sensing blood, is about to run TV attack ads pegged to the music of "Thank Heaven for Little Girls."

When trouble strikes, or so White House operative Winifred Ames (Heche) reveals, the president has only one motto: Get Conrad Brean. As played by De Niro, Brean may look like a shambling suburban Redskins fan, but beneath that disheveled exterior he's an unflappable political spin doctor, capable of salvaging any situation and keeping the dogs of war at bay.

Brean's mandate is to use any means necessary to distract the American public from the budding scandal. He's a master of planting disinformation that official spokesmen can honestly deny, thereby making people believe it's true. His fabrications don't have to prove out, they just have to con the electorate for those few days until the election.

Brean's brainstorm is to concoct a crisis with Albania, insisting that this hapless country is "a staging ground for terrorism." Why Albania? Why not Albania? To make the story stick, Brean and company go out to Hollywood and elicit the support of one of the movie business's top producers, the legendary Stanley Motss (Hoffman). His job, should he accept it, is to manufacture not a real war but a media one, to create the images and campaign that will convince the country that something terribly dangerous is going on in that weak Balkan country.

It's common knowledge in the real Hollywood that the outward appearance of Stanley Motss, his house, his clothing and hairstyle, are inspired by producer Robert Evans, whom Hoffman has been imitating in private since Evans produced the Hoffman-starring *Marathon Man* in 1976.

But Hoffman is able to go way past caricature here. He brings such zest to his characterization that it is Motss's zany passion for producing that ignites Brean's plot and carries the picture. First, he pulls together his crack team, including the Fad King (Denis Leary), who can start trends before others even spot them, and resourceful songwriter Johnny Green (Willie Nelson), who complains that "Albania" is a hard word to rhyme.

Seeing Motss at work is a privilege. Who else could fabricate atrocity footage from war-torn Albania on a local sound stage, simultaneously reassuring a nervous starlet (Kirsten Dunst), telling technicians to "punch up a burning bridge," and arguing with the president ("I hate when they interfere") about what kind of kitten will be optically added to the girl's arms to complete the picture.

No matter the nature of the crises he faces (and this film has an endless number of them), Motss calls it nothing compared to what he has gone through in the past, when, for instance, "I was four months into 'Song of Songs' and realized I didn't have the rights."

Motss brazens it out with the CIA, insisting to wavering members of his team that "the war isn't over until I say it's over," and leaves no doubt in anyone's mind that "producing is being a samurai warrior." It's been so long, perhaps since *Tootsie* and *Rain Man,* that Hoffman has taken a satisfying comic role that it's good to be reminded of the gift he has for funny business.

It's not only Hoffman but everyone on both sides of the camera who seem to have been energized by the challenge of working fast with quality material. The only sad thing about *Wag the Dog* is that it suggests the kind of films we're missing out on because of an elephantine production system that makes reasonably priced films with major talent as rare as actors seeing any money on studio profit-participation deals.

Underneath the humor, not surprisingly, *Wag* is making serious points about what's wrong with our political system and media culture. Of course we'd like to believe we're not all that gullible, that there is a limit to what we can be manipulated into, but the evidence points elsewhere. When a character says, apropos of everything, "It's a good thing Jimmy Stewart didn't live to see this," *Wag the Dog* leaves you without the power to disagree.

Waiting for Guffman
1997

The fictional municipality of Blaine, Missouri, "a little town with a big heart in the heart of the country," is about to celebrate a very special event.

Although it seems like only yesterday that an unscrupulous guide abandoned a wagon train after convincing the gullible travelers they'd arrived in California, in fact it's been 150 years since Blaine's glorious founding. And the town is determined to pull off an event that promises to be "the standard by which sesquicentennials will be judged."

For those not fortunate enough to make it to Blaine for the festivities, a documentary crew is on hand to record it all for *Waiting for Guffman,* a sly comedy showcase that pokes clever fun at the American musical, amateur theatrics, and anything else that's not nailed down.

The standard by which all mock-documentaries are judged is, of course, *This Is Spinal Tap,* and the moving force behind *Guffman* is Christopher Guest, alive in our memory as Tap's lead guitarist Nigel Tufnel.

Guest directed and co-wrote *Guffman* (with *Second City*'s Eugene Levy) and also stars as Corky St. Clair, the creative tornado behind *Red, White and Blaine,* the musical pageant that celebrates Blaine in all its misbegotten glory.

For there is more to this town than the legend of its accidental founding. There's the story of how the weary feet of President William McKinley led to Blaine's becoming the Stool Capital of the World. And then there was the celebrated UFO sighting/potluck dinner of 1946. All of which has to get into *Red, White and Blaine.*

Collaborating with Guest on *Guffman*'s music and lyrics are his *Tap* cohorts Michael McKean and Harry Shearer. Together they come up with some splendid numbers, including the peppy "Stool Boom" and the parallel "Nothing Ever Happens in Blaine" and "Nothing Ever Happens on Mars."

But *Waiting for Guffman* offers more than music. We're privileged to be behind the scenes in everything from the choosing of the cast to the inevitable crises of confidence when it looks as if *Red, White and Blaine* might never get to pack the high school gym after all.

Which, given the kind of talent there is in Blaine, would have been a shame. Ron and Sheila Albertson (Fred Willard and Catherine O'Hara), for instance, in private life travel agents who have never ventured out of town, have done enough local theater to be known as "the Lunts of Blaine."

Then there are the newcomers, such as Dr. Allan Pearl (Eugene Levy), the tone-deaf dentist who thinks he had a relative who worked in Yiddish theater. Or Libby Mae Brown (Parker Posey at her most irresistible), the soignée Dairy Queen counter girl, who wows Corky St. Clair with her spirited version of "Teacher's Pet."

Finally, it does all come down to the charismatic Corky, a veteran of too many years spent as far off Broadway as you can get. Back in Blaine as the high school drama teacher who wanted audiences to "feel the heat" in his legendary staged version of *Backdraft,* Corky has the passion and the vision to override skeptics, such as music teacher Lloyd Miller (Bob Balaban), apparently the only sane individual in town, and get *Red, White and Blaine* up on its feet.

Similarly, there would be no *Waiting for Guffman* without Guest, who came up with the concept, gathered a sprightly group of practiced farceurs around him, and even brought the arch Corky St. Clair, with his goatee, bowl haircut, and perennially puzzled look, to querulous life.

If Corky has a hidden agenda, it's that *Red, White and Blaine* could become his ticket to Broadway. He confidently expects the arrival of a certain Mr. Guffman, the representative of a powerful New York producing organization, sure that his show has what it takes. That may be an open question, but *Waiting for Guffman* will inspire no such doubts.

Waking Ned Devine
1998

The names Ian Bannen and David Kelly may not be familiar, but their mischievous faces will be. Senior citizens with nearly a century of experience between them, they're a pair of droll old souls with the comic wisdom of the ages in their smiles. Together they turn *Waking Ned Devine* into a roguish comedy of duplicity that's as entertaining as it is sly.

Though it's the first film for writer-director Kirk Jones, a top commercial director from the United Kingdom, *Waking Ned* is part of the great tradition of daft, cheerful British comedies. Linked in spirit to the understated Ealing studio classics of decades past, such as *Kind Hearts and Coronets* and *The Lavender Hill Mob,* but with a peppy, modern brashness added in, this picture proves that laughter and smiles can be coaxed out of the old moves if they're done with deftness and panache.

Waking Ned is set firmly in the mythical movie-Ireland of tiny towns and lilting brogues (though in truth filmed on the Isle of Man), where genial eccentrics trade amusing lines and the only telephone is outside the city limits. What would happen in such a place—Tully More by name, population 52—if a local won a £6.8 million prize in the Irish national lottery? What indeed.

It's Jackie O'Shea (Bannen) who first figures out from a small item in the *Irish Times* that someone in Tully More has hit the jackpot. Good-natured but with a bit of larceny in his bones, Jackie, admittedly "not a great man for telling things the way they are," has a plan to fit the situation.

As he explains it to his lifelong friend Michael O'Sullivan (Kelly),

Jackie wants to apply "the very best of Irish brains" to figure out who the winner is before the prize is claimed. Then he'll so ingratiate himself with the lucky individual that "I'll be their best friend by the time they cash the check."

Sounds simple enough, but, as in all classic comedies, nothing goes quite as planned. For once the winner is discovered (no easy task, as it turns out), so many elaborate feints and dodges prove necessary that Jackie's level-headed wife, Annie (Fionnula Flanagan), has reason to worry how it will turn out.

Even the honest Michael, who has never told a lie in his life, gets drawn into this increasingly complex and humorous web—to the point where he finds himself riding hell-bent for leather on a motorbike wearing nothing but a helmet and some sensible shoes. And that's just the beginning of his pains.

All this playful greed plays out against a background of wall-to-wall characters ranging in age from ancient town witch Lizzie Quinn (Eileen Dromey) to fatherless young Maurice (Robert Hickey), who tells the impoverished local priest that he wouldn't want his job because "I don't think I could work for someone I never met and not get paid for it."

Maurice's mother, the wild and beautiful Maggie (Susan Lynch), who earns money writing verse for greeting cards, is the heart of *Waking Ned*'s subplot, the battle for her fetching hand. Maggie's in love with the luckless Pig Finn (James Nesbitt), but she can't abide the smell his poor animals give off.

"If it wasn't for the pigs," she tells Finn many a time, "we'd be settled by now." Will the basket of "fruity soaps" provided by Jackie help Finn clean up romantically? Stay tuned.

All the actors in *Waking Ned* are smooth and practiced performers who inhabit these roles as though they've lived them all their lives. But few can touch stars Bannen (nominated for an Oscar back in 1966 for *Flight of the Phoenix*) and Kelly. Playing off each other beautifully, with a lifetime of skills in their every move, they create a charming comedy of winks and nods that is inescapably engaging.

Waking Ned is, of course, nothing if not traditional, old-fashioned, and small-scaled, its humor depending on such familiar situations as a battle of wits between country lads and an official from the big city. No new ground gets broken, nothing is done that hasn't been done before. But if this film doesn't make you want to smile, you've no one to blame but yourself.

The Waterdance
1992

When you call *The Waterdance* uplifting, smile. When you are tempted to describe it as a tribute to the human spirit, bite your tongue. When you confuse it with well-meaning but wimpy motion pictures that do the Lord's work in the most lethargic way, go hang your head in shame.

The truth about this remarkable piece of work is that it is the last film anyone has to make excuses for. Wickedly funny, undeniably moving, featuring a knockout series of performances and the most sensual of love scenes, it has everything audiences have been missing in American films. It just happens to be about three men in wheelchairs.

Neal Jimenez, *The Waterdance*'s screenwriter and co-director (along with Michael Steinberg), has been in a chair himself since an accident in 1984. Already a nervy, accomplished screenwriter with the disturbing *River's Edge* to his credit, Jimenez based *The Waterdance* on his own experience. Yet his closeness to the situation resulted not in any mushy special pleading, but the exact opposite: an unforced, unsentimental film that flatly refuses to overdramatize, thereby enhancing its considerable power.

The Waterdance's first image is a bracing, static one: a close-up of a battered head immobilized in a peculiar traction device known as a "halo." A small hand tentatively strokes this wary, immobile face. "Hi, honey," the hand's off-screen voice says timidly. "Oh, I'm sorry."

The head belongs to Joel Garcia (Eric Stoltz), a young novelist with a broken neck. The hand belongs to Anna (Helen Hunt), a sweet and spirited woman who is seriously in love with Joel but married to someone else. With that torturous situation as a backdrop, they both have to deal with the confounding fact of Joel's life in the chair, permanently paralyzed from the waist down.

Anna is determined to stand by him, but even in the best of circumstances, this is not an easy man to love. Demanding, coolly sarcastic, ever ready to say needling things such as, "I'd feel sorry for him but I'm saving all my pity for myself," Joel would be a handful even in perfect health. Faced with six months in Holbrook Hospital and a considerable leap into the unknown after that, his relationship with Anna becomes even more topsy-turvy, an emotional bomb with a hot-wired fuse.

Given all that, as well as the way Jimenez's screenplay refuses to downplay the inescapable anger that finding yourself suddenly changed for life calls forth, it is a tribute to Stoltz (who reportedly never used his legs during production even when off the set) that he makes Garcia not only believable but sympathetic as well.

Helping him considerably along the way is Hunt's understated but very affecting work as Anna, a performance that manages to project selflessness as strength and scrupulously avoids any hint of dishrag self-sacrifice. The two have acted together before (in a 1989 Broadway production of *Our Town*), and that familiarity must have helped *The Waterdance*'s pair of exceptional love scenes, sequences so delicately erotic that you can hear a pin drop both on-screen and off.

But Joel must do more than just try to sort out his life with Anna. He is forced, whether he likes it or not, to interact with the other men on his ward, and it is a mark of *The Waterdance*'s across-the-board power that his relationship with Anna comes close to being overshadowed by the outstanding acting and writing that characterize the appearance of Bloss and Raymond Hill.

Certainly, no two men could be more dissimilar, both to each other and to the cagey, distant Joel. Bloss (an even better performance than usual from the always formidable William Forsythe) is a surly, racist biker (complete with beer belly, tattoos, and an ever-present mom) whose Harley was totaled by a Mercedes-Benz and who dreams of a litigious revenge.

Hill, by contrast, is a trash-talking, streetwise, self-confident black man. Cavalier about his wife and young daughter before the accident that paralyzed him, he says, "God is slowing me down so I can appreciate them." Though at first he seems a bit of a clown, Hill turns out to be a man of infinite parts and energetic emotions, and the protean Wesley Snipes, projecting everything from bravado and despair to tenderness and angry tears, makes him close to unforgettable.

The funny, sad, passionate story of *The Waterdance,* then, ultimately turns out to be about the way these three men, in coming to terms with one another, come to terms with what has happened to their lives. As Raymond Hill, who often serves as Jimenez's mouthpiece (and whose haunting dream gives the film its title) puts it, "Every man got to find his place." Watching these basically ordinary men, not celebrities or superstars, find theirs is a deeply satisfying movie experience.

Whale Rider
2003

Whale Rider was something of a sensation on the international film festival circuit, winning audience awards at such diverse and influential festivals as Sundance, Toronto, Rotterdam, and San Francisco. Yet far from overhyping the project, all those honors barely do justice to this significant and surprising film.

Surprising because audience awards often go to undemanding, unapologetically cheerful ventures. Although it's a work of great warmth with an overwhelming finale, *Whale Rider* (written and directed by Niki Caro from the 1995 novel by Witi Ihimaera) is also a substantial film of unexpected emotional force. And when at a certain point it seems to slip the bonds of this world and take a leap of faith into an almost mythological dimension, it easily takes us along for that memorable ride.

Even before all that happens, *Whale Rider* draws great strength from the Maori community of New Zealand where it is set. Although its classic story of a twelve-year-old girl battling to be accepted by a crusty grandfather is always involving, the film wouldn't be as compelling as it is if powerful cultural and societal issues didn't serve as underpinnings to that struggle.

Whale Rider opens with a wrenching scene narrated in voice-over by young Pai (Keisha Castle-Hughes in a splendid debut). "When I was born," she says in a reedy voice as we watch the tragedy unfolding, "my twin brother died and took our mother with him."

That event would be catastrophic anywhere, but it is especially so for the Ngati Konohi, residents of the small New Zealand fishing village of Whangara (where the film was actually shot). Pai's stern grandfather Koro (Rawiri Paratene) is the village chief, the latest leader in a patrimonial line that stretches back to Paikea, the tribe's progenitor, who, legend has it, arrived on the island centuries earlier riding on a whale.

Determined that the male line be unbroken, Koro has no use for a granddaughter. He tells his bereft son, Porourangi (Cliff Curtis), to start over with another wife. The son refuses, instead going off to Europe, where a career as an artist beckons. He has been driven away, we come to understand, by the weight and intensity of his father's expectations, and, as she grows up, his daughter, Pai, has to deal with Koro's unbending worldview as well.

Whale Rider reintroduces Pai as a stick-thin twelve-year-old, as small and stubborn as Joan of Arc. Raised by her grandfather and her more loving but equally strong-minded grandmother, Nanny Flowers (Vicky Haughton), Pai turns out to be as enraptured with the spirit of the Maori tradition as the older man is.

There is a clear bond between these two, but it is one that the grandfather cannot acknowledge because he is determined to find a new leader to replace his absent son and dead grandson, and tradition dictates absolutely that a girl, no matter how capable or involved, cannot fill that position.

Anchored by the persuasive performance of Paratene, *Whale Rider* makes the unbending Koro a realistic, surprisingly resonant character. Obsessed by his obligations, he is rigid about excluding Pai from leadership preparation because of his conviction that this is what his ancestors and his religion demand. When he screams, "You don't mess around with sacred things," you can feel the intensity of his belief and the force of the pressures on him, but Pai is equally determined, and so the battle is joined.

Although it does so gently, *Whale Rider* is also forthright about revealing why Koro feels that his tribe is in such desperate need of a strong new leader. We see the young people of the village, unanchored to tradition, either gone, like Pai's father, or falling under the thrall of alcohol, drugs, and dissolute behavior.

But unlike *Once Were Warriors* (1994), an ultra-bleak look at modern Maori culture, *Whale Rider* also conveys the easygoing directness and conviviality of Maori life, including a penchant for bawdy humor and earthy traditions such as rubbing noses as a ceremonial greeting.

A New Zealander (though, unlike the original book's author, not a Maori), writer-director Caro worked hard to gain the trust and cooperation of her all-Maori cast and the inhabitants of the village where the shooting took place. Among the other qualities that Caro (whose first film was the prizewinning *Memory and Desire*) brings to the mix are a willingness to let this story tell itself in its own time and the ability to create emotion that is intense without being cloying or dishonest.

She is also able, and this is critical, to leave the mundane behind and steer the film to a higher level when the story demands to go there. Echoing *The Fast Runner* (2001), which takes Inuit culture as its subject, she can make the stuff of myth seem both natural and believable. When the words "Dedicated to those who came before" appear on screen at the close, you can almost feel all those ancestors joining modern audiences in applauding what has been accomplished here.

Wonder Boys
2000

Distracted and dissipated dope-smoking man of letters Grady Tripp (Michael Douglas) has known bad days. Yes, he admits as *Wonder Boys* opens, his wife left him that very morning, "but wives had left me before." Yes, WordFest, the three-day literary event hosted by his university that this flailing novelist and writing professor genially scorns, will start that evening, but Tripp has always survived that as well. So what's the big deal?

What Tripp doesn't know is that the wasted weekend about to begin is going to be the worst (and that covers a lot of territory) he's ever experienced, so chaotic that the cataclysmic death of a dog at its beginning will seem positively benign before things are over. Tripp's precariously balanced life, always in shambles, is about to collapse with a slow-motion vengeance.

Tripp won't be taking this amiably disastrous trip into the dark night of his soul alone. Along for the ride, among others, are his predatory, satyr-like, gay New York editor, Terry Crabtree (Robert Downey Jr.); Sara Gaskell (Frances McDormand), his university's married chancellor as well as his mistress; James Leer (Tobey Maguire), a precocious, albeit death-obsessed, student; and Hannah Green (Katie Holmes), an equally gifted though considerably more attractive classmate who rents a room in Tripp's rambling house.

What makes Tripp's journey, and *Wonder Boys* as a whole, the pleasure it is isn't the destination so much as the way it's conveyed and experienced. Fastidiously directed by Curtis Hanson (*L.A. Confidential*) and written by Steve Kloves (*The Fabulous Baker Boys*) with an eye to preserving the rueful comic sensibility of Michael Chabon's splendid 1995 novel, this smart, literate film is especially noticeable for its generosity of spirit, for the sympathetic compassion it displays toward people who don't always receive it, on screen or off.

Though Chabon's book got exceptional reviews, its picaresque structure and richness of detail kept it from being automatic film material. But producer Scott Rudin believed in the project, and screenwriter Kloves showed why he's so well regarded in Hollywood despite a slender output (this is his fourth film in sixteen years) by expertly paring down the novel. Fans of Chabon's writing will find things missing, from a boa constrictor to character nuances, but what's more significant is Kloves's ability to capture the antic spirit of the proceedings as well as the book's droll sense of humor, which mixes restrained screwball antics with deft verbal repartee.

Hanson not only understands the jokes, he knows how to place them in the context of a handsomely mounted, graceful production that is well-played across the board. Though earlier films such as *River Wild* and *L.A. Confidential* may seem miles from this, they share Hanson's thoroughgoing classicism, his ability to give every on-screen element just the weight it deserves. What was new about *L.A. Confidential* is a quality that has carried over to this film: Hanson's increased confidence, his belief that he can bring off pretty much whatever he chooses.

A film buff before he was a director, Hanson convinced veteran editor Dede Allen to add her gift for narrative flow to *Wonder Boys*, and he retained his exceptional *L.A. Confidential* cinematographer, Dante Spinotti, who makes the film's Pittsburgh settings gleam like an eccentric urban Fantasyland. Hanson also has orchestrated uniformly excellent performances from his cast, from Oscar winners such as McDormand, ambivalent and conflicted as a mistress at a moment of truth, to youngsters such as Holmes (*Dawson's Creek*), just right as the beauty with kind of a crush on the old man.

The performance that anchors the film and makes everything possible is Douglas as Tripp, trying to even remember, let alone act on, what being responsible means after a lifetime spent as the boy who wouldn't grow up. Though the film's ad poster brings Elmer Fudd to mind, Douglas's Grady Tripp is rather a once-formidable man gone distressingly to seed, a weary Lothario who now stumbles around in a wool cap and his wife's bathrobe like one of the more dissolute elves in Santa's workshop. The been-there Douglas, reviving the offhanded comic moves that made *Romancing the Stone* so successful, has exactly the look and presence to make that characterization believable.

Tripp is especially worried about the upcoming WordFest weekend because of the appearance of editor Crabtree, who, desperate for a success, wants to take a look at the manuscript of an enormous, unwieldy novel Tripp has been working on for the seven years since its highly successful predecessor. The problem is that Tripp, at page 2611 and counting, is the opposite of blocked: He's got Sorcerer's Apprentice Syndrome; he can't stop or even prune the flow of words no matter how much he wants to.

Crabtree, the tempter incarnate (played by Downey with engaging flair), lives up to Tripp's worst fears by getting off the plane from New York with a treetop-tall transvestite and tuba player named Miss Sloviak (Michael Cavadias). The trio head for a party at the home of the chancellor, who catches a hint of Miss Sloviak's perfume and says with weary resignation, "I wear the same scent as a transvestite."

Outside, Tripp runs into Leer, a novel-writing student his professor views as a tricky combination of rival, protégé, and unstable surrogate son. Always morose and unhealthily focused on celebrity necrology, Leer (Maguire, in perhaps his best and most controlled performance) is especially morbid this evening, and Tripp thinks he knows just how to distract him.

For the chancellor's husband, a demon Yankee fan and memorabilia collector who sees Joe DiMaggio as an all-inclusive metaphor, keeps the fur-trimmed jacket Marilyn Monroe wore to marry the Yankee Clipper in a bedroom safe. Tripp decides to sneak in and give Leer a glimpse of the holy relic, and that's when, fueled by alcohol, ennui, and illicit drugs, things start to seriously unwind for wonder boys past, present, and future.

It turns out that one of Leer's most unnerving traits is that he's a compulsive fabulist, apparently unable or unwilling to tell the plain truth, and one of the themes of *Wonder Boys* is the exploration of what it means to be a writer, a teller of tales and creator of worlds. It's all part of the heady and sophisticated experience the script characterizes as "one nutty ride," and for once we're glad to have been invited along.

You Can Count on Me
2000

Kenneth Lonergan knows what he's written and why he's written it. He hears the words behind his words, understands the states of mind they reflect. He sees into his characters, into how they have to be who they are though they hurt themselves in the process. Even his tiniest moments ring true, which is why the ruefully funny dramatic comedy *You Can Count on Me* is such an exceptional debut.

A double prizewinner at Sundance, sharing the Grand Jury Prize and taking the Waldo Salt Screenwriting Award, this beautifully textured film shocks us for all the right reasons, by creating inescapably real people and allowing them to be themselves. Always individuals, the characters Lonergan has written and directed are forever doing unexpected things for no good reason, faking us out again and again because they have minds of their own.

A New York playwright (*This Is Our Youth* is his best-known work), Lonergan has written for film before: His original script became the very different *Analyze This* nine years and fourteen writers after he wrote the first draft. He turned to directing to ensure that *You Can Count on Me* would appear on screen just as he wanted it, and that has made a considerable difference.

Though there are romantic elements in it, what Lonergan has written is a different kind of love story, one between a sister and a brother. Orphaned at a young age, they are, at least in theory, each other's main support in the world, but what Sammy (Laura Linney) and Terry (Mark Ruffalo) can actually depend on from each other is something more complex and frustrating.

For Lonergan is especially good at making Sammy and Terry's oppositeness as clear as the affection they share. They love but disappoint each other; they're irked as often as they're caring. Chronically unable to provide what the other sibling is looking for, the only thing Sammy and Terry can truly count on is a mutual exasperation that looks to extend to the end of time.

Wonderfully played by Linney in a performance that makes the most of Lonergan's incisive writing, Sammy is the sister who stayed home in a small town in upstate New York, tending her parents' grave, working as a lending officer at the local bank, and having an off-and-on relationship with the square-jawed Bob (Jon Tenney).

The most reliable man in Sammy's life is the eight-year-old son she's raising as a single parent. Like many another serious child of divorce, Rudy (Rory Culkin, Macaulay Culkin's talented youngest brother) is a worrier with a somber sense of humor, a kid who likes things as structured as possible.

Having a special hold on Sammy's emotions is her brother Terry;

when a rare letter from him arrives, her face lights up like the sun. And when Terry announces that he's coming back for an even rarer visit, not even the officiousness of her new boss at the bank (a deftly comic Matthew Broderick, a friend of Lonergan's since high school) can stop her from throwing herself into preparations.

Equally strong as Linney's performance is Mark Ruffalo's special work as Terry. A veteran of many of Lonergan's plays, his experience with the director's language and themes helps bring levels of complexity and interest to what could have been the most dismissible of characters. Slacker, layabout, underachiever—whichever word you choose, Terry fits it. But it is one of the triumphs of *You Can Count on Me* that his kind of rootless disaffection has rarely been so honestly, convincingly, yet sympathetically portrayed.

"I am not the kind of guy everyone says I am," Terry whines to a girlfriend early on, but, truthfully, he pretty much is. Awkward and ill at ease with people, easily insulted, and always aggrieved, he frustrates everyone with whom he comes into contact, himself most of all.

So as much as Sammy is looking forward to his visit, Terry's generic fecklessness inevitably brings out her disapproval; he, in turn, feels cramped and smothered by her excessive concern. Complicating things is Terry's developing relationship with a dubious Rudy, who has never seen anyone like his uncle and is not sure he even wants to.

Because so much can be said about these characters—because, like people we know—they can be looked at from any number of angles, it's easy to forget to emphasize how completely funny *You Can Count on Me* is, how much its warm humor bubbles up naturally from the heart. Lonergan (who's cast himself as the overmatched local priest) makes both his perceptive writing and subtle direction, his ability to view ordinary life as a potentially great adventure, look much easier than it really is. If you've been looking for an American independent film that fulfills the promise of the movement, you have it now.

Zoolander
2001

The call went out, not for a hero, but for someone "extremely dimwitted." For "a self-absorbed simpleton who can be manipulated." For "a shallow, dumb moron." In a word, for Zoolander.

Derek Zoolander is not a superhero but a supermodel; the only things even remotely larger than life about him are his self-absorption and his ego. "Vain, stupid, incredibly self-centered," he is, all unawares, the preposterous centerpiece of the exuberant and insidiously funny satire that bears his name.

A fashion icon, Derek has parlayed a look he calls "Blue Steel" to win the industry's coveted male model of the year title three years running. Ben Stiller, who plays him in addition to co-writing and directing, employs a piercing look of a different, more insightful kind. Though he's best known as a pitch-perfect deadpan comic presence in films such as *Meet the Parents* and *There's Something about Mary,* Stiller's Emmy-winning *The Ben Stiller Show* of several years back showed the gift for the kind of mocking, take-no-prisoners skit humor that *Zoolander* thrives on.

Here, working with co-writers Drake Sather and John Hamburg and using a character created for a *VH1/Vogue Fashion Awards* telecast, Stiller savagely skewers not only the fashionista universe but a ripe-for-ridicule popular culture that has elevated models to nearly godlike status. *Zoolander* starts, in fact, with the model being interviewed by investigative journalist Matilda Jeffries (Christine Taylor) for *Time*. Completely clueless about how clueless he is, Derek can't pronounce "eulogy," confuses "bulimic" with "psychic," and doesn't know the difference between architectural models and full-sized buildings.

Unbeknownst to Derek, the real world is preparing to affect his reality. There's a new prime minister in Malaysia who wants to raise wages and end child labor, both serious threats to garment-industry sweatshops. A shadowy coalition of fashion moguls commands top designer Mugatu (Will Ferrell) to find someone really, really dim to assassinate the prime minister. Zoolander is the inevitable choice.

Our hero, meanwhile, is having troubles of his own. He's enmeshed in a rivalry with fellow top model Hansel (Owen Wilson), a blond surfer dude who is never without his nonchalant "I grip it and I rip it" attitude. Suddenly riven by self-doubts, Derek starts to wonder, "Is there more to life than being really, really, really ridiculously good-looking?"

What to do? Stay a model? Retire and start giving back with the "Derek Zoolander Center for Kids Who Can't Read Good"? Or go back to his roots, which in this case means a trip to the coal-mining country of southern New Jersey, where his hardscrabble dad (a wonderful Jon Voight) can't hide his disgust. No wonder Derek is ripe for the *Manchurian Candidate* machinations of Mugatu's associate, the merciless Katinka (a well-used Milla Jovovich). Only reporter Matilda realizes the danger he's in. And time is running out.

Though basically an extended skit, *Zoolander* never runs out of amusing satiric thrusts. There's Mugatu's latest clothing line, inspired by vagrants and street people and called "Derelicte." Or the coveted Slashie, given to the best actor/model and won by the deserving Fabio. The film also gets laughs out of where it places songs, such as the Bee Gees' "I Started a Joke" and "He Ain't Heavy . . . He's My Brother," and tosses in brief parodies of *2001* and the *Godfather* films just because it can.

Aside from numerous cameos (Donald Trump, Paris Hilton, and David Bowie among them) and sharply cast actors (David Duchovny as the man who knows the truth behind every political assassination of the past 200 years), Stiller also makes good use of his family. His father, Jerry, is Derek's over-the-top manager, Maury Ballstein; his mother, Anne Meara, and his sister Amy have cameos; and his wife, Christine Taylor, is very winning as the film's essential straight person.

Holding the picture together, however, are the well-meshed complementary performances of Stiller and Wilson, who share the ability to be deadly serious while their characters get increasingly ridiculous. The reality that neither one exactly has the supermodel look makes this dead-on joke even more delicious.

part two

FOREIGN LANGUAGE FILMS

*The body lay outside an abandoned, boarded-up theatre.
The theatre had started as a first-run movie house, many
years back when the neighborhood had still been fashionable.
As the neighborhood began rotting, the theatre began
showing second-run films, and then old movies, and finally
foreign-language films.*
—from *Cop Killer* by Ed McBain

Introduction

Growing up in the Brownsville section of Brooklyn, I heard more foreign languages on the street than I did on screen. Yiddish, Russian, and later Spanish drifted across the sidewalks, but inside the elaborate Loew's Pitkin or the proletariat Sutter Theater, films in languages other than English were both unheard of and unheard. It probably would have surprised me to find out they even existed.

When, in college and after, I discovered and devoured foreign film during the 1960s and '70s, most of what I saw came from just a few countries. France and Italy dominated, and when other cultures were represented at all, it was often through the work of a single auteur: Ingmar Bergman was the Scandinavian cinema, Akira Kurosawa the Japanese, Satijat Ray the Indian, and so on. The great man theory of history transitioned quite smoothly to the big screen.

What's notable and even exciting about today's foreign film world as reflected in the movies I've selected is the greatly increased diversity in terms of countries represented and filmmakers within them. When the Academy of Motion Picture Arts and Sciences asks for submissions for its foreign language Oscar, it gets entries from upwards of eighty countries. I haven't cast my net quite that widely, but some twenty non–English speaking entities are represented here, including ones that no longer exist (the former Yugoslavia with *Tito and Me*) and ones that aren't really countries at all (the Inuit-speaking regions of Canada, with *The Fast Runner*).

The great thing about these films is that they are not locally made copies of American movies. They have their own sensibility and attitudes, allowing us the exciting opportunity to see the world as an insider, through the eyes of the people who live in it. *The Blue Kite,* in effect banned in its native China, shows what that country's tumultuous recent history was like, and the devastating Indian independent film *The Terrorist* gives the kind of chilling insight into the mind of suicide bombers that today's international situation has made frighteningly relevant.

One thing that has not changed from the days of my introduction to foreign language films is how large French cinema looms in my life.

Fully one-third of the films in this section come from France, and that doesn't count the French language films from Belgium (*La Promesse, Ma Vie En Rose*), Canada (*Leolo*), and elsewhere.

French films are so prominent in part because France may be the only country that takes the movies even more seriously than America does, that has an enviable cinematic heritage, and that richly supports all aspects of its film life both financially and culturally. But more than that, to be honest, is that the French film sensibility, the premium its beautifully adult films place on psychological insight and human complexity, is one I personally find irresistible.

Whenever I worry that foreign language films are slowly losing traction in our blockbuster-dominated culture, I remember a conversation I had with the late Daniel Toscan du Plantier, then president of Unifrance, the organization charged with promoting French film overseas.

"If you are on a street full of hamburger shops, you finally want to eat something else," Toscan told me. "If you hear there is an old lady who prepares *cassoulet* in a small apartment on the second floor, you will go there, you will seek her out. In a film world where there is too much noise, too much *Independence Day,* French cinema is *cassoulet* on the second floor." And what is true for French cinema is true for the rest of the world as well.

After Life
1999

You could spend eternity watching movies and not see one with the qualities of *After Life*. That's how special, how original this intimate Japanese film is.

Written and directed by Hirokazu Kore-eda, *After Life* is simple in structure but poignant almost beyond words in effect. A meditation on the randomness of pleasure, of memory, of life itself, *After Life*'s story of a week spent at an unusual facility starts slowly and simply yet ends up as close to transcendent as cinema gets.

It begins on a Monday, the first day of the week, and employees are doing the usual grousing about their jobs as they report to an unprepossessing institutional building, a former school perhaps. They complain about the chill in the air as their supervisor advises them that this week's workload is heavier than usual.

Out of a blinding white fog, other people walk up a few stairs and sit expectantly in the building's waiting room, old and young chatting politely with one another. Then each person is called individually to a room, where the following information is imparted: "As you know, you died yesterday. You will stay here for a week, and there is one thing you must do. You must select one memory, the one most meaningful and precious to you. We will re-create it for you on film, so you can relive it, and you will take only that memory with you into eternity."

There is something innately appealing about this concept, as there is about the simplicity and everydayness of a ramshackle halfway house between Earth and the next life. But again, the magic in *After Life* is in more than the simplicity of the concept, it's in the subtle and perceptive way it's executed.

Though he uses it to very different effect, writer-director Kore-eda shares with Belgium's Dardennes brothers (*La Promesse* and the Cannes-prizewinning *Rosetta*) a background in documentary work that is both considerable and essential. That experience adds grace to the straightforward interview shooting of the twenty-two people who must choose memories this particular week, all of whom face the camera in classic neo-documentary poses. In developing the script, Kore-eda interviewed more than 500 subjects about the memories they would choose, and those on screen include actors working from a script as well as actors and nonprofessionals recounting their own experiences.

Possibly because we're told that these are dead men and women talking, there is something intrinsically moving about the ways, ranging from wistful to matter-of-fact, that these people provide exquisite snapshots of what has mattered to them in their lives.

A seventy-eight-year-old woman, for instance, talks about a new dress bought for a childhood dance recital. A prostitute remembers a client who was kind; a potential suicide recalls what made him pull back from the brink; a pilot thinks about clouds; an old man remembers the breeze on his face when he rode a trolley to school; and a wild-haired twenty-one-year-old wearing leather pants refuses point-blank to choose anything at all.

Some of *After Life*'s most moving moments are its smallest. A man who claims all his memories are bad feelingly says, "You can forget? That really is heaven." A pretty, vivacious girl is going to put down a trip to Disneyland until convinced otherwise. And a tiny, bird-like woman (Hisako Hara) quietly scavenges treasures from nature and hardly talks at all.

After Life spends different amounts of time with different people, gradually concentrating most on retired steel executive Ichiro Watanabe (Taketoshi Naito), a man whose ordinariness seems a barrier at first, and staff member Takashi Mochizuki (Arata), who's been assigned to help him.

As involving as the experiences of the newly dead, it turns out, are the adventures of the staff, who though no longer living are not immune from the pleasures of tea, the excesses of fits of temper, or the frustrations of having crushes on co-workers, like the one young Shiori Satonaka (Erika Oda) has on Mochizuki. When he offers to lend her his mystery novel, she replies that she's currently reading something else: a multivolume world encyclopedia. "Time," she says artlessly, "I've got plenty of."

Once a memory is chosen, the staff also aids in filming it, using simple special effects that couldn't be further from state of the art. The role of movies, even the most primitive, in molding, enhancing, and even changing our memories is one of this film's recurring themes, and one of its most telling.

All this is accomplished with a level of delicacy and restraint that is rare and welcome. In its examination of what is fleeting and what remains, *After Life* is not only perceptive, it leavens everything it touches with a surprisingly sly sense of humor. Few films about death, or about life for that matter, leave you feeling so affirmative about existence.

Aimee & Jaguar
2000

Aimee & Jaguar is about the power of falling in love, what it gives us and the price that can be attached to its joys. It's the most familiar story in the lexicon of cinema, but watching it in this emotionally powerful film makes you feel as though you've never quite seen it before.

As acted by Maria Schrader and Juliane Kohler, both of whom won Silver Bears at the Berlin Film Festival, *Aimee & Jaguar* shows individuals who are drawn to each other with such intensity we can actually feel the attraction ourselves. With key scenes so vivid they barely feel scripted, this is more than a same-sex success, it's one of the most affecting, most sensual of on-screen love affairs, period.

Based on a true story that became a bestseller in Germany in 1994, *Aimee & Jaguar* details a completely unlikely wartime romance. Unlikely not because it involved two women, but because one of them was a conventional German wife, the mother of four children with a husband at the front, while the other was a Jewish woman hiding in Berlin from an increasingly rapacious Nazi search-and-destroy machinery.

The latter would be Felice Schragenheim (Schrader), who called herself "Jaguar" in the erotic love poetry she wrote as a hobby. Though she lived clandestinely in the apartment of her lover Ilse (Johanna Wokalek), describing Felice as hiding, while accurate enough, gives a completely misleading impression.

A daredevil with a highly developed sense of bravado, Felice thrived on recklessness and danger. So adept at passing as an Aryan that she worked at a Nazi newspaper, Felice hung out at the best Berlin hotels yet passed information to the underground. Believing in the value of "living your life now," she was so innately duplicitous that, Ilse said, "as soon as you got hold of one Felice, another one betrayed you."

Lilly Wust (Kohler), whom Felice dubbed Aimee, was a different sort of woman. A flighty but vulnerable and unsophisticated romantic, Lilly compensated for a philandering husband away at the front by having numerous affairs with men who were worthier in her imagination than they proved to be in life.

It's through Ilse, who works as Lilly's maid, that the two women meet, and though *Aimee & Jaguar* is bookended by scenes in the present, it mostly deals with the wartime years from 1943 on, when the relationship began. It was a peculiar time for Berlin, when the city was both physically and psychologically unraveling as a result of constant Allied bombing.

Though the intensity of feeling the two women almost immediately experience unnerves them both, it's the flirtatious Felice, who knows what's going on but is terrified by the onset of real emotion, who's affected first. For Lilly, who has never had a nonheterosexual thought, the emotional distance that has to be covered is, if anything, greater and more treacherous.

It's through acknowledging and keeping faith with these considerable difficulties that *Aimee & Jaguar* does its best work. Because Felice and Lilly are always complex, always themselves, the barriers to their having a relationship are not easy to surmount. And things like the parallel jealousies of Felice's distrustful friends and Lilly's disbelieving husband only make things harder.

Aimee & Jaguar is the feature debut for German television director Max Farberbock (who also co-wrote the script with Rona Munro). His film feels uncomfortably middle of the road at first, but it gathers strength and integrity as it goes along, and its re-creation of how terrifying life must have been for these women ends up overpowering its more conventional tendencies.

The biggest factor in that success is the potent interplay of its two stars. Schrader and Kohler feed off each other beautifully, the intensity of their dynamic growing with every scene, and the sequence in which they confront Felice's Judaism is as impressive as you hope it will be and more.

"Great people leave a mark, and when they leave, the mark remains." So says a Nazi functionary, quoting Joseph Goebbels. In an irony the filmmakers no doubt intend, the romantic mark left by these two women turns out to be very great indeed.

Un Air de Famille
1998

"Ah, Monsieur Rabelais," an admirer said to the sixteenth-century French writer in a memorable New Yorker cartoon, "there is simply no word to describe your lusty, bawdy sense of humor."

Similarly, there is no one word (and it probably wouldn't be "Rabelaisian") to describe the kind of uproarious, quintessentially French verbal farce that is *Un Air de Famille.* Delicate and deliciously directed by Cedric Klapisch, one of France's best young filmmakers, and acted with great sureness, this droll symphony of comic disenchantment is as perfectly balanced and executed as the timepiece of your dreams.

Un Air de Famille is based on a hit French play, and its six-character ensemble is made up of original cast members who played their parts on stage for nine months before filming began. Two of the actors, Agnes Jaoui and Jean-Pierre Bacri, wrote the piece and received a Cesar, the French Oscar, for best screenplay, and two more, Jean-Pierre Darroussin and the marvelous Catherine Frot, won supporting actor Cesars for their roles.

Done in real time largely at a single location, a café incongruously named Au Pere Tranquille (Tranquil Dad's), *Un Air de Famille* is simplicity itself in outline. It's Friday night, a time when the Menaud family—mother, two sons and their wives, and an unmarried daughter—gathers for a weekly family dinner at the café run by son Henri (Bacri), who inherited the place from his father.

The film's title translates as "Family Resemblances," and in truth, only families can drive each other as crazy as these people do. Quick to take offense, always willing to needle one another for scores that will forever remain unsettled, these whining, complaining relations have been getting on one another's nerves for time out of mind. On this particular Friday, everything will come to a wildly comic head.

All this contentiousness stems from the pugnacious family matriarch (Claire Maurier, who played the mother in François Truffaut's *The Four Hundred Blows*), who's always ready with a critical word for whoever crosses her line of vision.

Usually it's underachieving son Henri who gets most of her grief, and tonight, with his wife, Arlette, absent without official leave, Henri returns the favor. He expresses outraged irritation at anything he can think of, from the willingness of female tennis professionals to wear shorts instead of skirts to the slothfulness of his bartender, Denis (Darroussin). "Are you cleaning your kneecap?" he snaps when the poor man rests his rag there for a minute. "It's spotless."

Henri even lashes out at his irritable sister Betty (Jaoui), who has problems of her own. She's worried about being thirty and unmarried, she has just told off her boss, and she is involved in a phlegmatic relationship with bartender Denis that no one else in the family knows about.

Smiling, self-satisfied brother Philippe (Wladimir Yordanoff), a top executive at the computer company Betty works for, usually has things his own way, but tonight is not an ordinary night. Philippe represented his firm on local TV earlier in the day, and he's worried about how he came off, not to mention what Betty's fight with her boss will do to his career. And then there is Yolanda, familiarly known as Yoyo (Frot).

Yoyo is Philippe's slightly dim wife whose thirty-fifth birthday is to be celebrated on this most uncelebratory night. Simple but sweet and genuine, prone to getting tipsy and putting her hand to her lips when she laughs, Yoyo is a singular comic creation, as sympathetic as she is naive, and Frot's performance makes her irresistible.

All of this highly verbal madness is delivered with great style and in a way that seems, as the entire film does, thoroughly French. The members of this family lavish more care on dogs than they do on people, punctuate their dizzying tirades with vivid gestures and grimaces, take offense easily, and are obstinately passionate about each and every one of their opinions. A collection of national stereotypes, in short, and no less amusing for that.

Though director (and co-screenwriter) Klapisch came into the project after it was a stage hit, *Un Air de Famille* benefits considerably from his touch. As he did with his early *Chacun Cherche Son Chat* (When the Cat's Away), Klapisch excels at bringing reality and empathy to unlikely comic material. We know these people as well as we know ourselves, and maybe that's why we laugh so hard at their foibles.

Autumn Tale
1999

Though you wouldn't know it from Hollywood's youthful obsessions, filmmakers actually can improve as they advance in age. The droll and delicious *Autumn Tale* is the twenty-second feature in writer-director Eric Rohmer's four-decade career, and besides being one of his wisest and most enjoyable films, it also has the light-fingered vigor and panache more chronologically youthful directors are not always able to muster.

Rohmer, along with Jean-Luc Godard, François Truffaut, and Claude Chabrol, is one of the New Wave directors who revolutionized French film starting in the late 1950s. Over the years, he's made such favorites as *My Night at Maud's, Claire's Knee, Chloe in the Afternoon,* and *Pauline at the Beach,* all marked, as *Autumn Tale* is, by elegant, character-driven plots as carefully worked out as intricate mathematical proofs.

Mostly, as those films indicate, Rohmer's work has focused on the male fascination with (invariably) younger women. Recently, however, not only have Rohmer's titles gotten simpler (*Autumn Tale* was preceded by *Summer's Tale, Winter's Tale,* and *Tale of Springtime,* all part of his decade-long *Tales of the Four Seasons* series), but he has tended to see things more from the female point of view.

Autumn Tale is also unusual for Rohmer because it's involved with women of a certain age, focusing on the romantic difficulties of a forty-five-year-old widow and the increasingly frenetic efforts of the well-intentioned but misguided friends who try to help her.

Rohmer here displays not only the assurance that comes with great experience but also his marvelous sense of character. It's a pleasure to have a writer-director who understands people so well; his sense of how the combination of good intentions and faulty judgment can land us in a terrible mess is both compassionate and exact.

More than anything, Rohmer's people love to talk. Passionate about their own thoughts and ideas (though not necessarily anyone else's), these formidably articulate individuals analyze, reflect on, and consider everything they do—not once but several times—all to magnificent effect.

The main talkers are two longtime friends living in the Côte du Rhône region of southern France: Magali (Beatrice Romand, who debuted in 1970's *Claire's Knee*) and her closest confident, Isabelle (Marie Rivière, also in Rohmer's acting stable). Happily married Isabelle is dealing with her daughter's impending wedding, while Magali, a bit estranged from both her grown children, devotes herself to the winery left her by her parents.

An early scene of these two women walking and talking among Magali's plantings illustrates the subtlety of Rohmer's approach. Nominally nothing of substance is discussed as the two women wander aimlessly amid the vines, but, in fact, everything we need to know about both of them, about Magali's forthrightness and stubborn candor as well as Isabelle's flighty, not quite practical nature, is gracefully revealed, as is the intimacy they share.

Chatting later in the farmhouse, Magali reveals that though she would like to have a man in her life, she's all but given up on the idea as impossible. "It's the hardest thing of all," she explains. "At my age, it's easier to find buried treasure!" Prospects are even more unlikely in her case because, as Magali is the first to admit, "I need to meet a man but I refuse to do anything about it."

Undaunted, Isabelle, who owns a bookstore, forms a plan to help her friend out. Not only does she place a misleading personal ad ("Fun-loving, lively, sociable") in Magali's name in the local newspaper, she also decides, in an excess of comradely zeal combined with a desire to bring a little flirtation into her own life, to impersonate her friend and test-date Gerald (Alain Libolt), the most likely of the candidates, herself.

Also for personal reasons, someone else is simultaneously trying to act as matchmaker for Magali. The beautiful young Rosine (Alexia Portal) is nominally the girlfriend of Magali's son Leo, but her strongest emotional attachment is to Magali.

Young though she is, Rosine has romantic complications of her own. She's trying to get over a love affair with her insufferable college philosophy professor Etienne (Didier Sandre). Ignoring his obsession with young women, she thinks that if she's successful in hooking him up with Magali, she'll have succeeded in killing two birds with the same stone.

These romantic shenanigans are all the more appealing because Rohmer understands that when adults are involved with affairs of the heart, their nominal maturity often disappears, leaving them as shy, awkward, and accident-prone as the most love-struck teenager. When you're going out on a first date, it's always high school in your mind.

With his characters hatching more and more complicated schemes, Rohmer delights in revealing how we inevitably complicate our lives simply by being human. When Isabelle writes in her personal ad that what's wanted is a man "interested in moral as well as physical beauty," she could be describing this consummate filmmaker just as easily as Magali's imaginary dream date.

The Blue Kite
1994

Of all the remarkable films to have come out of China, *The Blue Kite* could well be the most authentic, the most accessible, and, finally, the most powerful. Daring politically and quietly shattering emotionally, it tells the truth in such a completely human way that it hardly seems foreign at all.

Unlike the work of fellow Fifth Generation filmmakers Chen Kiage (*Farewell My Concubine*) and Zhang Yimou (*Raise the Red Lantern*), this film from director Tian Zhuangzhuang is not at all theatrical or operatic. A welcoming naturalism characterizes his style here, an ability to see great events through the lives of ordinary people caught unawares in the toils of history.

Set between the death of Joseph Stalin in 1953 and the living death of the Cultural Revolution of 1968, Xiao Mao's realistic script illuminates that most unstable period of modern Chinese politics by telling the story of an ordinary woman named Chen Shujuan (popular Chinese actress Lu Liping) and her extended family.

Simple as it is, this idea did not find favor with the powers who run China's film industry. After viewing a rough cut of *The Blue Kite*, they forbade shipping the footage to Japan (where most Chinese films go for post-production). The film was spirited out anyway, edited according to the director's detailed notes, and shown to great praise both at Cannes and the Tokyo Film Festival, where the Chinese delegation walked out during the screening and later announced plans to sue the Dutch company that had acquired the world rights.

It may seem unusual for such a quiet film to have stirred up such a considerable fuss, but it is the discretion and restraint with which *The Blue Kite* was created that makes its points so effective and its indictment of China's past political situation so damning.

Certainly when we first meet Shujuan, everything seems happy and hopeful. Much to the delight of her idealistic sister (Song Xiaoying) and her brothers (Zhong Ping and Chu Quanzhong), she is about to marry librarian Lin Shaolong (Pu Quanxin) and move into a small apartment in a bustling Beijing courtyard. Soon a son, called Tietou, or "Iron Head," is born, and, true to his nickname, he grows up to be the film's stubborn narrator.

Much of the action of *The Blue Kite* takes place in that busy courtyard and among the members of that family. Director Tian is a thoughtful, nuanced observer, and, helped by Hou Yong's sensitive camera work, he gets a great deal of poignancy out of intimate family scenes between brother and sister, mother and child, husband and wife.

These moments play out against the turmoil caused by the chaotic political movements of the day. First came Rectification, a call from the Communist Party for honesty and criticism, followed almost immediately by an Anti-Rightist campaign that condemned those who did speak out. Next was the Great Leap Forward, a frantic attempt to increase China's industrial production, which led finally to the mad terror of the Cultural Revolution.

The Blue Kite is especially good at showing how difficult it was for ordinary people to try to find space to simply survive as the baffling crosswinds of politics caused the loss of jobs, relationships, even lives. "The more I think about it," Shujuan says at one point, more in resignation than in anger, "the less I understand."

This kind of rigorous, unforgiving look at a major span of Chinese history, a willingness to take on political movements that are still off-limits to criticism, is one of the things that got *The Blue Kite* in such trouble with the authorities. The other subject that is taboo, apparently never before addressed on film, is official insistence that attractive women in the army eschew steady boyfriends and instead provide escort services for powerful party leaders as a "political duty."

The only token of hope in this troubled time is the kite of the film's title. A fragile paper object that keeps getting destroyed or lost and then rebuilt, it symbolizes freedom, beauty, innocence, and the hope of escape, all the things that that generation of Chinese, as this film so movingly shows, had to live their lives without.

Celebration
1998

A family comes together to celebrate its patriarch's sixtieth birthday, but everyone is not in a festive mood. Adult children gather to nominally salute their father, but darker thoughts prey on their minds. It may sound familiar, but *The Celebration* (*Festen* in the original Danish) overturns expectations.

Winner of the special jury prize at Cannes, *Celebration* is a remarkably mature work to be only the second feature from twenty-nine-year-old director Thomas Vinterberg. A beautifully calibrated and carefully thought out film about a completely out-of-control situation, it is raw without being off-putting and wrenching without losing its sense of humor.

Best of all, *Celebration* allows the audience to share the same sense of emotional danger and uncertainty that its characters feel. We're in there with them, watching the chaos happen all around, wondering where it can possibly end.

Celebration is so successful because it's a film that's as compelling for the way it tells its story as for the tale itself. The techniques used by the director and cinematographer Anthony Dod Mantle are as potent and effective as the excellent actors in conveying what Vinterberg and co-writer Mogens Rukov intended; any attempt to separate the film's elements, even in the mind, is bound to be futile.

Celebration's look stems from Vinterberg's commitment to the tenets of a collective of Danish directors (including Lars von Trier of *Breaking the Waves*) who call themselves "Dogma 95." Dogma's rules include shooting on location without added props, using natural sound and available light at all times, and filming with only a hand-held camera.

Although some of Dogma's rules, such as "The director must not be credited," have not been carefully attended to, the overall impact of this emphasis on naturalism is exceptional.

Hand-held camera work, which can seem like an affectation, is used here to remarkable effect. It adds intimacy, immediacy, and vitality to the piece, giving *Celebration* a connection to throbbing life it would not otherwise have had. Moving around like one of the family, the camera brazenly eavesdrops on delicate situations, shrinking from nothing, showing and telling all.

Everything starts quietly enough as the camera picks up Christian (Ulrich Thomsen) walking with a suitcase through the Danish countryside. The family's serious, sober prodigal son, he's just flown in for the celebration from Paris, where he runs two restaurants.

Headed down the same road in a sports car is younger brother Michael (Thomas Bo Larsen), a bullying, unpleasant hothead who immediately reveals his character by forcing his wife, Mette (Helle Dolleris), and their children to walk the rest of the way to the celebration so he can offer brother Christian a chance to ride in comfort.

Arriving by speeding taxi is sister Helene (Paprika Steen), a scattered, emotional woman who appears alternately strong-willed and on the verge of a collapse.

Waiting for everyone at what appears to be a family-owned hotel are mother Elsa (Birthe Neuman) and father Helge (veteran Danish actor Henning Moritzen). He's a bit stern, but caring and in general happy to see his children, especially Christian, who has not been in close touch.

Once upon a time, it's revealed, Helge and Elsa had four children. But Christian's twin, Linda, has committed suicide so recently that when Helene is given her room she almost can't bear to stay there. Helge asks his son if he could say a few words about Linda at the celebratory dinner, and Christian says yes, he was planning to say something.

Extended family members and guests arrive by the dozen, and everyone proceeds to get fearfully drunk. Michael has what feels like one of innumerable intense brawls with his wife, Helene explores her room to startling effect, and Christian has a reunion with childhood friends Kim (Bjarne Henriksen), now the evening's chef, and Pia (Trine Dyrholm), who's always had a crush on him.

Then, in the midst of considerable inebriated merriment, Christian rises to speak. Barely able to stand, he makes a horrifying accusation against his father. The words have an air of finality, but in fact a Pandora's box of jealousies, rivalries, countercharges, and recriminations is just beginning to open.

Wonderfully acted by a well-cast ensemble, *Celebration* never quite goes where you expect it to, even managing to throw in comic moments amid its terrifying family dynamics. While most films about dysfunctional relationships fit neatly into a problem picture box, this wrenching but uplifting film finds its own way with energy and aplomb.

The Circle
2001

Restrained yet powerful, devastating in its emotional effects, *The Circle* is a landmark in Iranian cinema. By combining two things that are relatively rare in that country's production—unapologetically dramatic storytelling and an implicit challenge to the prevailing political ideology—this new film by producer-director Jafar Panahi creates a potent synthesis that was the surprise winner of the Golden Lion at the Venice Film Festival.

Panahi's first film, *The White Balloon,* took the prestigious Camera d'Or at Cannes and became something of an art-house hit over here. Yet it, too, shared in the slow, allusive nature of much of Iran's cinema of indirection, where the response to an intrusive, censorious govern-ment has been to pull back and make films where narrative drive is suspect and hardly anything overt is allowed to happen.

The Circle is a different story. Its pace is insistent, its drama obvi-ous, and its theme, the plight of women in post-revolutionary Iran, the constricted, wasted nature of their lives, couldn't be more provocative. As with Soviet-era Eastern European cinema, societies in conflict invariably create the most potent dramas.

Though Panahi didn't make *The Circle* to challenge the govern-ment, the powers that be made his life difficult. The screenplay, by Kambozia Partovi, was only approved following public pressure from now-defunct reformist newspapers, and, once finished, the film was banned in its homeland and only allowed overseas with great reluc-tance.

The Circle shares in the neo-realistic style that dominates current Iranian cinema, with nonprofessionals taking on most of the roles. But Panahi's exceptional eye for faces combines beautifully with cine-matographer Bahram Badakhshani's intimate, naturalistic camera work. As a result, we feel like we're living a reality, not watching a film.

In this reality, we share in the lives of several women who are joined in a sisterhood of misery. Set on the streets of Tehran, the sto-ries don't intertwine but are told consecutively, as the camera, with seeming randomness, leaves one woman to concentrate on the next. What's gradually revealed is the unthinking, suffocating chauvinism of Iranian society and the hopelessness it engenders in women.

The Circle opens in a maternity hospital with the birth of a baby girl. But instead of treating this as a happy event, the grandmother, a woman with a truly tragic face, foresees calamity. The ultrasound had indicated a boy, and she knows that in male-oriented Iran, the in-laws will be furious that it's not.

As the grandmother flees the hospital, the camera leaves her and concentrates on a group of agitated women on the street. We are thrust immediately into their story, which turns out to be the film's central one, and it's only gradually that we find out who they are and what their situation is.

Both the hawk-faced Arezou (Maryiam Parvin Almani) and the

naive, dreamy Nargess (Nargess Mamizadeh) are on a temporary pass from prison, but they have no intention of going back. Nargess wants to return to her rural village, but she has no money, and Arezou is determined to get the cash for her, despite their lack of proper papers, a major handicap in a city where police checks and roving neighborhood watches are omnipresent.

Other women and their difficulties also make their way into *The Circle,* dramas about women who hide their pasts, who are desperate for illegal abortions or driven to consider abandoning their children. Through these stories we learn that even the smallest and most nominally inconsequential ways in which women's lives are circumscribed reflect a larger, more disturbing reality.

Women in Iran cannot smoke in public. They can't enter certain buildings without an all-enveloping *chador.* They can't even buy a bus ticket if they are traveling alone. Yet the men in the city, even the members of the supposedly zealous neighborhood watch, are free to hassle them sexually on the street, and, in one telling telephone scene, proposition them whenever it suits their fancy.

It's not by chance, we gradually realize, that the film's central figures are presented as prisoners, prisoners whose crime we are never told. Trapped almost as literally as if they were in a cage, strangers in their own land, their stories don't really end, they simply vanish from our field of vision. *The Circle,* however, makes them unforgettable.

Un Coeur en Hiver
1993

When Claude Sautet makes a film, no one goes hungry, either on-screen or off. While his characters are never far from an exceptional glass of wine or an enviable apple tart, the complex emotional lives they display are as rich and satisfying as any of the spectacular meals they consume.

Sautet's newest film, the expressively titled *Un Coeur en Hiver* (A Heart in Winter), follows in this pattern. Like *Vincent, Francois, Paul and the Others* and the director's biggest American hit, *Cesar and*

Rosalie with Yves Montand and Romy Schneider, *Coeur* succeeds in finding surprisingly supple and involving romantic entanglements in the well-upholstered lives of the Parisian bourgeoisie.

Though he is a popular and well-respected filmmaker in France (*Coeur* was nominated for nine Cesars and won for best director and best supporting actor), Sautet has never been avant-garde enough to be a passionate critical favorite. Instead, he follows in the humanistic tradition of the master, Jean Renoir, and turns out films that are realistic yet accepting about affairs of the heart even when they show a darker side of love.

Coeur (written by Yves Ulmann, Jacques Fieschi, and Jerome Tonnerre and inspired by a short story by Russian writer Mikhail Lermontov) follows that same pattern of passionate and unnerving feelings. Though it deals with the kind of unlikely couple movies traditionally specialize in, what it does with them is as involving as it is unfamiliar.

Stephane (Daniel Auteuil) is introduced to us (quite shrewdly given what comes later) via his measured voice-over description not of himself, but of his boss. That would be Maxime (Cesar-winning Andre Dussollier), the hawkishly handsome proprietor of a small but prestigious violin repair service.

Gregarious and sure of himself, Maxime is the firm's Mr. Outside, the man who gains the confidence of the professional musicians and convinces them to trust Stephane, Mr. Inside, with the agonizingly delicate repair of their most precious possessions. Stephane is clearly the more reserved of the two, content, his own words tell us, to remain in the background, living a monkish, almost hermetic existence with only his work for companionship.

The routine of both men's lives is disturbed, however, when the married Maxime tells Stephane he has fallen so rapturously in love with the beautiful young violinist Camille Kessler (Emmanuelle Beart) that he is leaving his wife and moving in with her.

Diffidence itself, Stephane does not really respond at first to his boss's announcement, but gradually, as Camille moves more into Maxime's world, she moves more into his as well. They turn out to not only share a beloved former violin teacher, but also apparently are on a similar psychological wavelength.

Stephane views his growing intimacy with Camille with his usual, almost scientific dispassion, while Camille, also reserved on the surface, becomes increasingly intrigued by Stephane's emotionally removed quality, his seeming ability to live a totally disconnected life. Both seem fascinated with the tentativeness of their attraction, and neither one seems to know what to do about it or even whether, given their emotional patterns and their connections to Maxime, doing anything is even an option.

The outcome of this unlikely romantic triangle is *Coeur en Hiver*'s subject matter, and it is worked out with a kind of full-bodied delicacy and unexpectedness, an embracing of psychological complexity, that is characteristic of the best of Sautet's work. An excursion to some of the wilder shores of love and obsession, this film proves its statement that "feelings can't be demystified" with every scene.

Un Coeur en Hiver is especially fortunate to have Beart and Auteuil (who appeared together in *Manon of the Spring*) as its leads. With sad brown eyes sunk deeply in a poker face, Auteuil has the perfect bearing for Stephane, who is attractive but not handsome, simultaneously distant and self-confident. Beart is equally impressive as a woman whose smoothly classical, almost severe beauty turns out to contain levels of passion that surprise even her.

Exquisite classical music is a major part of *Coeur*'s sensibility, the place where everyone's emotions converge, and listening to it is yet another of the physical pleasures Sautet delights in providing. Beart in fact spent a year learning to play the violin with so much facility that although it is not the actress, but violinist Jean-Jacques Kantorow who performs the exacting Ravel sonatas Camille both rehearses and records, only an expert could be sure. The honesty of this film demanded no less of her, and its success is everyone's reward.

Cronos
1994

Bela Lugosi may have made it look easy, but being one of the undead, *Cronos* insists, is hardly a simple thing. It can be a lonely state, painful but also crazily comic in a charming if grotesque way. It's all on view in this pleasant and spooky film that gives surprising new life, so to speak, to a genre that won't die.

The first feature by twenty-nine-year-old Mexican writer-director Guillermo Del Toro, *Cronos* exemplifies the good things that can happen when adventurous filmmakers choose to investigate traditional forms. Winner of both the Critics Week competition at Cannes and nine Ariels, Mexico's Academy Awards, *Cronos* surprises with its sophisticated and spirited look at a tale straight from the crypt.

The film opens with a prologue detailing the strange history of an alchemist who, fleeing the Spanish Inquisition, came to Veracruz in 1536 and continued working on his plans for a machine that granted eternal life, a machine he called the Cronos Device. Four hundred years later, the alchemist dies in a freak accident, and though his mansion and its contents are sold, no mention was ever made of this device: "As far as anyone knew," a portentous narrator informs, "it never existed."

Existing as well without any knowledge of all this is Jesus Gris (Frederico Luppi), a gray-haired antiques dealer in today's Veracruz, who lives, perhaps too quietly, with his wife (Margarita Isabel) and his mostly silent granddaughter, Aurora (Tamara Shanath).

One day, his attention drawn to a figure of an archangel in his shop, Jesus discovers a wondrous mechanical gold egg inside, an impressively elaborate mechanism that makes a fine, creaky sound when it's wound up—and also does strange and insidious things to its owner once it is fully operational.

Before he can figure out quite how it works, Jesus and the device attract the attention of the sinister De la Guardias, consisting of an Uncle Dieter (Claudio Brook) and a nephew, Angel (Ron Perlman). Though concerned, in one of the film's many oddball touches, with a forthcoming nose job, Angel is basically the muscle, following the orders of his obsessed uncle.

A Howard Hughes type, Dieter lives in a germ-free environment, listening to opera and dreaming of life eternal. Forty years earlier, he had found the Cronos Device's instruction manual, and now he wants the item itself, which, he warns Jesus, should never be used without proper guidance. But Jesus, already addicted to the machine's frightening, hypnotic actions, cannot turn back.

With this as the buildup, *Cronos* goes on to tell the story of how Jesus deals both with the De la Guardias and the device, which, we gradually and deliciously come to understand, is turning him into a vampire.

It is a mark of what makes this old-fashioned story so clever that this realization does manage to sneak up on us. Director Del Toro takes pleasure in turning the familiar horror story inside out, dispensing with the evil vampire of legend and concentrating on how an understandable desire for youth leads an average citizen into decidedly irregular paths.

One of the most characteristic features of *Cronos* is its fondness for over-the-top Grand Guignol scenes that both graphically and comically illustrate the wear and tear of vampiredom, how bad it is for the complexion, for instance, and how grueling and tiring it can be not to die even when circumstances make you wish for it.

Though veteran Latin American star Luppi gives a poignant and amusing performance as a man trapped by his obsession, the real centerpiece of this film is writer-director Del Toro, who has made a droll film out of what is often exploitation material. Edgar Allan Poe with a sense of humor, Del Toro not only has fun mixing genres, he knows how to convey his enjoyment and make the result distinctly his own. With any luck, he'll have a creative life as long as any vampire's.

Del Toro has since made three other unusual films, Mimic, The Devil's Backbone, *and* Hellboy.

Cure

2001

The string of bizarre murders. The master criminal. The stubborn detective testing his will against an evil genius. All the usual genre suspects show up in the haunting and persuasive *Cure,* but this is not the usual psychological thriller. Not even close.

The first film of prolific Japanese director Kiyoshi Kurosawa to be released in this country, *Cure* makes having it both ways look easy and natural. It creates excitement with pulp elements while playing games with genre expectations, pushing at the boundaries of narrative convention—not to mention your mind—while obliquely commenting on the alienating tendencies of modern society. And all without overplaying its hand or doing anything forced.

With perhaps twenty films, including direct-to-video items, to his credit in a career that began in 1983, writer-director Kurosawa (no relation to the more celebrated director Akira Kurosawa) has turned out a beautifully made film, put together with elegance, control, and a confident precision.

Kurosawa also has an eye for casting actors who wholly embody the characteristics he's seeking. For his world-weary detective Takabe, battling with the strangest forces of his career, the director has lured one of Japan's most popular performers, *Shall We Dance*'s Koji Yakusho.

Working with an astute psychologist colleague named Sakuma (Tsuyoshi Ujiki), Takabe is investigating a singular series of murders, highly unusual as much for how the victims are put to death as for the state of mind of the killers. For although each person is executed in the same bizarre way—a huge X slicing them open from throat to chest and cutting their carotid arteries, a technique the film only hints at visually—different people do the attacking every time.

Even more unusual, the killers seem to be completely normal people who suddenly lash out with knives as if that were the most natural thing in the world. Interviewed after the crimes, they describe themselves as "stunned" and act as though they've been somehow removed to a distance from everyday reality.

Gradually, *Cure* directs our attention to a shuffling, nondescript drifter (Masato Hagiwara) who seems lost, disoriented, without memories or a sense of identity or even self as he wanders the city. There's an eeriness about this character in Hagiwara's unsettling performance. He asks disturbing questions, such as "Why am I talking to you?" Wherever he goes, death seems to follow, but his connection with the deaths is not immediately clear.

As he tries to puzzle out the motivations for these crimes, Takabe starts to lose his personal bearings as well. And his wife, it turns out, is running an empty washing machine all day and being quietly overtaken by mental illness. The detective's seemingly normal world starts to present him with troubling characters, such as a man waiting patiently at a cleaners who suddenly starts to mutter horrible obscenities under his breath.

Perhaps what is most distinctive about *Cure* is that, although it solves the crimes, its resolution offers us none of the genuine peace we ordinarily expect, no sense that anything has really been resolved. Can mere knowledge make a difference against pervasive hopelessness? Can the forces of order ever be a fair match for the power of the unconscious? With its gift for infusing uneasiness into every frame, Kurosawa's moody, unnerving film continues to spook us even after the lights have gone on.

The Dinner Game
1999

Americans have barely heard of him, and even the French don't always respect the considerable talents of Francis Veber. As a writer and director, he's had a hand in some of his country's most popular films, including *La Cage aux Folles, La Chevre, Les Comperes,* and *Les Fugitifs* (all of which were remade, often indifferently, by Hollywood), but high-end approval has been lacking at home and abroad. His latest film, *The Dinner Game,* turned things around in France, and it is bound to do the same over here.

Perhaps Veber's best work as a writer-director, *The Dinner Game* was not only the lone domestic film to seriously challenge *Titanic* at the French box office, it was also, and this was a first for him, nominated for six Cesars, the French Oscar, winning three awards, including one for Veber for best script.

Expertly acted by Jacques Villeret, Daniel Prevost (both of whom won Cesars), and Thierry Lhermitte, *The Dinner Game* is a classic French verbal farce in which, inch by imperceptible inch, things get beautifully and hysterically out of control. No one orchestrates this kind of farce with quite the skill of Veber, who without visible effort creates structures as delicate and elaborate as, say, a scale-model Eiffel Tower built completely out of matchsticks.

François Pignon (Villeret) happens to be passionate about such matchstick models. A low-level functionary at the Tax Ministry, he spends nights and weekends working on them and is all too eager to let perfect strangers know it took 37 tubes of glue and 346,472 individual sticks to construct his tower. "And the angle of the matches," he says, his voice rising in excitement, "can't be even a 10th of a degree off."

In the ordinary course of events, Pignon would never socialize with an upper-crust type like publisher Pierre Brochant (Lhermitte, who's made a career of these kinds of narcissistic roles). But Brochant, arrogant yuppie creep that he is, is involved in a snobbish scheme that causes their paths to cross.

The publisher is the moving force behind an idiots' dinner (*Le Diner de Cons* is the film's French title) at which heartless co-conspirators are charged with bringing complete fools to the table so that everyone else can laugh at them behind their backs. Brochant's wife, Christine (Alexandra Vandernoot), thinks the scheme is vicious, but Brochant insists otherwise and feels supremely lucky when "an A-1 idiot" like Pignon crosses his path.

Luck, however, is soon to desert the disdainful publisher. He badly wrenches his back playing golf on the day of the dinner and so irritates his wife that she decides to leave him. It's while he's in this state, unwillingly chained to his apartment and unable to get to the dinner, that the oblivious Pignon comes to call.

Short, chubby, with frizzy hair and a hangdog face that easily gets crestfallen only to irrepressibly bounce back again, Pignon is the most well-meaning of individuals. He'd love to help Brochant, he really would, but he's a world-class blunderer, someone with a gift for doing the worst possible thing at any given moment. The more he tries to assist his new friend, the more devastating, and funnier, the results turn out to be.

Is Brochant's wife gone? Pignon can fix that. Or at least he thinks he can. Is the publisher's mistress (Catherine Frot of *Un Air de*

Famille) also giving him some trouble? *Pas de problem*. One would-be good deed follows another, and soon enough the putative tormentor's life is in so complete a shambles that *Idiot's Revenge* would be an appropriate title.

Putting the situation even more out of control is the appearance of Pignon's great and good friend Cheval (Daniel Prevost, the film's other Cesar winner), who just happens to be the most feared and ferocious tax inspector in France. "He'd audit his own mother," Pignon says admiringly, a sentiment that the horrified and tax-evasive Brochant does not share.

To watch *The Dinner Game*'s principals handle the film's delicious lines and situations with the aplomb of expert jugglers is like watching a master class in farce. This is a delicate style of acting that doesn't get called on much in this country, and though DreamWorks has wisely latched onto the film's remake rights, it's doubtful that anyone anywhere can do this story better justice than is done right here.

Divided We Fall
2001

It's been decades since the great days of the Czech New Wave and incandescent films such as Milos Forman's *Loves of a Blonde,* Jiri Menzel's *Closely Watched Trains,* and Ivan Passer's *Intimate Lighting,* yet watching Jan Hrebejk's *Divided We Fall* brings it all back. Not only is the film that good, it's also that wonderfully, inescapably Czech.

Poignant, humanistic, and irresistibly comic, *Divided We Fall* has that characteristic national ability to distill laughter from painful situations, to maintain a delicate, razor's edge balance of humor, pathos, and potential tragedy. If it hadn't come up against the juggernaut that was *Crouching Tiger, Hidden Dragon,* it would likely have won the best foreign-language Oscar in 2001.

Set during one of the most divisive periods in Czech history, the World War II German occupation, *Divided* is a tale of the moral complications and farcical chaos that result when a couple decides, rather reluctantly, to shelter a Jewish concentration camp escapee in their small apartment.

Though the film has some of the same elements as Roberto Benigni's *Life Is Beautiful,* director Hrebejk and screenwriter Petr Jarchovsky, friends and collaborators since high school, have opted for quite a different tone. This is a comedic film that never oversentimentalizes, where ironies are plentiful yet unforced, and in which characters, even theoretically negative ones, are not denied their humanity or their complexity.

Divided's sharpness is evident from its unusual opening, a trio of abbreviated but to-the-point vignettes set two years apart, each one adding to the back story as well as advancing the narrative in crucial ways.

The first scene, set in 1937 outside an unnamed Czech town, shows a gentle moment involving the three men at the center of the story: David (Csongor Kassai), the son of a wealthy Jewish industrialist; the family chauffeur, Horst (Jaroslav Dusek); and Josef (Boleslav Polivka), the head of the company's sales division.

Next, it's 1939, and David and his parents are forced by the Nazis to abandon their grand house. Then it's 1941, and David and his parents are leaving the spare room in the apartment of Josef and his beautiful wife, Marie (Anna Siskova). (The spare room is intended for the children they cannot have.) The apartment has been the trio's home for two years, and now they're headed for a work facility called Theresienstadt that they hear is quite nice.

The bulk of *Divided* takes place two years later still, in 1943, and starts with the sudden reappearance in town of a fugitive, ghost-like David, a man who looks as if he's returned from the dead and, as an escapee from a concentration camp, almost literally has.

A series of coincidences puts David and his former employee in touch once more, and Josef and Marie agree to hide the hunted man in a secret pantry in their apartment. Not because they're eager to, not because they're stereotypically heroic, but because the other alternatives are even more unpalatable.

It's a decision that is laden with complications, from the silly—Josef, a decent man but a perennial grumbler, is reluctant to give

David his favorite blanket—to the more serious. Horst, the former chauffeur, is not only a powerful and active Nazi collaborator but also a not-so-secret admirer of Marie—and likely to drop by the apartment at the most unexpected and inopportune moments.

It's these complications that lead both to *Divided*'s fine comedy (a classic farce sequence takes place in the couple's bedroom) and its more serious themes, including the inevitability of compromise, the true nature of integrity, and the promise of redemption. "You wouldn't believe," a weary Josef tells David, "what abnormal times can do to normal people," to which David quietly replies, "Yes, I would."

Though its performers are unknown to American audiences, this story is exceptionally well-cast and acted with uniform grace. It's never judgmental, and the film's serious, reserved tone makes its comedy that much funnier and unexpected. In completely mad times, just holding on to your sanity can be an exceptional feat, and this excellent film shows how it's done.

The Dreamlife of Angels
1999

Frank, intimate, touching, with an emotional immediacy that is killing, Erick Zonca's *The Dreamlife of Angels* draws its intensity and feeling from a pair of actresses whose portrait of a troubled friendship is as moving a collaboration as you'll see.

Since the film's Cannes debut, young stars Elodie Bouchez and Natacha Regnier have been showered with honors. They shared the best actress award at the festival, Bouchez won the Cesar (the French version of the Oscar) for best actress, Regnier the Cesar for best new-comer, and the film itself was named France's best of the year.

All this from the assured feature debut of a forty-two-year-old director who has fashioned an empathetic portrait of the kind of aimless outsiders we perhaps pass every day, dispossessed young women living on the fringe of society, trying to construct a life out of the most flimsy material.

Bouchez (already a Cesar-winner for Andre Techine's *Wild Reeds,* and an actress with the most open, enchanting smile) is Isa, a twenty-one-year-old vagabond waif who arrives in the northern French city of Lille with her whole life in a knapsack. Resilient and game for anything, Isa has managed to retain her basically sweet nature despite having to cope with the perils of being on the road.

A chance encounter enables Isa to bluff her way into a job as a sewing machine operator in a clothing factory where Marie (Regnier), a sullen young wildcat with an attitude about everything, already works. Marie is house-sitting a large apartment belonging to a mother and daughter hospitalized after an auto accident, and soon Isa is sharing it with her.

These young women may be the angels of the title, but Zonca, careful not to idealize, doesn't hesitate to portray them as unconcerned instigators and frequent troublemakers who are more pleased with themselves than they have objective reason to be.

Despite the wide difference between Marie's furious stance and Isa's gamin-like simplicity, Zonca prefers, at least at first, to concentrate on what these two have in common. In addition to their shared smug looks, neither young woman is as in control of her life as she imagines, and though they don't realize it, fragility is as much a part of their makeup as toughness.

Marie and Isa also share an unspoken and unacknowledged longing to establish connections, and not necessarily romantic ones, to people outside themselves. The wary, gradual way in which these two become friends is one of *Dreamlife*'s many pleasures, and the astonishment Marie displays at actually having a soul mate is subtly but unmistakably conveyed.

With less of a chip on her shoulder, Isa relaxes completely into her new life. When she finds the journal of the hospitalized young person in whose room she's staying, Isa's search for connection leads her to visit the comatose girl and get tentatively involved in her rehabilitation.

Marie is less accepting of what life offers her. Unlike Isa, she won't think of applying for work as a waitress or walking around with an advertising sandwich board. She enters into a lethargic romance with an overweight but gentle club doorman named Charly (Patrick Mercado), but there is the sense that she is simply marking time, waiting for a prince to rescue her from her self-destructive fury.

Then Marie meets Chris (Gregoire Colin), the self-satisfied son of one of the town's most successful restaurateurs. Marie, who, like many untrusting people, risks falling too hard when she lets her guard down, simultaneously resists Chris and wants him desperately. Her furtive vulnerability turns out, finally, to be more frightening than her hardest edge.

The Dreamlife of Angels focuses on how these outside connections affect Isa and Marie individually and impact their relationship with each other. It's an exceptional rendition of a friendship that holds us by the grace and skill with which it re-creates the very shape and texture of reality.

Zonca, a former actor who co-wrote *Dreamlife*'s script with Roger Bohbot, has an impeccable sense of what's natural and unaffected on screen, so much so that it never seems that what's seen and heard began as words on a page. When Bouchez's and Regnier's honest and unguarded performances, captured in hand-held moments by cinematographer Agnes Godard, are added in, getting drawn into these unfocused, precariously balanced, and heartbreaking lives is all but inevitable.

Dry Cleaning
1999

The thickets of human desire are staples of the movie experience, but *Dry Cleaning,* an exceptional French film, explores them with unusual insight, empathy, and daring. A dark and troubling film that investigates what we accept, what we encourage, and what we finally can't tolerate in our emotional and sexual relationships, *Dry Cleaning* mesmerizes with its ability to be both explicit and ambiguous, candid and restrained.

Dry Cleaning (*Nettoyage a Sec* in French) is the second film for co-writer (with Gilles Taurand) and director Anne Fontaine, and on the surface it couldn't be more different from her debut, the bright and eccentric comedy *Augustin.*

But like that film, *Dry Cleaning* displays a keen sympathy for people who live outside the norm. It deals with extreme situations not with predictable cinematic exaggerations, but with considerable sensitivity and tact.

Fontaine is helped enormously by a cast that includes Charles Berling (*Ridicule*), newcomer Stanislas Merhar, and the luminous Miou-Miou (Bertrand Blier's *Going Places* and Diane Kurys's *Entre Nous,* among others). Perfectly in tune with the director's intentions, these actors, especially Miou-Miou in perhaps the best work of her career, give off a believability that convinces us to follow them down a psychologically winding road.

Berling and Miou-Miou play Jean-Marie and Nicole Kunstler, a hardworking French couple who run a dry-cleaning establishment in the provincial town of Belfort. Living above the store with their young son and Jean-Marie's mother, the Kunstlers seem a contented pair whose labor-intensive work rarely allows them the luxury of time off.

On one of those rare nights out, Jean-Marie and Nicole visit a gay nightclub where they enjoy an intoxicating drag number by a two-person ensemble called the "Queens of the Night." The next day, handsome young Loic (Merhar, who won a Cesar for best new actor for his performance) brings his unmistakable Queens costume into their shop for cleaning. "I've heard," he says, almost reflexively flirting with both husband and wife, "you do miracles."

Loic and his sister Marilyn (Mathilde Seigner) are the two halves of the Queens, and the first sign that their presence in the lives of Jean-Marie and Nicole will have an invigorating effect on the married couple's sex life is when Jean-Marie surprises his wife by trying on Loic's costume, which leads to a bout of passionate lovemaking.

Sexually active and a bit mercenary, Loic and his sister try to loosen their new friends up, but in addition to attraction, there is also resistance. Still, when the Queens move on to another city, the husband and wife feel compelled, without ever acknowledging why, to take a rare vacation to catch their show.

That visit leads to an intensifying and increasingly complicated relationship between the angelic, androgynous-looking young man and both husband and wife, a tripartite relationship that is far more complex and unexpected than the conventional plotting would have you imagine.

Initially, of course, there is the frisson, the whiff of excitement that clings to the danger of crossing the boundaries that separate the conventional from the forbidden, and what takes place in *Dry Cleaning* adroitly tantalizes the audience as much as its characters.

But passions aroused can have a darker side, and the more intimately the couple gets involved with Loic, the more the relationship reveals fissures in their marriage and in their lives. The question becomes not only whether they can go back to square one, but whether they even want to.

As an intimate examination of the consequences of first exposing and then attempting to gratify longings that have remained well-lhidden, this film is a knockout. As it builds toward an almost unbearable climax, *Dry Cleaning* reminds us that sometimes getting what we want, or even what we need, is only the beginning of the story.

Eat Drink Man Woman
1994

By all means, see *Eat Drink Man Woman,* but not on an empty stomach. Filled with spectacular Chinese dishes, this wise and rueful romantic comedy about those unavoidable human desires, food and sex, looks tasty enough to incite a monk to abandon the simple life.

The latest work from director Ang Lee (who co-wrote the script with Hui-Ling Wang and James Schmaus), *Eat Drink* shares an empathetic sensibility with Lee's Oscar-nominated hit, *The Wedding Banquet.* A look at the intertwined lives of a father and his three live-at-home daughters, this is more than anything a personal-scaled film, funny, emotional, and compassionate about the human comedy, Taiwan-style.

For unlike the New York–based *Wedding Banquet, Eat Drink* is set in Taipei, Taiwan's capital, an upscale, up-to-date metropolis where young women often have Western names, such as Sophia and Rachel, and are comfortable in both miniskirts and Buddhist temples.

The three beautiful sisters in *Eat Drink,* however, all have traditional Chinese names, because their father, Master Chu (*The Wedding Banquet*'s father, Sihung Lung), is a believer in the old ways.

A wizardly chef, perhaps the greatest in Taipei, Chu is crusty and brusque but a national treasure behind the stove. *Eat Drink* opens with an engaging sequence where the great man, chopping, slicing, and dicing like a Veg-o-Matic gone wild, prepares a series of knockout dishes.

It looks like the feast of a lifetime (and in fact *Eat Drink* utilized three master chefs full-time, plus several consulting food specialists), but Chu does this every Sunday for his daughters, who, not surprisingly, are tired of the fuss.

Referring to the meal as "the Sunday dinner torture ritual," they spend most of it bickering with each other and their father, who has been a widower for so long he can't accept that his children are all grown women.

The daughters, for their parts, though old enough to be out on their own, stay at home partly for financial reasons but also because their desire for independence is balanced by the Chinese tradition of filial responsibility, the desire to give their father, irritating though he is, the respect and attention his position as head of the family merits.

Most likely to leave first is middle daughter Jia-Chien (Chien-Lien Wu), a career-oriented executive with a Taiwanese airline. Still involved sexually with an ex-boyfriend but with her eye on a married co-worker (Winston Chao, the co-star of *Wedding Banquet*), she is eager to move into an about-to-open condominium complex known as the Paris of the East.

Most likely to be stuck taking care of Chu (and not particularly pleased about it) is eldest daughter Jia-Jen (Kuei-Mei Yang), a serious Christian who teaches chemistry at an all-boys high school. Still fixated on her long-gone first boyfriend, she can't help but notice the school's muscular new volleyball coach.

Not even thinking about romance is Jia-Ning (Yu-Wen Wang), the twenty-year-old baby of the family who works behind the counter at Wendy's and amuses herself by chatting up a co-worker's Dostoyevsky-reading boyfriend, whose credo is "Love is suffering."

As for Chu, when the master chef is not performing emergency culinary rescues at elaborate hotel banquets, he relaxes by cooking tasty lunches for the grade-school daughter of a neighbor (top Taiwanese star Sylvia Chang) who is involved in a messy divorce.

Eat Drink cuts back and forth between the daughters' interactions with each other, their father, and the other men around them, watching with fond but clear-eyed sympathy as they cope with the confusions and misapprehensions of their lives.

Like a Chinese banquet—something that all but the most resolute will become hungry for as they watch this movie—*Eat Drink Man Woman* is a leisurely affair, not in any hurry to dole out its amusing surprises or to resolve its conflicts.

This is a film that trusts us not to get impatient—and also trusts us to appreciate the humor and poignancy in its situations without having to be force-fed (so to speak). Though it is only Ang Lee's third feature, it is a strikingly confident one, and viewers will be understandably eager for the next course to appear.

Lee's later films include the Chinese language blockbuster Crouching Tiger, Hidden Dragon, *but this earlier effort remains perhaps his most charming.*

The Fast Runner
2002

The Fast Runner (*Atanarjuat*) is the cinematic equivalent of adventure travel. Nearly three hours long, and deliberately paced at that, this first feature ever in the Inuit language is a demanding experience. But the rewards for those who risk the journey are simply extraordinary.

The Fast Runner does more than use a rarely heard language, does more than cast a spell with its mind-expanding panoramas. The film deposits you deep within the compelling, unfamiliar culture of the native people of the Arctic North. And it tells a story of elemental passions, a mythic tale of courage and mendacity, of undying love and corrosive lust that can't help but hold our interest.

The society of the Inuit (the word means "a man, preeminently") has fascinated those in more hospitable climes at least since Robert Flaherty's 1922 *Nanook of the North* and *Kabloona,* Gontran de Poncins's marvelous 1941 memoir of what was then called Eskimo life. But it's never before been presented from the inside and in so persuasive a way. The film deservedly won the Camera d'Or for best first feature at Cannes and six Genies, the Canadian Oscar, including best picture and best director.

Although this is the first feature for director Zacharias Kunuk, he has since 1990 had his own television and video production company, based in the 1,200-person hamlet of Igloolik in Canada's Nunavut Territory, where this film was shot. And the venerable nature of *The Fast Runner*'s story, an oral narrative forever in the heads and on the lips of his people, has given the production a confidence and assurance unusual for a first-timer from a culture without a filmmaking tradition.

Paul Apak Angilirq, *The Fast Runner*'s screenwriter, had eight elders tell him their versions of this ancient Inuit story, which is set in an indefinite past when Europeans were not even a rumor, when spirits could take physical form, and when men who were to become myths were still merely human.

The Fast Runner's story of the pervasiveness of evil and the power of taboos begins when a malignant shaman visits a small Inuit clan and infects it with dissension and death. As a result, the clan chief is murdered. "It just happened," someone explains, baffled, powerless, "and we had to live with it."

Because at first glance the film's characters dress alike and resemble one another, and because the beginning of the story unfolds in a deliberately fractured way, the opening sections of *The Fast Runner* are as confusing as things would be if we personally found ourselves in that foreign a situation. And Kunuk's unhurried pacing, his decision to duplicate the temporal rhythms of Inuit culture, makes a willingness to give yourself over to the experience on its own terms essential.

But just as travelers acclimate to strange surroundings, less than an hour into the film everything comes into focus, and the story, which now remains in a single period with well-defined characters, gets increasingly involving.

At its heart, this is about two brothers with great powers. Amaqjuaa (Pakak Innukshuk) is the older and stronger, but Atanarjuat (Natar Ungalaaq), the title character, is the fleeter of foot. Atanarjuat and Atuat (Sylvia Ivalu) fall in love, but she is promised in marriage to the sullen Oki (Peter-Henry Arnatsiaq), son of the clan's evil leader. Complicating things even more is that Oki's sister, the fey Puja (Lucy Tulugarjuk), has eyes only for the fast runner. As Norman Cohn, the film's cinematographer, said, "The film is about love, jealousy, murder and revenge. What else is there?"

Actually, there is a good deal more, starting with Cohn's compelling cinematography. Though *The Fast Runner* was shot on widescreen digital video (then transferred to 35 millimeter), the images are nevertheless truly breathtaking—pictures that also tell the indelible story of what it feels like to be frail humans in an immense natural world. And the film's signature sequence, Atanarjuat running naked across the snow with his life in jeopardy, is simply a knockout.

The Fast Runner has paid equal attention to painstakingly constructing the physical world its people live in and creating a living record of a culture that's threatened with extinction. Not just tools and clothes, but also songs and dances, bawdy customs, and deadly serious rituals—ways of being in the world—are vividly reproduced.

Because the story, performers, and landscape are so unfamiliar, everything combines in *The Fast Runner* to create a film that does not feel acted but rather as if it were simply happening in front of our eyes. This is so much the case that, when the closing credits are run next to documentary shots of the film's crew at work, it comes as a shock to see how the artifice was put together.

At the film's beginning, one of the tellers of this tale says, "I can only sing this song to someone who understands it." What's special about *The Fast Runner* is that by its epic close, that select group includes us.

How I Killed My Father
2002

For Jean-Luc Borde, a successful gerontologist who's practiced in affluent Versailles for ten years, it is the crowning night of his career. The town's elite have come to his luxurious home to award him the coveted Order of Merit at an elaborate party hosted by his elegant wife, Isa. "I was like an orphan," he tells the crowd, "and you adopted me."

It is a telling choice of words. For the doctor's father, in fact, abruptly abandoned Jean-Luc and his brother decades before, disappearing to Africa without a word of explanation. And in the central conceit of Anne Fontaine's penetrating and emotionally complex *How I Killed My Father,* that absentee parent has somehow chosen that special night to unexpectedly return to his sons' lives.

Fontaine's film may have a thriller title reminiscent of *I Wake Up Screaming* and *Kiss the Blood Off My Hands,* but its interest is in the psychological more than the literal aspects of its name. Still, there is a palpable air of tension and suspense about this insightful film, a realization that the greatest and most provocative mystery of all is the human soul.

In this respect, *How I Killed* resembles director Fontaine's earlier exploration of the tangled complications of interpersonal relationships, *Dry Cleaning,* which focused, with her trademark combination of empathy and evenhandedness, on the effect a charismatic transvestite has on the lives of a married couple.

Here, working with top French screenwriter Jacques Fieschi and an exceptional cast (including Charles Berling as Jean-Luc and Natacha Regnier, a world apart from her breakthrough role in *The Dreamlife of Angels,* as Isa), Fontaine has made an even greater success. Alive to nuance, unafraid of the intricate implications of emotional situations, she's made a compelling exploration of the unfinished business between fathers and sons, of the lasting influence parents have over children even if neither side wants it to be that way.

As with *Dry Cleaning,* Fontaine and her collaborator have come up with a singular central character with a forceful, yet enigmatic

nature. Brilliantly played by the veteran Michel Bouquet, a star of theater and film for more than forty-five years, Jean-Luc's father, Maurice, by his very nature sets off disturbances in the field from the
moment he arrives. He puts pressures, perhaps unintentionally, on
preexisting fissures in his son's life, ensuring without necessarily trying to that what's been papered over becomes exposed.

Maurice and Jean-Luc not only look like father and son, they have
other similarities, starting with the profession of medicine, though
Maurice's work in impoverished Africa couldn't be more different
than the kind of ultra-bourgeois, Botox-intensive practice that has
made Jean-Luc wealthy. The main similarity between the two men,
however, is the combination of wariness and strained formality with
which they treat each other, the barbed remarks they exchange, the
chill in the air that is always between them.

Certainly Maurice (and this is one of the gifts of Bouquet's performance) has an unknowability and impenetrability about him, characterized by an enigmatic half grin that can be infuriating. Maurice is
completely imperturbable, without the slightest interest in apologiz-
ing for, justifying, or even explaining the desertion of his family. Even
in his seventies, there is a dangerous presence about the man, the
sense that every remark he makes is a move in an elaborate chess
game in which he holds an unfair advantage.

Yet Maurice also has a kind of appeal that even Jean-Luc can't
deny. "If I met him by chance," he tells Isa, "I'd have fallen for his
charm." Which, gradually, is what those closest to Jean-Luc do, especially his wife. Even his brother, Patrick (Stephane Guillon), a ne'er-
do-well who works as Jean-Luc's chauffeur while moonlighting as a
stand-up comic, is not immune. This even though Patrick was initially so hostile to his father for leaving when he was but four that he
refused to so much as be in the same room with him.

For Jean-Luc, things are different. With his withdrawn, watchful
intelligence and an anger that lurks coiled under his placid surface, he
is still furious at his father, so much so that he seems almost to have
changed places with him, to have inherited the very traits that disturbed him most as a child. When Jean-Luc tells Isa that "he has eyes

like ice, he judges you calmly, down to the bone," he could be talking about himself as much as Maurice.

One of the most gratifying aspects of *How I Killed My Father* is that it couldn't be less interested in taking sides in this primal conflict. As the film's characters head into uncharted, inevitably explosive emotional territory against the backdrop of Jocelyn Pook's unnerving music, you can feel director/co-writer Fontaine's intelligence probing and illuminating this high-tension, high-stakes situation. Truly, there can be nothing as complex as the most basic human relationships, and nothing as satisfying as a film that understands that as this one does.

Intacto
2002

Everyone knows what it is to be lucky, but what exactly does being lucky mean? Is it simply a matter of chance, or are there other factors, as unusual and unnerving as they are unknown, clandestinely at work?

What if, just for argument's sake, luck was something quantifiable, a commodity that could be traded, gambled away, even stolen? What if luck were a gift that could be discovered and maximized or, just as easily, deactivated? What if good luck for you meant bad luck for someone else? Even scarier, what if other people could bet with your luck without your knowledge, risking the entire course of your life in the process?

The spooky Spanish film *Intacto* takes these questions and concepts and turns them into a sharp brainteaser of a film, a compelling mind game you compulsively play along with. Think of *The Hustler* in a *Twilight Zone* setting and you'll have an idea of the territory director Juan Carlos Fresnadillo and his co-writer, Andrés M. Koppel, are getting into.

Fresnadillo, who won the Goya, his country's Oscar, for best new director with this, his debut film, is one of a group of Spanish filmmakers, including Alejandro Amenabar of *Abre los Ojos,* who have a gift for contemporary fantasy, for making supernatural thrillers of the everyday that posit that the world is stranger than we can possibly know, that odd forces are at play and just out of reach of our understanding.

The director was helped in this by a well-chosen cast and a cinematographer (Xavier Gimenez) able to craft a clean, matter-of-fact style that is the ideal counterpoint to the strange dramatic situation. "He was able to create a realistic look that also had the quality of fable," explained Fresnadillo, who for his part added a strong sense of narrative that propels the film from event to mysterious event.

The emotional center of *Intacto* is Samuel Berg (persuasively played by Max von Sydow), otherwise known as the king of luck or the god of chance. He's a concentration camp survivor who lives in the antiseptic bunker of a gambling casino located on a blasted lava field (shot in the director's Canary Islands homeland), and no one has ever had more control over luck than he. Even Berg's top lieutenant and protégé, Federico (Eusebio Poncela), who lived through a destructive earthquake, discovers he cannot leave the man and take his good fortune with him.

Banished from the kingdom, Federico devotes himself to finding a protégé of his own, someone he can match against the king. He thinks he's found him when he comes across Tomas (Leonardo Sbaraglia), the only person to come out intact (hence the film's title) after a plane crash that claimed 237 others.

Federico introduces Tomas to the bizarre world of clandestine gambling based on luck, a disturbing subculture that involves peculiar contests of chance, such as running blindfolded but full speed through a forest heavy with trees. It's an undeniably creepy world, but as presented here a completely convincing one.

Complicating Federico's quest is the fact that Tomas turns out to be a fugitive bank robber actively pursued by the law. Causing more difficulties is that Sara (Mónica López), the policewoman chasing Tomas, is another one of these preternaturally fortunate individuals with luck to burn.

Co-writer/director Fresnadillo, it turns out, has been thinking about this film since he was nine, when, completely by chance, he witnessed the aftermath of a horrific 1977 Canary Islands plane crash that killed 578 people. "I think it was that exact moment," he says, "that gave birth to *Intacto*."

Because it is so smart and so carefully worked out, *Intacto* can be a bit hard to follow at times, but the effort it takes to understand what's happening is well worth it. We may not be quite sure from moment to moment where the narrative is going, who's playing who for a fool, and why, but we always care, and that is saying a lot.

In the Mood for Love
2001

Given that it settled on a title scant days before its world premiere at Cannes, *In the Mood for Love* is remarkably well-named. A swooningly cinematic exploration of romantic longing, both restrained and sensual, luxuriating in color, texture, and sound, this film raises its fascination with enveloping atmosphere and suppressed emotion to a ravishing, almost hypnotic level.

With Hong Kong stars Tony Leung Chiu-wai and Maggie Cheung playing a couple caught in a vortex of quiet passion, *In the Mood for Love* will likely be the breakthrough work for that city's celebrated writer-director Wong Kar-wai, an international critical favorite whose previous films, including *Days of Being Wild* and *Chungking Express,* have had limited exposure in this country.

This time, however, the conventional nature of the material—a love story that is not only set in Hong Kong in 1962, but is PG-chaste enough to have been filmed then and there—makes it easier to appreciate the visual assurance and provocative, intimate directing style that have made all seven of Wong's films major award-winners. (At Cannes, *In the Mood* received the Grand Prix de la Technique for its exceptional look and also took the best actor award for Leung.)

Married, but not to each other, Chow Mo-wan (Leung) and Su Li-zhen (Cheung) meet when they rent adjacent apartments. His wife has the late shift as a hotel receptionist, while her husband, Mr. Chan, works for a Japanese company and is often away on business, which means that no one, including the audience, gets more than a fleeting glimpse of either spouse.

Both these people are quiet, considerate, exquisitely polite, and much less boisterous than their landlord's extended family. Earnest and boyish, with carefully slicked-down hair, Mr. Chow works as a journalist, but with his anonymous suit and tie, he could be any kind of businessman. Mrs. Chan, however, would stand out anywhere.

Poised and impeccably turned out, with never so much as a hair out of place, Mrs. Chan has the ability to stop your heart just by walking from her room to a neighborhood take-out stand with a combination of grace and loneliness that seems almost tragic. As costumed by William Chang Suk-ping, she dresses in nothing but cheongsams, more than twenty in a wonderful variety of fabrics, giving the traditional high-necked sheath once popular in Shanghai more screen time than it's had since *The World of Suzie Wong*. Even her neighbors are impressed. "She dresses up like that," one of them says, "to go out for noodles."

Ever so gradually, as hints mount and their paths cross on the way to forlorn take-out dinners, Mr. Chow and Mrs. Chan come to realize that not only are both their spouses having an affair, but they're having it with each other. This naturally brings these two closer, but because they are innately decent people and still care for their partners, how involved they will allow themselves to become turns into a potent, disruptive question with surprising emotional pull.

Essential in giving their quandary its due is the director's choice of visual styles. Working with two cameramen, his regular director of photography, Christopher Doyle, and Mark Li Pingbin, who usually films for Taiwanese director Hou Hsiao-Hsien, Wong Kar-wai turns his lens into a visual eavesdropper, peering around corners and looking at things from covert angles, the better to emphasize both the confining, restrictive nature of the characters' lives—"One can't put a foot wrong," Mrs. Chan wails—and the potentially illicit nature of their relationship.

Adding to the superb sense of ambience is the film's alluring use of muted yet vivid color. With sublime production design (once again William Chang, who also edited the film), *In the Mood* is a dream of complementary pastels, with window blinds, wallpaper, kitchen appliances, shower curtains, even telephones all part of a rapturous color scheme. The melancholy, insinuating music by Michael Galasso and Umebayashi Shigeru enhances the mood, as do some artful examples of Nat King Cole singing in especially haunting Spanish.

Though Wong began in films as a screenwriter, as a director he is known not to believe in scripting anything until the very last minute. This method isn't usually very successful, but in this case, because his stars have worked several times both with him and with each other, a surprising amount of intimacy is achieved. The result is a kind of ultimate romantic film, joining an almost Jamesian sadness and discipline to that extraordinary visual sensibility. It's not the kind of thing you see every day.

Italian for Beginners
2002

It gets, in case you hadn't noticed, awfully cold and bleak in Copenhagen in the winter, and the Danes, who definitely have noticed, often escape in thoughts of Italy, a place that symbolizes passion, romance, and several kinds of warmth.

Sometimes they even try to learn the language, which is where *Italian for Beginners,* a completely charming romantic comedy, enters the picture.

A delicious and delicately funny look at the residents of a Copenhagen neighborhood coping with the befuddling complications life tosses at them, *Italian for Beginners* won a Silver Bear and other awards at Berlin, where it was much talked about for being the first picture made in the cinema verité Dogma style to be written and directed by a woman, Lone Scherfig.

None of this, however, matters as much as how expertly Scherfig has molded her characters and constructed her plot, which is laden with crafty complications and unexpected catastrophes but is so well put together you never notice how much work has gone into it.

Like its fellow Scandinavian production, Sweden's *Together, Italian for Beginners* is a textured comedy, not afraid to season its humor with anger, mortality, and unapologetically bleak moments.

It's a film that recognizes the laughter and sorrow of a question such as "How soon after someone dies can you fall in love?" And it's a film that manages, without making a fuss, to make points about the nature of faith, the difficulty of parents, even the consequences of fetal alcohol syndrome.

More than anything, however, *Italian for Beginners* is about falling in love. It focuses on six individuals, none of whom is particularly adept at romance, which they approach in different ways and at different speeds. Most of all, these are people who understand the truth of Pastor Andreas's remark: "It is in loneliness that God seems farthest away."

The pastor (Anders W. Berthelsen) knows this as much as anyone. A young and very recent widower, he arrives in town to replace a cranky older colleague who got so out of hand he threw the church organist off a balcony and still hangs around to heckle Andreas's sermons. The new pastor is told that a community center class in conversational Italian might help pass the time, so he goes.

Already attending are two men who work at the hotel Andreas is living in. Jorgen Mortensen (Peter Gantzler), who manages the place, is a quiet, diffident man with serious romantic difficulties, and his best friend, Hal-Finn (Lars Kaalund), is an abrasive lout who runs the hotel's sports bar and systematically abuses his customers.

Hal-Finn became passionate about the language after an Italian soccer team made his bar its local hangout. Not needing language lessons, at least not in Italian, is the sports bar's young and beautiful Italian waitress, Giulia (Sara Indrio Jensen).

Two other women end up at the classes. Karen (Ann Eleonora Jorgensen) runs a hair salon and has no end of trouble with her failing alcoholic mother. Olympia (Anette Stovelbaek) works at a bakery while dodging the wrath of her intemperate father. Her longevity at the shop is open to question, however; incorrigibly clumsy, she's had forty-three jobs since she left high school.

As even these thumbnail sketches indicate, the great thing about

Italian for Beginners is that all of its people are completely and unmistakably individual. This is a film that likes and is intrigued by its characters, that allows them to be eccentric, funnier than they realize, and very much themselves.

"I think that life is about comedy and melancholy," writer-director Scherfig has said, and *Italian for Beginners* shows what an irresistible blend that can be.

Lamerica
1996

Lamerica is a miracle, a reason to believe. Dramatic, intelligent, insightful, and ambitious, this exceptionally moving film is strong enough to rank with the masterworks of Italy's cinema. In a movie culture that increasingly believes that box office is the sole test of greatness, it is both chastening and heartening to encounter the real thing.

The film's always-human story touches delicately but tellingly on questions of personal and national identity, on the immigrant's desire to better himself elsewhere and the stranger's parallel passion to return home. Its title, an unlettered reference to the United States, is as much metaphor as anything else, an allusion to the fabled place of dreams that is, finally, as elusive as El Dorado.

Lamerica is only the third theatrical feature (the first, *Open Doors,* was Oscar-nominated, and the second, *Stolen Children,* won the Grand Jury Prize at Cannes) for director Gianni Amelio, a quiet but forceful filmmaker whose natural empathy with his characters and adept use of nonprofessional actors places him directly in the Italian neo-realistic tradition.

Like *Stolen Children,* which followed a carabiniere as he escorted a child prostitute and her brother across Italy to a new home, *Lamerica* uses the device of a geographical journey to move characters on unexpected voyages of interior discovery.

And with *Lamerica,* the director himself took a journey, for this film is entirely shot in Albania, just 70 miles across the Adriatic from Italy's boot. Perennially impoverished, Albania, as shown in old newsreel footage that runs alongside *Lamerica*'s opening credits, was invaded by Italy in 1939 and forced into an unequal political union "in the name of fascism."

In 1991, the year in which *Lamerica* is set, a new pair of opposing invasions is taking place. On the one hand, thousands of Albanians, desperate to improve their lot, are pouring into Italian port cities, intent on fleeing over the water to the earthly paradise they've glimpsed on TV.

Coming into Albania from Italy, on the other hand, are exploiters looking to make a profit out of the country's desperation and naïveté. Fiore and his young partner, Gino (Michele Placido and Enrico Lo Verso, respectively, the film's only professional actors), are practiced and prosperous deceivers who are looking to set up a dummy corporation that will take advantage of the Albanians while bilking money from the Italian government.

Arrogant about their wealth and contemptuous of the desperate locals, Fiore and Gino need a docile Albanian figurehead for their board of directors. In the disease-ridden ruins of a former prison camp, they come across their ideal man: Spiro Tozai (Carmelo Di Mazzarelli).

Encrusted with the misery of half a century in detention, Spiro has so lost touch with reality that he thinks he's twenty years old. Incontinent, unwilling to speak, possibly feeble-minded, Spiro is capable only of signing his name, which is all the Italians care about.

Fiore heads back to Italy, which means that Gino is left alone when a crisis occurs. Spiro is needed to sign more papers, but the old man has precipitously fled from the orphanage where he's been incongruously warehoused, and Gino, much against his will, has to head out into Albania proper to find him.

It's a journey into a world of unimaginable chaos that, like a bog, sucks Gino in deeper and deeper, involving him in complex and unforeseen emotional situations. With his illusions and his bravado gradually peeled off the way the wheels are stripped from his expensive car, Gino is forced to confront the implications of his own and his country's history and culture when he discovers that Spiro Tozai has a voice after all.

Enrico Lo Verso, who starred in *La Scorta* and *Farinelli* as well as playing the wistful carabiniere in *Stolen Children,* is an ideal actor for director Amelio's aims. With soft, pouting lips and sad eyes, he has a face to which emotional confusion comes easily, a face that can make the transition from arrogance to uncertainty believable.

The wonder of this film, however, is eighty-year-old Carmelo Di Mazzarelli, a retired fisherman Amelio met by chance on a pier. With no previous acting experience, Di Mazzarelli has, in the tradition of neo-realism, been able to give a performance that seems to go beyond acting to convey something essential about the human spirit.

As much as any of the actors, Albania and its people are critical to *Lamerica*'s success. Amelio has a particular gift for faces and types, picking images—such as a tiny girl doing slick hip-hop dance moves in a ruined hotel—that are indelible. It's only one of the many things to marvel at in this unforgettable film.

Leolo
1993

Nothing describes *Leolo,* nothing does it justice. It's a film you feel more than analyze, a movie that makes emotional rather than literal sense. And though it is as intoxicated with language as it is with images, *Leolo* comes from such a deep connection between memory and the subconscious that it resists tidy summation. A film without boundaries, a fever dream of imagination, poetry, and love, it simply must be seen.

Everything about *Leolo* turns out to be the opposite of what you might expect. Its territory, that of the coming of age of a sensitive, artistic boy in an unforgiving environment, is chronically overused and prone to teary sentimentality. But *Leolo*'s writer-director, Jean-Claude Lauzon, has turned his film into an assault, filling it with piti-less, profane images and offensive situations that can't help but make you squirm.

But think of *Leolo* as a barbaric attack on delicate sensibilities and you will be wrong once again. For French-Canadian Lauzon, who says this film is in large part based on his own childhood, has marvelously suffused the madness and the squalid desperation with the all-accepting warmth of remembered experience. By uniting formidable technical skill with intensely held, intuitive feelings, Lauzon reaches a pitch of emotional fervor that induces us to experience the rages, fears, hopes, and pleasures of childhood all over again.

Leolo initially was subtitled "Because I Dream," and that phrase defines its theme as well as anything. Its twelve-year-old protagonist (Maxime Collin), growing up in the mundane decay of Montreal's tough Mile End neighborhood, says, early on, "People who trust only their own truth call me Leo Lozeau. Because I dream, I am not."

Instead, Leo imagines he is really Leolo Lozone, a miniature Italian who ends up being born in Montreal after his mother, in an especially boggling sequence, makes accidental contact with a sperm-laden Sicilian tomato. With a life sandwiched between two sisters who move in and out of mental hospitals, an obsessive bodybuilder of an older brother, and a brutish, packhorse father who is remarkably involved in the regular bowel movements of his offspring, it is no wonder that Leolo dreams. And his dreams focus on the power of writing, on passionately believing "there was a secret in words strung together."

Getting hold of the house's sole book, Leolo ritualistically dons hat and mittens to read it late at night by the chilly light of the refrigerator. And he writes. Continually, compulsively, for no practical reason, not even bothering to save the pages, he commits to paper his heightened, poetic reflections, overflowing with emotion and insight. Only the mysterious Word Tamer, an almost mythological literary scavenger, created by Lauzon as a tribute to the real-life teacher who rescued him, appreciates what the boy is writing, but the Word Tamer is powerless to help him change his life.

As read by a cultivated adult voice (and exceptionally well subtitled), Leolo's writings set an assured, polished verbal tone that counterpoints the rawness of the savage atmosphere in which he lives. For this film is definitely not decorous, well-behaved, or suitable for children. It circles again and again, sometimes elegiacally, sometimes with taunting brutality, sometimes with unexpected humor, around the same key events and personages in a small boy's life.

There is Leolo's bulked-up older brother, Ferdinand, whom "fear had given a reason for living," turning him into a bodybuilder following a humiliating encounter with a cocky local bully. His sister, Queen Rita, curator of an insect collection, is lulled into tranquillity by the sound of dozens of wings. His mother, enormous in a series of gargantuan house dresses, is the only sane person in the family, with "the strength of a frigate plowing through troubled waters." And, finally, there is the boy's muddled grandfather (veteran French actor Julien Guiomar), the cause of the family's insanity as well as Leolo's rival for the smiles and favors of their lovely Sicilian neighbor, Bianca (Giuditta Del Vecchio), Leolo's Italian fantasy.

Because Lauzon remembered this story so exactly, because the emotions were as vivid for him as they would have been if it all had just happened, he was able to effectively use nonprofessional actors in several key roles. Surprisingly strong for their lack of experience are Yves Montmarquette, one of Montreal's top bodybuilders, as Ferdinand, and Pierre Bourgault, a political journalist and force for Quebec independence, as the Word Tamer. And Ginette Reno, in real life the queen of Quebec's pop singers, embraces the role of Leolo's mother with impressive results.

Though *Leolo* was only Lauzon's second feature (his first, an offbeat thriller called *Night Zoo*, won an unprecedented thirteen Genies, the Canadian Academy Award), he worked consistently on commercials in Montreal and had the eye to prove it. His arresting, unsettling images always fascinate, and in some cases they arrive so directly from an uncompromising dream world that they reduce us to sighs of wonder.

The same can be said for *Leolo*'s splendid, eclectic soundtrack, which Lauzon had set in his mind before he began to write the script. Using everything from Tom Waits and the Rolling Stones to music from Arabia, Argentina, and Tibet, it is yet one more element that pulls you deeper and deeper into Lauzon's very particular and yet uncannily universal story. For the wonder of *Leolo* is that in his passion to tell his own personal truth, Lauzon ended up telling everyone else's as well.

Lauzon, perhaps the most prodigiously gifted of Canadian filmmakers, did not live to make a third feature. He died on the way home from a hunting expedition when the small plane he was piloting crashed in the Canadian north.

Lumumba
2001

Lumumba is potent stuff. Complex, powerful, intensely dramatic, its compelling depiction of an African political tragedy echoes Woodrow Wilson's apocryphal remark about a very different film: "It is like writing history with lightning." The tragedy is not only that of Patrice Lumumba, a man whose career had the trajectory of a skyrocket. He was not yet thirty-five when he became the first prime minister of the newly independent Congo in June 1960 and one of the continent's most promising and charismatic leaders. Two months later, he was out of power; six months after that, he was dead. It was a calamity for his country and for Africa's place in the world.

These events happened forty years ago, but *Lumumba*'s realistic style has infused them with a driving urgency and immediacy. Though born in Haiti, director Raoul Peck (who wrote the script with Pascal Bonitzer) knows the Congo well: He spent part of his childhood there and made a prizewinning documentary on Lumumba.

In Eriq Ebouaney, Peck has found the ideal actor to play the French-speaking Congolese leader. Ebouaney's Lumumba is an intensely magnetic individual, a mesmerizing speaker with an exceptionally forceful personality. It's a riveting performance, one that makes everything that happens persuasive and believable.

Given that it was done with the cooperation of Lumumba's family, it's not surprising that the film's portrait is respectful and admiring. But *Lumumba* doesn't hesitate to show the man's confrontational self-confidence, his intransigent insistence on saying the truths he felt needed to be said no matter what the consequences. Some of the film's most dramatic moments turn out to have happened just as depicted on screen.

It is another of *Lumumba*'s virtues that it acknowledges that the Congo situation was too complex for either cardboard saints or convenient villains. What happened can't be entirely chalked up to one individual's characteristics, to the maneuvers of Congolese adversaries, or to the regrettable Cold War machinations of the United States. The awful legacy of colonialism, it turned out, was too overwhelming to be immediately overturned by the stroke of a pen.

Some of that baggage is hinted at in the vintage photographs displayed under the opening credits, snapshots that only touch the surface of the horrific atrocities that took place during the decades when the Congo was not the standard colony but the personal property of Belgium's King Leopold II.

Lumumba begins at the end of the man's history, with the deposed prime minister, handcuffed in the back of a car, being driven to his execution site. The rest of the film plays as a kind of extended flashback, a beyond-the-grave letter to Lumumba's wife detailing his life, his death, and the pains his enemies took to dispose of his corpse. "Even dead I was a threat to them," the victim says. *Lumumba* unaccountably (and initially confusingly) skips the start of the future prime minister's drive for his country's independence and his founding of the Congolese National Movement party. Rather, it picks up his life as a convincing salesman for Polar Beer in the capital city of Leopoldville.

Lumumba's political activity puts him in contact with quiet journalist Joseph Mobutu (Alex Descas), nobody's pick to be the country's future dictator. Lumumba is imprisoned for his political activity but is freed to go to Brussels and participate in a Belgian round table on the Congo's future.

Aside from his drive and charisma, what set Lumumba apart from his main rivals—veteran politico Joseph Kasavubu and Moise Tshombe, mineral-rich Katanga province's strongman—was his vision of a unified Congo. While others wanted a weak federation, Lumumba was passionate about a single Congo that he hoped would rise above tribalism's petty rivalries.

Agreeing in a political compromise to be prime minister (Kasavubu would be president), Lumumba was faced with problems as soon as independence was declared, problems that were inevitable because of the Belgians' refusal to train native Congolese for management positions. Unhappy with its white officers, the army began rioting. Katanga province seceded, and the Belgians began looking for the first opportunity to intervene with troops and run the country again. This, above all else, Lumumba could not abide, and his courage and iron convictions helped pave the way for his downfall.

Overmatched by history, with a vision for his country that the international community did not share, Lumumba was more doomed than he knew. "I came fifty years too soon," the film has him say, adding: "History will have its say someday." This authoritative, always involving film is a major step in that process.

Ma Vie en Rose
1997

The family is giving a party, and upstairs someone small is getting ready. The dress, the earrings, the lipstick, everything is selected with care. But when the seven-year-old is introduced, the neighbors gasp, and so do the parents. For this perfectly dressed little girl is actually Ludovic, a little boy.

A serious comedy about gender confusion, *Ma Vie en Rose* (My Life in Pink) is a lively, high-spirited film that is at once light and serious, sentimental and smart. Though it's the debut for Belgian director Alain Berliner, *Ma Vie* is so delicate and assured it manages to avoid the traps a venture like this might be in danger of falling into.

Against expectation, *Ma Vie en Rose* has nothing to do with sexual orientation but says a great deal about childhood, fantasy, acceptance, and the gap between adults and younger folks. For it's in no way clear what Ludovic's sexual orientation might or might not be as an adult, and that's the point: For right now, no matter what anyone says, he is a child all the way.

A good deal of the credit for *Ma Vie*'s success must go to Georges Du Fresne, without whose exactly calibrated performance as the seven-year-old Ludovic this picture can't even be imagined. With huge saucer eyes in a grave, sphinx-like face that occasionally breaks into a pleased smile, the preternaturally calm Du Fresne gives the most guileless and natural impression of a boy who doesn't understand why his conviction that he is really a girl should be a big deal to anyone.

But a big deal it most certainly turns out to be, though at first his father, Pierre (Jean-Philippe Ecoffey), and mother, Hanna (Michele Laroque), try to be amused by their son's desire to dress up, resisting any trims to his carefully maintained Prince Valiant hairstyle.

Equally understanding at first is his sports car–driving grandmother Elizabeth (Helene Vincent), who smiles on Ludovic's identification with the Barbie-like TV character Pam and counsels understanding for someone searching for his identity.

But then Ludovic, who is nothing if not determined, starts insisting that he and Jerome, the son of a neighbor who just happens to be his father's boss, are going to get married—in the future, "when I'm not a boy," he says. Ludo, as his parents call him, doesn't want to cause trouble, but when what to him is a simple and straightforward desire gets combined with the boy's iron will, things soon spin out of control.

The problem, not surprisingly, is the adults, starting with the family's neighbors and the parents of the other children at Ludo's school. By turns unnerved, threatened, and made insecure by the boy's insistence, the nominal grown-ups show themselves to be more limited in their thinking than the children, eager to place inappropriate and offensive labels on anything that makes them uncomfortable.

Speaking of *Ma Vie* at its Cannes debut, director Berliner said his film "begins like Tim Burton's *Edward Scissorhands* and ends like Ken Loach," and then added, "In the middle it's Billy Wilder." This unexpected combination of bright fairy-tale fantasy, sharp satire, and naturalistic empathy for its characters is what gives Berliner's work (he also co-wrote the screenplay with Chris vander Stappen) more resonance than might be expected.

The other great thing about *Ma Vie en Rose* is its fairness. Though Ludo's mother and father do not behave like a couple out of *Parenting* magazine, the film resists the temptation to portray them as ogres and is instead careful to cast them in an extremely sympathetic light.

If in truth no one is lonelier than the child who is different, the plight of the people who love him, this graceful film insists, can be just as hard.

Monsoon Wedding
2002

If you want to talk about the world, Anton Chekhov once said, talk about your own village. In *Monsoon Wedding,* director Mira Nair has persuasively taken this advice, returning to India's Delhi and coming up with an energetic and amusing romantic drama about the power of love to make things whole.

Nair, whose breakthrough was the Oscar-nominated *Salaam Bombay!,* has said that this film, conceived in a spirit of low-key casualness, was meant to be no big deal. But because she and screenwriter Sabrina Dhawan know their world so well and are so comfortable in it, *Monsoon Wedding* has an engaging warmth and an effortless sense of life. It also has an instinct for the humanity and universality of situations that are comic, romantic, and quite seriously dramatic by turns.

Monsoon Wedding takes place in an India that is finding a balance between tradition and modernity, paralleling the way its middle-class characters alternate between Hindi, Punjabi, and English in their everyday speech and fit venerated cultural practices into a world of e-mail and cell phones.

Similarly, Nair's film, smartly shot by Declan Quinn in very mobile Super 16 millimeter blown up to 35 millimeter, mixes the reality-caught-on-the-fly techniques of independent filmmaking with the always entertaining music and dance conventions of India's mass-audience Bollywood films.

Given how they combine passion, tension, unresolved emotional issues, and inevitable chaos, weddings are natural subjects for filmmakers. Nair has upped the ante by making this a Punjabi wedding as well. "The Punjabis are to India," she explains in a director's statement, "what the Italians are to Europe: We party hard, work hard and have a huge appetite for life."

Rather like Robert Altman's *Gosford Park, Monsoon Wedding* begins with a welter of characters thrown at you all at once, so many that it's understandable when one of the group confesses, "I don't even know who's who half the time." Almost everyone on screen is a member of a very extended family that is gathering in Delhi from all over the world to celebrate the arranged marriage of Aditi (Vasundhara Das), the only daughter of father Lalit (celebrated Indian actor Naseeruddin Shah) and mother Pimmi Verma (Lillete Dubey), a ceremony that is only four days away.

All this chaos is especially hard on Lalit, who is responsible for everything going smoothly as well as for paying the ever-increasing bills. He snaps at a college-age nephew just back from Sydney, calling him "bloody No. 1 most stupid duffer," and he snaps at his own young son (Ishaan Nair, the director's nephew) for his fascination with TV cooking shows. Most of all, he snaps at P.K. Dube, the wedding's caterer and event coordinator.

As played by Vijay Raaz, Dube is a character of almost Dickensian comic humanity. Excitable, brash, upwardly mobile to the point of wearing an ascot, Dube is a parvenu entrepreneur who juggles the truth the way he juggles his workers' schedules, and he continually munches on marigolds, the Indian wedding flower.

Despite all these preparations, Aditi is not at all sure she wants to be married to Hemant (Parvin Dabas), the nice young Houston resident she's only just met. It seems she's not quite over the steamy affair she has had with a married man. She confesses her doubts to her unmarried cousin Ria (Shefali Shetty), who, it turns out, has been living with secrets of her own.

It's not only Aditi who has barriers to overcome on the way to potential romance, and, in the best Bollywood tradition, both the attractions and the obstacles are partially worked out in song and dance. The bloody No. 1 most stupid duffer catches the eye of a young woman with a passion for Indian dance, something he knows nothing about. And the exasperating Dube finds himself attracted to Alice (Tilotama Shome), the family's quiet, unassuming maid. This charming, unlikely relationship is *Monsoon Wedding*'s secret weapon; it is the pitfalls and potential of this pairing that involve us the most.

Because it starts out so frantic, *Monsoon Wedding*'s later moments of introspection and drama come as something of a calming relief. And when the film's unexpected darker chords do manifest themselves, they don't clash with the overall sense of acceptance but rather extend and deepen it.

Inescapably foreign yet endearingly familiar, *Monsoon Wedding* manages to gather all its threads so satisfactorily that audiences will feel like celebrating at the wedding as much as any of those guests. "Life is such a comedy," a celebrant says, but it's not often as satisfying as the one we have here.

Nowhere in Africa
2003

On the surface, *Nowhere in Africa*'s story of a German Jewish family that fled to Kenya in 1938 to escape the Holocaust sounds familiar and uplifting, a safe and predictable piece of inescapably heartwarming cinema. But *Nowhere in Africa* is not the film you may be expecting. It's better. A whole lot better.

The first hint that there is more going on here is the film's success, both critical and popular. It won five German Film Awards, including best feature, best director, and best cinematography, became that country's top-grossing German-language film, and took America's Oscar for best foreign-language film into the bargain.

That success is a result of the way director Caroline Link (who previously directed the Oscar-nominated *Beyond Silence*) took a story that could have drowned in sentiment and turned it into an emotionally complex scenario laced with poignancy and conflict, urgency and compassion. This is an intelligent epic told without special pleading, a film able to cut deep enough to reveal a keen specificity of experience.

Not surprisingly, *Nowhere in Africa* does have a strong basis in fact. It's taken from Stefanie Zweig's autobiographical novel, a bestseller in Germany, about her childhood in Kenya, where she fled with her parents before the war.

Though the daughter, Regina (played at different ages by Karoline Eckertz and Lea Kurka), remains a key character, Link, who also wrote the adapted screenplay, chose to focus on the troubled, complicated, but always passionate relationship between husband and wife. It's a textured, realistic story that has the nerve to risk having not one but both partners lose our sympathy at different junctures of the film, just as they might do in life.

Helped by the nuanced, yet powerful performance of Juliane Kohler as the wife, Jettel Redlich, *Nowhere in Africa* is striking in that one of its key focuses is the indomitability of women. Kohler, memorable as the military wife in *Aimee & Jaguar,* shows Jettel in a variety of psychological states: angry, despairing, coping, fearlessly wrestling with compelling conflicts and difficulties with both her husband and her daughter.

Nowhere in Africa's other great asset was its decision to have director of photography Gernot Roll shoot the film in logistics-challenged Kenya, where it took place, rather than in the cozier but more generic environs of South Africa. Link believes that specific, nonduplicable details are essential to creating a sense of place, and the way the bleak, terrifying, and finally exhilarating vistas of Kenya come alive on screen just as they did for the Redlichs shows how correct she is.

As if to underline the difference between the two countries, *Africa* opens by cutting back and forth between Kenya, where husband Walter Redlich (Georgian-born actor Merab Ninidze) is stricken with malaria, to Germany, where wife Jettel is making plans to join him with their five-year-old daughter despite her family's insistence that "this will all be over in a year."

Once Walter's family does join him, the pivotal questions become how long they will all be in Kenya, and under what physical and psychological circumstances. *Nowhere in Africa* is particularly good at emphasizing the middle-of-nowhereness of its setting and at showing how difficult it was for this cultured German family to adjust to the unfamiliar status of tenant farmers, to understand a new language and an unimaginably different culture, and to decide how much of their homeland they could and should hold on to.

Making things even more problematic is that husband and wife grapple with these problems in different ways and at radically different paces. Walter, once a prominent attorney, throws himself into the pioneer life as best he can, while Jettel initially resists it, filling her trunk from Germany with fine china and an evening gown instead of the vital small fridge she'd been asked to bring.

Caught in the middle are a pair of very different individuals who end up forming a touching and unusual bond. Young Regina acclimatizes easily to the new surroundings, as children often do. She's helped by the family's self-possessed cook, Owuor (beautifully played by Kenyan actor Sidede Onyulo), a figure of considerable dignity faced with the challenge of balancing his culture's demands with those of his employer.

Staying with this family for nearly a decade, *Nowhere in Africa* broadens and deepens as World War II arrives in Kenya and as the experiences and even the attitudes of Jettel and Walter undergo radical shifts. Theirs is a relationship that causes real pain and demands real sacrifices, not once but several times, yet the deep connection between these people, who seem to frustrate and love each other in equal measure, is never in doubt.

At the heart of *Nowhere in Africa*'s success is its ability to keep what happens to this family from seeming schematic or preordained. Again and again, we are surprised by the disconcerting feeling that, at any given moment, everything could ruinously fall apart for these strangers in the strangest of lands. Only human lives could be so complex, and only watching people grow and change could be as involving as this surprising film manages to be.

Prisoner of the Mountains
1997

One hundred and fifty years ago, Russian writer Leo Tolstoy wrote a short story set in the Caucasus at a time when his country was locked in a miserable war with intractable rebels. How little some things change.

Simple, powerful, convincing, *Prisoner of the Mountains* is the

Tolstoy plot updated to the recent conflict with Chechnya, but its story needs no specific time or place to be effective. A spare, poetic tale of the traps of conflict and fate, of how much and how little humanity counts for in a state of war, it could be told about any location where killing is casual and options for survival few.

Directed by veteran Russian filmmaker Sergei Bodrov (who had a hand in the script and cast his son Sergei Bodrov Jr. as one of the leads), *Prisoner* won the International Critics' Prize at Cannes. Bodrov's work is remarkable for not taking sides in the conflict. Rather, the film's measured, unsentimental sympathies are for those whose lives are fractured by war's pointless savageries, no matter what their political allegiance.

Bodrov Jr. plays a young crew-cut recruit named Vania, first glimpsed being inducted assembly-line style into the Russian army. Boyishly eager to serve, he asks where he's headed. "Wherever your country sends you," is the gruff reply.

That turns out to be the Caucasus mountains, where the large but lackadaisical Russian force engages in massive drinking and random weapon firing, a combination that arouses the contempt of the devoutly Muslim local people who have bitterness, feuds, and long memories of their own to contend with.

Out on patrol in the hinterlands, Vania gets shot in an ambush, and only he and Sacha, another badly wounded soldier, survive the attack. Chained together, they're taken to a remote mountain village, where they find themselves the personal prisoners of an unbending local patriarch named Abdoul-Mourat (Jemal Sikharulidze).

Played by the quicksilver Oleg Menshikov, who was Nikita Mikhalkov's nemesis in *Burnt by the Sun*, the mustachioed Sacha is not the kind of person you want to be shackled to. A cocky, selfish veteran who loves only his AK-47, Sacha is at home in the cynical ambience of combat. Contemptuous of his chain-mate's reluctance to kill the enemy, he insists, "You have to, Vania. It's war."

Not surprisingly, Sacha and Vania do not remain at each other's throats but form a wary camaraderie. Also to be expected is the relationship of sorts that forms with their guards, especially Abdoul's young and suspicious daughter Dina (Susanna Mekhralieva). But these familiar elements are handled with clarity and integrity and don't play out in completely expected ways.

The core of *Prisoner of the Mountains* is the reason these men have been taken captive in the first place. Abdoul's own son has been imprisoned by the Russians, and he hopes, with a parent's defiant logic, that he will be able to exchange his first-born for these two foreign invaders.

But in the corrosive atmosphere of war, with not a thimbleful of trust on either side, what ought to be a simple trade becomes anything but. The villagers want the soldiers killed out of hand, the Russians don't believe the hostages even exist, and the intractability of the situation narrows the possibilities for those who believe that there is value in even a single human breath. But, because they do believe, they can't help but persevere.

Beautifully shot by Pavel Lebeshev, the cinematographer for a number of Mikhalkov films, *Prisoner* is strengthened by its scenes showing village customs and traditions that have endured for generations. And the acting, both by veteran Menshikov and newcomer Bodrov, stresses the characters' individuality.

But *Prisoner of the Mountains* is successful mostly because of its determination to trust the pared-down ruthlessness of its situation. By doing so, the filmmakers underline one of the truisms of world cinema: The best of films often come from the worst of times.

Sergei Bodrov Jr., who became a star partly because of this film, died tragically young a few years later while filming in a remote part of Russia.

La Promesse
1997

Morality is a given in the movies; everyone, even the worst of creatures, knows whether they're bad or good. In *La Promesse,* an exceptional film from Belgium, all of that is reversed as a sense of right and wrong struggles to emerge in a young man who never knew there was a difference. The conflicts involved are intense and absorbing, proving that compelling moral dilemmas make for the most dramatic cinema.

An exciting discovery at the Directors' Fortnight at Cannes, *La Promesse* makes being politically relevant and philosophically thoughtful so simple and involving that the story seems to be telling itself. Written and directed by Luc and Jean-Pierre Dardenne, a pair of filmmaking brothers, it is made with such unobtrusive sureness that it's able to exert great power without forcing anything.

Though relatively new to features, the Dardenne brothers have twenty years of documentary work in Belgium behind them, and their use of hand-held cameras and probing close-ups gives *La Promesse* the urgency and immediacy of total authenticity. Toss in unknown but persuasive actors and characters whose reality is unmistakable, and you get an idea why this film is as bracing as it is.

La Promesse is set on the outskirts of the Belgian city of Liège and centers on a fifteen-year-old apprentice auto mechanic named Igor (Jeremie Renier). An opportunistic sneak thief and smooth liar, Igor is like a small animal with dirty blond hair, casually amoral because, in his world, nothing else has ever been presented as an option.

Igor's universe is completely controlled by his father, Roger (Belgian stage actor Olivier Gourmet). A pudgy and bearded petty despot, Roger has a lie or a threat or a beating ready for every occasion. Hot-tempered, violent, a master of casual betrayals, Roger puts together scams without end, but he also cares for his son and values their almost symbiotic relationship.

Roger's business is dealing in illegal immigrants—Turks, Ghanaians, Romanians, and Koreans—who sneak into Belgium looking for a better life. Roger hides them in a clandestine rooming house, charging them exorbitant fees for false identity papers, while collaborating with the police when a raid is needed to satisfy the local politicians.

In all of this, Igor, made in his father's image and hardened by sharing his lifestyle, is a willing second-in-command. Part man, part boy, he spends the spare moments when he's not conniving with the old man putting together a go-kart with his young friends.

Igor's life begins to change when Assita (Assita Ouedraogo) and her small child arrive from Burkina Faso to join husband and father

Hamidou (Rasmane Ouedraogo) in Roger's boardinghouse. Assita's individuality intrigues Igor, and then a jolt of fate shoves their lives closer. Hamidou has an accident while working illegally, Roger refuses to take him to the hospital, and Hamidou dies after making Igor agree to take care of his wife and child—the promise to which the title alludes.

It's difficult to do justice to how subtly the film develops from here, how unflinchingly it depends on documentary-style realism and expressive faces to make its points. Though the question of romance never arises, Igor becomes increasingly protective of Assita, which puts him in conflict with his father, the only person who's ever cared about him. It's a predicament that is as difficult as it is compelling.

La Promesse's actors have differing levels of experience, with Jeremie Renier, an impressive natural, having the least, and Assita Ouedraogo (whose first trip to Europe was to make this film) having appeared in three films of fellow countryman Idrissa Ouedraogo. But they all work so seamlessly here we feel we're eavesdropping on a moral rebellion that is being played out for the highest possible stakes.

Among the many things it does right, *La Promesse* refuses to even consider glib solutions. This film understands that moral choices are a painful, troublesome business, that decisions to do the right thing are not simple to take and hardly make things easier. Nothing in life takes more courage, and no kind of filmmaking offers greater rewards.

Read My Lips
2002

Read My Lips is a battle of wills and desires set in a thriller context, a violent meditation on the unlikely persistence of love, and an investigation of a difficult and compelling relationship between two abused individuals seeking revenge for the unfairness of their lives.

That's a lot for one film, and the powerful success of *Read My Lips* with such provocative material shows why, after only three films, director/co-writer Jacques Audiard, though little known in this country, belongs in the very top rank of French filmmakers.

The son of successful screenwriter Michel Audiard, Jacques Audiard turned to directing because he couldn't find anyone willing to handle his scripts. His first two films, *See How They Fall* (sadly, never released in this country) and *A Self-Made Hero,* are characterized by an unusual ability to create tension within the bounds of traditional genre plotting while focusing on mature examinations of the complexities of human behavior.

Above all else, Audiard, who has a novelist's gift for creating personalities, is an intensely curious investigator of psychological states. He's fascinated with character, with who people are versus who they imagine themselves to be in the private corners of their minds. It's no surprise that Vincent Cassel, the male lead here, told an interviewer, "For the first time, I had the impression of working on a set with adults."

Though he began as a writer (on *Lips* he collaborated with Tonino Benacquista), Audiard's specificity about character has helped make him an excellent director of actors. Of the three Cesars this film captured, one was for screenplay, one for sound, and an especially deserved one for best actress Emmanuelle Devos, voted in over Audrey Tautou's crowd-pleasing performance in *Amelie.*

Devos plays Carla Bhem, a secretary-assistant for a Paris-based real-estate developer, a not noticeably attractive woman in her mid-thirties who reads lips (hence the title, *Sur Mes Levres,* in French) but can't hear without the help of a pair of mechanical aids.

Harried, hassled, and overworked, completely without a personal life, Carla does all the firm's grunt work, up to and including lying to wives, but is so habitually taken for granted that when her boss suggests she's so stressed she might hire an assistant, Carla's first thought is that she might be fired.

Though you can read victimization in Carla's face, you can also read fury. Her sharp eyes take offense easily; as someone whose life is a struggle, she is sullen and resentful toward those who have things easy and don't know it. Yet because she does struggle, Carla is a character we want our heart to go out to, even as we're not sure we can trust her with it.

Paul Angeli (Cassel), the man an agency sends over as Carla's assistant, is in many ways her opposite. Ten years younger, he's a rootless, ambitionless drifter newly out of jail who's got oily good looks but isn't very bright. Paul is so unqualified and over his head as an office assistant that he doesn't know what "outgoing mail" means.

But Carla hires him on the spot. She likes having someone in her life who'll appreciate her help, and she instinctively senses a kind of bond with Paul, the us-against-them connection of two beaten-down people who are too wary to trust each other completely, but who finally have nowhere else to turn.

Gradually, intricately, the relationship between this pair gets more complex. Carla asks for the kind of help only Paul can provide for a situation around the office. Then he returns the favor when he goes to work as a bartender for nightclub owner Marchand (Olivier Gourmet of the Dardenne brothers' *La Promesse*) and starts to have extracurricular ideas.

Though the plot twists in *Read My Lips* may be too intensely melodramatic for some tastes, the impeccable performances of the two leads just about compel our belief. Cassel, a top young French actor (*Brotherhood of the Wolf, The Crimson Rivers*, among many others), has reined in his natural magnetism to excellent effect, but it is Devos whose performance absolutely has us in its power.

Audiard is especially good at creating intimate moments for Carla, private reveries when the fantasies about Paul she keeps in check during business hours come out and play. An instant of her standing nude in front of a full-length mirror wearing only one of his shirts is a snapshot of longing impossible to forget. The linked questions of whether Carla can, and, more than that, whether Carla should get involved with this man are ones with which this bravura film tantalizes us until the very end.

Red
1994

Except for his imposing name, there is little about Polish filmmaker Krzysztof Kieslowski that fits the conventional American image of a great director. His public statements are spare, his subject matter intimate rather than epic, and his interest in anything as flamboyant as a cult of personality is nonexistent.

Yet, as *Red* underscores, Kieslowski is likely the world's most accomplished director, that rare artist with a virtuoso's exhilarating grasp of all aspects of filmmaking, from editing and cinematography to music and acting.

More than that, Kieslowski is the type of master whose hallmark is unobtrusiveness, whose skill is the more impressive for its lack of self-important posturing. And his interest in narrative, emotion, and the human condition make his films so accessible that it is possible to underestimate how accomplished they are.

Coming after the invigorating *Blue* and the bitingly comic *White*, *Red* is the final film in Kieslowski's *Three Colors* trilogy, inspired by the French flag and the motto of "Liberty, Equality, Fraternity." Co-written with longtime collaborator Krzysztof Piesiewicz, *Red* concentrates on fraternity, on the yearning for connection in even the most detached lives.

Simple on one level, profound on another, *Red* is also the best kind of adult fairy tale, a romance conceived and executed by a pessimist. For when a filmmaker as stern and uncompromising as the man who directed *Decalogue,* a somber, ten-part meditation on the Ten Commandments, decides to tell a story of love and hope, it is bound to be both different and convincing.

Kieslowski also believes in the importance of coincidence, and *Red* is rife with it. A tightly controlled film about the randomness of events, *Red* has as a major theme the pivotal role of chance and happenstance in shaping and defining its characters' lives.

At the center of things is Valentine (Irene Jacob), a young model living in a small apartment in Geneva. Though she is unaware of it, *Red*'s elegant camera movements reveal that a handsome young man named Auguste (Jean-Pierre Lorit), busy with his preparation for exams to be a judge, lives in a similar apartment just around the corner.

Auguste has a beautiful blonde girlfriend named Karin (Frederique Feder). Valentine is involved in a ticklish phone relationship with a young man named Michel, who is working outside the country. Fiddling with her car radio one night while driving, Valentine hits a dog named Rita. The animal's collar lists an address, but returning the wounded Rita is not a simple affair.

For Rita's owner turns out to be an icily reserved man named Joseph Kern (Jean-Louis Trintignant), an unshaven former judge who is both reclusive and apparently contemptuous of all feeling. A formidable individual, unapologetic about his misanthropy, he coldly tells Valentine that he is indifferent to the dog's fate and would like nothing so much as for her to go away.

Leave she does, as disgusted at his attitude as he is at her evident concern and generosity. But circumstances bring her back to the judge's house, and though nothing conventional is to be expected, one of the accomplishments of *Red* is how convincingly it depicts the fragile and highly unlikely emotional connection that is forged between these two.

But there is more to Kieslowski's web than that. There is always Auguste, the young man who unknowingly lives in the periphery of Valentine's existence, and whose own life is gradually revealed to have curious parallels to that of the former judge. Kieslowski has dealt with this theme before, most notably in *The Double Life of Veronique*, which also starred Jacob, but he handles it here with lovely delicacy.

Presented naked on a page, *Red*'s plot has the potential to sound contrived, but the skills of Kieslowski and his team, starting with Zbigniew Preisner's ethereal music and Piotr Sobocinski's gliding camera work (which looks effortless but at times required hours of work for the briefest shots), obviate that possibility.

Critical as well are the remarkable performances of the film's two leads. Jacob, a radiant actress with an open, expressive face, must have served as much as a muse for Kieslowski during filming as she does for Joseph Kern in the finished product. And Trintignant, perhaps the preeminent French actor of his generation, is faultless opposite her, brittle antimatter to her vibrant matter.

As with *Blue* and *White*, Kieslowski uses this film's title color as a visual accent, forcing us to notice the bright red of a car, a Swiss Army knife, even a cigarette package. And though all three films stand alone, the director couldn't resist a finale that will be most fully understood by viewers who've seen the previous pair.

Kieslowski has also repeated a scene from both of the earlier films, showing an old woman vainly trying to stuff a wine bottle into a recycling bin, but with a difference. Here, for the first time, someone comes to the woman's aid. If *Red* does turn out to be, as Kieslowski claims, his final film as a director, there can be no doubt but that he's gone out in brilliant style.

Red did turn out to be Kieslowski's final film. He died unexpectedly in 1996 at the age of fifty-four.

Russian Ark
2003

Russian Ark is an astonishing technological feat, but what is even more remarkable is that the technology does not overwhelm the artistry. From the craft point of view, this film by Russian director Alexander Sokurov is all but unprecedented, but that hasn't gotten in the way of its beauty and its soul.

Simply put, *Russian Ark* is a feature-length film that was photographed in one take, a single, uninterrupted shot lasting an unheard-of 87 minutes.

Durable director of photography and Steadicam operator Tilman Büttner, who filmed all the running in *Run, Lola, Run,* used a high-definition digital video camera that fed images to a specially constructed hard drive before they were transferred to 35-millimeter film. After three brief false starts, *Russian Ark* was shot all the way through, one time only, after which, not surprisingly, embraces were shared all around.

Sokurov has been quoted as saying he made *Russian Ark* because he was "sick and tired of editing," but in truth, this film is a natural outgrowth of his earlier works—moody, elegiac films that at their best (*Mother and Son* in 1997) use visuals to create powerfully emotional states of mind.

Sokurov has never been known for incisive dialogue or witty byplay (*Mother and Son* is nearly wordless), and parts of *Russian Ark* are undeniably a long slog. What saves this film is its setting, the absolutely stunning museum and former czarist palace in St. Petersburg known as the Hermitage.

Preparations for *Russian Ark*'s hour-and-a-half visit (which took four years to finance and organize) were understandably extensive. The thirty-three museum rooms that were utilized had to be carefully restored, and the film's 2,000 beautifully costumed actors and extras rehearsed for seven months before Büttner began his nearly mile-long Steadicam walk.

Russian Ark begins, ironically given the splendors that are to come, with its unseen narrator (Sokurov himself) saying, "I open my eyes and I see nothing." Some kind of accident has transported him, he knows not where, and the first thing he does see is a spectacular image: smartly uniformed Russian officers out of the long-gone past carrying gorgeously costumed women out of their carriages and trudging through falling snow in search of an elaborate ball.

The narrator follows them into the Hermitage and almost immediately encounters another time traveler. He's a black-suited nineteenth-century French marquis and diplomat (Sergei Dreiden), who goes nameless in the film but whom Sokurov has identified as the Marquis de Custine, author of a celebrated Alexis de Toqueville–type book on Russia.

Though the snobbish, know-it-all marquis is an irritating character, the dialogue he and the narrator have about the place of Russia and its culture in Europe is as close as the film gets to having a dramatic spine.

The spiteful remarks of the marquis ("Russians are so talented at copying," "Russian music makes me break out in hives"), and the narrator's attempts to counter them, will probably be of interest largely to those already familiar with this long-running argument. What the film shows us, however, has a much greater appeal.

For as the two men wander through the Hermitage's seemingly endless series of rooms, they take a trip through Russian history as well.

Glimpsed in exquisitely crafted settings are Peter the Great twisting the ear of an underling, Catherine the Great taking delight in an elaborate opera staged just for her, Nicholas I and his court receiving emissaries from Persia, and the czarina Alexandra fussing over her daughter Anastasia.

That these scenes are not dry re-creations is a tribute to several things, starting with director Sokurov's great sense of beauty. There's hardly a scene that doesn't please the eye, and some of them—for instance, a sequence of Catherine hurriedly retreating through a snowy courtyard—are truly magical.

Also, Büttner's long walk with the Steadicam does not necessarily go in expected directions. The film's camera work is never showy for its own sake but rather weaves and wanders very much the way an actual person would. The camera lingers, it hovers, it moves sinuously and unhurriedly, managing to turn a highly organized maneuver into something that feels natural and spontaneous.

What *Russian Ark* also does is enable the viewer to reconsider what cinema means, to rediscover an older, more basic way of using the camera, a way that, ironically enough, fell from favor thanks to an earlier Russian generation of directors, such as Sergei Eisenstein, Vesevolod Pudovkin, and Lev Kuleshov, who raised rapid editing to an art form. Just as the Hermitage is finally viewed as a floating ark preserving Russia's history and culture, so film itself comes across as a river of dreams, seamless and free-flowing.

All of this comes together in the film's staggering final scene, a nearly 10-minute look at a 1913 ball in the Great Nicholas Hall (complete with Valery Gergiev conducting the Mariinsky Theatre Orchestra), the last ball the Hermitage was in fact to hold.

This scene, which includes a leisurely following of the crowds as they leave when the music is over, is surprisingly moving, in part because we can't help but be aware that the soldiers we're seeing, "the flower of the officer corps," as someone puts it, will likely meet death soon in either World War I or the Russian Revolution.

More than that, the ball is an emotional experience because the unbroken way in which it is shot has the wherewithal to take us back in time, to allow us to actually live in the past. The ability to unhurriedly wander through the ballroom just as we would if we were on the premises makes the event seem not a re-creation but a real experience. As this particular ship sails on and on, it feels more and more of a privilege to be on board.

A Self-Made Hero
1997

Duplicity is always intriguing, but impostors, people who painstakingly create false identities from the ground up, fascinate most of all. "The best lives are invented, someone said that," remarks Albert Dehousse, the protagonist of Jacques Audiard's smart and provocative *A Self-Made Hero*, before blandly adding, "I think it was me."

Directed and co-written (with Alain Le Henry) by Audiard, an experienced French screenwriter who now directs as well, *A Self-Made Hero* is an acute psychological study of a man who made himself up as he went along, a delicious piece of work that succeeds in making the audience a willing accomplice in the deception. Winner of the best screenplay prize at Cannes, it is as precisely written as it is thought out, and beautifully acted in the bargain.

For most of the film, Dehousse is played by Mathieu Kassovitz (best known as the director of *La Haine*), but when we first meet the character it's as a much older man played by Jean-Louis Trintignant, the subject of a documentary looking into the unique circumstances of his life. (Using these two actors is also something of an inside joke, for they were the stars of Audiard's first film as a director, the excellent but still unreleased *Regarde Les Hommes Tomber*, made in 1994.)

It is the nature of Dehousse's deception that makes him worthy of this documentary. More or less unaffected by World War II, he was able, in the chaotic peacetime months of 1945, to pass himself off as a valued and heroic member of the French Resistance. This concern with the malleability of morality in wartime and after, with how easily the French nation as a whole was able to slough off its history of collaboration, was what attracted Audiard to the Jean-François Deniau novel on which the film is based.

Audiard is especially fortunate in the way actor Kassovitz brings the correct combination of earnestness, timidity, and bravado to the role of the simultaneously guileless and ruthless Dehousse. Though we may think we'll be put off by the man's dishonesty, there is something ingratiating and amusing about how desperately Dehousse wants to become an insider. A callow youth with surprising reserves of cleverness, able to hide pure calculation under the mask of boyishness, Dehousse is an entertaining master magician who turns his own life into the greatest act of all.

One of the unstated themes of *A Self-Made Hero* is that though he wasn't aware of it while it was happening, Dehousse's entire life was a preparation for his supreme deception. He in effect grew into his vocation, picking up tips and techniques from a variety of unrelated sources.

As a child growing up in genteel poverty in rural France, young Albert gets his first lesson in deception when he realizes that his own mother has misled him about his late father's past. Already a lover of words and make-believe, he reads and acts out novels of youthful adventure, and when he meets his future wife, Yvette (Sandrine Kiberlain), he tells her he's a writer—and proves it by copying out passages from the book he has just finished reading, passing them off as his own.

However, Dehousse will not invent on the page, but rather with life itself. After a wartime spent as a salesman learning about self-presentation, he runs off to Paris on Liberation Day out of embarrassment at how little he did during the conflict. There, he comes under the influence of "the Captain" (Albert Dupontel), a real Resistance hero who "loved deceit in every form." He tells his young protégé that he's at a rare moment in history when anything goes, advising him, should he try to be false, "to make it all up, to invent everything from A to Z."

Which is what Dehousse sets out to do. Beginning with easy things, such as bluffing his way into Resistance reunions, he soon turns to deception's heavy lifting. *A Self-Made Hero* is especially good at showing the painstaking hard work that goes into making yourself over: the reading, the memorization, the socializing, the willingness to practice lines as conscientiously as any actor.

The more he does it, the more Dehousse discovers he has a gift for this business, an ability for outfoxing the suspicious, for knowing how to say, "Need I say more?" when saying more would be fatal. He eventually meets a woman (Anouk Grinberg) who is very nearly a match for him, and he finds himself almost turning, like the protagonist of Roberto Rossellini's classic *General Della Rovere*, into something like the person he's pretended to be.

Writer-director Audiard has not only put together a script that works like an intricate piece of machinery, he's also collaborated with cinematographer Jean-Marc Fabre (*Moi Ivan, Toi Abraham*) to give the film a sense of cinematic style. Among the playful touches he includes are shots of a chamber ensemble playing the film's Alexandre Desplat score. No matter how real I've made it seem, he's saying, never forget that we're making it up here just like that rascal Albert Dehousse.

A Single Girl
1997

The simplest films can be the most daring, the most impressive, the most satisfying. So it is with *A Single Girl.*

Directed by Benoit Jacquot and starring the radiant Virginie Ledoyen, this French effort focuses, largely in real time, on a critical moment for a young Parisian woman. Intimate and engaging, *A Single Girl*'s immediacy, sense of life observed, and belief in the power of cinema make it a delicate throwback to the now distant pleasures of the French New Wave.

This is not apparent all at once, however, as *Single Girl* opens, like many another French film, in an unprepossessing café, where testy young Remi (Benoit Magimel) is awaiting the arrival of his girlfriend.

Once Valerie (Ledoyen) appears, she is also in a dicey mood, for this couple has reached the edgy stage of their relationship where every word is taken the wrong way. It's also Valerie's first day of work at a new job, and she's chosen this moment to tell Remi that she's pregnant and wants to keep the baby no matter what.

Even in these early stages, it's possible to see hints of what director

Jacquot is up to. His decision to have cinematographer Caroline Champetier shoot largely in intimate close-ups gives the film a sense of tight connection to these lives that verges on emotional eavesdropping.

It's also immediately noticeable that actress Ledoyen has one of those priceless faces, like Greta Garbo in *Queen Christina* or Falconetti in *The Passion of Joan of Arc,* that the camera is infatuated with even when it's doing nothing at all.

Suddenly Valerie tells Remi she's got to go to work, she'll come back and continue the conversation in an hour. The camera follows her as she heads into the street, enters the posh luxury hotel where she works as a room service waitress, follows her to her locker, and, why be coy, follows her for every second of that hour until she returns to Remi at the cafe.

What happens to Valerie in that hour is, paradoxically, nothing and everything. She learns her routine, talks to her mother on the phone, meets her bosses and co-workers both amiable and obstructionist (including *Augustin*'s droll Jean-Chretien Sibertin-Blanc), delivers breakfast to a variety of guests, all the time worrying about Remi and her future. These largely mundane events might not even be shot in a conventional movie, let alone make the final cut.

But by showing everything, *A Single Girl* invests these happenings with an unexpected impact, creating unlooked-for connections between Valerie and the viewer. It's impossible to watch someone this intensely without getting terribly involved in what they do, without sensing hidden vulnerabilities and worrying that things turn out well. Such is the power of the film medium. The sense that a single life, no matter how ordinary, can contain multitudes has rarely found better expression than it does here.

If *A Single Girl* were a documentary, little of this emotional transference would take place. It only happens because of how artfully veteran director Jacquot and his co-screenwriter, Jerome Beaujour, have set up, paced, and edited the small moments of Valerie's hour, from attempted seductions to angry confrontations, to the point where scenes of her simply walking down hotel corridors become intensely involving.

Also essential is the work of actress Ledoyen. By turns saucy, edgy, vulnerable, petulant, cheerful, resentful, resilient, and forlorn, she is on screen for almost all of this film's 90 minutes, but we never tire of paying attention to what she's up to.

Yet, as closely as we follow her during this crucial period, Valerie remains, finally, unknowable to us, even perhaps to herself. *A Single Girl*'s final shot, of this woman fading from view as she blends into a crowd, tells us that what we've seen is just a life, not a hero's tale, but involving and important nonetheless.

Spirited Away
2002

Prepare to be astonished by *Spirited Away*.

Written and directed by one of the world's master animators, Japan's Hayao Miyazaki, this visual wonder is the product of a fierce and fearless imagination. His creations are unlike any you've seen before.

If you're dispirited by look-alike, sound-alike, think-alike movies, disturbed by an art form that seems not only to tolerate but also to reward a paucity of imagination, you're not going to believe your luck.

That was certainly the feeling at the Berlin Film Festival, where this dark, strange, mysterious, but ultimately joyous film so held the jury in its power that *Spirited Away* became the first animated feature in the event's fifty-year history to win the top prize, the Golden Bear. It was true in Japan, where the film earned $234 million and unseated *Titanic* as that country's all-time box office leader, as well as in Hollywood, where it took home the Oscar for best animated feature.

As those Americans who saw Miyazaki's previous *Princess Mononoke* know, his version of Japanese anime is quite different from American animation. The style is more painterly, the feeling unmistakably Japanese, and the mood, even when it's light, is almost never jokey or cartoonish.

Yet, even for Miyazaki, there is something special about *Spirited Away*. It's a heroic adventure story worthy of *The Arabian Nights* with an ordinary ten-year-old girl named Chihiro as the heroine. And it has a magical air of once-upon-a-time, a fairy-tale quality reminiscent of the unexpurgated works of the Brothers Grimm, where boys can turn into dragons, door knockers talk back, and even evil spirits can't go back on their word.

Although likely too scary for small children, *Spirited Away* also manages, in a casual, off-handed way, to teach lessons about the power of love and friendship, the importance of knowing who you are, the corrupting nature of greed, and how much is possible for those who believe.

On a more everyday level, *Spirited Away* also shows the potential for dubbing, usually the most onerous of film techniques, when it's done sensitively. Under the supervision of *Toy Story*'s John Lasseter, a friend of Miyazaki's for twenty years, this film's English-language version shows the original the best kind of respect.

The voices chosen are not strident, and the believably colloquial dialogue (written by Cindy Davis Hewitt and Donald H. Hewitt) was timed to fit the Japanese lip movements, helping to make this extremely foreign world accessible while conveying critical background information.

The voices have an easier time of things because of the power of *Spirited Away*'s facility with wonder and enchantment. It's not only that Miyazaki's inventiveness never flags despite a two-hour-plus length, it's the great gamut the visuals run that is most impressive.

Although it comes to the sweetest possible ending, *Spirited Away* is as at home with disturbing scenes of creatures throwing up as it is with images of piercing tranquillity and purity, such as the unforgettable vision of a train gliding to nowhere on tracks submerged in water that could have come from a painting by Magritte.

Miyazaki no doubt intended the opposition of these images to have an effect on us. Dream and nightmare, the grotesque and the beautiful, the terrifying and the enchanting all come together to underline the oneness of things, to point out how little distance there is between these seemingly disparate states, much less than we might imagine.

For a film that does so much, *Spirited Away* starts quietly, with a skittish, reluctant Chihiro (voiced by Daveigh Chase, Lilo of *Lilo &*

Stitch) sulking in the back seat of a car that is taking her and her parents to their new suburban home. She's unhappy at leaving familiar surroundings behind and not at all mollified when her mother says her new life will be an adventure.

That adventure starts sooner than anyone anticipates. In classic fable fashion, Chihiro's father takes a wrong turn and thinks he sees a shortcut through the woods that will solve his problems. The family ends up in front of a mysteriously beckoning tunnel that leads to what looks like an abandoned theme park.

Wise beyond her years, Chihiro doesn't want to enter, but her mother and father, lured by intoxicating smells, insist the family plunge ahead. Although no one's around, they discover tables piled high with food so irresistible that the parents, suddenly losing all restraint, dig in with savage gusto. "Don't worry," Chihiro's father says between heaping mouthfuls, "you've got daddy here." Then, suddenly, everything goes incredibly wrong, and Chihiro finds herself on her own in this decidedly spectral environment.

In a panic, she comes upon an enormous building and watches in an astonishment we share as a ferry pulls up and unloads one of the strangest cargoes in film history. For the structure turns out to be a bathhouse for the gods, a place where all kinds of nonhuman spirits come to refresh, relax, and recharge. Miyazaki shows them all to us with a dazzling variety (don't miss the enormous, walrus-like Radish Spirit, as if you could) that words can't hope to equal.

Coming to her aid is Haku (Jason Marsden), a severe-looking boy with a Prince Valiant haircut. "Don't be afraid, I just want to help you," he says, and Chihiro begins to feel that she and he have met somewhere before.

Haku sends Chihiro to one of the bathhouse's oddest corners, the boiler room, where tiny, skittish motes of dust deliver coal to the furnace one lump at a time. The wily, six-armed Kamaji (David Ogden Stiers), looking like a hipster-anarchist with his round dark glasses and bushy mustache, is the creature in charge.

Kamaji sends Chihiro to see Yubaba (Suzanne Pleshette), a strange and powerful witch who runs the bathhouse despite looking like a petticoat-wearing, hair-in-a-bun nineteenth-century Victorian lady.

She lives with her gargantuan infant son, Boh (Tara Strong), and three goateed, green heads that roll around her apartment for no apparent reason like a trio of grumbling, muttering beach balls.

Chihiro is given a job assisting bathhouse attendant Lin (Susan Egan), and although it may sound like a lot has already happened, it's here that her adventures truly begin. Starting as a spoiled girl who never worked a day in her life, Chihiro gains in confidence and ability as she copes with the singular challenges that Miyazaki has prepared for her. The writer-director's name, as it turns out, is the last image to appear on the screen after the final credits roll. It's hard to think of a filmmaker who deserves that prominence more.

The Terrorist
2000

The Terrorist is a wonder several times over. Joining a compelling tale with exquisite photography and involving acting, it's a remarkable film by any standard, but especially given the circumstances of its creation.

The story of a crisis of conscience in the young life of a committed suicide bomber, *The Terrorist* is an Indian independent film, almost a contradiction in terms for a country whose passionate moviegoers are, if anything, more addicted to their Bollywood commercial cinema than Americans are to studio output.

Directed, co-written, and photographed by the gifted Santosh Sivan, *The Terrorist* (though shot for $50,000 in sixteen days) has a delicacy and artistry that is rare at any cost and at any budget.

This is Sivan's first feature as a director, but he's not a film neophyte. He's worked as director of photography on some twenty features and twice that many documentaries and has won India's National Film Award for cinematography nine times. The exhilarating visual sensibility he's brought to *The Terrorist* is the first thing you notice about it.

Exclusively using natural light in largely jungle situations, Sivan gives his settings a brighter than bright radiance. Colors are luminous (the greens especially pop out at you), and there's a crispness to his look that gives running water an extra sparkle. While images such as a leaf in a stream, a glass of iced tea, or a faded red guerrilla mask being river-washed may sound familiar, *The Terrorist* makes them indelible.

Though set in Sri Lanka, where the government has been contending with Tamil separatists for years, *The Terrorist* was more directly inspired by the assassination of Indian Prime Minister Rajiv Gandhi in 1991. One of its intentions is to provide insight into the mindset of people willing and even happy to die as martyrs; another is to examine what happens when the human cost of terrorism takes on a personal dimension.

The terrorist of the title is nineteen-year-old Malli (Ayesha Dharkar), the veteran of thirty successful operations, who opens the film by coldly executing a traitor within her guerrilla group. A woman who kills without mercy or compunction, Malli will take human life several more times and never look back.

It is this ability to be "a thinking bomb" that earns Malli recognition from the leader of her revolutionary group, and he chooses her from a group of equally young, equally eager volunteers to carry out a suicide mission: Get close to an important government official, he instructs her, and set off a quantity of explosives strapped to your waist.

The Terrorist is deliberately shadowy about the makeup of this group and the legitimacy of its drive for independence. The barely glimpsed leader insists that "our struggle has a purpose, justice is on our side, we will shed our blood but not our tears," and pains have been taken to make him and his cohorts sound rational and sane. No judgment is offered about the rightness or wrongness of Malli's clandestine movement, and the easy way out—presenting her group as obviously deluded—is carefully avoided.

The leader's words make a particular kind of sense to Malli, given her background. Her father was a nationalist poet; her brother, a famous martyr, was killed when she was small. Throughout her life she has known almost nothing but the Struggle and its world of guns, violence, and betrayal. "If you were a man," a besotted female comrade-in-arms says, "I'd marry you."

But as Malli makes the physical journey from the jungle to the city where her suicide bombing is to take place, she takes an interior journey as well. She meets a traumatized young boy named Lotus (Vishwas), who serves as a guide, and also has memories of an unexpected assignation with a wounded fellow fighter (K. Krishna), who told of having buried his beloved schoolbooks, vowing to dig them up again only after freedom is won.

Though viewers will inevitably want Malli to have second thoughts about her mission, because the film is so delicately balanced and so fair to all sides, it's perfectly plausible for the opposite to take place.

Dharkar, the Indian actress who plays Malli, is in almost every shot of the film, and *The Terrorist*'s success would be less without her expressive performance. With her dark and deeply penetrating eyes, she looks out at us in a way that is familiar, terribly touching, and, as it should be in the final analysis, all but unknowable.

Time of Favor
2002

Time of Favor is one of the most successful, provocative, and intensely contemporary of Israeli films, so much so that to watch it is to feel the country having a passionate argument with itself.

The winner of six Israeli Academy Awards, including best picture, best screenplay, best actor, and best actress, *Time of Favor* is the impressive debut of thirty-three-year-old writer-director Joseph Cedar. A former infantry paratrooper, he is one of the few Israeli directors to come out of the Orthodox religious community, and that dual background is one of the things that gives his work a distinctive quality.

Part political thriller, part romantic melodrama, *Time of Favor* is set in an Orthodox settlement on the West Bank led by a charismatic rabbi. It looks candidly at the differing currents within this community, at the personal price that is invariably paid for messianic dreams, and at how the philosophy of the settlements affects individuals and the country as a whole. And it does so, despite the theatricality endemic to Israeli films, with an evenhandedness that extends to points of view the film in no way supports.

Although it's no more than glimpsed, the center of *Time of Favor,* much talked about but hardly ever on screen, is Jerusalem's Temple Mount, the site of places sacred to two religions—Islam's Dome of the Rock and Judaism's Western Wall. A visit here in September 2000 by then–political candidate Ariel Sharon led inevitably to violence and controversy.

Also focused on the mount is the magnetic Rabbi Meltzer (Assi Dayan, son of former Defense Minister Moshe Dayan and a major figure in Israeli film). The rabbi dreams, as did his father before him, of a new temple rising on the mount, and he conveys that dream to the young men who study in his yeshiva.

Not necessarily a hard-core fanatic, the rabbi is sane, brilliant, and articulate, which makes secular Israelis view him as even more dangerous than the zealots of the past—proof that, as one of them nicely puts it, "the line between abnormal and normal has changed."

Menachem (Israeli heartthrob Aki Avni) is one of the rabbi's students and an officer in the army. As the film opens, Menachem is given command of an entirely Orthodox company that includes his best friends Pini (Edan Alterman) and Itamar (Micha Selektar). It's a good moment for Pini, too. The most brilliant mind in the yeshiva, he has been selected by the rabbi as a potential husband for his daughter Michal. Michal, however, is more interested in Menachem, and, it becomes increasingly obvious, he's interested in her as well.

As played by Israeli actress Tinkerbell and written by Cedar (who at one time wanted Natalie Portman for the role), Michal is the film's most involving character. Unapologetically direct, she speaks her mind about her situation at every opportunity, instigates and quashes romantic situations, and provides an eloquent counterpoint to her father's heedless advocacy and the film's welter of traditional male voices.

There is more going on in *Time of Favor* than boy meets girl. There is also, in an echo of the assassination of Yitzhak Rabin by a Jewish religious student, the possibility of a plan to blow up the Dome of the Rock, a plan that would be catastrophic for any chance of peace in the region.

Cedar—who was born in America but lived in Israel since he was six, and who holds a film degree from New York University—provides glimpses of many sides of Israel. We see violent secret-police interrogation techniques that Human Rights Watch would not approve of, as well as an enormously touching scene of two Orthodox young people, fearful of physical contact, courting by having their hands intertwine as shadows on a wall.

Cedar's script also allows for divergent philosophical viewpoints not often given screen time. We hear Rabbi Meltzer's genuine yearning for Jerusalem, an Orthodox man's explanation of how and why doing everything for God is his ultimate goal, even the voice of a fanatical terrorist talking about the "privilege" of being able to "put history on its correct course."

What Israelis no doubt take for granted turns out to be one of *Time of Favor*'s most interesting aspects for foreign audiences, and that is a glimpse into how gruff and abrasive their society can be, how lacking—as parties throughout the Middle East are—in the ability to simply trust in people who don't share your point of view. In this kind of a world, a happy ending is not likely. The only question is exactly how distraught everyone is going to be.

Time Out
2002

Time Out is not just an especially subtle and thoughtful psychological drama, it's a provocative, even an unnerving one as well. It's the story of a daring impostor named Vincent, a world-class dissembler who goes to extraordinary lengths to carry out an increasingly elaborate deception. What does Vincent take all these pains to pretend to be? A man with a job.

At one time, of course, Vincent had the kind of well-paying, white-collar employment that enabled him to buy a home and support a wife and three children. But after he's let go, his reluctance to tell his family what has happened leads him down an increasingly risky and surreal path that starts to double back on itself in unforeseen ways.

Though its trajectory is different, *Time Out* (*L'Emploi du Temps*) was partly suggested by the real-life story of Jean-Claude Romand, who resorted to violence when it was discovered that he spent eighteen years pretending to work for the World Health Organization. French director Laurent Cantet, who co-wrote *Time Out* with Robin Campillo, was understandably attracted to this situation. Unlike most contemporary filmmakers, his pictures, such as his previous *Human Resources,* are about the centrality of work, about work as the definer of who we are. "When we are out of work," he has said in interviews, "we are nothing."

Cantet was especially fortunate in persuading Aurelien Recoing, a top French stage actor who has never before had a leading role on film, to star as Vincent. It's a quite demanding part because this soft, harmless-looking individual is in many ways a cipher, someone who's largely unknowable to his former co-workers, his wife, maybe even to himself.

Pudgy, balding, his face a pliant mask, Vincent is the man who always blends in, the man who is interchangeable with the rest of the herd. Which is what makes his deceptions so difficult to detect and so discomforting to observe as they unfold.

Time Out begins with Vincent, asleep in his car in a school parking lot, roused by a cell phone call from his wife, Muriel (Karin Viard). Before he's even fully awake, he's telling the first of the endless lies that mark his day, talking about clients that don't exist, meetings that will never take place, the grueling nature of a travel-intensive job that is no longer there. Once he's off the phone, he's freed, at least initially, from the working world's cares.

When Vincent returns home, the deceptions get increasingly difficult to manage as his wife and his parents pressure him for details about his work. When his lies threaten to trip him up, he escapes by telling bigger ones, taking greater and greater risks as he tiptoes on the verge of being unmasked.

It is one of the pleasures of Recoing's performance that it enables us to sense how initially exhilarating all this is for Vincent. He's fascinated, even energized by his gift for deception, turned on by how willing others are to accept his claims. And when he concocts a job for himself as a Geneva-based consultant for the United Nations, he clearly gets satisfaction out of finally doing meaningful work, even though that work is mostly in his head.

It's not entirely in his head because, in one of the film's killing paradoxes, maintaining the illusion of having a job becomes a time-consuming occupation in and of itself, though one that Vincent finds much more to his liking.

So we see Vincent sneaking into his make-believe office in a Geneva building, clandestinely reading documents, and preparing to talk knowledgeably back home about his new position. Now that he has no source of income, he's forced to involve old school friends, even his parents, in increasingly complex and frantic scams that prey on gullibility and trust and involve Vincent in all kinds of unforeseen dilemmas.

Though you wouldn't necessarily guess it, except for Recoing as Vincent and Cesar-winning actress Viard as his wife, the performers in *Time Out* are not professionals. Director Cantet encouraged the cast to have input into their dialogue, a process that adds to the film's uncanny naturalness. *Time Out*'s reality level is one of the many things that make this look at living a lie truly haunting. Does Vincent lose track of who he is through this complex deception, or does he get tantalizingly closer to his actual core being? It's not as easy a question to answer as you might think.

Tito and Me
1993

The year is 1954. Josip Broz Tito is the unchallenged ruler of Yugoslavia—marshal, prime minister, and president all in one. Zoran is a somber and phlegmatic ten-year-old boy whose idea of a good time is eating the plaster off the walls of his Belgrade apartment. Talk about your odd couples.

Zoran mimics the great man's gestures in newsreels and gets up in the middle of the night to ensure a good spot when the maximum leader parades by. The protagonist of writer-director Goran Markovic's slyly autobiographical *Tito and Me* even daydreams about Tito, who appears to the boy in visions whenever he is in trouble. Which is often.

Wacky, ironic, and always light on its feet, *Tito and Me* turns out to be an engaging and amusing farce about the time when the maximum leader's fierce cult of personality kept his country together. One of the last films to be shot in a Yugoslavia that has since fallen apart, it also makes some quiet points about what made the good old days so difficult.

Tito is narrated in clever voice-over by young Zoran (Dimitrie Vojnov), a moon-faced and melancholy Slavic version of the Pillsbury Doughboy. Living with his ballerina mother and musician father in a small apartment shared with an aunt and uncle, grandmother, and "my hideous cousin Svetlana," Zoran casts a droll eye over the never-ending foibles of grown-ups.

"Love is the most complicated thing in the world," he observes with deadpan seriousness of his parents' wranglings. "It causes a variety of insoluble problems for adults." No sooner does he say this, however, than Zoran himself falls in love, with a string-bean orphan named Jasna who is almost twice his height.

Desperate to accompany Jasna and other politically motivated youths on a two-week "March Around Tito's Homeland," Zoran throws himself into an essay contest on "Do You Love Marshall Tito and Why." To his parents' mixed pride and horror, his epic poem, proclaiming "the grass sees Him when it grows, the swallows sing only for Him," wins the prize. So, wearing lederhosen and a Tyrolean hat, Zoran dutifully sets off on a trip for which the word "misadventure" is way too mild.

Director Markovic, none of whose eight previous films have had a theatrical release in this country, has a gift for this kind of comic satire, enlivening the proceedings with both a jaunty soundtrack (by Zoran Simjanovic) and lots of newsreel footage of the real Tito doing all kinds of nonsense, from playing the drums in North Africa to tossing darts and talking to parrots.

Markovic also has the benefit of a cast, including his former wife, Anica Dobra, as Zoran's mother and his own parents, Olivera and

Rade Markovic, who perfectly understand the wry effects he is after, as the boy's grandparents.

Especially amusing as well are Lazar Ristovski as the zealous Comrade Raja, the leader of the trek, and Vesna Trivalic as Zoran's misty-eyed teacher. As for the unsmiling boy himself, nonprofessional Vojnov has such a natural comic dignity that it is impossible to see him trudge purposefully through the indignities of his life without being charmed and charmed again. The best kind of personal filmmaking, *Tito and Me* is the final gentle grace note from a country that won't be smiling for some time to come.

Together
2001

It's a word painted on a been-around VW bus, the name of the collective in Stockholm that jointly owns the vehicle, and the title of this relaxed, intimate, wonderfully clear-eyed and altogether charming Swedish comedy of manners that deals with the accident-waiting-to-happen phenomenon known as communal living.

It's November 1975 in Stockholm, and the eight adults and two children who make up Together are introduced dancing in delight at the news of the death of that eternal bogeyman of the Left, Spain's Francisco Franco. Dedicated to "revolting against the bourgeois way of living," the commune's self-centered members claim to like the idea of being, as the earnest Goran (Gustaf Hammarsten) puts it, "like a porridge: part of something bigger, warm, soft, together." Are they fooling themselves? Maybe, and then again, maybe not.

Together is the second film by thirty-one-year-old Swedish writer-director Lukas Moodysson, and those who saw his first, the effective *Show Me Love* (awkwardly retitled from the profane Swedish original), have already experienced the traits that make this new and more accomplished venture so satisfying.

Moodysson has the rare ability to combine an exact sense of the silly, misguided ways people tend to behave, the knack we all have for embarrassing ourselves, and a keen empathy for how irresistible the messiness of life turns out to be.

This is a filmmaker who easily works the pain and humor of existence into comedies in which the jokes are not in one-liners or pratfalls, but in character and situation, in the foibles of a commonly shared humanity. To watch *Together* is to go on a journey both familiar and unexpected, where the slightly ridiculous merges with the almost sublime.

The plot is precipitated by a crisis in the life of Goran's sister Elisabeth (Lisa Lindgren). She's leaving her abusive, alcoholic husband Rolf (Michael Nyqvist), and she needs a place to stay with their children, thirteen-year-old Eva (Emma Samuelsson) and ten-year-old Stefan (Sam Kessel). Goran, an emotional pushover universally known as "the nicest, kindest, sweetest man," wants to give up his room, but his opportunistic girlfriend, Lena (Anja Lundqvist), says no. Instead, Elisabeth and family get a small space meant for meditation and relaxation, from which they venture forth to meet the collective.

What they find is a place where clothing is optional but no one can be bothered to answer the phone, where sexual relationships are open but doing the dishes is considered counterrevolutionary. As for the children, one of them is named Tet (after the Vietnamese offensive) and likes to play Pinochet and the Torturers in his free time. Despite their claims of idealism, the main characters prove to be, to no great surprise, remarkably self-absorbed.

Aside from those already mentioned, the key players include the recently divorced Anna (Jessica Liedberg), who's just made a more or less political decision to become a lesbian, and who's immediately attracted to Goran's very conventional sister; Lasse (Ola Norell), a wry medical student and Anna's ex-husband; Klas (Shanti Roney), a lonely gay man who pines for Lasse; and Erik (Olle Sarri), a humorless political radical and member of the Communist Marxist-Leninist Revolutionary League, who prefers discussing dense political theory to everything, including sex.

In this world, where children seem saner and more responsible than adults, the straitlaced family next door to Together is horrified at these goings-on. All except young Fredrik (Henrik Lundstrom), who senses that the newly arrived Eva might be a kind of soul mate.

While all this is going on (and it's a lot), discarded husband Rolf is increasingly desperate to reconnect with his family. His only friend is an equally at-sea divorced guy named Birger (Sten Ljunggren), who tells him, as if he needed to hear it, that "loneliness is the most awful thing in the world."

Aside from superb ensemble work from an eighteen-member cast, *Together*'s sense of human potential is its greatest pleasure. Moodysson treats all his characters well, even when he puts them through terribly bleak moments. Although he well knows that this commune is a rather silly place, he still is able to put forward a convincing case for the concept behind it, difficult though it may be to put into practice. "The only thing worth anything," one character says, likely echoing the filmmaker's thoughts, "is being together."

The Town Is Quiet
2002

Intimate and human yet deeply ambitious, a powerhouse of a film made with a disturbing vision, Robert Guediguian's *The Town Is Quiet* has a title that turns out to be savagely ironic. For if the town in question is anything, it's anything but quiet.

That would be Marseille, the birthplace of writer-director-producer Guediguian, one of the most prominent of France's new breed of regional filmmakers. Guediguian has lived in Paris for twenty-five years, but each of his ten films has been set in Marseille. Although his earlier works, notably the sunny French box-office hit *Marius and Jeanette,* have been well received, they give no hint of the scope of what he has attempted here.

The Town Is Quiet opens with a magisterial 360-degree pan of Marseille, with the camera moving slowly around the city's harbor as an unseen pianist plays a classical medley. The effect is simultaneously melancholy, lonely, and also somewhat intimidating. *The Town*

Is Quiet is an X-ray of a city, an involving neo-realistic look at how people on several strata of society try to cope with the desperate circumstances of their lives. It's a pitiless film, uncompromising in what it shows us.

Yet it is precisely Guediguian's all-seeing dispassion, his intimate knowledge and unblinking eye for human frailties, that makes his film so effective. Despite its bleak nature, *The Town Is Quiet* is honest and unexaggerated, with nothing done for effect. And it is wise enough not to offer answers, not to pretend to solutions to personal and societal problems that are far from simple. As the director has said, "I wanted to talk of everything that scares me."

Although he is a former member of France's Communist Party, Guediguian (who co-writes his scripts with Jean-Louis Milesi) is anything but didactic. What is just as rare for a politically committed filmmaker, his people are never merely symbolic, but always believable and individual. The acting in the film is not just a means to an end, but a satisfying end in itself. The overall picture *Quiet* paints is of a culture that has lost its moorings and a city that is flirting with decline and collapse. Once a workers' citadel where class identification was strong, Marseille is now a bastion of glib, far-right politicians who say their "preference" for native French citizens rather than the foreign-born is as simple as a wife's preference for her husband.

In this atmosphere, *Quiet* follows three main story lines and the people in them, characters united by a frustrating sense of entrapment. These are people who want their lives to be better, but whose options are inevitably limited, who don't know how to escape a life where, as one of them says, "it's always the same time, always the same beat."

Guediguian has returned to the same performers repeatedly during his career, starting with the actress who is his wife as well as *Quiet*'s star, the gifted and versatile Ariane Ascaride. Her hair dyed blond for the role, Ascaride plays Michele, who does back-breaking labor at a fish market to keep her family solvent. With a husband who's been reduced to a sad drunk by three years on the government dole, a daughter who sleeps around to support her heroine habit, and an infant granddaughter, this is not a simple task. For help, Michele turns to the mysterious Gerard (Gerard Meylan), a former beau whose current situation is decidedly shadowy.

Also eventually associated with Michele is Paul (Jean-Pierre Darroussin), a former dockworker who once knew "The Internationale" in four languages but now has turned his back on his union colleagues for a payout that enabled him to put a down payment on a fancy taxi. Although he is close to his parents, loneliness is Paul's main characteristic, a loneliness that seems to seep through his every pore.

Although she is married, Viviane (Christine Brucher), who teaches music to the disadvantaged, is lonely as well. She makes a connection with one of her former students, a young North African ex-con named Abderamane (Alexandre Ogou) who is troubled by prejudice no matter which race it springs from.

The Town Is Quiet perfectly captures the mood of a city where personal contact is tenuous and uncertain at best. Though its verité feeling places it indelibly in Marseille, it is a film that is also able to make judicious use of outside influences, such as a pair of Janis Joplin songs ("Summertime" and "Cry Baby") that connect exquisitely with its despondent mood.

By its close, *The Town Is Quiet* has built to a more emotionally potent conclusion than even its strengths would have you imagine, despairing while holding out an unexpected kind of hope. If life does find a reason to go on, this exceptional film says, it's on its own terms and no one else's.

The Vertical Ray of the Sun
2001

The Vertical Ray of the Sun is a wholly enveloping experience. Gentle, ravishingly beautiful, and awash in everyday sensuality, it so intoxicates you with the elegance and refinement of its filmmaking that even noticing, let alone caring, whether it has a plot starts to seem beside the point.

Written and directed by Tran Anh Hung, *Vertical Ray* does in fact have a story line, one that investigates love, marriage, and faithfulness as they play out in the romantic lives of three Vietnamese sisters, but no one will come out of this film compelled to deconstruct the narrative.

The lure of *Vertical Ray* is its sophisticated blending of delicate music, restrained acting, and a seemingly casual but immaculate use of breathtaking color. Cinematographer Mark Li Pingbin, who worked with Christopher Doyle on Wong Kar-wai's *In the Mood for Love,* delivers just as much of a visual tour de force with this film's exquisite pastel shades.

Vertical Ray marks a return to form for writer-director Tran. His Oscar-nominated debut, *The Scent of Green Papaya,* set in a luscious 1950s Vietnam he created in a French studio, was very much this kind of film. Tran followed that with the determinedly different *Cyclo,* which depicted the chaos of today's Ho Chi Minh City to little effect except irritation.

With *Vertical Ray,* Tran stays in the present and, for the third movie in a row, features his graceful wife, Tran Nu Yen-Khe. The setting this time is Hanoi, depicted in such an inviting way that it could incite a tourism boom of harried westerners panting to experience a civilization that values leisure and beauty, a polite, unhurried earthly paradise where there's always time for jewel-like meals and everything is casually color-coordinated. This world may not really exist, but it is hard to resist on film.

Vertical Ray focuses on a close family of four siblings—three sisters and a brother—and opens as the alarm goes off in the small apartment that Lien (Tran Nu Yen-Khe), the youngest sister, shares with her brother, Hai (Ngo Quang Hai).

The insinuating acoustic music of Lou Reed spills onto the soundtrack as curtains billow in the wind. Hai does chin-ups, and Lien languidly stretches in bed and moves into a tai chi routine. Lien is the playful type, and she enjoys poaching on Hai's bed at night and teasing him about the way people think they're a couple when they're seen on the street.

Lien works in a cafe run by their eldest sister, Suong (Nguyen Nhu Quynh), who is married to Quoc (Chu Ngoc Hung), a photographer who prefers shooting plants to people because "they have a tranquillity you can't find in a face." Middle sister Khanh (Le Khanh) is married to a writer named Kien (Tran Manh Cuong), who is struggling to finish his first novel.

Vertical Ray opens on the anniversary of the mother's death and ends a month later on the anniversary of the father's. During that time, everyone finds relationships tested when, among other happenings, Quoc takes a trip to snap some plants and Kien goes to Saigon to look into a suspicion the sisters have but don't want to believe—that their beloved mother might have had an affair, or at least a flirtation.

Romantic entanglements ensnare all the sisters, but scenes that lack plot relevance are often as memorable as those that have it. A couple caught in the rain, the sisters giggling as they prepare a meal, a quiet moment between a husband and a wife in a lovely garden, all linger in the mind.

Helping sustain the film's soothing mood is the music of Vietnamese composer Ton That Tiet, the vivid sounds of birds, insects, and water on the soundtrack, and the way the lighting enhances that subtle use of color. A cooling drink in an exotic shade of green, a rain slicker in the most delicate light blue, the blades of a fan in a blue that's a bit darker: They all combine to gem-like effect.

"One should live where one's soul is in harmony," photographer Quoc says, adding: "Harmony can be a great consolation." *Vertical Ray of the Sun* demonstrates how great an asset it can be as well.

Y Tu Mamá También
2002

Outrageous without being offensive, provocatively and unapologetically sexual, alive to the possibilities of life and cinema, Alfonso Cuarón's *Y Tu Mamá También* is a sophisticated film happily masquerading as something off the cuff.

Nominally a simple road movie about two Mexican teenagers taking off to look for a mythical beach in the company of a suddenly available woman of twenty-eight, *Y Tu Mamá* manages to be comic, dramatic, erotic, sociological, and even political, all without breaking a sweat.

Cuarón's picture, co-written with his brother Carlos, is more than anything reminiscent of the classics of the French New Wave. Echoing films such as Jean-Luc Godard's *Band of Outsiders* and François Truffaut's *Jules and Jim*, it makes exceptional use of a detached, omniscient narrator, but the parallels don't stop there.

Y Tu Mamá also echoes the unmistakable freshness and excitement of the Nouvelle Vague, the sense of joy in being alive and making movies, that made those works distinctive and unforgettable.

To be able to turn out something this apparently effortless and natural paradoxically takes a background of craft and experience. Cuarón caught the eye of the studio system with his Mexican debut film, *Love in the Time of Hysteria*, which got parlayed into a pair of Hollywood literary adaptations, the well-done *A Little Princess* and the much less so *Great Expectations*.

Wanting, after that encounter, to "go off and get my hands dirty," Cuarón and his longtime collaborator, gifted cinematographer Emmanuel Lubezki (twice Oscar-nominated, for *Little Princess* and *Sleepy Hollow*), returned to their homeland to make what turned out to be a sexually candid, deeply Mexican film that pulses with energy and spirit.

Y Tu Mamá (even its title is a bragging sexual reference) begins with a graphic bedroom scene, in front of a huge poster for *Harold and Maude,* between seventeen-year-old Tenoch (Diego Luna) and a girlfriend about to head off for a summer in Italy. Tenoch's homeboy, Julio (Gael García Bérnal of *Amores Perros*), it turns out, is being left behind in similar fashion.

Formidably self-centered best friends who do everything from getting high to pleasuring themselves together, Tenoch and Julio are dripping with attitude and conceit. Though their humor runs to flatulence jokes and their interest in the outside world is confined to interchanges such as "left-wing chicks are hot"/"totally," they nevertheless view themselves as epitomes of knowledge and sophistication.

The film's attitude toward these two is one of the keys to its success. *Y Tu Mamá* is neither complicit with the boys nor hostile to them; rather, aided by the voice-over, it views them from an amused distance, entertained by their energy and sass but knowing full well what essentially clueless space cowboys they are, not bad kids but spoiled by Tenoch's position as a child of privilege and affluence.

One of the casual ways that voice-over asserts its influence, makes political points, and sets a shrewd tone is by letting us know that these two are not from the same world. Julio is supported by a working single mother, and Tenoch's father is a Harvard-educated politician once accused of selling tainted food to the poor. He was going to call his son Hernán (after, as Mexican audiences are likely to assume, the conqueror Cortés) but impulsively chose an Aztec name instead because such names were momentarily fashionable.

Bored beyond belief by their vapid, druggy summer, the friends perk up at a wedding so establishment the joke is that there are more bodyguards than guests. The boys all but drool over the beautiful Spanish-born Luisa (Maribel Verdú), the wife of one of Tenoch's cousins. When she asks about Mexico's beaches, they make one up out of thin air, call it Heaven's Mouth, and offer to drive her there if she's ever in the mood.

Following a phone call from her absent husband, who tearily confesses to what is not his first infidelity, Luisa is suddenly in the mood. Though they have no idea where they're going, the boys are too excited at the trip's fantasy prospects not to agree, and more unready than any of them realize, off they all go on a classic coming-of-age jaunt.

Not surprisingly, a getting-to-know-you period happens first. Luisa is not the ethereal philosopher the boys fantasized but a lively and down-to-earth dental technician. The friends like her so much they reveal the existence of their secret society, the Charolastras, which has precepts such as "The truth is cool but unattainable."

Gradually, as the three get more complicit, emotional and, yes, sexual complications, both erotic and comical, take center stage. These underline quite a different precept: Be careful what you wish for; you might actually get it. Yet no matter how unsettling things become, *Y Tu Mamá*'s emotional balance, its ability to avoid the gratuitous and keep everything recognizably human, prevents the material from being off-putting.

A key factor in this is the skill of the actors, all at ease with the film's dramatic complexities and sexual content. This is especially true of Spanish actress Verdú, who starred in Fernando Trueba's Oscar-winning *Belle Epoque* several years back. Her Luisa is a rich, empathetic character, uncertain yet brave in her willingness to be alive to her emotions, with all the risks that that attitude entails.

Though the film's advance word will prepare audiences for *Y Tu Mamá*'s sexual antics, passion is not this trip's only component. Cuarón and his collaborators are intent on giving us a vivid, kaleidoscopic vision of roadside Mexico, from local festivities to steers blocking the highway. When Luisa says, "You're so lucky to live in Mexico; it breathes with life," she is speaking for the film as well.

Simultaneously, *Y Tu Mamá* is making offhanded but pointed comments about the country's political situation. Though they rarely mention it, the three drive through an endless series of police-military checkpoints. And the voice-over, calmly noting things such as a laborer hit by a bus because no place to cross a highway exists for miles, or a fisherman who will soon be forced to become a janitor because of the construction of a luxury hotel, casually lets us know what the power of a ruling oligarchy can mean for ordinary lives.

Though *Y Tu Mamá* has its serious aspects, pointing them out may make this graceful film sound different from what it is. What could be more satisfying than strong characters, a sense of humor, and a handful of unabashedly erotic scenes, including one that climaxes with a wonderful twist? Jazzed by film's potential to tell all kinds of stories in all kinds of ways, director Cuarón did more than get his hands dirty. He struck a kind of gold.

Yi Yi
2000

Edward Yang, writer-director of *Yi Yi,* a wise and gentle comedy of manners from Taiwan, has chosen *A One and a Two* as his English title, and his choice of the words that musicians use before they begin seems increasingly inspired as this humanistic film unfolds.

Opening with a wedding and closing with a funeral, *Yi Yi* investigates the entire melody of life: the delicate balance between love and disillusion, the short distance between farce and tragedy, the way different generations have to confront the same difficulties in their own ways, and how what's important is always with us yet simultaneously just out of reach.

Most of all, *Yi Yi* deals with the conundrums of romance, the wonder and perplexity of mutual attraction, what it springs from and where it goes. It's a quiet film but a strong one, graced with the ability to see life whole, the grief hidden in happiness as well as the humor inherent in sadness. Its subject, to borrow a phrase, is the dance to the music of time in which we all must participate.

The popular winner of the best director award at Cannes, *Yi Yi* marks the first time a film by director Yang, a key figure in the Taiwanese New Wave, has had significant American distribution. It's nearly three hours long, but with events intertwining as subtly yet resiliently as encroaching ivy, time is forgotten as we become involved in problems and situations that are complex yet universal.

Central to this family narrative is NJ (Wu Nienjen), a partner in a Taipei computer company who's married with a son and a daughter, an aging mother-in-law, a feckless brother-in-law, even a first love he hasn't seen in decades. Each of these people has a strong narrative position in *Yi Yi*, and we experience their myriad emotional entanglements, their attempts to make the best of their lives' perplexing conditions—professional as well as personal. When NJ says, "There's very little I'm sure about these days," he's speaking for this entire extended family as well.

NJ's wife, Min-Min (Elaine Jin), the dynamo who holds everyone together, sets off ripples when her fears that her life is without meaning send her to an ashram for an indeterminate stay, leaving everyone to their own devices at what seems an especially unsettled time.

Her brother, A-Di (Chen Xisheng), though recently married to his pregnant bride (Xiao Shushen), is still very much a child who can't seem to terminate his relationship with his strong-minded former girlfriend (Zeng Xinyi). And NJ and Min-Min's two children have their own dilemmas as well.

Unsophisticated high-schooler Ting-Ting (Kelly Lee) gets caught up in the romantic entanglements of a single mother and her teenage daughter who move in next door. And her eight-year-old brother, Yang-Yang (an irresistible Jonathan Chang), divides his time between asking profound questions about the nature of life that no one is prepared to answer and getting picked on by his fellow students and an unreasonable teacher.

Father NJ, however, is oblivious to most of this, so all-consuming do his own problems seem to him. His company is going through a potentially fatal financial crisis, and fate puts him back in touch with old flame Sherry Chang-Breitner (Ke Suyun), the woman who may or may not be the love of his life.

In telling this complicated story, Yang utilizes a deliberate, masterful style that defines "unhurried." His accepting sensibility has a way of immersing an audience in his characters and situations. With actors completely inhabiting their roles, *Yi Yi* feels as if it's happening right in front of us, with a satisfying immediacy.

One of Yang's techniques is the way he periodically holds the camera, unmoving, at a small remove from the action. This may sound distancing, but it actually comes off as accepting. Yang not only trusts viewers to understand he's far from unconcerned but also believes in the powerful emotion inherent in his situations. He knows *Yi Yi*'s passions are strong enough to involve us, and his confidence is more than repaid.

part three

DOCUMENTARIES

Introduction

Documentaries have always been my secret pleasure. Not because I haven't wanted to share, but because moviegoers have traditionally resisted these films as in some indefinable way not worthy of their time. All that, however, is changing, and fast.

Ten years ago, I began a *Los Angeles Times* piece on *Black Harvest,* the earliest of this book's documentaries, this way:

> An exceptional motion picture, recent winner of a worldwide 380-film competition and the capstone of a trilogy that has dazzled critics and won dozens of international awards, is opening theatrically today in Los Angeles.
>
> Two years late. For an abbreviated run. Showing at 11 A.M. only.
>
> The key to this seeming riddle is that that film, *Black Harvest,* is a card-carrying member of that most shunned of all genres: the documentary.
>
> Nothing, unfortunately, shouts "unclean" at today's theatrical audiences so much as that category, with the result that *Black Harvest* is being shown as part of a series carefully labeled "Nonfiction Film" to avoid contamination by that accursed 11-letter word.

What a difference a decade makes. Here's a quotation from an article in *Daily Variety* about what was hot and what was not in the 2003 Toronto Film Festival:

> Highly original docs have festgoers talking. These films look poised to close distribution deals, capitalizing on the newly expanded theatrical visibility of doc features in key markets like the U.S.
>
> "Documentaries have always had something to say but now they're saying it in a much louder voice," said Mark Urman, head of distribution at Thinkfilm. "It's become self-perpetuating. Filmmakers know they can get distribution and distributors know they're getting good stories.

"Documentaries aren't just about information anymore, they're about the whole experience. And they're almost always less expensive and easier to market."

The Sundance Film Festival, which gives its documentary competition the same prominence as its prestigious dramatic contest, was a key factor in this turnaround. Fully half of the films in this section received their debuts at the Park City event, which recently acknowledged the international prominence of the genre by inaugurating a new section called "World Cinema: Documentary."

Even before that category opened, Sundance regulars knew that pound for pound you were much likelier to have a satisfying experience with a festival doc than a feature film. With docs, you never feel that you've wasted your time, never run the risk of dealing with the tantrums of a self-indulgent infant auteur. With documentaries you can actually learn something, and be entertained into the bargain.

So why is all this happening now, why does it feel like we are living in perhaps the greatest era for documentaries in the history of film? Numerous factors are involved, starting with the fact that the inexpensive nature of shooting with digital equipment has, not to sound too Marxist about it, placed the means of production firmly in the hands of the proletariat.

Take, for instance, the experience of Scott Hamilton Kennedy, a music video and commercial maker and the director of one of the brightest documentaries of 2003, *OT: Our Town*. When a teacher he was involved with romantically said she was doing a production of the Thornton Wilder work in an inner-city California high school that hadn't put on a play in more than twenty years, he knew he had to record the experience, no matter what. "I never tried to raise money, or put a crew together," he said. "I knew that if any time was wasted trying to do all that, this moment was going to pass undocumented."

So Kennedy went down to Dominquez High School in Compton with a camera so unimpressive he said it looked like a model you can buy at Circuit City. But the unintimidating nature of his equipment enabled the students to relax around him, helping to create an intimacy and trust that is the film's greatest strength.

Not only are documentaries getting easier to make, audiences are getting hungrier for what they provide. It's hardly a secret that the major studios have, with periodic exceptions, all but given up on making films with adults in mind. So where can these viewers turn for involving stories, intriguing characters, real drama? They're turning to documentaries in the same way that frustrated novel readers are making the memoir one of the most popular literary genres. That's where the stories are.

Although it may be desperation that's driving audiences to documentaries, they're apparently liking what they're seeing, which, as any studio executive will tell you, means that they're likely to venture out and see more. Even as noxious a phenomenon as reality TV may be helping here. Already in the habit of enjoying a gimmicked-up version of the real world on the small screen, a wider audience may be finally ready to believe what critics already know: Documentaries can be simply more satisfying than most fiction films can manage. If this is indeed a documentary golden age, that's good news for everyone who believes that the truth will set you free. Or if not, that it at least provides some much-needed entertainment.

Black Harvest
1994

Black Harvest is more gripping, flabbergasting, and purely entertaining than 90 percent of what usually appears on movie screens. The unexpected resonances of its story, the vividness of its cast of characters, and the passion with which it's been made all translate into an indelible movie experience.

Bob Connolly and Robin Anderson, the Australian filmmaking team (he does camera, she does sound, and they both edit with Ray Thomas), spent more than a dozen years making the trilogy that *Black Harvest* concludes. Though this final film contains a recap of the first two (*First Contact* and *Joe Leahy's Neighbors*) and stands completely on its own, a bit of background information is helpful.

All three films are set in Papua New Guinea, the large island nation just north of its former colonial master, Australia. One of the last places on Earth to be affected by Europeans, Papua New Guinea was largely untouched until 1926, when the discovery of gold brought the inevitable invasion of outsiders. Still, because the interior of the island looked to be one continuous and impenetrable mountain range, no one thought to search inland. Until the Leahys.

Led by Michael, the eldest, and joined at varying times by brothers Patrick, James, and Daniel, the Leahy mining expeditions of the 1930s were in many respects typical of prospectors looking for the big strike. But as they ventured inland, a pair of related developments confounded everyone. Those supposedly impenetrable mountains turned out to contain huge and fertile hidden valleys, valleys inhabited by close to a million people who had never seen, heard, or so much as imagined the existence of white people.

Encounters like this had been taking place for hundreds of years, ever since Columbus, Cortés, and Pizarro came to what they called the New World. What made the situation in Papua New Guinea different was a simple quirk of fate. Michael Leahy was a photography buff, and along with his mining gear he had casually brought along both movie and Leica cameras.

The extraordinary result (related in *First Contact*) was several hours of 16-millimeter film and 5,000 still photos that for the first time documented the way indigenous peoples reacted to the incomprehensible appearance of pale-skinned invaders. The looks of awe and terror Leahy's cameras recorded let us see just what Columbus and all the rest must have seen on their arrival in an unprepared world.

The tribal men thought that these pale people were spirits or gods, but the women found out soon enough how human they were, and several mixed-race children, never recognized by their fathers or fully accepted by the tribes, were born. Of these, Joe Leahy, Michael's unacknowledged son and the protagonist of *Joe Leahy's Neighbors*, was easily the most prominent.

Made in the mid-1980s when Joe was in his forties, *Neighbors* details his interaction with the Ganiga, a prominent highland tribe.

More educated and entrepreneurial than the Ganiga, who still live quasi-traditional lives, Joe buys land from them and turns it into a successful coffee plantation, which in turns leads to tribal resentment about Joe's determination to keep all his profits for himself.

Black Harvest opens with Joe at the peak of his influence. That first plantation has made him a wealthy man. Partially to quiet that resentment, he has gone into partnership with another of the Ganiga clans, led by Popina Mai, a charismatic "big man" with the face and manner of an Old Testament prophet.

Joe, who promises the tribe "You'll be up to your necks in money," provides the expertise, while the tribe provides the land, with profits to be split 60–40. Five years after the deal, with the new plantation preparing for its first harvest, the filmmakers returned to see what would transpire.

Connolly and Anderson's commitment to stay in the highlands for as long as it took for the story to unfold—even though it meant living for a year with their infant daughter in a grass hut they built themselves—is one of the keys to *Black Harvest*'s success. For what did unfold was a tale no one could have anticipated, a wrenching story that reverberates with personal and global implications while revealing a singular culture from the inside.

It is a culture that greatly admires oratory, and one of the film's unexpected pleasures is to hear premier public speakers such as the expressive Popina Mai powerfully declaim in Temboka, the melodic local language, about the burning issues of the day. Of which there turn out to be several.

First of all, no sooner is the new plantation ready to harvest than worldwide coffee prices drop steeply, and not only won't the Ganiga be up to their necks in money, they'll be forced to do the bean picking for less wages than they have in the past in order to keep the plantation out of the hands of the bank.

And if this crisis wasn't enough, the Ganiga get halfheartedly drawn into a tribal war that is not really their affair. But like all wars, this soon escalates out of everyone's control, keeping Joe's workers away from the plantation and wreaking havoc with all of his—and an increasingly haunted Popina Mai's—careful plans.

From a visual point of view, the footage Connolly and Anderson recorded is riveting, a startling glimpse into prehistory. During the bow-and-arrow tribal battles, one of their closest friends, a key player in *Joe Leahy's Neighbors,* was killed, and their own hut burned.

Ironically enough, that footage may have kept *Black Harvest* from being nominated for a best-documentary Oscar. Persistent rumors had it that a minority of the nominating committee felt these shots had been staged. In a public letter issued in response to the controversy, Connolly and Anderson underlined the methodology that makes their films so effective: "To not interfere, manipulate, stage, interrupt, but to unobtrusively observe is absolutely central to our filmmaking philosophy."

And though the war footage is visually arresting, it is, in fact, a sidelight to why this film is such a knockout. For what *Black Harvest* focuses on is Joe and Popina Mai trying to cope with these crises. It is concerned with what happens when the twentieth century meets traditional ways, with a people forced to confront the shaky coexistence between revered tribal customs and lust for what Western modernism can provide.

But potent as it is on that level, *Black Harvest* is even more effective when it personalizes these dilemmas. For at its heart this is a story about the death of dreams and all the anger, exasperation, and sadness that goes along with that. It is a story of two men caught between competing cultures—both of whom have reason to feel angry, trapped, and betrayed, for they are both victims of societal forces that are well beyond anyone's control.

And though Joe Leahy tells Popina Mai at one point, "Nobody cares about us and our little enterprise, we're insignificant," *Black Harvest* shows that that doesn't have to be true. As told in this singular film, their story becomes not only our story, but in some ways the key story of the past 500 years.

Blind Spot: Hitler's Secretary
2003

A door opened in the Wolf's Lair, a military field headquarters in East Prussia, and "a kindly old gentleman came to us, smiling, with a soft voice. Meeting him was completely different than I imagined."

The speaker is eighty-one-year-old Traudl Junge; the man is, unbelievably, Adolf Hitler; and the film, *Blind Spot: Hitler's Secretary*, is completely different from anything we could have imagined.

A riveting 90-minute encounter with the woman who was the German leader's private secretary of choice from 1942 until his suicide in 1945, *Blind Spot* parts the curtain of time with such immediacy that it's as startling as having Napoleon's aide-de-camp suddenly materialize to report on the Russian campaign. Inevitably, its premiere at the Berlin Film Festival was a genuine sensation.

Crowds struggled to get in and then sat absolutely still in pin-drop silence, unable to take their eyes off this articulate, insightful, and ferociously honest woman who recounted in dramatic detail not only her experiences up to and including Hitler's final chaotic days in his Berlin bunker, but also her own agonizing struggles with the guilt about being a presence on the scene.

For no one is harder on Junge than she is on herself. No one is as unforgiving of the naive, apolitical young woman who was "so unaware and so thoughtless" that she could look on this terrible man as a kind of benign father figure.

Shielded from knowledge of Hitler's barbaric projects while thinking her job had put her "in the center of information," she tells Austrian co-directors Andre Heller and Othmar Schmiderer that "in fact, I was in a blind spot."

Junge's continual battles with herself, the formidable self-analysis that resulted from how deeply she has thought about this, not only add insight to her memories but also give them a kind of compulsive power. It's as if Junge felt compelled by the weight of history to get her story out with the kind of vividness that takes us back in time along with her.

Junge had, over the past half-century, spoken to historians about her experiences, but she'd never publicly spoken this extensively. Intent on doing so before she died (which she did, amazingly, on the day after the Berlin premiere), Junge sat down for some ten hours of interviews over at least three sessions, identifiable by the different outfits she wears.

In a daring and successful stylistic choice, directors Heller and Schmiderer include almost nothing in the film but Junge, shot in both middle distance and close up, looking at the camera and talking from her one-room Munich apartment. A few shots have her viewing and then expanding on earlier interviews, but nothing is allowed to distract from the impact of a single human presence with a powerful story to tell.

Raised by a divorced mother and a distant, tyrannical grandfather, Junge ended up as Hitler's secretary, she says, "by complete coincidence and chance." A friend got her a secretarial job in the Führer's chancellery, where she opened Hitler's mail, largely from lovelorn women.

Victory in a typing contest got her an audition with the German leader, who told her, "If I take a pretty young secretary, someone marries them and takes them away." Junge replied, "I've lived twenty-two years without a man, so that's no problem for me." Hitler laughed, and the job was hers.

Part of the fascination with *Blind Spot* is the way Junge's revealing personal glimpses combine to create a portrait of a man whose recognizably human traits seem chilling in the context of who he was. Hitler disliked cold rooms, having flowers around (he hated dead things), and being touched. He could spend an entire evening playing with his German shepherd, Blondie, but he always washed his hands after petting her.

Junge, who daily had either lunch or dinner with Hitler, also has more philosophical observations to make. The Führer never spoke about love—"he never used the word"—and he never spoke about the Jews. "Human life meant nothing to him," she feels. "He didn't think in human dimensions but about abstractions like nation or Reich."

Junge's recollections get most compelling as she discusses the period when the walls started to metaphorically close in on Hitler. She saw him immediately after he had survived a 1944 attempt on his life by German officers, "with his hair standing on end, his trousers in tatters, saying, 'I have been saved, destiny has chosen me, providence has preserved me.'"

Most surreal of all are Junge's memories of the shadowy final days in the bunker. People discussed different methods of suicide, and Hitler, who dictated his final will and testament to Junge, sat in a corridor with one of Blondie's puppies in his lap, staring into space.

Junge was even present at Eva Braun's wedding to the Führer ("She told the staff, 'You may now call me Frau Hitler'") and recounts a beyond-belief end-of-days discussion between the two about a statue of a nymph on the foreign ministry grounds.

For Junge, who lived it all, escape into disbelief was not possible. Yet it is one of the real triumphs of this most specific of films that its lessons about blind spots are, by strong implication, intended for us as well, for no one can experience Junge's story without realizing how oblivious we all can be to what seems obvious later on.

Blind Spot underlines how easy it is to be complicit in great evil and how hesitant we all should be about being sure of the moral correctness of what we do. To paraphrase the famous Santayana quote, those who do not understand the past may be condemned to repeat it.

Bus 174

2003

It was not major news in this country when a Rio de Janeiro city bus was hijacked by a lone gunman on July 12, 2000, but in Brazil the resulting multi-hour standoff got the highest TV ratings of the year. An exceptional Brazilian documentary, *Bus 174* provides both a gripping recap of the situation and a disturbing examination of the reality that led to it.

Stymied by a fleeing bus driver while attempting a simple robbery, Sandro do Nascimento impulsively ended up holding the vehicle's eleven passengers hostage. Because the Rio police neglected to secure the perimeter against TV crews, and because the bus had enormous glass windows on all sides, every moment of this terrifying situation was visible and broadcast live.

Director Jose Padilha, a Rio native, was one of the millions transfixed by the unfolding situation, and the first thing he did when he began to work on this film was to look at the more than 24 hours of raw video the different networks had recorded. It is remarkable footage, a very different order of material than the *Survivor* stuff we're used to.

Unwilling to look but unable to turn away, we see Sandro, his face sometimes visible, sometimes hidden by a towel, walking up and down the bus, a gun always at one of the hostage's heads, screaming imprecations at the police and the whole watching world.

"I'm gonna shoot, I'm gonna do her first," he yells, following that with "Check this out, I'm gonna blow her head off" and "There's blood on my mind, lots of blood." At one point, he orders a hostage to write a message in lipstick on the front window: "He is going to kill us all at 6 P.M." It's then that the real drama begins.

Bus 174, however, does a lot more than rebroadcast that unsettling actuality footage. What director Padilha had in mind is something considerably more ambitious and even unexpected. He uses the bus incident as a lens through which to explore major currents in Brazilian life, as a way to examine the different ways modern urban society has failed its citizens. What results is a thoughtful, analytical, yet powerfully emotional film, meticulously investigated and absolutely compelling.

Padilha intercuts scenes of the hijacking with interviews of an unexpectedly wide selection of involved parties. He talks to some of the hijack victims, to a masked street criminal, to members of the city's elite SWAT team, and to social workers, sociologists, and family members. What concerns him are the societal forces that came together to cause Bus 174, how a tragedy no one wanted ended up happening.

We learn the sad specifics of Sandro do Nascimento's life, how his mother was murdered in front of him when he was six years old, how a turn in reform school left him more criminal than he was when he went in. We see the hell-hole prisons he spent time in, hear about the infamous Candelaria street-kids massacre he survived, listen to other street-kid survivors explain "When we grow up, we're enraged. I think I'll never know happiness."

The culture of homeless, underage, amoral criminals that Sandro came from has also been the subject of Brazilian fiction films such as *Pixote* and *City of God.* The reality behind the stories is bleak, and it is especially unsettling to hear a sociologist explain the incendiary combination of massive TV coverage and the classic street-kids' drive, "a battle against invisibility and a hunger for recognition."

Sandro, the sociologist explains, felt empowered by the TV coverage and acted violently because the cameras made him feel powerful. In other words, "He recovered his visibility, he redefined the social narrative," and seeing himself as someone important became, tragically, as necessary a goal as staying alive.

Bus 174 is equally concerned with the pressures and problems of the police. The film reveals that though the city's SWAT team was well respected, the rest of the Rio force was not. Poorly paid, untrained, lacking in esprit de corps, these people were in many ways hard to distinguish from the criminals they were nominally policing.

It is this kind of rigorous evenhandedness, an ability to tell this story without special pleading for any of its participants, that makes *Bus 174* hard to shake. Closing our eyes to the lessons history teaches is likely as ruinous a strategy on our city's streets as it is on the international stage.

The Cockettes
2002

The Cockettes confounds the cliché that if you remember the 1960s, you weren't really there. An irresistible documentary look at the ensemble of the moment in the hippie kingdom that was San Francisco, this comprehensive and charming film not only recalls those days exactly, it also manages the wonderful trick of taking us back there along with it.

Directors David Weissman and Bill Weber have used excellent interviews and remarkable vintage footage (some of it compiled by former Cockette Martin Worman for a doctoral dissertation) to illuminate a corner of half-forgotten countercultural history.

By doing so, they've also managed to capture the feeling of an era now dealt with largely in terms of bromides about license and free love. If you want not only to see what the '60s looked like but to experience what it was like to be in them, it's hard to improve on what's here.

The Cockettes were a performing troupe best defined (by director and early fan John Waters) as a bunch of "hippie acid freak drag queens." Made up of both men and women, some straight but mostly gay, the group was united by a passion for LSD, by a belief in "complete sexual anarchy, always a good thing" (Waters again), and by something else: an unlikely, almost heroic naïveté.

As much as the drugs and the blurring of sexual lines, the Cockettes were characterized by a belief that they were part of a revolutionary movement that was going to change the world into something better. It's hard not to be charmed by their messianic good cheer, their enthusiastic guilelessness and sense of play. These were people who built their own reality, who were, as someone vividly says, "allowed to live at the end of their imagination."

Cockettes begins with a moment—a November 1971 appearance at a New York theater thick with celebrities—that seemed to mark a collective high point for the group. But, as we come to see, it actually finds them already on a downward slide.

In the early days, the dozen or so former Cockettes interviewed for the film seemed to find each other in the spaced-out melting pot of San Francisco's Haight-Ashbury. What united them was a passion for dressing up like you wouldn't believe; it was, someone says, as if they communicated through drag.

The leader of this pack was New York transplant George Harris, now known as "Hibiscus" and accurately described as looking like "Jesus Christ with lipstick."

Still intensely charismatic in vintage videos, Hibiscus was the group's acknowledged visionary, and it was his idea that what the company (named for Radio City's Rockettes) needed was to be on stage.

As chance would have it, North Beach's Palace Theater was running a midnight film series called the Nocturnal Dream Shows. Agreeing to appear in exchange for free tickets, the Cockettes' can-can dancing combination of anarchy, nudity, glitter, drugs, and lace became an instant success, and a San Francisco institution was born.

Filmmakers Weissman and Weber have done a heroic job of getting the surviving Cockettes on film, from the guileless Sweet Pam and the waspish Goldie Glitters to token male heterosexual Marshall and self-described bad girl Fayette, whose life ambition was to be an adventuress.

The group put on a series of loosely constructed shows with names such as *Gone with the Showboat to Oklahoma*. Remembers Sweet Pam, these "were so untraditional, so far from the mainstream, they were almost illegal." Film was also dabbled in, from *Elevator Girls in Bondage* to the mock *Tricia's Wedding*, which debuted at the Palace on the same day as the actual event in the Nixon White House.

As show followed show, the big question with the Cockettes became, as one member put it, "Can mediocrity stand success?" Celebrity led to ego problems, and a split developed between Hibiscus and his allies, who believed in the purity of free performance, and those who believed in professionalism and felt that money should be changing hands.

But the truth was that what the Cockettes did was always more the public expression of a lifestyle than a stage event that could be planned or transplanted—hence the group's celebrated flop in New York. In addition to personality clashes, the ensemble was also done in by early deaths, first from drug addiction and later from AIDS.

Still, it's possible to see in their idiosyncratic work a prefiguring of everything from gay liberation to glam rock. As journalist Lillian Roxon predicted back then, "Every time you see too much glitter, or a rhinestone out of place, you know it's because of the Cockettes."

Crumb
1995

As shocking yet haunting as a Diane Arbus photograph, disturbing because it is so unmistakably human, *Crumb* makes it difficult to look away. Not even Leo Tolstoy's dictum that "Every unhappy family is unhappy in its own way" is adequate preparation for the unsettling personal dramas that unfold in this remarkable film.

Though Terry Zwigoff's documentary begins as an examination of the art and career of the celebrated cartoonist R. (for Robert) Crumb, it is considerably more than that. Because it provides an intimate view of Crumb's singular background, it ends up dealing with larger, more complex issues, from the impact of family in shaping personality to the concept of the artist as a messenger to society from a scathing personal hell.

Considered the key figure in the underground comic movement, Crumb is responsible for such outrageous creations as Mr. Natural, Fritz the Cat, and the catchphrase "Keep on Truckin'." In the view of *Time* magazine art critic Robert Hughes, his scabrous monsters of the id make Crumb "the Breughel of the last half of the 20th Century," and comparisons to Daumier and even Goya have not been lacking.

Though Crumb is often the centerpiece of his drawings, little has been known about him personally. Shy, bemused, and seriously eccentric, a devotee of bow ties and old 78 records, Crumb is hardly eager to let the world interact with what he calls "the little guy that lives inside my brain."

But documentarian Zwigoff, who worked on this film for six years, has known Crumb for twenty-five years and even played alongside the artist in the Cheap Suit Serenaders, his old-timey string band. Only an intimate of such long standing could have gotten this kind of privileged view of a subject's life, and only a talented and experienced filmmaker, which Zwigoff is as well, would have been able to handle material this unnerving.

Unwilling to drive, uneasy with people, described by his wife, Aline, as someone who'd "rather be a brain in a jar than have a body," Crumb is initially presented in a typical mode of ironic self-disgust.

"If I don't get to draw, I feel suicidal; if I do, I feel suicidal, too," he says, paralleling his general belief that "Words fail me, and pictures aren't much better."

In fact, Crumb is an engaging monologuist when he gets going, willing to reveal more about his tangled sex life (with his ex-wife and girlfriends providing corroboration) than many people may want to hear. And his graphic, straight-from-the-unconscious artwork, which Crumb says began to flower after a particularly weird LSD experience, can be so unapologetically misogynistic that Zwigoff appropriately devotes time to feminist critics of his sensibility.

But the biggest shock of *Crumb* is not what he draws but finding out that this man is the most normal, functional member of his family. The artist is one of five children of a violent ex-Marine who wrote and taught on "Training People Effectively" while physically terrorizing both his trio of sons and their amphetamine-abusing mother. (Crumb's two sisters refused to cooperate with the film and are not interviewed.)

Robert's eldest brother, Charles, got the brunt of the physical punishment, and his presence on film has an unusually disturbing quality. Witty, painfully sad, someone who is on easy terms with Kant, Hegel, and the great nineteenth-century novelists, Charles has lived with his mother in their shambles of a home since high school and is only tenuously linked with reality.

As far as artistic expression in the Crumb family, however, Charles was the acknowledged trailblazer. He was the first of the children to become interested in comics, the one who insisted that Robert draw and get good at it. The film shows him now as an adult dependent on tranquilizers and antidepressants, too detached from the human race to so much as set foot outside the front door.

Equally arresting, but not quite so poignant, is brother Max, who sleeps on a bed of nails in a San Francisco flophouse, remembers every childhood slight, and performs off-putting yoga cleansing rituals for the benefit of the camera.

Taken together, the tale of these three brothers functions as a textbook example of the way horrific family conditions can nurture an artistic sensibility. Resistant to fame, congenitally unable to sell out,

Crumb draws because he has to, because it is the only way he can make the strain and madness of his upbringing manageable.

Last glimpsed about to move his family to France because it's "slightly less evil than the United States," Crumb also says at one point that he doesn't consider himself an exciting subject for a movie. Maybe not exciting, but when it comes to unflinching, riveting looks at a compulsive artist who can't be other than who he is, nothing comes close to *Crumb*.

Zwigoff went on to direct the eccentric dramatic features Ghost World *and* Bad Santa.

Dark Days
2000

"When I first came into the tunnel, I was scared," the man says. "It was dark, even in the daytime. It looked dangerous." That day is now years in the past; the tunnel is now home. "You'd be surprised," the man says, "what the human body, the human mind can adjust to."

Dark Days, Marc Singer's exceptional documentary on the people who live in train tunnels beneath Manhattan, won three awards at the Sundance Film Festival and may have deserved more. It's remarkable for where it takes us, how it takes us there, and the quiet way it changes our view of the world by giving a voice to people no one has much listened to before.

Producer-director Singer was so far from being a filmmaker when he started *Dark Days* that he had to be shown how to load a camera. More an advocate for the homeless, he had as his aim not to win prizes but to somehow earn money to get these people above ground. Not only did he end up living in the tunnels himself for extended periods of time, he also used his subjects as his entire film crew. Rarely has the typical closing dedication to those "who put their hearts and souls into making this project against all the odds" meant as much as it does here.

This kind of personal involvement makes *Dark Days* all the more powerful for being nonjudgmental. Told from deep inside by people who trusted Singer enough to be open and candid, the film treats its subjects straight-on, without the kinds of patronizing or romanticizing that often mar well-meaning documentaries on the dispossessed.

Inspired in part by *Hoop Dreams,* Singer ended up investing nearly six years, all told, in *Dark Days.* And as happened with the landmark basketball documentary, the director discovered that spending that much time with a subject allows reality to come up with unexpected twists that fiction would have a hard time matching.

Dark Days begins in daylight, with a man walking down a flight of stairs. Then, like Alice, he continues his journey through a hole in the ground. Although he doesn't end up in a wonderland, the destination is not a complete nightmare, either.

In fact, it's one of the ironies of *Dark Days,* and a bleak comment on the kind of society we've created, that the tunnel's residents almost uniformly feel far safer and more secure down there than anywhere up on the surface. "Ain't nobody in their right mind coming down here," a man named Greg says. "They're not going to mess with you."

The tunnel community turns out to be—and why should this surprise us?—a very human place, a kind of parallel universe where young and old, black and white, male and female try to survive and even get a little bit ahead. Though the percentage of crack addicts is considerable, many tunnel dwellers are eager, as Greg says, "to make that almighty dollar," even if it means collecting cans and bottles and selling things scavenged from the trash.

Ignoring as best they can the omnipresent rats and horrific noise of Amtrak trains hurtling past, tunnel residents plug into available electricity and use scavenged material to build and furnish wood-walled shacks so sturdy that, when some say they don't consider themselves homeless, you know what they mean.

In addition to the talkative Greg, *Dark Days* introduces us to a tunnel cross-section including former crack addict Ralph, energetic and motivated dog fancier Tommy, and a woman named Dee who unburdens herself of a life story that is heart-rending. None of them are archetypes, or even types, but rather people more like us than we really want to acknowledge.

Like regular citizens, many of the characters in *Dark Days* have a great desire to be busy, to be productive, to be doing something. And like homeowners everywhere, they are forever tinkering with their roofs, their walls, even their makeshift security systems. So when a crisis arises and armed Amtrak police give them thirty days to evacuate, it's an action that's both profoundly shocking and the catalyst for a powerful ending.

Despite filmmaker Singer's lack of previous experience, *Dark Days* is smartly shot on black-and-white film and makes excellent use of a moody, evocative soundtrack by DJ Shadow. Like a Dante back from the deepest circles of despair, Singer has personalized his friends and neighbors and made it as hard as it should be to look on homeless people as a shapeless, formless mass.

The Decline of Western Civilization, Part III
1998

It's a tradition for documentaries to explore inaccessible, even dangerous locales, mounting voyages of discovery to places few people have been. *The Decline of Western Civilization, Part III,* fits that definition, but instead of going to the headwaters of the Orinoco or the far reaches of the Kalahari, it unveils a disturbing world that's just down the street.

Shot on and around Hollywood Boulevard over a span of eleven months, *Decline* focuses on the subculture of gutter punks, the elaborately pierced and tattooed young people with kaleidoscope hair shaped into skyscraper mohawks. They're a familiar local sight, but until this intelligent, provocative, and sympathetic film by Penelope Spheeris came along, not many people gave them much thought.

Decline is the twelfth feature of Spheeris's wildly divergent filmography. She's made both Hollywood ephemera, such as *Wayne's World, The Beverly Hillbillies,* and *The Little Rascals,* as well as a series of honest, groundbreaking documentaries on rock 'n' roll themes, of which this is the third.

The first *Decline,* which focused on the early L.A. punk scene, was made in 1979, before most of the punks in *Part III* were even born, and Spheeris uses interviews with some of the old-timers to try to put the new kids into perspective.

Rick Wilder of the Mau-Maus, now a sepulchral presence with long flaming red hair, calls punk "a shrieking siren" conveying "anger at everything." And today, says Keith Morris, formerly with Black Flag and the Circle Jerks, "there's more people, more crime, more corruption, more reasons to be angry and upset."

Decline features performance footage of current punk bands with names such as Final Conflict, the Resistance, and Naked Aggression as well as interviews with the members of that last group, who turn out to be politically aware individuals with musical backgrounds in classical guitar, piano, and French horn.

The heart of the film, and equally surprising, is the extended talking-head interviews Spheeris does with the kids on Hollywood Boulevard, who've taken street names such as Squid, Troll, Hamburger, and Why-me.

To see these gutter punks is not to love all aspects of them. They brag about drinking every night until they black out, talk openly about thievery, and at times display typical teenage sullenness and bravado.

But Spheeris has captured another side of these people, which makes the sight of wasted lives sadder than it would otherwise be. Along with their baby-faced nihilism, the gutter punks also display a poignant idealism about the decency they'd like to see in the world, a wistful sense of being let down by forces beyond their control and by a society that is often judgmental, violent, and uncaring.

Surprisingly bright and articulate, many of these kids turn out to be victims of adult abuse who became angry and anarchistic because they felt no hope of fitting in. Their toughness ("We're the cockroaches, we're the ones that can live through anything"), as it turns out, does not always run deep. "We get our feelings hurt," one girl says, "and we cover it up with spikes and color." Adds another punk, speaking for them all: "It's not really fun to be in reality."

With her unblinking but nonjudgmental eye, Spheeris doesn't shy away from the horrifying, at times violent messes these kids make of their lives, but she is always sensitive to the pain behind everything, to the unhappy futility of squandered potential.

Spheeris plans to donate any profits from this self-financed venture to charities for homeless young people and abused children. When she introduced this film at its debut at Sundance (where it won the Freedom of Expression award), the director said that of all her films, "this one is closest to my heart, the one that I feel, if I die tomorrow, I've done something." She certainly has.

East Side Story
1997

You've never seen anything like *East Side Story,* but then again, neither has anyone else. At least not on this side of the former Iron Curtain. Smart and sassy, this smashingly entertaining documentary introduces the West to the world of socialist musicals, a genre so unlikely that even its creators were often chagrined at what they'd accomplished.

Imagine, if you can, hearty machinists bursting into a chorus of "In the hot blast of the coal oven, the coal press begins to stomp." Or ecstatically happy peasants taking part in a stupendous wheat harvest choreographed to the rhythms of massive machinery. Or a glamorous swineherd singing, "Hey, piggies, time to eat, come to your trough and have a little meal." It's all here, and more.

But *East Side Story* is not just a *That's Entertainment!* compiled from communism's most eye-popping production numbers. As put together by Dana Ranga and Andrew Horn (she directed, he produced, they co-wrote), the film examines how these unlikely epics came to life in the face of serious obstacles. And it does so with irresistible style, typified by a puckish thank-you to Karl Marx, "without whom none of this would have been necessary."

"A socialist musical film has to be a crazy idea," says the movie's sly voice-over, partly because "fun and music in a world of ambiguity and suspicion" is an unlikely scenario. Also, the seriousness of socialism, its humorless determination to raise the political consciousness of the working class, led party functionaries to dismiss mere enter-tainment as unworthy of the great cause.

Yet some forty socialist musicals with catchy titles such as *Tractor Drivers* and *Cossacks of the Kuban River* were made behind the Iron Curtain, mostly in the USSR and East Germany, but with stubborn outcroppings in Bulgaria, Poland, Romania, and Czechoslovakia. *East Side Story* uses a generous selection of clips and pithy interviews with experts, participants, and ordinary fans to show how the impos-sible came to be.

It all started with Russian Grigory Alexandrov and his unlikely pa-trons in high places. Alexandrov was the great Sergei Eisenstein's as-sistant director, but after the two of them returned from a 1931 trip to Hollywood, Alexandrov went out on his own and made the first So-viet musical, the merry, syncopated *The Jolly Fellows*.

Naturally, the film was promptly banned, but Alexandrov took it to writer Maxim Gorky, who liked it so much he personally showed it to Joseph Stalin himself. Against considerable odds, Stalin was wowed, allegedly commenting that "anyone who made a movie as funny as this has to be a brave man."

With backing that potent, Alexandrov and his actress wife, Lyubov Orlova (who was so popular she regularly got fan letters signed by thousands), were able to make several musicals, including the cele-brated *Volga Volga* about local talent determined to make it big in Moscow. That film was Stalin's favorite: He watched it more than 100 times and even gave a copy to wartime ally Franklin D. Roosevelt, whose own reaction is not recorded.

Both Alexandrov and the other key Soviet musical director, Ivan Pyriev, created dreams, but they were specifically Communist ones, where optimistic workers were always smiling, and fulfilling quotas was a joy, not a duty. But when Stalin died, the heart went out of the USSR musical, and it fell to the German Democratic Republic (GDR) to pick up the slack.

But not right away. The East German film bureaucrats preferred to turn out turgid tales, such as *Ernest Thalmann, Class Leader,* that ide-alized the heroic, albeit boring struggle against capitalism. But in the days before the Berlin Wall, what East German audiences preferred was to cross over to the West and spend their money on the potent fantasies that Hollywood produced. Entertainment, it turned out, had a powerful imperative of its own.

So, reports actress Karin Schroder, known in her heyday as "the Doris Day of the East," members of the GDR power structure, having determined that "we have attractive people, we have sex, we have all that here," decided to go into the musical business themselves and pocket the profits.

Their first product, *My Wife Wants to Sing* (1958), starring a former Miss Bavaria and the actor who'd played Ernest Thalmann, boasted the daring theme that communism supported women who wanted to work. It was an immediate hit even in the Soviet Union, where it earned 11 million rubles in just four weeks.

Eventually, East Germany got bold enough to attempt brassy teen musicals with names such as *Hot Summer* and *No Cheating Darling*, but the lack of governmental support and recognition—not to mention that the shoots used so much electricity they threatened the power supply of entire cities—led inevitably to their extinction.

Even in their heyday, what with lack of experienced personnel and official pronouncements condemning them as "the most flagrant offspring of the capitalist pleasure industry," these musicals were never easy to create. In fact, one of the most charming of the East German films, *Midnight Review*, focused on the difficulties and featured a lyric complaining:

> It's enough to make you tear your hair out!
> It's easier to wait 10 years for a car.
> It's simpler to go ice-skating in the desert
> Than to make a socialist musical!

Viewed today, the clips featured here are both musically engaging and endearing in their earnestness, a view of an intriguing parallel universe influenced by Hollywood but doing things not quite the same way. "Who knows," *East Side Story* asks with a tinge of regret, "how things would have turned out if socialism could just have been more fun?" How indeed.

Fast, Cheap & Out of Control
1997

At a certain point in *Fast, Cheap & Out of Control,* Errol Morris's strange but wonderful documentary, wild-animal trainer Dave Hoover explains why a brandished chair is an effective foil for a lion: The four legs present four points of interest, and that confuses a beast who had been completely focused on "eating the guy in the white suit."

A one-of-a-kind extravaganza by the most original talent now working in documentary film, the four-pronged *Fast, Cheap* has a similar potential to disorient audiences. Director Morris, whose other efforts include *Gates of Heaven, The Thin Blue Line,* and *A Brief History of Time,* is intent, as always, on pushing the envelope of nonfiction filmmaking, on cutting the form as much slack as he can while remaining in complete control.

What that means here is linking four stories that have only the most tenuous thematic connections by means of fluid juxtapositions of image and sound. *Fast, Cheap* is an intoxicating collage put together (by Morris, Oscar-winning cinematographer Robert Richardson, composer Caleb Sampson, and editors Shondra Merrill and Karen Schmeer) using nothing more than instinct and sensibility. This is nervy filmmaking, and like facing lions in a cage, it's as powerful to experience as a dream.

Links could, of course, be found between the four men profiled in *Fast, Cheap.* They all tell what the director himself has called "deeply weird animal stories," they're all restless intelligences searching for knowledge while trying to control the natural world. But even as these links are acknowledged, they seem beside the point. The truth, as Morris said when *Fast, Cheap* debuted at Sundance, is that this is "the ultimate low-concept film," a quartet of stories linked only by the director's fascination with each of its characters.

Dave Hoover is, as noted, an animal trainer specializing in the big cats, like his mentor and idol, the legendary Clyde Beatty. Now semi-retired, he's a genial raconteur, spinning tales of life inside the ring and letting us know why you never, ever want to wear an expansion band wristwatch when lions are around.

Much more intense, though his animals are considerably smaller, is Ray Mendez, an authority on African mole-rats. These strange little beasts, with monster teeth capable of gnawing through concrete, have the distinction of being the only mammals who live in the same kind of complex society that insects do. A photographer who designed a mole-rat habitat at the Philadelphia zoo, Mendez wears a butterfly-shaped bow tie and is positively gleeful about his favorite species.

Just as excited, though his specialty is not flesh and blood, is Rodney Brooks, one of MIT's top robot scientists, who builds machines that are unnervingly lifelike. The same goes for the wild beasts sculpted with garden shears by George Mendonca, a topiary artist who's worked at a Rhode Island estate called Green Animals for more than twenty years, turning privet and boxwood into giraffes and bears.

Using the Interrotron, a machine of Morris's invention that enables interview subjects to look directly at the audience, these four tell tales of ordinary madness, offering tricks of the trade and revealing how and why they do what they do. But that is only the first level of what *Fast, Cheap* has to offer.

Added on next is footage by Richardson, who shot almost all of Oliver Stone's films (his Oscar was for *JFK*) and who has done an exceptional job of infusing an air of strangeness and beauty to pictures from the lives of these men, such as that topiary garden, or the three-ring action of the current Beatty circus.

Equally important is a hypnotic, driving score by Sampson (a founder of the Alloy Orchestra, admired for its compositions for silent films) and a wide and impressive variety of other kinds of footage, everything from circus home movies to clips from Beatty-starring serials such as *King of Jungleland*.

Although there is minimal cohesion between the lives of the certified eccentrics the film investigates, all these varieties of film and sound are layered tightly together in the most artful way. Circus footage, for instance, will be on the screen while someone is talking about robots, and shots of robots will be intercut with kangaroos and ostriches. Even without conventional links, the whole thing hangs together beautifully. Don't question this film's structure, just let its images and connections wash over you. We're all at the circus here, and Morris is an unconventional ringmaster whose sense of wonder never flags.

Freedom on My Mind
1994

Not that much time has passed since the epochal Mississippi Voter Registration Project of 1961–1964, but that's been enough for the events to almost disappear from America's consciousness, for the civil rights movement's successes in dislodging blatant segregation to be forced into near oblivion by the extent of the problems between the races that remain.

So it is an especial tonic to see *Freedom on My Mind,* winner of the Sundance Film Festival's Grand Jury Prize, a spirited evocation of a struggle with an enormity we have largely forgotten. Co-directed by Connie Field and Marilyn Mulford, this lively documentary underscores how dramatic that battle was, how much was accomplished, and how terrifyingly difficult it was to do.

Unlike public television's *Eyes on the Prize,* this documentary is not a general survey of the period but a passionate and personal oral history. It intercuts strong contemporary footage and the pointed singing of spirituals, such as "Ain't Gonna Let Nobody Turn Me Round," with the still vivid memories of the people transformed by the movement, people who unhesitatingly put their lives at risk because of the power of what they believed.

Freedom is structured around the recollections of ten civil rights veterans, but especially evocative are the memories of Mississippi natives such as Curtis Hayes of McComb, so infuriated by racism as a child that he used to "hit trees, pretend they were white folks." Or sharecropper's daughter L.C. Dorsey, now a Ph.D. in public health, who remembers that her illiterate father had such faith in education that he would walk her daily to the school bus stop, shotgun in hand.

Most stirring of all, however, are the memories of Endesha Ida Mae Holland of Greenwood, raped by her white employer on her eleventh birthday and afterward a teenage prostitute. When the civil rights organizers came to town, Holland was first excited at the possibility of "turning tricks with them." But the movement instead became "the beginning of me finding myself," unlocking the possibility of a new kind of life, though it was a life that was to come at a considerable personal cost.

For Mississippi in 1961 was, in one observer's words, a place where "blacks were free in name only," where men could be lynched for "eye rape," and where segregationists outdid each other in boasting of their devotion to racial separation. The state, says Bob Moses, was "a little South African enclave within the United States."

Soft-spoken, thoughtful, and deeply charismatic, Bob Moses was one of the leaders of the voter registration project, and the experience, especially the loss of life involved, ,was such a wrenching one for him that he rarely discusses it in public. Moses's wise and careful comments here, putting the past in perspective, are one of *Freedom*'s strengths.

The idea behind the movement to register a half-million disenfranchised black voters was that it was the best way to pull a reluctant federal government into the fight for equality. The struggle almost immediately became a brutal one. Segregationists fought back with deadly force, and the black community responded with remarkable acts of everyday heroism that commanded national attention.

To further focus the country's attention, the movement's leadership decided on the controversial strategy of calling on white college students from out of state to help with the work. The idea, as one veteran puts it, was that "if you want to bring law to the South, you have to bring the people the law covers," and that meant northern whites.

To its credit, *Freedom* does not try to hide the difficulties that strategy caused as people who had never mingled before began to try to do just that. And the film's strongest section is a careful look at the rarely examined and traumatic conclusion to the voting rights project, the attempt by the newly formed Mississippi Freedom Democratic Party (MFDP) to unseat that state's segregationist Dixiecrat delegation at the 1964 Democratic National Convention.

Believing, naively as it turned out, that they had the moral force to "take on the system at the highest level," the MFDP ran up against the machinations of master politician Lyndon Johnson. Apparently fearing that seating the rebels would jeopardize his election chances with the rest of the South, Johnson effectively stymied their movement and in the process, insists Bob Moses, did damage that is still being played out.

"The Democratic Party lost a group of young black people, disillusioned a generation of young white people, and missed the chance to capture the attention and the energy of the generation that set the tone for the '60s," Moses poignantly points out. The result was "a polarization we're not out of yet. It's one of the great tragedies of this country." It is a sobering and provocative conclusion to a stirring piece of documentary work.

Genghis Blues
1999

It is a sound once heard, never forgotten. A sound with the power to rearrange your mind and transform your life. That's what it did for San Francisco–based blind blues singer Paul Pena, and *Genghis Blues,* an enchanting documentary on a magnificent obsession, shows how it all went down.

The sound is throat singing, the ability to create two, even three distinct vocal tones simultaneously. The *Washington Post* calls the results "feats of harmonic acrobatics," and Pena describes it as sounding "just like Popeye singing the blues."

Throat singing is a national passion in Tuva, a North Dakota–sized Asian nation largely populated by nomadic herdsmen. Located north of Mongolia and now a part of the Russian Federation, Tuva was briefly independent from 1921 to 1944 (collectors have the vivid postage stamps to prove it). Its people take pride in its association with Genghis Khan, whose top general, the conqueror of Europe, called Tuva home.

Tuva had also piqued the curiosity of celebrated physicist Richard Feynman, who believed that a nation with a capital city named Kyzyl had to be of interest. He and a friend, Ralph Leighton, formed

Friends of Tuva, corresponded with Tuvans in their own language, and even got three Tuvans into a Rose Bowl parade.

Pena, not surprisingly, knew none of this back in 1984, when he picked up a random Radio Moscow broadcast while scanning his shortwave radio. A respected musician who had played with John Lee Hooker, Muddy Waters, and T-Bone Walker (and whose grandparents were from the Cape Verde Islands, home of world music star Cesara Evora), Pena heard throat singing for the first time and was transfixed. "That's for me, man," he remembers saying to himself. "That's something I could get off doing."

It took Pena years to find anyone who even knew what he'd been listening to, further years to both learn some of the Tuvan language, via English-Russian and Russian-Tuvan Braille dictionaries, and to teach himself how to sing in *kargyraa,* one of the key throat-singing styles.

When virtuoso Tuvan throat singer Kongar-Ol Ondar (who has recorded with Frank Zappa, the Kronos Quartet, and Mickey Hart) gave a concert in the Bay Area in 1993, Pena surprised him afterward by breaking into some impromptu vocalizing in the lobby. Greatly impressed, Ondar invited Pena to come to his country's next National Throat-Singing Symposium and Competition, scheduled for 1995.

With some financial help from Friends of Tuva ("One of our ideas is just to do crazy things," admits co-founder Leighton), an improbable, ragtag expedition to Tuva was put together. Besides Pena, members included friend and recording engineer Lemon DeGeorge; the late Mario Casetta, an irascible world music authority; and two young filmmakers, brothers Roko and Adrian Belic, who between the two of them wrote, directed, produced, edited, and shot the film, their first.

Under the aegis of Ondar, whom the voice-over describes as "a combination of John F. Kennedy, Elvis, and Michael Jordan" in his home country, the expedition went everywhere and met everyone, from the legends of throat singing to Ondar's mother. They also were guests at numerous celebrations at which the slaughter of sheep (shown in graphic detail in the film) was the main event.

Singing in the competition, Pena was a monster hit, living up to his nickname of "Earthquake" and astonishing the Tuvans with both his vocal work and his willingness to speak their obscure language.

Despite being dogged by illness and other problems, Pena and his companions clearly had the experience of their lives.

As culled by the Belic brothers from 150 hours of video, the 88-minute *Genghis Blues* (which won an audience award at Sundance) is nothing to write home about in terms of technique, but the story it tells couldn't be more charming, and the film's makeshift qualities echo the off-the-wall spirit of the trip itself. A more improbable and endearing yarn can't be imagined.

Licensed to Kill
1997

What is most surprising—and most provocative—about *Licensed to Kill,* Arthur Dong's strong and disturbing documentary on men who kill homosexuals, is the way it overturns our expectations. Nothing you've heard about the plague of violence against gay men will lessen the shock value of this chilling look at the real face of evil.

Winner of the Filmmaker's Trophy at Sundance, *Licensed to Kill* is written, directed, produced, and edited by Dong (*Coming Out Under Fire*), a gay man who counts personal experience as the impetus behind this work.

In 1977, Dong explains in a brief voice-over prologue, he was attacked by four gay-bashing teenagers in San Francisco and escaped only by throwing himself on the hood of a passing car. Still attempting, years later, to understand the roots of this violent behavior, he decided to do "the most difficult thing" and confront men "whose contempt for homosexuals led them to kill people like me."

"Confront" may not be the right word, because one of *Licensed to Kill*'s strengths is the coolness of its technique, the almost clinical matter-of-factness of its presentation. Dong never appears on camera and wisely allows the half-dozen convicted murderers he interviews to tell their own stories unimpeded by any kind of hectoring or editorializing.

That does not mean that *Licensed to Kill* is no more than a collection of talking heads. Intercut with Dong's six prison interviews are various kinds of relevant material, including TV news reports and unsettling police evidence tapes and photos of the murders that his interviewees committed.

Equally disturbing are the selections from homophobic statements by prominent fundamentalist leaders, psychotic phone messages of the "Save America/Kill a Fag" variety, a home video of a gay man being viciously beaten up by a neighbor, and a police interrogation tape in which a young man calmly describes how he came to stab a gay man twenty-seven times.

But though this material is all relevant and to the point, *Licensed to Kill* is that rare documentary that would fascinate and horrify even if it were nothing but talking heads. Because while Hollywood's movies have acclimated us to clichéd bigots, cardboard monsters like James Woods in *Ghosts of Mississippi,* it's a shock to see how various, how unexpectedly well-spoken, how deeply troubled and haphazard the evil that walks our streets can be.

Who would expect to encounter someone like Jay Johnson, an articulate, initially closeted gay man who was raised in a religious, violently anti-homosexual household? Feeling loathing toward all things gay, even, he says, "to the extent that I was doing it, I was disgusted with myself," Johnson was even more horrified to discover that his mixed race was a handicap to cruising that made him "unsuccessful at something I already hated." A series of slayings attempting to frighten gay men off the streets of Minneapolis is what followed.

For some of the prisoners, the murders they committed were almost an afterthought or a whim, the casual byproduct of robberies of gay men who were the classic easy targets. Faced with the choice of robbing a 7-Eleven, with its ever-present video camera, or robbing victims who, "because of the fact that they're a homosexual and they don't want people to know it, they're not gonna go report it to the police," says Donald Aldrich, "who you gonna go rob?"

The most disconnected story belongs to Kenneth Jr. French, a career army man who killed four people at random in a North Carolina restaurant to protest President Clinton's relaxing of the ban on gays in the military. And one of the sadder histories is that of William Cross. Raped by a friend of the family when he was seven, he "never felt the same afterward, never felt like I was even a man anymore." The irrational but deadly result was anti-homosexual rage.

What many of these men have in common, Dong's film suggests, is the way society's attitudes in general, and the hostility of fundamentalist religion in particular, gave them an almost literal license to kill, a feeling that slaying gay men meant, as Jeffrey Swinford puts it, "just one less problem the world had to mess with." "Religion," muses Jay Johnson, "is a vicious thing."

To look these people in the face, to hear their horrific but always recognizably human stories, is much more affecting and unsettling than printed summations can indicate. In his interview, an unrepentant Aldrich, coolly commenting on the new Texas hate crimes statutes that were passed in response to his act, says "Maybe something good will come of this after all." To hear these words is to be confronted with the human condition in all its awful complexity.

Lost in La Mancha
2003

Standing in the midst of pre-production hell for his dream film, *The Man Who Killed Don Quixote,* filmmaker Terry Gilliam looked around and summed it up. "There is," he said, with an actual gleam in his eye, "a lot of potential for chaos here."

Lost in La Mancha, the essential documentary about the collapse of Gilliam's most cherished project, records that chaos and more. A hip and intelligent insider's look at what a completely absurd experience filmmaking can be, *Lost* records an accident while it's happening, revealing a situation that makes you laugh again and again while weeping, metaphorically at least, for the sheer frustration of it all.

Because he is a master of elaborate and eccentric visions, responsible for wonders such as *Brazil* and *Time Bandits,* Gilliam's movies have never had an easy time of it. But even by the standards of his 1988 *The Adventures of Baron Munchausen,* which ended up costing double its budget, what happened on *Quixote* was a study in having everything that could possibly go wrong promptly do so.

In place to record the wreckage were documentary filmmakers Keith Fulton and Louis Pepe. They'd first worked with Gilliam during the shooting of his *12 Monkeys,* turning out an admired behind-the-scenes documentary called *The Hamster Factor and Other Tales of* 12 Monkeys.

Gilliam, to his great credit, made sure Fulton and Pepe were given complete access to all aspects of the *Don Quixote* shoot, and he didn't renege on his promise even as his film began to inexorably collapse. "This project has been so long in the making and so miserable that someone needs to get a film out of it," he told the pair, "and it doesn't look like it's going to be me."

Undaunted by the experience of Orson Welles, who spent decades trying to get a *Quixote* project made, Gilliam had been working on his version for ten years. A man with an infectious spirit, called "a responsible enfant terrible" by a friend, Gilliam seemed a good match for a project about a dreamer who sees things others can't see.

Assembled to do the deed was an enviable cast. Because the role of Quixote needs an older actor who looks right, acts well, and can ride a horse, Gilliam felt fortunate to get the entire package in veteran French performer Jean Rochefort. And for Sancho Panza, who in Gilliam's version was a modern advertising man transported back to the seventeenth century, Gilliam got the co-star of his *Fear and Loathing in Las Vegas,* the criminally handsome Johnny Depp.

Because the budget for this epic film was $32 million (bargain basement by Hollywood standards, but "a heavy film for European shoulders," said one of the producers), tension was high even early in pre-production. Gilliam charged his crew to "protect me from myself, to stop me sooner rather than later" if things headed in an untenable direction, and first assistant director Phil Patterson allowed that working with Gilliam was "like riding a pony bareback. You're in for the ride of your life."

Once filming actually started, things got unimaginably worse. An isolated location turned out to be used by NATO for fighter-bomber exercises, a flash flood washed away equipment, and, most critical of all, star Rochefort began showing signs of health problems that were as debilitating as they were mysterious.

That this *Don Quixote* got derailed is especially distressing because the little of it that we see looks so enticing. One sequence in particular, Quixote's vision of marauding giants, is shown in casting, in rehearsal, and finally in a 35-millimeter test. Just those few minutes let us know that Gilliam's *Quixote* would have been something special.

Though a film about a film that didn't get completed seems unusual, it has in fact been done before. In 1965, the BBC produced *The Epic That Never Was,* a film about the abortive 1937 *I, Claudius,* starring Charles Laughton and directed by Josef von Sternberg. In reviewing it, Pauline Kael wrote, "This is probably the only film ever made about an abandoned film." Now there's a second, and it's a pip.

One Day in September
2000

Nightmarish public events awaken an aspect of human nature that's frustrated more often than not: the need to find out just what went down. Though we may never know beyond a doubt, for example, whether Lee Harvey Oswald acted alone, as far as learning exactly what transpired during the kidnapping and deaths of eleven Israeli athletes at the 1972 Munich Olympics, an unnerving, highly dramatic documentary called *One Day in September* lets us in on all the secrets.

When *One Day* defeated the much-loved *Buena Vista Social Club* to take 1999's best-documentary Oscar, those who hadn't seen it suspected it had won because of its worthy subject matter alone. Nothing could be less true. As directed by Kevin Macdonald, this utterly compelling behind-the-scenes account of that horrific event unfolds with a potent sense of authority and authenticity. This is a story that can't help but involve us, one we can't turn away from even for a moment.

For one thing, the chain of events the film exposes is almost beyond belief, a roller-coaster saga not lacking for heroes, villains, incompetents, and dupes, a narrative balancing International Olympic Committee hubris, Israeli bitterness, Palestinian pride, and boggling German ineptitude and malfeasance.

Macdonald and his team have done a remarkable job, not just of amassing a collection of significant archival footage, but also of getting almost everyone critical to the situation to speak on the record—some for the first time—about how that particular nightmare evolved.

We hear from German officials, including military men as well as Hans-Dietrich Genscher, then the German minister of the interior. We hear from the only member of a key Munich police squad ever to talk about the incident: His colleagues were all threatened with loss of pensions if they spoke up, but he had none to lose. There are international journalists who witnessed what happened, and from the Israeli side, everyone from wives and children of the murdered athletes to Zvi Zamir, the former chief of Mossad, the super-secret Israeli intelligence organization, who required, according to the press notes, "six months of persuasion and arm-twisting" before he agreed to cooperate.

Yet if there is one person whose testimony is critical to this film's success, it is Jamal Al Gashey, the only member of the Palestinian Black September terrorist squad still alive. Getting him to speak on camera for the first time apparently took a considerable amount of determination, fortitude, and luck, but the film wouldn't have the authenticity and balance it has without his story.

When Al Gashey talks about how "the Palestinian revolution" empowered him after a young life spent in squalid refugee camps, when he talks about feeling "very proud that for the first time I was able to confront the Israelis," what we hear sounds uncannily familiar. It's an early version of the Middle Eastern dynamic of reciprocal violence that is being played out to this very day.

One Day in September starts with a German travelogue that presents Munich as it wanted to be seen in 1972, "a kind of German paradise . . . where tradition and modernity exist happily side by side."

Unspoken in this is Munich's place as one of the birthplaces of Nazism, not to mention international memories of the last German Olympics, the Nazi-controlled 1936 Berlin event. But those events were very much factors in Germany's decision to counter a militaristic image by having light security in the Olympic Village.

For the eight Palestinians disguised as athletes and helped over the village fence by inebriated Americans sneaking in after curfew, the Olympics provided a perfect world stage to publicize their grievances. The aim of the terror squad, a naive one considering Israel's historical absolute refusal to bargain, was to hold Israeli athletes hostage and trade them for 200 political prisoners.

Making extensive use of contemporary footage and sportscaster Jim McKay's voice-over on ABC television (which holds up remarkably well), *One Day in September* shows how the siege inside the Olympic Village played out, revealing early signs of German incompetence. The ruses that police used to attempt to sneak into the building where the athletes were held, for instance, were as pathetic as they were transparent.

The last third of the film concentrates, with the help of computer-generated re-creations (as well as graphic and bloody photographs), on what happened when the Palestinians and their hostages moved to a Munich airport. It reveals a level of almost criminal German naïveté and ineptitude that seems especially striking given the way that, as one journalist put it, "everyone was transfixed by a myth of utter German ruthless efficiency." When Israeli Mossad chief Zamir throws up his hands in bitter frustration and says "unbelievable," it's impossible not to agree.

Rivers and Tides
2003

When *Rivers and Tides* begins, it's not clear that its subject, British environmental artist Andy Goldsworthy, will be able to command our attention for 90 minutes. By the time it's over, however, we take our leave with reluctance, even sadness. It has been a kind of privilege to see the world through this man's eyes.

Goldsworthy is celebrated for creating art in the wild using whatever natural materials are at hand, stones and driftwood as well as leaves if it's summer and ice if it's winter. He puts enormous effort into making these pieces look effortless, as if they could have been on site all along.

Because his works are often delicate and always open to the elements, they frequently last a finite amount of time. "The thing that brings a work to life," the artist says, "will cause its death." For most people, these creations are known only through the photographs Goldsworthy takes and turns into popular gift books.

With his emphasis on being in harmony with the natural world, Goldsworthy is an ideal artist for today's urban audience eager for a connection to the wilds. Earnest and completely absorbed by his work, Goldsworthy can sound like a New Age tree-hugger when he rhapsodizes on the intangible energy running through a landscape.

But any doubts about the validity of what he's doing are removed by actually seeing the art in this film, both in process and in a finished form. When Goldsworthy's works appear as photographs in books, they inevitably tend to flatten out and even to appear gimmicky, but experiencing them on the big screen—closer to the way they exist in the landscape—is to see them come alive in a particularly transfixing way.

There is, for instance, a driftwood igloo that Goldsworthy pain-stakingly creates at the ocean's edge in Nova Scotia. To watch the tide come in, remove it from its moorings, and then gently push it toward collapse is a surprisingly magical experience.

The same is true as we watch Goldsworthy build one of his trade-mark large stone pinecones, a process that includes him grimacing in frustration as it collapses after considerable work. Seeing the finished product first covered and then uncovered by water as the tide goes in and out, and observing a similar structure as it weathers the changes of season at the artist's farm in Penpont, Scotland, is satisfying in an almost indescribable way.

Though we see Goldsworthy travel to several different locations to execute commissions, he quite definitely prefers to be at that farm, where he feels a mystical link to the land that he needs to function creatively. He jokes about being an intuitive artist, but that is really the case, as his projects appear to stem from an uncanny ability to com-mune with his materials.

German documentarian Thomas Riedelsheimer, who directed, photographed, and edited *Rivers and Tides,* spent more than a year with Goldsworthy, and this intense commitment strengthened the film in a pair of complementary ways.

For one thing, the artist clearly got so used to having Riedelsheimer around that he treats the filmmaker like a confidant, sharing articulate musings about the nature of his work that are candid and illuminating.

Riedelsheimer also got to experience Goldsworthy's works so intimately that he gained an instinctive sense of the best camera angles for the different pieces. Consequently, he was able to photograph everything with a clear and precise eye for beauty. Intoxicating and meditative by turns, helped by Fred Frith's minimalist score, this film opens a portal into a singular creative mind.

The Saltmen of Tibet
1998

The Saltmen of Tibet wasn't filmed in a galaxy far, far away, but it feels as though it might have been. A gentle, meditative documentary filled with spectacular visuals, it allows audiences the rare pleasure of experiencing a traditional way of life that is close to vanishing.

Even in Tibet, apparently, the lifestyle of nomadic salt gatherers, who spend three months of the year taking yak caravans to Lake Tsentso in the country's far north to collect salt and bring it back to their encampment, is considered exotic. Yet seeing it all through the eyes of director Ulrike Koch is a cleansing, revivifying experience that's as restorative as a mountain vista.

Having worked in different capacities on Bernardo Bertolucci's *The Last Emperor* and *Little Buddha* and other films set in Central Asia, Koch is a filmmaker who specializes in this part of the world.

But even she, the notes tell us, had a difficult time finding the saltmen, who face stiff competition from the traders who use trucks for hauling salt. However, aided by "Professor Zhang, manager of the 'Frozen Yak Semen Station' and a national hero," Koch, cinematographer Pio Corradi, and their crew finally made contact and began shooting.

What we see on screen is quintessentially unhurried and unobtrusive filmmaking. There is no voice-over, the only words that are spoken are in Tibetan, and whatever problems the crew had are scrupulously kept off the screen.

Neither is there any attempt to romanticize what is clearly a physically difficult existence. The aim is rather to immerse us in a simpler life in which no one moves any faster than the slowest yak and everything, including trading the salt for essential barley, is done just as it has been done for time out of mind.

Saltmen focuses on a group of four who make the journey, each of whom is given a traditional designation. The Old Mother is the most experienced; his tasks include preparing several strengths of all-..important tea. The Old Father takes care of the many sacrificial offerings. The Lord of the Animals (whose mother is shown worrying that he'll catch a cold) watches the livestock, and the young Novice is there to learn how things are done.

Though these men have added such modern touches as wristwatches and sunglasses to their colorful traditional clothes, they still live a life in which religion and ritual are all-important. They're intensely proud of their work and of the innumerable stories and legends that are associated with it, including one that led to a ban on Tibetan women making the trek.

The Saltmen of Tibet immerses us in the dailiness of these men's lives as they head out to the salt marshes. We see them fording streams, coping with bad weather, and worrying about a suddenly sick yak, all against the backdrop of some of the most memorable scenery in the world.

We also hear a lot about the rules that circumscribe the saltmen's lives as they near the lake where salt is gathered. They must sit correctly, not curse, not commit any bad deeds, and, most important, converse in a secret salt language that is unknown to outsiders—and which is not translated into English when used on film.

The salt-gathering process is also apparently one that necessitates a good deal of singing. There's a song for scraping the salt and another one for sewing the sacks closed before they're loaded onto the yaks. And one woman featured in the film is celebrated for singing hypnotic ballads, especially the tale of King Gesar of Ling, one of Tibet's great folk epics.

Somehow, the filmmakers have managed to seamlessly blend in with the nomads, recording their story without getting in the way. Seeing *The Saltmen of Tibet* doesn't create a desire to be included on their next trip, but we're more than pleased to have been taken along—and hopeful that the tradition lasts until the current Novice is old enough to be an Old Mother himself.

Speaking in Strings
1999

Speaking in Strings is an intimate, affecting, and revelatory documentary on how pain and passion can come together in a creative artist. Its portrait of controversial virtuoso violinist Nadja Salerno-Sonnenberg is as vivid and unstoppable as the woman herself: You don't need to know who she is or even much care about classical music to be gripped, even flabbergasted, by what's on the screen.

That's because the genuine drama of Salerno-Sonnenberg's life reaches the level of grand opera and because the woman herself is exceptionally intense. "She doesn't know how to phone it in," says a friend, a description that barely does justice to someone whose emotions are all out on the surface, a diva who admits that "feeling more than anyone I know" can be, frankly, "a damn curse."

Director Paola di Florio has an extensive background in producing and directing documentaries for television, but what served her best here was a childhood friendship with the violinist. Without that kind of personal connection and the trust it engendered, it's doubtful that the kind of intimacy that is the film's hallmark would have happened.

More than being intense, Salerno-Sonnenberg is compelled to be completely honest, to forthrightly confront the demons and crises that have accompanied her to a position as one of the world's premier violinists. "It's amazing what you endure," she says, "when you must."

These crises include a 1984 kitchen accident in which Salerno-Sonnenberg cut off the tip of her left little finger ("I thought my life was over as I had known it") as well as a more recent suicide attempt that was nearly successful. "I don't want to talk about this," Salerno-

Sonnenberg says at first, literally doubled over in psychological pain, but finally, movingly, she does.

The core of everything for Salerno-Sonnenberg is her playing. "Classical music is like a drug, it's like food for your soul," she says of this all-consuming way of life. Strong-willed and iconoclastic, she's able to make powerful connections through her music even during moments of terrible personal crisis. "In fact when I put a fiddle under my chin I'm able to convey how I feel a lot better than speaking," she says—hence the film's title.

The other constant in Salerno-Sonnenberg's life is her stance as a battler. Moving to the United States from Italy when she was eight, her thick accent (and her old-country lunches) made her an outcast at school, "but I had," she says, "that fighting attitude."

Salerno-Sonnenberg's father, now dead, abandoned both her and her mother when his daughter was three months old, and Nadja's refusal to meet with him when she got older typifies her unbending frame of mind. "What if we became friends? How would my mother feel?" she asks. "I didn't want to hurt my mother's feelings."

The turning point in Salerno-Sonnenberg's career came in 1981, when, as a student at Juilliard and against her teacher's advice, she entered the prestigious Walter W. Naumberg International Violin Competition, practiced twelve and thirteen hours a day, and ended up winning the prize.

From the beginning, Salerno-Sonnenberg's approach to her art divided people, a schism *Speaking in Strings* fully acknowledges. "I feel possessed sometimes when I play," she says, and the film's many clips of her at the violin show her face transported by emotion. But critics have charged that she puts too much personality into her work, battling the composer and overpowering the music in the process.

Speaking in Strings shows Salerno-Sonnenberg talking to her mother, her friends, fellow musicians, and journalists. It also shows her in any number of situations, from dinner parties to recording sessions to tending to her aging cat.

Volatile, high-strung, but with a fine wise-cracking sense of humor, Salerno-Sonnenberg, unable to be anything but herself, is the opposite of the usual run of stage-managed artistic personalities. Your heart can't help but go out to her because, in this exceptional film, hers goes out to you.

Spellbound
2003

It isn't possible to resist the eight young competitors in *Spellbound;* it really isn't. They're so filled with hope and belief, so industrious in wonderfully individual ways in their quest to win the National Spelling Bee, that wishing each and every one of them could triumph becomes inevitable. And maybe, this Oscar-nominated documentary suggests, they already have.

These eight were part of a group of 249 who came out of some 9,000 school and city bees to qualify for the 1999 finals in Washington, D.C. Although a contest where the aim is to correctly spell words such as "lycanthrope" and "cephalalgia" may not sound compelling or even particularly humane, director Jeff Blitz and producer Sean Welch (who together also served as the film's camera and sound crew) and editor Yana Gorskaya prove to us that it is.

Blitz and Welch spent a good deal of time selecting the kids they would focus on, a process that pays off beautifully. The group settled on is so engaging and so diverse, from different economic strata, ethnic backgrounds, family structures, and areas of the country, that they effectively—and intentionally—provide a vibrant cross-section of America today.

The competitors highlighted are uniformly bright kids who are simply in love with big words for their own sake. The still-stunned parents of Nupur Lala, for instance, remember her at age two and a half saying, "I have no opportunities," before she knew the meaning of the word. Though there are exceptions, most of the parents, far from being whip-cracking stage managers, are rather astonished at having offspring willing to chain themselves to dictionaries for hours a day to learn the really hard words.

Just as important, the other thing these kids have in common is a charming inability to be other than themselves. Old enough to spell well but too young to have mastered dissembling or guile, they can't hide their feelings, can't disguise who they are, and, thanks to the genuine rapport the filmmakers achieved with them, truly open their lives and thoughts to the camera.

One of *Spellbound*'s most remarkable contestants is the one we are introduced to first, Angela Arenivar of tiny Perryton, Texas. Her parents were illegal immigrants from Mexico who've never learned to speak much English; her father likes to joke that the cattle he takes care of don't speak it either. The academic achievement that spelling-bee prowess represents, says Angela's brother, "is what he came here for." To see Angela's parents being proud to the point of tears is what we come to the movies for, too.

What makes *Spellbound* such an appealing film is that all the other contestants have captivating stories to tell as well. For instance:

- Ashley White, a sunny African-American child being raised by a single mother in Washington, D.C., likes to talk about her life as being "like a movie. I go through trials and tribulations, and then I finally overcome";
- Neil Kadakia, the son of a prosperous San Clemente couple, attacks the national bee as though it were a military invasion, making use of computer programs, multiple coaches, and, reportedly, the prayers of recruited well-wishers in his parents' ancestral Indian home;
- Harry Altman, a braces-wearing baby stand-up comic from Glen Rock, New Jersey, is a compulsive wisecracker given to stream-of-consciousness conversations with himself as he tries to puzzle out words. "I guess," he says in his only stab at understatement, "you could call me talkative."

These kids and their peers are so involving that half of *Spellbound*'s length is legitimately taken up getting acquainted with them. Then everyone goes to the Washington, D.C., finals, and the tension really kicks in.

Because we've come to know these kids and appreciate their honesty, it's especially touching to see all the emotions—from joy and relief to stunned disbelief—come tumbling across their faces. Though results will not be given away here, some of the "Spellbound Eight" go far enough to add extra interest to the narrative, and director Blitz, whose favorite childhood film was the Agatha Christie–based *And Then There Were None,* does an excellent job of conveying the one-strike-and-you're-out nature of the competition.

Though the National Spelling Bee has, given the tension involved, been understandably characterized as "a different form of child abuse" by a speller's parent, *Spellbound* is quite clear and unapologetic about the value in what might seem a valueless exercise.

For these contestants are, for the most part, not just memorizing; they are learning meanings, getting familiar with root languages, and, most important of all, participating in an arena where hard work and intelligence pay off, even if, obviously, they can't ensure victory.

At the end of the day, these children all seem better for the effort they put into the competition, as we are better for watching what the experience did for them. At a time when so many in this country are at odds about what represents America at its best, it's refreshing and then some to see a film that everyone can agree is an example of exactly that.

Theremin: An Electronic Odyssey
1995

Nothing on this Earth makes a sound quite like the theremin, a strange and wonderful musical instrument with an eccentric history that has become the subject of a whimsical, beguiling documentary called *Theremin: An Electronic Odyssey.* No matter what your thresholds for pleasure and astonishment, this film, winner of the Filmmakers Trophy at Sundance, will cross them easily.

Making eerie, undulating tones that are difficult to describe but unmistakable once heard, the theremin—though unknown to the general public—is a legend in several fields. It has made the soundtracks of numerous movies unforgettable, played a key part in the history of both electronic music and rock, and earned a reputation for its inventor,

Leon Theremin, as, says celebrated musicologist Nicolas Slonimsky, "the prophet of the future of music."

Invented by Theremin in his native Russia in 1920, the theremin is quite a bizarre piece of electronic equipment. Its circuits are largely hidden by a wooden cabinet; all that's visible are a vertical antenna and a horizontal metal loop. What makes the theremin unusual is that it is played without being touched; merely moving your hands through the air over the cabinet varies loudness, pitch, and timbre.

After demonstrating his invention to an approving V.I. Lenin, Theremin embarked on a world tour that eventually landed him in New York, where packed concerts at Carnegie Hall and a rapturous press reception followed. "Soviet Edison Takes Music from the Air," read one headline, and other stories were impressed by the instrument's "ethereal and heavenly sounds."

In New York, Theremin met the teenage Clara Rockmore, who soon became a virtuoso on the instrument, capable of playing Bach for Leopold Stokowski, as well as the object of the inventor's attentions. One of the pleasures of Steven M. Martin's film is that we see Rockmore both then and now: in home movies as a glowing eighteen-year-old in an era when "we were always in evening clothes, it was very romantic," as well as in her current incarnation as the fierce priestess of the theremin cult, playing with delicacy, precision, and beauty as her long red fingernails flash.

We also see Theremin himself in those home movies, a Gyro Gearloose elegantly turned out in white tie and tails with the kind of piercing eyes that unnerved people. A singular genius who speculated about raising the dead with electricity, Theremin went his own way in his private life as well, scandalizing his society friends by marrying not Rockmore but Lavinia Williams, an African American ballerina.

If detailing all this was all *Theremin* had on its mind, it would suffice, but suddenly the movie and the man's life take an unexpected and riveting turn. In 1938, like a character in a thriller, Theremin disappeared from New York without a trace. There were rumors of Soviet secret police involvement, but to his friends in Manhattan, he simply vanished, appropriately enough, into thin air. A sizable chunk of *Theremin* is concerned with the man's fate, and the film's investigation into exactly what happened has the pleasant and surprising air of a juicy mystery.

Theremin might be gone, but his influence, if anything, expanded, and another aspect of the movie details its extent. Robert Moog, for instance, the celebrated inventor of the Moog synthesizer, started out by building theremins at home when he was fourteen. He considers the instrument "the cornerstone of electronic music."

Most amusing are the clips and interviews that illustrate how the theremin was employed by Hollywood. Whether it was the DTs in *The Lost Weekend,* amnesia in Miklos Rosza's Oscar-winning score for *Spellbound,* or, most memorably, space aliens in *The Day the Earth Stood Still,* whenever weird noises were called for, the theremin was ready.

And then came Brian Wilson of the Beach Boys, whose brief torrent of nonstop eccentric enthusiasm for the theremin captures as much of his essence as the entire *I Wasn't Made for These Times* documentary. Frightened by the instrument when he heard it as a child, Wilson reconsidered while putting a particularly tricky song together, thinking, "Why not put a theremin in there?" and the defining sound of "Good Vibrations" resulted.

Expertly orchestrating all these different strands is director Martin, also a theremin fan from childhood, who has an appreciation of how simultaneously serious and silly this forgotten corner of musical history and popular culture is. By the time he brings everything together in a memorable climax played against the classic notes of "Good Vibrations," Martin's movie has made as vivid an impression as the music it celebrates with such charm.

When We Were Kings
1996

In addition to everything else he was and stood for, Muhammad Ali in his prime was a potent, prodigious talker with a genius for the playful and the poetic. More charismatic than most actors, his presence alone makes *When We Were Kings* a special event.

A documentary centering on the famous "Rumble in the Jungle," the 1974 heavyweight championship fight between Ali and George Foreman in Kinshasa, Zaire, *Kings* was a work in progress for twenty-two years.

Director Leonard Gast came back from Africa after the Foreman-Ali fight with something like 450 hours of footage dealing with the event as well as its accompanying world music festival. But problems of various kinds (paying the lab bill alone took almost fifteen years) kept his film from being completed.

In 1995, director Taylor Hackford (who has a producing as well as an editing credit here) became involved with the project. He shot a series of strong new interviews with writers Norman Mailer and George Plimpton, who were ringside in Zaire, and other interested parties, such as filmmaker Spike Lee and Ali biographer Thomas Hauser.

The resulting film does have a makeshift quality to it, with the new footage, old newsreel shots, circa 1974 interviews, film of the fight, and concerts stitched together in a kind of cinematic crazy quilt. But because a classic heavyweight championship fight, especially with these protagonists, epitomizes the drama inherent in sport, *When We Were Kings* always compels our interest.

When Don King, who lived the phrase "wily promoter," got Zaire's despotic ruler Mobutu Sese Seko to offer each fighter $5 million, champion Foreman was the twenty-five-year-old young lion and challenger Ali looked to be fading from the scene. Even Ali partisan Howard Cosell is shown in an on-camera clip saying, absent a miracle, "the time may have come to say goodbye to Muhammad Ali."

Only Ali seemed to feel differently, and one of the lures of this film is to hear the many and various ways he verbally takes on the man he calls "a big, bad monster who knocks everybody out and no one can whup him." Ali called the champion "the Mummy" for his alleged awkwardness in the ring, rhapsodizing, "If you think the world was surprised when Nixon resigned, wait till I kick Foreman's behind."

A mesmerizing talker on any and all subjects, Ali is seen discoursing on Chinese music, on how excited he is to be in Africa, even on the perils of, no kidding, Mr. Tooth Decay, advising young fans to quit eating so much candy and focus on natural foods. Though he liked to claim he was "so mean I make medicine sick," Ali on camera was irresistibly gregarious—he may be that rare public figure who never said a dull word.

As for the champion, despite his physical prowess (Mailer says that watching Foreman hit the heavy bag was "one of the more prodigious sights I've ever seen in my life"), he never seemed comfortable in Africa, and a six-week delay in the fight because of a cut over his right eye made things worse. Ali, by contrast, thrived in Zaire, and among other things used the extra time to formulate a ring strategy that surprised everyone.

If the vintage footage of Ali is the heart of the film, the new interviews conducted by Hackford are also effective. Lee and African actor Malik Bowens describe the impact Ali had on their respective communities, and Mailer, Plimpton, and Hauser do excellent work analyzing everyone's state of mind and the fight itself. Least interesting at this point is the footage relating to the music festival, which has not held up well.

Though Ali's problems with Parkinson's disease may have kept him off camera, it's a shame that a much-changed George Foreman was not interviewed for his thoughts today. Because it's the difference between what we know now about the two fighters and what we see happening in 1974 that gives *When We Were Kings* a poignancy it would have lacked had it not been kept in the can for all those years.

part four

CLASSICS

Introduction

In an unexpected reversal on the celebrated lamentation of Job, the home entertainment industry first took away and then gave when it came to the viewing of classic films.

In the days before video, laser disc, and DVD, if you wanted to see a masterpiece from the past you had to keep a sharp eye on the rapidly changing schedule of a repertory cinema, a movie house that specialized in showing older films to a clientele that either had missed them the first time around or wanted to re-experience their glories.

As the lure of watching films at home increasingly captivated audiences, these repertory cinemas gradually began to go out of business or change their screening philosophies. If you could see *Casablanca* in your living room any time you wanted to, even the lure of a big screen was not enough to entice viewers out of the house. You needed something more.

Also needing something more, or so it turned out, were distribution companies. The executives of such companies found that if they made a new print of a classic film, or added previously deleted footage to the original version, that made the item easier to sell as a video or DVD. And if the new print had a theatrical run prior to going on sale, the publicity it accrued also helped profits down the road.

Which brings us to the films in this section. These are motion pictures you can never see or write about too often, acknowledged classics of one sort or another that fully deserve whatever refurbishing they were given, films it is always a pleasure to either rethink or have the excuse to research.

Some, such as Alfred Hitchcock's *Vertigo,* Elia Kazan's *A Streetcar Named Desire,* and Sam Peckinpah's *The Wild Bunch,* are celebrated high spots of American cinema. Others, such as *Peeping Tom* from Britain and *Pepe Le Moko* and *Eyes Without a Face* from France, are as little seen as they are memorable. Many turn out to be on the dark side, though at least one, Jean Cocteau's *Beauty and the Beast,* ranks with the greatest romantic films ever made. As old as the 1930s and as new as the 1980s, they have captivated audiences for decades and will likely do the same for decades to come. They are, more than any other group in this book, simply unforgettable.

Beauty and the Beast
1946

Jean Cocteau's transporting 1946 *Beauty and the Beast,* as romantic a film as has ever been made, now looks better than ever.

In 1995, as part of France's celebration of the 100th anniversary of cinema, the film underwent a comprehensive restoration. Its original nitrate negative was painstakingly cleaned, sprocket holes were repaired, and missing frames—150 of them from 49 places in the film—were replaced. This new version is closer than anyone has a right to expect to the way it looked more than half a century ago.

Although this *Beauty* also has newer, more accurate subtitles ("May the devil himself spatter you with dung" is a particularly pungent example), the prime lure is the way the print underlines the film's incredible richness of atmosphere. Cinematographer Henri Alekan's images are simple but crystalline, and the film's numerous heart-stopping moments, such as the magical way white curtains billow in the wind, stand out even more.

Based on the fairy tale by Jeanne-Marie Leprince de Beaumont, the story begins with Beauty (the lovely Josette Day) scrubbing floors in Cinderella fashion while her snobbish older sisters terrorize the neighborhood. Beauty has a suitor, but she is hesitant about leaving her penniless father, a merchant whose ships have a habit of not coming in.

Returning from yet another fruitless journey, Beauty's father comes across an enchanted castle deep in the forest. He stays the night without seeing anyone, but when he stops to pick a rose for Beauty, the magnificent Beast appears. "You may take anything but my roses," he announces with the magisterial clarity that characterizes Cocteau's script. "For this you must die."

Jean Marais, a lover and protégé of Cocteau's, plays the Beast as a

figure of enormous dignity. Richly dressed and with an extremely realistic leonine face (created by Christian Berard and requiring hours
to apply), the Beast is a picture of self-command and ironic self-
knowledge. "Don't call me 'Sir,'" he says to the stunned merchant. "I
am called the Beast. I do not like compliments."

Once Beauty takes her father's place at the castle in order to spare
his life, we see a different Beast, an ogre with a soul, crueler to himself
than to humans and with a somber, heartbreaking voice that Cocteau
described as that of "a monster in pain." Tortured by a compulsion to
kill that leaves his hands literally smoking, the Beast is sensitive
enough to be capable of dying of a broken heart if Beauty, given time
off for good behavior to visit her dying father, does not return at the
appointed hour.

Making Cocteau's success with this material even more remarkable
is that *Beauty* was filmed under extremely trying conditions. As detailed in Cocteau's *Beauty and the Beast: Diary of a Film* (available in
English translation from Dover Books), the obstacles the production
had to overcome were formidable. These included an agonizing combination of flu, burns from the arc lights, and skin problems that put
the director in the Pasteur Institute in Paris for a week feeling "as
though my neck were being sawn through with a blunt saw."

Always playful, Cocteau cast Marais as not only the Beast but also
Beauty's suitor, Avenant, and even as the Prince who magically appears in the Beast's place at the close, when it becomes immediately
apparent that Beauty misses her more savage suitor. In this she was
not alone. Greta Garbo's reaction to the finale, or so the story goes,
was equally simple and to the point: "Give me back my Beast," she
exclaimed.

Das Boot
1982

At 2 hours and 28 minutes, the original 1982 *Das Boot* was pretty big
to begin with. A crew of 250 labored for two years on this story of life
aboard a German submarine cruising the wartime North Atlantic,

spending the equivalent of $40 million, still the biggest budget for a German film.

The results, however, justified every expenditure. With its rigorous attention to both physical and psychological realism, *Das Boot* became a sensation domestically as well as the highest-grossing postwar overseas German venture. Even more impressive for a foreign language film, it was nominated for six Academy Awards, including best screenplay, best cinematography, and best director for Wolfgang Petersen.

Das Boot was also made under special circumstances, simultaneously shot, to the tune of more than 1 million feet of celluloid, as a theatrical motion picture and a six-hour miniseries for German television.

Now Petersen, who went on to direct *In the Line of Fire, Outbreak,* and *Air Force One,* has traded on his increased industry clout to go back and in effect combine the two versions, making what he calls his ideal *Das Boot.* Improvements include pumping the running time up to a hefty 3 hours and 30 minutes and bringing the all-important sound (which got two of those Oscar nominations) up to more modern technical standards.

With the extra footage adding texture to the psychological portraits of the men of the U–96, the new version of *Das Boot* reaffirms the film's position as perhaps the most convincing war movie ever made, complete with tension that wrings you dry and an overpowering sense of verisimilitude.

It does this despite the handicap, at least for American audiences, of being about our enemy in World War II. But the film's script (adapted by Petersen from Lothar-Gunther Buchheim's widely read, semiautobiographical novel about a journalist's U-boat experiences) does such an excellent job of humanizing the crew, of creating an almost John Fordian sense of male bonding, that which side anyone was on doesn't seem to matter.

Excellent ensemble acting, of course, was a factor, and the all-male group that plays U-96's crew is close to faultless. Jürgen Prochnow, for instance, forged an international career (including *The English Patient*) as a result of this completely commanding performance as the boat's captain, a pragmatic, humanistic, thoroughly professional warrior whose crew would do anything he asked.

Prochnow's co-stars—including Klaus Wennemann as the chief engineer, Hubertus Begsch as the only Nazi true believer on board, and Martin Semmelrogge as the mischievous, redheaded second lieutenant—have gone on to strong careers in Germany. And Herbert Grönemeyer, who plays the visiting journalist, has become one of the country's top pop stars.

Set in 1941, at a time when Germany was gradually losing the naval war in the North Atlantic, *Das Boot* follows the U-boat on one extended voyage. The crew endures boredom, chases convoys, attacks ships, and gets attacked in return by thunderous depth charges, all of it with a level of crushing realism that, if anything, feels stronger now than it did when the film first came out.

The reason for this success is that, though Petersen has since been typed as an action impresario, his background before *Das Boot* was as a director of intense character studies. And he turned out to be especially good at building tension on board, in capturing the hellish, almost unimaginable chaos of a submarine under attack.

What remains the most vivid and unsurpassed about *Das Boot* is this ability to thrust us on board the submarine with absolute assurance. Cinematographer Jost Vocano, who shot more than 90 percent of the film with a hand-held Arriflex rigged with a special steadying gyroscopic mount (in effect, a precursor to the Steadicam), creates a sense of physical verisimilitude strong enough to be overpowering.

Helping this was several decisions Petersen made. He refused to let his actors take other jobs during the nine months of shooting and wouldn't even let them go out and spend a day in the sun for fear they'd lose their pale faces. And he did the filming in sequence, so that by the finale those faces reflected the toll of living and working in a terribly cramped space.

For though the full-size model of the U-96 was constructed, Petersen said in a 1982 interview, with retractable walls that allowed "someone to sit back comfortably in a chair with a cigar in his mouth and say, 'Action,'" the director insisted on shooting in the enclosed space to ensure reality.

"I wanted to force the cameraman to shoot the whole film in this tube," he explained. "I wanted the audience not to see this as decoration but to feel that we are all together in this boat for months and months." It worked.

Also dissatisfied with the typical technique of simulating depth-charge attacks—"you shake the camera and tell the actors to have frightened faces"—Petersen mounted his submarine on top of a 16-foot-high hydraulic apparatus "that could shake, rattle and roll the whole boat. Inside, you can't see anything, you just hear the terrible noise of this machine. It was the hardest production you can imagine. The actors, sometimes they had fear for death in there."

Decalogue
1988–1989

Originally made for Polish television in 1988–1989 by the masterful Krzysztof Kieslowski, and with each of its 53- to 58-minute segments focusing on one of the Ten Commandments, *Decalogue* is as great a treasure as modern cinema has to offer, and if that sounds hyperbolic, it's just going to have to be that way.

Though the cumulative impact of all ten films makes seeing the entire *Decalogue* one of cinema's transcendent experiences, each segment, like each commandment, has an independent existence. Viewing even one is rewarding, and no matter which episodes are chosen, they'll probably be among the best films you see all year.

A member of the post–Andrzej Wajda generation of Polish directors that includes Krzysztof Zanussi and Jerzy Skolimowski, Kieslowski died in 1996 at age fifty-four. He's best known in this country for *The Double Life of Veronique* and his *Three Colors* trilogy of *Blue, White,* and *Red.*

The director first received international notice when his darkly satirical 1979 *Camera Buff* won several international awards. He co-wrote *Decalogue* with Krzysztof Piesiewicz and originally intended to have ten directors involved.

"But I liked doing the first film so much," he told interviewer Annette Insdorf in 1990, "that I didn't want to give the others away." Using nine cinematographers, he shot and edited the entire series in a remarkable twenty-one months: "Sometimes I'd shoot part of one film in the morning, part of a second in another location in the afternoon, and a different one in the evening. That kept me from getting bored."

Though these films are based on the Ten Commandments (organized according to Roman Catholic tradition and not the King James version), Kieslowski has at times made the connection oblique. The commandments are dealt with in order, but each film is identified only by its number, and nowhere in any of the films is the commandment in question explicitly referred to.

What elevates *Decalogue* is not only that it deals with the most serious questions of life, death, and belief but that it knows how passionate and dramatic these explorations can be made. Utilizing the gravity and precision of parable, Kieslowski places his characters in agonizing dilemmas, confronting them with problems that defy solution.

As compassionate as they are pessimistic, Kieslowski and co-writer Piesiewicz understand that when human needs are in conflict, life is without easy choices. "Man doesn't choose between good and evil," is how the director put it in interviews. "He chooses between greater and lesser evil."

The director's concern is not resolving problems but investigating the gap between the ideals represented by the commandments and the way we end up living our lives. A lifetime of small decisions makes adults the way they are, and in moments of crisis it's often too late to become someone else. The acute probing of psychological states in the hope of uncovering a sliver of illumination, "the contradiction," in the director's own words, "between complicated characters and simple stories," is why *Decalogue* was made.

Always emotionally unsettling, these despairing, ambiguous pieces never flirt with pretension, and that, in part, is because of Kieslowski's complete assurance as a director, his command of cinema's resources. The director's spare, minimal visual preferences dominate each episode. The camera work is fluid and precise, and the films are so rich in nuance and gesture that they seem to be feature-length even though they're not.

Kieslowski is helped greatly by the superb actors whom he has chosen for his cast, the best Polish cinema has to offer. All perform with exceptional restraint, and all, including the children who appear in some episodes, have faces that speak movingly even when words are absent.

The stories and the commandments are as follows:

One: "Thou Shalt Have No Other Gods but Me." A mathematician father (Henryk Baranowski) and his devoted son (Wojciech Klata) share a passion for computers and a belief in the invincibility of reason.

Two: "Thou Shalt Not Take the Name of the Lord in Vain." A married woman (Krystyna Janda) whose husband is dying, and who is pregnant by another man, asks a doctor (Aleksander Bardini) whether her husband will live—as she tries to decide whether to have an abortion.

Three: "Honor the Sabbath Day." A married man (Daniel Olbrychski) has his Christmas Eve interrupted by his desperate former lover (Maria Pakulnis).

Four: "Honor Thy Father and Mother." The relationship between a twenty-year-old daughter (Adrianna Biedrzynska) and her father (Janus Gajos) powerfully changes when she reads a letter that was to have been opened only at his death.

Five: "Thou Shalt Not Kill." Perhaps the most celebrated film in the series, this one also exists in an 85-minute version (known as *A Short Film About Killing*) that won several major European awards. A gloss on the nature of murder, both by the individual and by the state, it features one of the screen's most graphic killings, spread out over more than 7 minutes.

Six: "Thou Shalt Not Commit Adultery." This film also exists in an expanded version called *A Short Film About Love.* The most overtly erotic of the group, it deals with a young peeping Tom (Olaf Lubaszenko) who falls desperately in love with the woman he spies on (Grazyna Szapolowska).

Seven: "Thou Shalt Not Steal." A wrenching story of Majka, a young woman (Maja Barelkowska) who has allowed her mother (Ana Polony) to pretend that Majka's daughter is her own.

Eight: "Thou Shalt Not Bear False Witness." A professor of ethics who survived the Nazi occupation (Maria Koscialkowska) is con-

fronted about her past by a young American student (Teresa Mar-
czewska).

Nine: "Thou Shalt Not Covet Thy Neighbor's Wife." An impotent
husband (Piotr Machalica) fears that his wife (Ewa Blaszczyk) is having an affair.

Ten: "Thou Shalt Not Covet Thy Neighbor's Goods." The only
even remotely comic episode—though a very dark comedy it is—details what happens when two brothers (Zbigniew Zamachowski and
Jerzy Stuhr) discover that their dead father had the most valuable
stamp collection in Poland.

Aside from Kieslowski's themes and his skill, a key factor unifying
these stories is the somber score by veteran collaborator Zbigniew
Preisner. Known for his work on *Blue* and *The Double Life of Veronique,* Preisner here has come in almost on tiptoe, choosing a minimal musical mode that haunts each part of the series.

Decalogue is also united by its site, an anonymous Warsaw apartment complex where all its protagonists live. Similarly, though he preferred not to explain why, Kieslowski placed the same watchful
character in almost every episode, a man whose silent presence seems
to be saying something just beyond our understanding.

As much as has been written about *Decalogue,* words don't convey
how magisterially these films fulfill their mandate. Fortunately, words
no longer have to. Finally on DVD and video after being unavailable
for years, *Decalogue* can now speak eloquently, unforgettably, for itself.

Eyes Without a Face
1959

Once seen, never forgotten, *Eyes Without a Face* is a film to haunt
your dreams. Disturbing, disorienting, quietly terrifying, it's one of
the least known of the world's great horror movies, and in its own
dark way, it's a startlingly beautiful and artful piece of cinema as well.

Directed by Georges Franju, *Les Yeux sans Visage,* to give it its original French title, was first released in 1959, when its pulp subject matter and disturbing imagery led many European critics to dismiss it. In

the United States, its fate was even worse: It was dubbed and released under the improbable title *The Horror Chamber of Dr. Faustus.*

Though this film and *Judex,* released in 1963, have a small but passionate following, Franju, who died in 1987, remains underappreciated in this country. The co-founder, along with the better-known Henri Langlois, of the Cinematheque Francais, Franju worked for years as a director of documentary shorts, including the slaughterhouse-themed *La Sange des Bêtes,* that earned him the respect of the younger filmmakers of the French New Wave.

Les Yeux sans Visage was only Franju's second feature, made when he was forty-seven. He explained to an interviewer that it was filmed under a series of restrictions. "I was told, 'No sacrilege because of the Spanish market, no nudes because of the Italian market, no blood because of the French market and no martyrized animals because of the English market.' And I was supposed to be making a horror film!"

A surrealist who believed, along with compatriot Jean Cocteau, that "the more you touch on mystery, the more important it is to be realistic," Franju had the ability to overcome all obstacles. "What is artificial ages badly and quickly," he wrote. "Dream, poetry, the unknown must all emerge out of reality itself. The whole of cinema is documentary, even the most poetic. What pleases is what is terrible, gentle and poetic."

As shot by the great cameraman Eugen Schüfftan (who won the Oscar for black-and-white cinematography for the very different *The Hustler* two years later), *Eyes* is a series of images that burn themselves into your subconscious. Every visual is carefully thought out and brilliantly composed for effect, creating a world that is simultaneously real and surreal. With its ability to go deeply into our fears, this is a motion picture that captures the texture of nightmare as convincingly as it has ever been done on film.

The idea for *Eyes* was conceived by several writers, including first assistant director and future director Claude Sautet as well as by Pierre Boileau and Thomas Narcejac (whose novels became Henri-Georges Clouzot's *Diabolique* and Alfred Hitchcock's *Vertigo*).

A young woman, her eyes untouched but the rest of her face "a vast open wound," has disappeared from a clinic where she was taken after a terrible automobile accident. Meanwhile, her father, the celebrated Dr. Genessier (Pierre Brasseur, more impassive and unbending than he was in *Children of Paradise*), lectures on the future possibilities of the heterograft, a procedure to transplant living tissue from one human being to another.

It turns out that the doctor's ideas are more than theoretical. Aided by his diabolical assistant Louise (*The Third Man*'s Alida Valli), this brilliant madman has been kidnapping young women in Paris, removing the skin from their faces, and attempting a transplant on the visage of his daughter Christiane (Edith Scob), whom he has hidden away in the attic of his château. How the relentless doctor (who experiments on a pack of constantly howling dogs in his spare time), the devoted Louise, and most of all Christiane cope with the effects of his horrific experimentation is the frame upon which this singular film is built.

Despite its gruesome plot, one of the hallmarks of *Eyes* is the austerity with which it is made, how little Schüfftan, with his discreet black-and-white camera work, allows us to see anything blatantly horrific (including Christiane's face). The reason, Franju explained, is that he envisioned *Eyes* as "an anguish film. It's a quieter mood than horror . . . more internal, more penetrating. It's horror in homeopathic doses."

In part because of this delicacy, Franju and Schüfftan's remarkable gift for the visual makes this the spookiest of movies, filled with elegant and poetic images that express longing, terror, and despair. Aided by Maurice Jarre's unsettling music, everything that appears on screen is meticulously calculated to create unease, from the doctor's shiny black Citroen and Louise's shinier black raincoat to the bird-like Christiane's oversized Givenchy housecoats and the film's final image, one of the most unforgettable ever created.

The film's most classic horror scene is an unflinching look at one of the doctor's blasphemous face-peeling operations. Though in terms of blood and special effects the sequence is pristine, even artificial, by today's dubious standards, it remains disturbing enough to make the skin crawl far into the night.

Even more psychologically unsettling are the sequences that show Christiane floating around the château like a dispossessed ghost, say-

ing things like "My face frightens me, my mask frightens me more."
For over her ravaged face she wears one of Franju's most telling inspi-
rations, a thin, plastic mask with holes cut out for her untouched
eyes, a neo-Noh object both expressionless and expressive that creates the powerful sense of poignancy and loss that is the film's most
impressive achievement.

Other motion pictures have obvious predecessors and successors,
but *Eyes* stands apart from all others, a film alone. But be warned.
Like a nightmare that never ends, this is a vision of madness, loneliness, and, yes, horror that, once seen, demands to be viewed over and
over again. It is that haunting, and that good.

Once upon a Time in America
1984

The best pictures are often the hardest to see. Which is probably why
Once upon a Time in America, Sergio Leone's richly cinematic mag-
num opus, went fifteen years without having the access to the U.S. big
screens it so thoroughly deserves.

When the Ladd Company originally released *Once upon a Time*
nationwide in 1984, it not only cut nearly an hour and a half off its
running time, it also changed everything that was distinctive, even audacious, in the director's dazzling narrative structure. It made a film
that was artificial and naturalistic, excessive as well as tightly controlled, seem sadly ordinary.

A 3-hour, 39-minute gangster epic set among Jewish hoodlums on
New York's Lower East Side, *Once upon a Time* has three main time
frames: 1922, 1932–1933, and 1968. But far from telling the story in the
straightforward manner the abbreviated version favors, Leone's
scheme toys with chronology. The film slips easily back and forth in
time, dancing between the decades, often making the connection
from one era to another solely by means of brilliant cuts that work like
magic.

Once upon a Time follows the fortunes of two boyhood friends and
partners in all kinds of crime, David "Noodles" Aaronson (Robert De

Niro) and Maximilian "Max" Bercovitz (James Woods). The film starts in 1933, at the beginning of the end for Noodles, with rival hoods looking to end his life, and skips both back to his larcenous boyhood and ahead to his exhausted old age in the 1960s.

Though the film is defined by its bravura aspects, Leone managed to keep the acting of his two stars as understated and muted as the picture's carefully modulated color scheme. Though both men have flirted with mannered work in the years since, they show restraint and power in what they do here.

Also impressive are Tuesday Weld as the sexually voracious Carol, William Forsythe as gang member Cockeye, and even producer Arnon Milchan, who has an amusing cameo as an outraged chauffeur. Less successful is Elizabeth McGovern, who never finds her footing as Deborah, the girl of Noodles's dreams. Future Oscar winner Jennifer Connelly, however, discovers ways to be memorable playing Deborah as a headstrong teenage girl.

Intensely violent, with bursts of mayhem that even modern viewers need to be warned about, *Once upon a Time* is also troublesome in its treatment of women. The film features two exceptionally violent rapes, and its screenplay doesn't recognize the existence of mature females who aren't, in critic Tony Rayns's words, "either nymphomaniacs or complaisant victims of male sadists and rapists."

Despite, or perhaps because of, having six Italian screenwriters, including Leone, plus giving an additional writing credit to Stuart Kaminsky, dialogue is not *Once upon a Time*'s strength. The use of English is awkward at times, the 1968 section is not as convincing plot-wise as it might have been, and nothing anyone says is as close to memorable as, for instance, the best parts of *The Godfather*.

More than making up for these drawbacks is Leone's exceptional filmmaking skill, his gift for lush storytelling, and his ability to create a visual tapestry luxurious enough to make you swoon without sacrificing the fierceness of his vision.

Working with cinematographer Tonino Delli Colli, Leone got so involved with the spectacular, large-scale physical re-creation of the Lower East Side that energizes this film that, according to Leone biographer David N. Meyer, he built the same set in three different cities.

Yet, paradoxically, many of this film's most memorable images are smaller, quieter ones. Some are impossible to forget: the sight of children skipping past the gargantuan Williamsburg Bridge, a series of bright red balls popping up on the foggy East River, a shootout in a feather factory, and even a tombstone in the grip of an earthmover, rising as if by magic above a cemetery wall.

Even though *Once upon a Time* contains considerable mayhem, its overall mood is far from the macho triumphalism of most contemporary violent films. Helped by Ennio Morricone's trademark score, especially the haunting playing of panpipes by Gheorghe Zamfir, this is a work with an overall mood of overwhelming melancholy and sadness, youthful yearning, mature regret, and the transcendent but fleeting nature of memory itself.

The important thing about filmmaking, Leone once said in an interview, is "to make a world that is not now. A real world, a genuine world, but one that allows myth to live. The myth is everything." Of the five films he directed between 1964 and 1984, this, his last film, makes that point the strongest.

Peeping Tom
1960

Michael Powell's genuinely spooky *Peeping Tom* ranks as one of the most terribly strange and twisted of motion pictures. Even in a day and age when the outré is encouraged, this brilliant, dark gem stands out in a crowd.

Peeping Tom is more than a sympathetic portrait of a deviant personality. Made in 1960 in England, it's been cited (along with Federico Fellini's *8 ½*) by director and film buff Martin Scorsese as one of the two pictures through which "you can discover everything about the people who make movies."

Until he directed *Peeping Tom,* Powell had a reputation as a consummate pictorialist whose films (often made in collaboration with Emeric Pressburger and including *The Red Shoes, Black Narcissus,* and *A Matter of Life and Death/Stairway to Heaven*) were not known for outraging too many sensibilities.

But when *Peeping Tom* came out, all that changed. The reviews it received were merciless and scathing (Powell reprints generous chunks of them in his autobiography, *Million Dollar Movie*), and though the director was considered one of the great names of British film, his career was abruptly ended by the notoriety.

What is clearer today than in 1960 is *Peeping Tom*'s probing and iconoclastic nature, the way its overriding aim was not to horrify but to provoke thought. In part about scopophilia, "the morbid urge to gaze," more commonly known as voyeurism, *Peeping Tom* is more than the history of a personal obsession. It's quite consciously about the moviemaking and moviegoing experience, and it functions as a cautionary tale for the film addict in all of us.

Peeping Tom's action begins with an unseen man stalking a Soho prostitute. Though she initially doesn't know it, we observe the man also filming her with a movie camera hidden in his overcoat sleeve. The way he records the inevitable murder on film not only terrifies the woman as much as her approaching death, it also, quite frankly, sexually excites the killer when he watches the resulting footage on elaborate home projection equipment.

Peeping Tom is no whodunit; the murderer is revealed almost at once to be Mark Lewis (Carl Boehm), a clean-cut, polite, but distant young man who mystifies almost everyone he comes across.

Mark has two jobs, working on a camera crew at a British movie studio and shooting photographs for magazines with "girls on the front covers and no front covers on the girls." Shy and furtive, he has no friends to speak of, and his most intimate relationship is clearly with his Bell & Howell camera.

Chance throws Mark together with a beautiful young neighbor named Helen Stephens (Anna Massey in her film debut). It's to her that he tells his astonishing story. His father was A.N. Lewis, a celebrated scientist and the author of the multivolume *Fear and the Nervous System*. To get his results, he experimented on his son, waking young Mark up in the middle of the night, completely terrifying him, and then filming what transpired.

Unnerving though its subject is, *Peeping Tom* is never explicitly violent and, by today's standards, is almost reserved in what it puts on the screen. In fact, the most disturbing images we see are the home movies of the senior Lewis (played, in a pointed bit of casting, by Powell himself) genteelly tormenting his son.

Peeping Tom follows Mark on his search for potential victims (Moira Shearer, from *The Red Shoes,* is especially good as a studio stand-in named Vivian). It also follows the London police as they try to determine why these women have the most awful looks on their faces that anyone's ever seen. Fear, as it turns out, is the most frightening thing in the world, and *Peeping Tom* makes us feel it palpably as few films have been able to do.

Pepe Le Moko
1937

Pepe le Moko is the stuff that dreams are made of.

An acknowledged classic of doomed romanticism and atmospheric fatalism, this 1937 French film was such a hit at its release that Hollywood promptly remade it as *Algiers,* keeping the original off U.S. screens for more than four years.

Despite this, *Pepe le Moko* has been enormously influential, not only in film but in numerous corners of American popular culture. It rooted the exotic Casbah in our collective imaginations; it's what Chuck Jones pillaged when he named a character Pepe le Pew; it's the film without which *Casablanca* likely would not have been made.

Directed by Julien Duvivier, it featured the iconic actor Jean Gabin in one of his signature roles and intoxicated almost everyone who saw it, from Jean Cocteau ("a masterpiece") to Pauline Kael ("superb filmmaking") and Graham Greene, who called it "one of the most exciting and moving films I remember seeing," a feature that succeeded by "raising the thriller to a poetic level."

Despite these accolades, *Pepe* is hardly some revered relic suitable only for a museum shelf. Beautifully crafted, movingly acted, still involving and entertaining, this is just the kind of film people are talking about when they say they don't make them like this anymore.

Much of the credit goes to star Gabin in the title role. He plays a French gangster who stole millions of francs from a bank in Paris and then fled to the Casbah, the Arab quarter of Algiers, with his gang.

Fearless, humane, an intensely masculine and unflappably charismatic presence who was completely natural on screen, Gabin is a star for whom there is no American equivalent. Often cast as a doomed man, the actor combines characteristics of Gary Cooper and Jimmy Cagney and comes up with an immaculately dressed gangster who makes women feel faint. Pepe may notice a woman's jewels first, but he's too much of a gentleman to say so.

Naturally, the French police are exasperated beyond words at their inability to capture Pepe, who has eluded them for two years in the labyrinthine Casbah, "where dark, winding streets form a jumble of mazes . . . colorful, dynamic, multifaceted." As one character says, "There's not one Casbah but thousands."

A true prince of thieves, Pepe is so beloved in the Casbah that police can't make a move against him without his knowing every step they take. "He's God up there," someone says. "You can't arrest God." Only the oily, insinuating Inspector Slimane (Lucas Gridoux) thinks he can capture the man, if only he can find the proper bait to lure him downtown.

With Ines the Gypsy (Line Noro) as his current flame, Pepe may be irresistible to the opposite sex, but he's never been in love. "I give them my body," he says, "but I keep my head."

Pepe also has a dark secret: His refuge has become a prison. Starting to feel hemmed in by the Casbah, Pepe finds himself missing Paris more and more.

All these feelings intensify when Pepe has a chance meeting with the glamorous Parisian Gaby (Mireille Balin), the mistress of a champagne tycoon. True to form, Pepe notices her platinum and diamond bracelets first, but soon he is mad for her, oblivious to the numerous complex webs woven around him as the film moves toward its celebrated poetic ending, redolent with longing and despair.

None of this could have succeeded as well as it does without the exemplary work of director Duvivier. Combining location work with studio scenes, he fills *Pepe* with teeming street life, the physical parallel to the film's psychological world of scheming, double-dealing, and betrayal.

Duvivier's Casbah is magical and dangerous, a place of whispers and shadows, where the unforgettably exotic lies just beyond a beaded curtain.

A Streetcar Named Desire
1951

Of the great American films—and make no mistake, it belongs in that group—*A Streetcar Named Desire* remains one of the most misunderstood, underappreciated, and surprisingly forgotten.

Released to great acclaim in 1951, nominated for a dozen Oscars and winner of four, including acting awards for Vivien Leigh, Kim Hunter, and Karl Malden, this Elia Kazan–directed version of Tennessee Williams's Pulitzer Prize–winning play has been seriously slighted in the intervening years, despite a lead performance by Marlon Brando that is little less than epochal.

In a critical world increasingly obsessed with visual mastery, *Streetcar*'s literary and theatrical origins have been held against it, and the fact that new prints were last struck in 1957 has obscured the cinematic strengths of virtuoso cameraman Harry Stradling's atmospheric black-and-white cinematography.

Also, *Streetcar* has always been a film with an asterisk attached to it. For the content of Williams's brilliant play was considered so risqué that the film version was in effect censored not once but twice before it made it to the screen.

First, the shooting script was toned down by Williams and Kazan themselves following monumental struggles with the Breen Office, the enforcers of the industry's moralistic Production Code. Then, just before its opening, threats of a boycott from several Catholic organizations led to cuts in the finished film. Without Kazan's knowledge, and to his enormous distress, Warner Bros. approved something like a dozen changes, taking out close to four minutes of film, key moments never to be seen again. Until now.

Those critical last-minute deletions were discovered in 1989 by Michael Arick (then director of preservation at Warner Bros. and now a private consultant) in a vault in Van Nuys, sharing space with bargain-basement westerns and exploitation pictures. They've been restored to *Streetcar,* and the first new prints in decades have been struck.

With what Warner Bros. is calling the director's cut of *Streetcar* available for the first time, several things are apparent. First, the restored footage, small though it is, clearly adds a different, more openly sensual tone to the film. But more than that, the new print allows us to recognize that—with or without those missing minutes—*Streetcar* was both a landmark in the fight against censorship and perhaps the most thrilling display of ensemble acting in all of American film.

A key reason the acting was so good is that all the members of the cast (with the sole exception of Leigh, who replaced Jessica Tandy because producer Charles K. Feldman felt at least one star name was essential) were in the original cast when the play opened on Broadway in December 1947.

Kazan was the original director as well, and one of the prime movers behind getting the twenty-four-year-old Brando, who only three years before had played a fourteen-year-old in the stage version of *I Remember Mama,* to take on the part of Stanley Kowalski on Broadway after both John Garfield and Burt Lancaster had been considered for it.

But when it came to making the film version, Kazan, who had never made a film from a play he'd already directed, wasn't sure he was interested. "It would be like marrying the same woman twice," he told Williams. "I don't think I can get it up for *Streetcar* again."

Kazan finally agreed to do the film, partly because his wife, Molly, was a longtime Williams fan, and partly because of the director's own affection for the writer. "I feel closer to Williams personally than to any other playwright I've worked with," he said. "Possibly it's the nature of his talent—it's so vulnerable, so naked—it's more naked than anyone else's. I wanted to protect him, look after him."

And *Streetcar,* which had few film nibbles despite its Pulitzer Prize because it was considered too hot to put on film, turned out to need a good deal of protection. What happened when the fragile Blanche Dubois visited her sister Stella and Stella's "be comfortable, that's my motto" husband, Stanley Kowalski, was not a tale for children. And as Joseph Breen, the Production Code's enforcer, wrote to Irene Mayer Selznick, the play's producer, "Material which may be perfectly valid for dramatization and treatment on stage may be questionable, or even completely unacceptable, when presented in a motion picture."

In a memo to Warner Bros., Breen identified several problem areas in the play. One, typical of the attitudes of the time, was what Breen called "an inference of sexual perversion. This principally has reference to the character of Blanche's young husband. . . . There seems little doubt that this young man was a homosexual." Dialogue fixes were used to obscure this, so that when the husband shoots himself in the film, it is after Blanche tells him off because he's "weak."

The biggest problem involved the play's pivotal moment, the rape of Blanche by Stanley. Rape of any kind was frowned on by the code, and the one in *Streetcar,* which Breen described as "both justified and unpunished," was especially objectionable. But here Kazan and Williams, who wrote the screenplay with adapter Oscar Saul, drew the line, saying it was not possible to eliminate the rape and do the picture.

As Williams wrote to Breen in an eloquent, impassioned letter, their feeling was that "the rape of Blanche by Stanley is a pivotal, integral truth in the play, without which the play loses its meaning, which is the ravishment of the tender, the sensitive, the delicate, by the savage and brutal forces of modern society."

Faced with this argument, and the possibility that *Streetcar* might try to outflank the Production Code and film without script approval, Breen indicated the rape might be acceptable if it was punished. So although the play had ended with the image of a united family, Williams wrote a new ending for the film, with Stella fleeing to a neighbor's house and insisting to her new baby, "We're not going back there. Not this time. We're never going back. Never, never back, never back again." As Murray Schumach wrote in *The Face on the Cutting Room Floor,* a history of censorship, "Thus the 12-year-olds could believe Stella was leaving her husband. But the rest of the audience would realize it was just an emotional outburst of the moment."

Kazan, feeling that his censorship problems were behind him, had sets built that emphasized the claustrophobic nature of the Kowalskis' New Orleans apartment. He had tried and largely discarded a version of the script that included scenes at Belle Reve, the lost Dubois estate.

Both of his lead actors, it turned out, presented problems of different kinds. Vivien Leigh had played Blanche for nine months in England under her husband Laurence Olivier's direction, and Kazan had to break her of the habit of saying, "When Larry and I did the play in London . . ."

Brando was more of a problem for the other actors. Leigh complained to Kazan, "You never know what he's going to do next, where he's going or what he's going to say." And the director, himself a former actor, admitted that Brando "had mannerisms that would have annoyed the hell out of me if I'd been playing with him. He'd not respond directly when spoken to, make his own time lapses, sometimes leaving the other actors hung up."

Still, seen today, the results are terrific. Though Brando once told an interviewer that in being "aggressive, unpremeditated, overt, and completely without doubt about himself" Stanley was "the direct antithesis of what I am," his anti-heroic performance, sweaty T-shirt and all, is one of the most completely realized ever put on screen, notable as much for its sensuality and its regret as its display of naked power. Only Humphrey Bogart, the sentimental favorite for *The African Queen,* was to stand between him and an Oscar.

As for the three who did win Oscars, Kim Hunter as Stella, Karl Malden as Stanley's pal Mitch, and Leigh as Blanche, their performances are all as alive now as the day they were put on film. As the author's voice and the deliverer of some of his most poetic lines ("Sometimes there is God so quickly"), Leigh is the most poignant, and Hunter, the restored footage shows, was the one most victimized by those last-minute cuts.

For though they thought otherwise, Kazan and Williams were not finished with their censorship battle when shooting was completed. The Legion of Decency, the Catholic Church's moral police, was threatening to give the completed *Streetcar* a "C," or condemned rating, with a cancellation of a Radio City Music Hall opening as the likely result, and the Catholic War Veterans were rumored to be considering a boycott of all Warner Bros. films.

Into this breech stepped Martin Quigley, the publisher of a movie trade paper, a prominent Catholic layman, and hardly a fan of the finished film. In fact, the first time he saw it he turned gray and informed Breen office representative Jack Vizzard, "Jack, I tell you, this fellow Kazan is the type who will one day blow his brains out."

Still, at the invitation of Warner Bros., and working with the film's embarrassed and horrified editor, David Weisbart, Quigley made a dozen cuts in the film, telling an amazed Kazan that "constitutional guarantees of freedom of expression are not a one-way street. I have the same right to say that moral considerations have a precedence over artistic considerations as you have to deny it."

A "C" was dutifully avoided, and a disgusted Kazan noted that Warner Bros. "didn't give a damn about the beauty or artistic value of the picture. . . . It was business, not art. They wanted to get the entire family to see the picture. They didn't want anything that might keep anyone away. At the same time they wanted it dirty enough to pull people in. The whole business was rather an outrage."

A measure of the way editor Weisbart felt about the trims that he was forced to make is that when Arick found them forty years later, in a mismarked can that had remained attached to the original nitrate negative, he realized "they had been lifted out in a way that made it easy for them to be put back in again. It was very clear where they went. The editor probably felt very bad."

The cuts, now restored, are mainly of single lines of dialogue, some of which emphasize the sexual yearning in Blanche's nature. One, of Stanley saying, "You know, you might not be bad to interfere with," just before the rape, underlines the brutality in his actions.

Most of the cuts, however, drain Kim Hunter's performance of what in the restored version seems one of its most notable qualities, its sensuality. The most important change comes in the scene of Stella returning after their post–poker game fight, walking down a flight of iron stairs with what can now be seen as a pure and expressive carnality. Martin Quigley, who had told Kazan he wanted Stella seen as "a decent girl who is attracted to her husband the way any 'decent' girl might be," was shocked at the scene, but for current audiences its return will be a revelation.

Still, the major thing to be remembered as far as censorship and *Streetcar* are concerned is that even with all its cuts and changes, the very fact that it existed and was successful as a film intended exclusively for adult tastes was a major blow to those who believed that any film little Jimmy couldn't see shouldn't be made. "For the first time we were confronted with a picture that was obviously not family entertainment," said Production Code official Geoffrey Shurlock. "Before then we had considered *Anna Karenina* a big deal. *Streetcar* broke the barrier."

Even more important, the restored *A Streetcar Named Desire* reminds us just how intense movies can be when expressive cinematography and emotional acting and directing are joined to some of the most beautiful lines ever written for the screen. Of later productions of the play, Kazan graciously wrote in his autobiography that "no matter who directed it, with what concept, what cast, in what language, it was always hailed, often as 'better than the original production,'" but this filmed version is without doubt the *Streetcar* for the ages.

The Third Man
1949

Who speaks up for *The Third Man* and its director, Carol Reed? A major success in its day—it won the Palme d'Or at Cannes half a century ago—it tends to be faintly recalled by film fans as something they saw and enjoyed once upon a time.

A newly restored print shows what a shame that neglect is. It also shows why *American Cinematographer* magazine named it as one of the ten best-shot films of cinema's first half-century. Robert Krasker's Oscar-winning black-and-white cinematography, and its depiction of a nocturnal atmosphere of deep and dangerous shadows, a dark world in every sense of the word, is truly deserving of this recognition.

The Third Man is also now back in its original form. That means that 11 minutes of excised footage, mostly trims from existing scenes, have been restored. And in the opening voice-over, instead of star Joseph Cotton, it's director Reed, with a voice much better suited to the bemused cynicism of Graham Greene's script, who gets to archly comment, while the camera reveals an unidentified corpse floating face down in the water, that in terms of corruption, "amateurs can't stay the course" in postwar Vienna.

The new print even features a few more minutes of the film's most characteristic element, the indelible zither playing of Anton Karas. The story goes that director Reed stumbled upon Karas playing in a small café outside Vienna and decided to use him on the spot. Karas's music became a worldwide sensation, leading to a U.S. ad campaign that promised, no kidding, "He'll have you in a dither with his zither!"

Just as much of a character as anyone played by an actor is Vienna itself in those lean and nasty days, when the city was divided into sectors run by each of the Great Powers. *The Third Man* makes excellent use of particular real-life locations, all specified by Greene, such as the Great Wheel of an amusement park, the lonely Central Cemetery, and a slightly seedy nightclub.

Even more evocative are the city's magnificent buildings, often glimpsed half-crumbling or standing destitute next to enormous piles of rubble. The atmosphere Reed and company created is as thick as the local coffee, an ideal setting for a world without heroes where everyone is either a fool, a cynic, a criminal, or, quite possibly, a combination of all three.

Into this cesspool of casual amorality comes Holly Martins (Cotten), a bumbling, self-righteous American (Greene didn't think there was any other kind) who has naive notions of justice and righteousness plus a great deal of misplaced confidence in his ability to get to the bottom of things. *The Third Man* is the story of his unsentimental education, of the hard road he travels in the getting of wisdom.

A self-proclaimed writer of "cheap novelettes" with names such as *The Lone Rider of Santa Fe* and *Death at Double X Ranch,* Martins has come to Vienna at the behest of his oldest friend and possible future employer, Harry Lime.

Unfortunately, everyone tells him, he has come just a bit too late. Lime has been killed, the victim of a random traffic accident, and is mourned only by his girlfriend, Anna Schmidt (Alida Valli), and a pair of epicene Viennese named Baron Kurtz (Ernst Deutsch) and Dr. Winkel (Erich Ponto).

Also at Harry's funeral is Major Calloway (a crisp Trevor Howard), a British military policeman who tells Martins that his erstwhile boon companion was a trafficker in adulterated penicillin, "the worst racketeer who ever made a dirty living in this city."

Filled with alcohol-inspired righteous indignation, and never considering that he might be getting into something considerably out of his depth, Martins is determined to prove the major wrong and find out what really killed Harry, starting with trying to discover who the mysterious third man seen at the site of the accident might be. "Death's at the bottom of everything, leave death to the professionals," the major says, but Martins is in no mood to listen.

Working closely with director of photography Krasker and showing a fondness for disconcerting camera angles, director Reed does exceptionally well conveying the topsy-turvy nature of this world of smiling insincerity, where a man typically speculates on Lime's afterlife state by saying, "He's either in heaven [pointing down] or in hell [pointing up]."

Reed and Greene also combine to create vivid characters who are very much of their time and place, such as the smirking Baron, who, incongruously, walks through a Viennese cafe holding a copy of Martins's *Oklahoma Kid,* or the small boy (Herbert Halbik) living in Lime's apartment building, who starts to resemble a sinister, malignant dwarf.

The Third Man provides superior roles for all its lead actors as well, especially for Orson Welles in a part that influential French critic André Bazin called a milestone in Welles's career. Not that the American actor wasn't fussy: Reed later recalled that Welles initially rebelled against filming in underground Vienna by saying, "Carol, I can't work in a sewer. I come from California!"

Because it is conceded that Welles wrote parts of his own dialogue, including the celebrated speech comparing the relative merits of peaceful Switzerland and Italy under the bloody Borgias, film historians have sometimes argued that much of the credit for this exceptional film belongs to him.

But anyone familiar with the best of Reed's work, tightly drawn, literate, popular items such as *Odd Man Out, Fallen Idol,* and *Outcast of the Islands,* can see how smoothly *The Third Man* fits into that equation. Truly, film has come a long way in fifty years, and too much of it in the wrong direction.

Touch of Evil
1958

Perhaps the most surprising thing about Orson Welles's 1958 *Touch of Evil* is the way it continues to surprise. No amount of repeated viewing can dull the edge of its sinister ambience or soften the visual excitement Welles brought to this quintessentially cinematic film. It's an excitement that's multiplied because, for the first time, we now have a *Touch of Evil* that's closest to Welles's intentions.

Although directors' cuts have become a standard come-on to publicize re-releases, the new 111-minute *Touch of Evil* offers considerably more than unseen scenes. By following the detailed instructions Welles offered in a celebrated 58-page memo he wrote after seeing what Universal had done to his cut, reedit producer Rick Schmidlin and editor Walter Murch have made numerous small changes that result in a clearer, more understandable film.

For the paradox of what the studio did to Welles's version, the reshoots and re-cutting it demanded, is that instead of making the film easier to follow (as was presumably intended), it bollixed things up. Possibly because Welles (who also wrote the script from a pulp novel by Whit Masterson) was ahead of his time in his ideas about crosscutting and use of sound, the director's version actually makes more sense, at least to modern viewers, than the slapdash edition Universal released at the time.

Though they make a considerable difference when added together, most of the modifications Schmidlin and Murch made are too specific to detail. Definitely not in that category, however, is the most visible of the changes: The credits that were once superimposed on the superb three-minute tracking shot, one of the most celebrated openings in American film, have now been banished from the sequence.

That complex shot tracks a bomb, starting from the moment it's placed in a car trunk in Mexico and ending with the resulting explosion, which kills a stripper named Zita as well as Rudy Linnekar, one of the most prominent men in the mythical American border town of Los Robles.

Nearby when the bomb goes off just happens to be crusading Mexican police official Miguel "Mike" Vargas (Charlton Heston), chairman of the Pan American Narcotics Commission, and his brand-new American wife, Susan (Janet Leigh). Since the bomb originated in his country and Vargas is nothing if not conscientious, he immediately involves himself in the investigation.

That doesn't sit too well with the local law-enforcement legend of Los Robles. Touchy about his prerogatives, alternately bullying, whining, and dismissive, Captain Hank Quinlan is as memorable a piece of acting as Welles (who wore padding for the role) ever did; a brilliant and grotesque characterization that commands attention from the first moment to the last.

Quinlan is described in *Touch of Evil*'s shooting script as "a grossly corpulent figure in an overcoat, a huge cigar in the middle of his puffy face," but even that image doesn't do justice to the huge, malignant toad Welles creates on camera. Venality and inner demons have marked Quinlan, and they're especially visible in his face, where tiny, gleaming eyes fight for life amid expanses of corrupt, bloated flesh.

The presence of Vargas and his wife soon draws the interest of crime boss Joe Grandi (a wheedling Akim Tamiroff). Vargas has imprisoned Grandi's brother, and Grandi is soon laying complex plans to embarrass and compromise the Mexico City cop. He has no qualms about involving Vargas's naive young wife in his schemes.

Though their presence is the catalyst for much of the plot, Vargas and his wife are the least compelling people in *Touch of Evil*. We remember, rather, the film's gallery of grotesques, such as the unnerving blind woman who sits prominently in the frame as Vargas tries to have a romantic telephone conversation with his wife.

Other performances, even if they are small, have become close to legendary, such as Mercedes McCambridge as the sinister leader of a drug-using gang, or Dennis Weaver as an unbalanced motel night man who totally loses control at just the mention of the word "bed."

Best of all is Marlene Dietrich, who wore a black wig to play Tanya, the owner of a local dive who delivers nothing but drop-dead lines. "You're a mess, honey," she tells Quinlan early on, and later, when he asks her to read his future in the Tarot cards, she comes back with a blood-freezing "You haven't got any. Your future's all used up."

Photographed by Russell Metty, *Touch of Evil* is one of the standard-bearers for the kind of eye-catching, bravura camera work Welles favored. Expressionistic in the extreme, filled with shadows, angles, and cinematic flourishes, the film raises the standard brooding nightmare ambience of film noir to a level few other pictures have attempted.

Welles's original memo about *Touch of Evil* is in line for book publication, and it's doubtful if a more heartbreaking document has ever come out of Hollywood.

Visible on every page is how much Welles cared about his work, how much he knew about the craft of filmmaking, his passion for detail, and, sensitive to his lack of influence, how polite and well-spoken he could be in making his case.

Though Welles is sadly aware that he's "the very last person whose opinion will likely carry any weight," he can't help but plead for his plan: "Do please—please give it a fair try." They didn't, and the man was never to make a film in Hollywood again. And though it's the expected thing to say, it remains true that *Touch of Evil* shows how much we lost by his absence.

Vertigo
1958

Proof of the fallibility of film critics, should it be needed at this late date, is as close as the reviews that greeted Alfred Hitchcock's *Vertigo* when it opened in 1958.

"Another Hitchcock-and-bull story," sneered *Time* magazine. *The New Yorker* said the director "has never before indulged in such far-fetched nonsense," and the *Los Angeles Times* lamented that the film "bogs down in a maze of details." Partisans, too, were forced to concede that this was minor Hitchcock at best.

Even seven years later, when iconoclastic British critic Michael Wood had the temerity to call *Vertigo* "one of the four or five most profound and beautiful films the cinema has yet given us," he made sure to follow his statement with the acknowledgment that "this is a claim that may surprise, even amuse, the majority of my readers."

That kind of disclaimer is no longer very much in evidence, as *Vertigo* is acknowledged to be, in the words of Hitchcock biographer Donald Spoto, the director's "richest, most obsessive, least compromising film." By 1992, when the British Film Institute did its once-a-decade survey of the world's film critics to compile an all-time ten-best list, *Vertigo*, which hadn't been listed in 1962 or 1972, came in at fourth place, bested only by Orson Welles's *Citizen Kane,* Jean Renoir's *Rules of the Game,* and Yasujiro Ozu's *Tokyo Story*. In the 2002 poll, it came in second, nearly dislodging the sacrosanct *Kane*.

What's going on here? Why has a film dismissed by the keenest minds of 1958 become an icon of modern cinema? Were they crazy, or are we? Or is it simply that *Vertigo* defines the concept of art that is ahead of its time, a motion picture with virtues that resonate much more strongly with contemporary viewers than they could have done in the past?

For nearly twenty years, from 1967 to 1984, that question was difficult to answer, because *Vertigo,* for a variety of reasons, was taken out of theatrical distribution. It returned briefly in 1984, but the print quality was sketchy. In 1996, after two years of work and $1 million, a restored and revitalized print of *Vertigo* became available at last.

Restoration partners Robert A. Harris and James C. Katz, whose credits in this area include *Lawrence of Arabia, Spartacus,* and *My Fair Lady,* did more than bring back the original's vivid colors so beautifully that the print looks like it did the day it premiered. Bernard Herrmann's original monaural score has also been remastered in brilliant DTS digital sound that leaves no doubt about why it's considered one of the pinnacles of modern film music, unsettling and Wagnerian with hints of something evil this way coming.

As a result, *Vertigo* stands revealed as what it probably always was, an audacious, brilliantly twisted movie, infused with touches of genius and of madness. A disturbing meditation on the interconnected nature of love and obsession disguised as a penny dreadful shocker, it's more impressive today than when it debuted because of several interconnected factors.

For one thing, the 1960s New Wave, the rise of independent film, and the proliferation of academic film studies have combined to give considerable cachet to the notion of subjective moviemaking. And though it was made in the heart of the studio system, *Vertigo* is as intensely personal as any entry at Sundance, with some of the biggest stars of the day helping Hitchcock work through the nakedest version of his perennial fascinations with glacial blondes and the ghastly jokes of fate.

Hitchcock was able to get away with this because he worked within the context of a thriller plot. *Vertigo* started out as a novel called *D'entre les Morts* (Between the Dead) by the French team of Pierre Boileau and Thomas Narcejac, the same pair who had written the book on which Henri-Georges Clouzot's *Diabolique* was based. In fact, though Hitchcock didn't find out until his celebrated series of interviews with François Truffaut years later, the new novel had been specifically concocted to get Hitchcock's attention.

Vertigo, the film that resulted, focuses on John "Scottie" Ferguson (James Stewart), a San Francisco–based police detective forced into early retirement by the sudden onset of acrophobia, a fear of heights that brings on intense dizziness, or vertigo.

Reduced to spending his spare time with Midge, a sensible ex-girlfriend (played by Barbara Bel Geddes, later known as Miss Ellie on

Dallas), Scottie is intrigued by a proposition from an old college buddy named Gavin Elster (Tom Helmore), now a wealthy local businessman.

Elster is concerned about his wife, Madeline. Though he knows it sounds farfetched, Elster feels something or someone has taken possession of Madeline, possibly from beyond the grave, and because he fears for his wife's safety and sanity, he wants her followed by someone he knows and trusts.

Scottie, who prides himself on his hardheaded practicality, is dubious at first, but his first glimpse of the blonde and ethereal Madeline, breathtaking in a black evening gown with a teal wrap, changes his mind. One look also tells us what Scottie himself is not ready to admit: He's intoxicated enough to follow this woman anywhere.

Where anywhere turns out to be is one of the many shocks this famously unpredictable plot has in store for us. Yet, difficult though its twists are to anticipate, *Vertigo* is most talked about for the way, in vintage Hitchcock fashion, it gets its strongest effects not out of surprise but from the more satisfying notion of suspense. The idea is to let the audience in on things the characters don't know and exploit our anticipation of how they'll react when they find out.

Madeline is played, in one of her strongest and most persuasive performances, by Kim Novak. Projecting a powerful, otherworldly sensuality, she underlines Truffaut's comment to Hitchcock that "very few American actresses are quite as carnal on screen." It's hard to imagine *Vertigo* without her, yet that's what the director was determined to do.

Hitchcock had initially preferred Vera Miles, who had co-starred in his 1957 *The Wrong Man* with Henry Fonda. But Miles became pregnant, and the director was not amused. "It was her third child," he explained to biographer Spoto, "and I told her that one child was expected, two was sufficient, but that three was really obscene. She didn't care for this sort of comment."

Although he was too peeved at Miles to use her even when shooting ended up starting so late that she became available again, Hitchcock was far from keen on Novak. She was a top box-office draw who had come to the project as part of a deal engineered by Lew Wasserman that had her and co-star Stewart then segue to *Bell, Book and Candle.* For one thing, she was independent-minded and had her own ideas about things like wardrobe, a stance the director had little patience with. "My dear Miss Novak," he is famously said to have replied, "you can wear anything you want, anything—provided it is what the script calls for."

Hitchcock, who could be something of a sadist on the set, is said to have taken his revenge by insisting on multiple retakes (one estimate is twenty-four) of a scene that called for Novak being dunked in a studio tank. Still, the actress apparently didn't hold a grudge, telling a reporter years later: "Hitchcock was dictatorial, but at heart he was a sweet, charming man. He didn't know how to relate to actors as people. He could put you into his plots, but it was a chess game. You were just a piece."

Equally problematic for a long time was how to turn the novel's plot into an acceptable script. Playwright Maxwell Anderson did a first draft with the unpromising title *Darkling I Listen.* Alec Coppel did a second version and ended up sharing screen credit with Samuel Taylor (the screenwriter for *Sabrina*), who came up with the key element that made everyone happy.

Taylor, who never read the original novel, explained in a later interview that he had told Hitchcock that the problem with the Coppel script was "'a matter of finding reality and humanity for these people. You haven't got anybody in this story who is a human being; nobody at all. They're all cutout cardboard figures.' I told him immediately that I would have to invent a character who would bring Scottie into the world, establish for him an ordinary life, make it obvious that he's an ordinary man. So I invented Midge." Stewart, for one, was so delighted that he charged into the director's office and said, "Now we have a movie, now we can go ahead!"

Once Hitchcock began to work, another of the qualities that make him a figure of increasing interest came into play: the amount of craft he brought to the table, rare today because it can only be acquired by directing dozens of pictures over a period of decades. Hitchcock was a master of every detail of the filmmaking process, meticulous enough to have Novak practice some of her movements to a metronome. His solution to simulating Scottie's vertigo, done by having the camera simultaneously zoom in and track out, was the result, he told Truffaut, of fifteen years of thinking about how best to show dizziness on screen.

So strong was Hitchcock's control of the medium that, working with cinematographer Robert Burks, he was able to bend San Francisco to his will, creating a deliciously ghostly metropolis, nearly deserted and not of this world. He also shrewdly combined studio shots with location work, re-creating in carefully measured detail such San Francisco landmarks as Ernie's restaurant and Ranshohoff's department store on L.A. sound stages.

The mission at San Juan Bautista, 90 miles south of San Francisco, is a key *Vertigo* location, but in real life it doesn't have a critical bell tower. So Hitchcock constructed one in the studio and superimposed it on the shot. His pure skill as a director is crucial to making the story plausible. Screenwriter Taylor later said, "I don't believe there's anybody who in purely cinematic terms is Hitchcock's equal."

Finally, more than Hitchcock's ability, what connects most impressively to today's audiences is the strange darkness of *Vertigo*'s themes, its moments of obsessive eroticism, its tipping of the hat to sadism, masochism, fetishism, necrophilia, and more garden-variety neuroses. The film's continued ability to unsettle and disconcert without resorting to graphic visuals underlines how modern and timeless its themes and execution remain.

Interestingly enough for a film that became so celebrated, all of *Vertigo*'s creators had problems with the finished product. Not only had Hitchcock wanted Vera Miles, but he grumbled later that the film had done poorly at the box office because Stewart looked too old. Screenwriter Taylor said he would have preferred Ingrid Bergman for the female lead, and composer Herrmann said: "They never should have made it in San Francisco and not with Jimmy Stewart. I don't think that he would be that wild about any woman. It should have been an actor like Charles Boyer. It should have been left in New Orleans, or in a hot, sultry climate."

Yet despite all this carping, *Vertigo* continues to have the strongest possible effect on audiences. Because Alfred Hitchcock put so much of himself into the film, *Vertigo* plainly demands an equally strong and personal response.

The Wild Bunch
1969

The Wild Bunch never fails to get a reaction out of people, but never was the response to Sam Peckinpah's visceral western drama as strong as it was at the film's initial public showing.

According to *If They Move . . . Kill 'Em!*, David Weddle's authoritative Peckinpah biography that takes its title from a key line of *Wild Bunch* dialogue, that 1969 Kansas City preview audience barely remained coherent. "Thirty people bolted up the aisle and out of the theater, some to vomit in the adjoining alley. . . . 'I want to get the hell out of this place!' someone cried a few rows away. . . . 'Only a madman could call this creation!' one livid patron scribbled furiously on the reaction card." And so on into the night.

Though history does not record whether any reviewers threw up when their turn came, the critical reaction to *The Wild Bunch* was equally passionate. "There is little justification for discussing this ugly, pointless, disgusting film," went one notice, while another advised, "If you want to see *The Wild Bunch*, be sure and take along a barf bag."

But some critics, including *Time*'s Richard Schickel, who called it "a raucous, violent, powerful feat of American filmmaking," spoke up for the defense. And in the intervening years, thanks to encomiums from directors such as Martin Scorsese, who considers Peckinpah "one of the great masters of American cinema," the film has come to be considered a modern classic.

After a few false starts, *The Wild Bunch* is now back in circulation in the form Peckinpah intended it to take. Not only is the soundtrack remixed, but the current version clocks in at the correct 2-hour, 25-minute length. Back as well are 10 lost minutes, victims of two separate cutting sessions that took place not to tone down the violence, as is usually assumed, but because nervous Warner Bros. executives felt the film's length was excessive.

Shot from a script by Walon Green and Peckinpah (from a story by Green and Roy M. Sickner, a stuntman pal of Lee Marvin's, who was originally supposed to star), *The Wild Bunch* is set in 1913 along the Texas-Mexico border. It opens with one of the film's celebrated set pieces, the attempted daylight robbery of a bank by Pike Bishop (William Holden) and his gang.

Lying in wait for Bishop, however, is his old friend Deke Thornton (Robert Ryan), now employed by the local railroad to hunt his ex-partner down. After a bloody shootout that shreds the town, the gang flees, and Thornton and his motley contingent of "egg-sucking, chicken-stealing gutter trash" (including Strother Martin and L.Q. Jones) take up the chase.

By the time the Wild Bunch crosses the border into Mexico, they are only six in number: Bishop; his second-in-command, Dutch Engstrom (Ernest Borgnine); a young Mexican named Angel (Jaime Sanchez); the sullen and psychotic Gorch brothers (Warren Oates and Ben Johnson); and the aged and eccentric Freddy Sykes (a completely unrecognizable Edmond O'Brien).

In Mexico, the gang enters territory controlled by a rapacious warlord named Mapache (the great Mexican director Emilio Fernandez) and his lieutenants (one of whom, Alfonso Arau, went on to direct *Like Water for Chocolate*). Embittered and cynical, Bishop agrees to what he hopes will be one last job, stealing a trainload of American weapons for the general. Meanwhile, led by the implacable Thornton, the bounty hunters continue to haunt his trail.

Filmed on location in Mexico, *The Wild Bunch* had an especially grueling eighty-one-day shoot, with the film's apocalyptic finale taking a full dozen of those days. Twenty-two crew members would be fired before it was over, including the gunsmith, who saw what he thought would be enough blank ammunition for the entire shoot used in a single noisy day. Finally, biographer Weddle notes, "*The Wild Bunch* would use 239 rifles, shotguns, revolvers, and automatics and over 90,000 rounds of blank ammunition—'More than was used in the entire Mexican revolution!' Warner Bros. publicity would later claim."

It was the violence that all the media focused on when *The Wild*

Bunch was released, and seen today, its bloodshed paradoxically makes both less and more of an impression than it did then.

For the troubling fact is that, in an age that roars in throaty approval when Quentin Tarantino graphically splatters brains over an automobile's back seat, the violence depicted in *The Wild Bunch* is not as likely to disturb audiences in the ways it did on its initial release. Perhaps this is progress of a sort, but somehow it doesn't feel that way.

Yet, on another level, the violence in this film continues to astonish because of the extraordinary level of skill with which it was executed. Some of the stunts, such as the slow-motion blowing up of a trestle with five horsemen on it, have never been improved on and have a clarity that makes them especially thrilling to watch today.

And though slow-motion action has become a cliché, its use was pioneered by Peckinpah and editor Louis Lombardo, and no one has ever done it better. According to Weddle, the director "would film the major shootouts with six cameras, all operating at variable frame rates—24 frames per second, 30 frames per second, 60 frames per second, 90 frames per second, 120 frames per second—so that when cut together the action would constantly be shifting from slow to fast to slower still to fast again, giving time within the sequences a strange elastic quality."

All that craftsmanship points out one of the things that is often forgotten, how skilled a filmmaker Peckinpah was, gifted with both natural talent and considerable experience honing it. The film's compositions, worked out with cinematographer Lucien Ballard, are models of wide-screen work, and Peckinpah had the ability to make *The Wild Bunch*'s story unfold on screen as if it were actually taking place, not following a script. In fact, some of film's most haunting moments, notably the final walk of Holden, Borgnine, Oates, and Johnson that is in many ways *The Wild Bunch*'s emotional high point, were improvised by the director on the spot.

Not only does all the fuss about *The Wild Bunch*'s violence feel like a false issue, it also tends to obscure much of what continues to be marvelous about the film, which includes how well Peckinpah worked with actors.

By director Paul Schrader's count (reprinted in *Doing It Right*, a compendium of *Wild Bunch* criticism edited by Michael Blisss), the film's six key cast members had appeared in sixty-six westerns between them. Yet here, far from being tired, the actors give performances that are honest, straightforward, and affecting, with Holden and Ryan doing work that has to be considered among the best of their careers.

Seen today, the greatness of *The Wild Bunch* lies in several related areas. One is the film's at times overlooked emotional content, the mythic end-of-an-era chords it so potently strikes, its old-fashioned belief in the importance of codes of honor allied with its modern willingness to explore ambivalent attitudes toward violence.

What stands out with equal strength is the personal and eccentric vision of the West that *The Wild Bunch* expresses. From its bizarre opening image of red ants overwhelming a scorpion (suggested by Emilio Fernandez) to its emotionally torn and damaged characters, and including even its largely clichéd treatment of both women and Mexicans, this is not a by-the-numbers genre film but a reflection of Peckinpah's own tortured psyche.

It's because *The Wild Bunch*'s emotional content is so strong that the 10 minutes of restored material is critical to the film's impact. As Peckinpah authority Paul Seydor, author of *Peckinpah: The Western Films,* notes, three of the six cuts were of flashbacks that deepen the complexity of key characters.

And another cut, of a fight between Mapache's forces and those of Pancho Villa, contains a charming interaction between Mapache and a small boy that understandably was one of the director's favorites. No wonder Peckinpah was so angry that he exaggerated the damage when he told a reporter that his producer, Phil Feldman, had "let those rotten sons of bitches at Warners chop out 20 minutes so they could hustle more popcorn."

"As long as you provoke a reaction, you've done your job," the director once told his son Mathew. "If they jump to their feet and scream for your head, or give you a standing ovation, either way you've succeeded." In the recent history of American film, no one did that any better than Mr. Sam.

part five

RETROSPECTIVES

Introduction

The writings that follow in this section depart from what has come before by not being reviews in the traditional sense of the word. Still, I couldn't imagine not including these longer pieces. That's how much they mean to me.

For there are moments when, despite the demands of daily reviewing, even the most harried critic will hunger for something more. For a chance to do extended research, to look at a genre or a director in depth, to engage in what could be called voyages of cinematic discovery, and to write about the results at some length.

The essays in this section are united by several things. First, each was written in response to a specific film event, invariably a series being mounted by a theater, museum, or repertory cinema. And whether dealing with movements, such as Yiddish film or pre-code Hollywood, or not-often-screened specific filmmakers, such as the Americans Anthony Mann and Edgar G. Ulmer or the French masters Jacques Becker and Jean-Pierre Melville, they all deal with bodies of work I had heard great things about but had never previously sampled in any meaningful way.

When I think of the times I have valued most as a critic, it is the hour after involving hour I've spent watching the films in these series, immersing myself in little-seen classics, getting to know pictures that had been no more than rumors to me, if that.

Not only is this a necessary antidote to the flavor-of-the-moment detritus that is such a large part of today's entertainment industry, it is also nourishing and sustaining in the way I once thought all of film would be, so much so that I invariably emerge after an all-day encounter with these features fresher than when I went in. I offer these essays as a special invitation to take the same voyages I took, to use DVDs and tapes to explore films you may not know, films that have stood the test of time. They're worth the effort, I promise you that.

Jacques Becker and Robert Bresson

At first glance, the parallels between Jacques Becker and Robert Bresson, two giants of mid-century French filmmaking, are striking. They were born in September, only a year apart, and each completed a baker's dozen features in their careers. Also, both directors were among the few from the older generation who impressed the young firebrands of the French New Wave. "Before us, the only person who tried to see France was Jacques Becker," wrote Jean-Luc Godard, and of the other, Louis Malle said simply, "We all wanted to be Bresson."

There, however, the similarities end. Bresson is justly considered an artist of the most rarefied kind, a saint of cinema whose work is all but worshipped. "Robert Bresson is French cinema," Godard wrote, "as Dostoevsky is the Russian novel and Mozart is German music."

If Bresson, still living and in his nineties, has a style so distinctive it's impossible to mistake his films for anyone else's, Becker has suffered critically because of the opposite problem.

Becker, who died in 1960 when he was only fifty-four, was a master craftsman whose lack of notice outside of France was due in part to a lack of anything completely distinctive in style or subject matter. "There are no theories about Jacques Becker," is how François Truffaut, a major partisan, put it, and critic Philip Kemp, writing in *Film Comment,* admitted that although he felt Becker's films had a distinctive quality, "just what that quality consists of isn't easy to pin down."

Yet those who sample Becker's films will be in for memorable experiences. *Touchez Pas au Grisbi* ("Don't touch the loot" in underworld slang), for instance, was voted the best French crime film of all time in a film critics poll in the magazine *Positif* and inspired a whole series of Gallic noir classics. And then there is *Casque d'Or,* an unforgettable fatalistic romance starring Simone Signoret in her signature role as Marie. It's a film so beloved in France that they even honored it with a stamp.

Although details of Bresson's personal life tend to be opaque and hidden, Becker's bio is wide open. His family and the family of Paul Cézanne were friends, and as a young man he met the son of another painter, filmmaker Jean Renoir. Becker worked as the latter's assistant for seven years in the 1930s (Renoir called him "my brother and my son"), and he had cameos in some of Renoir's films, most memorably as an English prisoner of war who destroys a watch rather than turn it over to the Germans in *La Grande Illusion*.

Casque d'Or, released in 1952, opens in a Renoir fashion in turn-of-the-century Paris, with a boatload of young toughs and their women rowing to a riverside boîte. There, the blonde Marie (the title, translated as *Helmet of Gold,* refers to her hair) meets dark, intense Manda (Serge Reggiani), a former tough himself now gone straight. The yearning looks they exchange pierce the heart, and their ill-starred romance, complicated by crime, jealousy, and the code of the underworld, ends with one of the most memorable reveries in French cinema.

Two years later, Becker came out with *Grisbi*. The film follows a world-weary gangster (it's apparently the only kind they have in France) as he tries to balance the demands of loyalty to his pals with his interest in millions of dollars in stolen gold.

Played with fine sangfroid by French superstar Jean Gabin, *Grisbi* is set in a near-mythical French world of chic cabarets and elaborate wrought-iron elevators. The film also stars a young, raven-haired Jeanne Moreau, whose scenes with Gabin have an unmistakable passing-the-torch quality to them.

Becker's last film, *Le Trou,* released in 1959, is also one of his most interesting. Set in Sante prison in Paris, and with an ex-convict named Jean Keraudy, "the King of Escapes," playing himself in a supporting role, it details an elaborate attempted prison break with the concern for character and attention to detail that were Becker's hallmarks.

If Bresson's severe, magisterial films are less immediately accessible than Becker's, they are equally rewarding—perhaps even more so in the long run. There is a magnificent simplicity to Bresson's work, a measured, unhurried precision, and a justified belief in the mesmerizing power of concentrating the camera with uncompromising fierceness on the most simple objects and actions. As writer-director Paul Schrader, who wrote a book on the director and calls him "the most important spiritual artist living," has said, Bresson's films "seem simple but they're impossible to copy, like a souffle that falls apart" should you try to make it yourself.

Highly recommended are two early Bresson works, *A Man Escaped* (1956) and *Pickpocket* (1959). The latter begins with the director's unnecessary warning that "the style of this film is not that of a thriller." Using scenes of pick-pocketing at a racetrack and on the Paris metro that are dazzling in their simplicity, Bresson explores the compulsion of a young man to steal in a way that is consciously reminiscent of Dostoyevsky's *Crime and Punishment*.

A Man Escaped is based on the real-life exploits of French Resistance hero Andre Devigny, who escaped from the Gestapo's dread Fort Montluc prison in Lyons. Becoming what director Eric Rohmer called "a miracle of objects," *A Man Escaped* focuses intently on how the hero uses simple, everyday utensils, such as a safety pin and a soup spoon, to facilitate his escape. Watching the film recently, Martin Scorsese commented that "it functions like a delicate and perfectly calibrated hand-made machine."

Though the purity of Bresson's style and the importance that his Catholicism plays in his work can make his films sound daunting, rather like taking a dose of cinematic medicine, the reverse is true. The best of Bresson—*Diary of a Country Priest, Pickpocket, A Man Escaped*—leaves you feeling exhilarated and enthralled. As *The New Yorker*'s Anthony Lane noted when writing of the director, "The fact that Susan Sontag wrote an essay entitled 'Spiritual Style in the Films of Robert Bresson' is no reason you shouldn't take a date to see *Pickpocket*." No reason at all.

Frank Borzage

Who knows Frank Borzage?

He made so many films that they resist an accurate count, the best guess being somewhere around 100 in a career that lasted from 1915 to 1959. Once his pictures were among the most popular ever produced, with his name in gigantic letters above the title. He won two best-director Oscars, one of the few directors to do so for both silent and sound films. And now?

In but a few generations, Borzage and his films have become as forgotten as Nineveh and Tyre. Though shelves groan with multiple titles on John Ford, Alfred Hitchcock, and Orson Welles, the best English language treatment of Borzage's work remains a small bilingual film journal published in Italy more than a decade ago. Who can explain it?

This descent into oblivion is even more remarkable because Borzage was not a specialist in some obscure genre. He was, audiences, fellow filmmakers, even critics all agreed, the Rajah of Romance, the best man to tell a love story the screen had ever seen. "He had the most marvelous touch," said Ernest Palmer, one of his cinematographers, "especially when you'd get a boy and girl together."

What resulted, wrote Andrew Sarris, were "privileged moments of extraordinary intimacy and vulnerability." "No director," thundered the distinguished French critic Georges Sadoul, "has shown better than he the intimate warmth of human love in a profoundly united couple."

So why is Borzage, in this age of thriving romance novels and *Soap Opera Digest,* the man nobody knows? The answer is a complex one, starting with the reality that the intensity of feeling Borzage felt in the marrow of his being is so out of favor today that it's best described, to borrow a phrase from another world, as Xtreme Emotion, romance with all the stops pulled out.

Borzage believed in love as a transcendent, transformative feeling, a wrings-you-out sensation so strong it literally laughs at reality, an emotion so powerful it can, if necessary, overcome death. His strength is in showing us moments that go too far and making us cherish him for it. He makes films not to convince the cynical but rather to comfort the believer. If you like to cry at movies, Borzage will make it happen. If you don't believe in Really Big Love, you probably shouldn't even be in the room.

Yet what is singular about Borzage, what no modern director has been able to duplicate, is an almost contradictory quality: the unadorned and overpowering directness he brought to his melodramatic vision. Borzage's scenarios might be excessive, but the episodes within them were conveyed with unusual naturalness and restraint.

Using an innate, almost steely delicacy, Borzage enabled actors who'd never done it before to open themselves up, to speak from the heart, to be emotional in ways they never knew they had in them. "One can only stare with admiration," summed up Herve Dumont, the reigning Borzage scholar, about the director's classic *7th Heaven,* "at the skill with which the director turns this kitsch and improbable tear-jerker into an inspired diadem of purity."

Unfortunately for Borzage's modern reputation, his best, most completely realized work was done in the silent era, a time that truly appreciated emotion and, with its absence of spoken dialogue and reliance on music, knew how to put viewers into the kind of dream state that made them especially receptive to it.

The director's first hit was *Humoresque* (1920). The story of a Jewish violinist striving for love and success (remade with John Garfield and Joan Crawford in 1946) was notable for the intensity of its Lower East Side milieu, and it was named the best picture of the year by the powerful *Photoplay Magazine.*

The aforementioned *7th Heaven* was Borzage's great success, winning him the first best-director Oscar ever awarded as well as statuettes for the screenplay and for 5-foot actress Janet Gaynor, who was catapulted to stardom along with her 6-foot-2 co-star Charles Farrell.

Starting with the unlikely idea of a Parisian sewer worker as a romantic hero, *7th Heaven* capitalized on Gaynor's warmth and presence and Farrell's rough-and-ready masculinity to create a fantasy romance that managed to include realistic World War I trench-warfare sequences and a beyond-words ending that might be the most transcendent of Borzage's entire career. At the box office, it outgrossed every movie released that year except Al Jolson's landmark *The Jazz Singer.*

Taking advantage of the success of the Gaynor/Farrell pairing, Borzage teamed them up again in 1928 for *Street Angel* as a poor Neopolitan girl and the itinerant artist who paints her as the Madonna of his dreams. Though the film's stereotypical notions of gender can be a bit much to take, *Street Angel* lives up to the famous intertitle that starts the film and sums up Borzage's lifetime interest in "human souls made great through love and adversity."

The hardest to see of Borzage's silents is *The River* (1928), a long-lost piece of lyrical romanticism rediscovered in the Fox vaults and painstakingly pieced together by the Cinematheque Suisse with the help of stills and intertitles. It matches Farrell as a nature boy who has been untouched by women with a dark, mysterious *femme du monde* (Mary Duncan filling in for Gaynor, who wanted more money than Fox wanted to pay). "I want to be lonesome," she insists. "I'm sick of men, I never want to see one again." Once again, the melodramatic component is considerable, and once again Borzage insists we take it seriously, and we do.

Man's Castle (1933) is generally thought of as Borzage's best early sound film. It's an early starring vehicle for Spencer Tracy, a Borzage pal and look-alike, as a smug hobo smitten by Loretta Young. But it is no match for the similarly themed and rarely seen *Bad Girl* (1931), a pre-code talkie that won the director his second Oscar and that was also nominated for best picture.

Featuring little-known James Dunn and Sally Ellers, *Bad Girl* has the true-to-life feeling that Borzage, who grew up poor in Salt Lake City as one of fourteen children of Italian immigrants, always valued in his work. An unlikely romance between a man too grouchy to flirt and a woman who's down on men, *Bad Girl* has a surprisingly modern sensibility, a tang of reality that refreshes its serio-comic examination of the problems and uncertainties that go along with being in love.

One of the highlights of Borzage's career was his 1932 version of Ernest Hemingway's *A Farewell to Arms*. Originally released in two versions to cater to those addicted to happy endings—a decision that infuriated the author—*Farewell* now has a close that follows the book, as well as some 12 minutes that were previously censored or removed for other reasons.

The film, nominated for the best-picture Oscar and a winner for its cinematography, stars an impeccable Helen Hayes as an English battlefield nurse and Gary Cooper, looking as genuinely bereft and heartsick as he ever would on screen, as an American ambulance-driving lieutenant in World War I. Hankies are recommended.

Surprising for such a romantic, Borzage was extremely prescient about the threat of Nazism, directing a trio of films set in the Weimar Republic. Two of them, *Three Comrades* and *The Mortal Storm,* starred Margaret Sullavan, the woman who was Borzage's muse in the sound era as Gaynor was in the silent, a performer whose freshness, warmth, and intelligent emotional directness were perfectly suited to his sensibility.

Three Comrades, a sensitive ode to the friendship between a trio of World War I veterans and the consumptive, impoverished aristocrat played by Sullavan, is most remembered today for giving F. Scott Fitzgerald his only (albeit shared) screen credit. Fitzgerald was referring to this film when he wrote his famous letter to Joseph L. Mankiewicz asking, "Oh Joe, can't producers ever be wrong? I'm a good writer, honest. I thought you were going to play fair."

The Mortal Storm, released in 1940, a year before the United States entered the war, was so forthrightly anti-Nazi in its story of a family destroyed by the party that it apparently played a role in convincing Joseph Goebbels to ban American films in Germany. Curiously enough, it was shot during the same year as Ernst Lubitsch's much-loved and very different *The Shop Around the Corner* and used its same empathetic co-stars, Sullavan and James Stewart. *The Mortal Storm* also featured Robert Young, of all people, as a fire-breathing Nazi Party stalwart.

Borzage spent much of the sound era as a journeyman, directing such unrelated projects as the witty, Lubitsch-produced *Desire,* the neo-noir *Moonrise,* even the part-romance, part-disaster film *History Is Made at Night,* where he paired the down-to-earth Jean Arthur with Charles Boyer and made her look as mysterious and romantic as Garbo.

Still, fans of Borzage's work have learned to wait for the inevitable Borzage moments that all his films, however various, inevitably have: those deeply emotional sequences that come out of nowhere to reach up and grab you, those times when love at flood tide sweeps us and everything else out of the way. They may not make a lot of sense, but if you appreciate Frank Borzage, you already know that, in the movies and in life, sense can take you only so far.

Anthony Mann

Even in this auteur-obsessed age, which idolizes directors past all reason, a handful of gifted filmmakers from Hollywood's past have resisted deification. Names such as Joseph H. Lewis, the B-picture virtuoso, or Monta Bell, a master of silent sophistication, are rarely on anyone's lips. But no director's career presents quite the problems, contradictions, or unnerving, disorienting fascination that characterize the work of Anthony Mann.

Mann's career was certainly a prolific one—he made forty features over a span of twenty-five years. He directed some spectacular films noir, completely changed James Stewart's image (remaking the western in the process), and captivated French critics such as Jean-Luc Godard, who liked to call him "Supermann."

But during Mann's lifetime, as one British writer tartly put it, American "critical opinion on his work was broadly unanimous: his films were either ignored or dismissed as negligible." And, notes biographer Jeanine Basinger, his untimely death at age sixty in 1967 meant that "he did not live to participate in the great reevaluation" of Hollywood directors that Andrew Sarris's 1968 *The American Cinema* began. Yet his films demonstrate not only why Mann ought to be better known and admired, but why the respect he deserves has been slow in coming.

In some respects, Mann, born Emil Anton Bundsmann in San Diego's Point Loma neighborhood, is an atypical candidate for auteur status. He worked in a wide variety of genres, finishing his career doing top-heavy historical epics such as *El Cid* and *The Fall of the Roman Empire,* and he was indebted for his success to such supremely talented co-workers as cinematographer John Alton, screenwriters Borden Chase and Philip Yordan, and, of course, Jimmy Stewart, who starred in a remarkable string of seven consecutive Mann pictures.

What has hampered Mann's reputation most, however, is a double-edged time warp caused by the unusual nature of his films. The brooding westerns that are the heart of his work clashed with the wholesome zeitgeist of the 1950s, unnerving people because their bitterness seemed to come out of nowhere. And though today's audiences are quite at home with darkness, they tend to be turned off by the recurring schmaltzy and sentimental elements, such as Stepin Fetchit's clichéd performance in *Bend of the River,* that earlier viewers accepted.

But Mann's greatest works rise above these problems, and to see them is to experience a director with a powerful and disturbing worldview and the means to get it across. Films such as Clint Eastwood's *Unforgiven* owe as much to Mann as to anyone, and as the American Cinematheque's Dennis Bartok points out, American film today looks a lot more like Anthony Mann than John Ford.

If there is an element of poetry in Mann's lack of recognition, it's that his best films invariably focused on fierce loners bent on revenge—often against the people closest to them—in a world where those who stopped to smell the flowers could count on getting knifed in the back. As Mann himself memorably said, his typical hero was "a man who could kill his own brother." And sometimes did.

It's no coincidence that four of the director's key titles (*T-Men, Men in War, The Man from Laramie, Man of the West*) have men in the title. His films are intensely masculine, focusing on complex man-to-man relationships involving questions of honor and betrayal rather than romance.

More than anything, Mann, without many illusions about the nobility of the human spirit, understood the fury of men under pressure. Scenes of dreadful humiliation occur again and again in his films, as do episodes of violence. But, unlike the cartoonish thuggery in vogue today, Mann's violence was no joking matter: Every punch carried a weight that was impossible to avoid.

Mann's best films asked what it meant to do the right thing in a world so venal that no one in it escapes unscathed by corruption. Even Mann's heroes, the figures of rectitude, were often self-centered, conflicted, suspicious of everyone, but most of all frightened of what they knew was inside themselves. If they do the right thing, it's because they have no choice, because they realize, as Gary Cooper's

Link Jones says with palpable disgust in *Man of the West,* that "there's a point where you grow up and become a human being or you rot with that bunch."

Mann's background was in East Coast theater, and he was brought to Hollywood in 1938 by producer David O. Selznick to work as a talent scout and in casting. His chance to direct came in 1942, but it wasn't until his thirteenth picture, *T-Men* in 1947, that Mann got what he called "my first real break towards being able to make films the way I wanted."

T-Men is usually linked with Mann's next film, *Raw Deal* (1948). Although their subject matter is different—*T-Men* is a pseudo-documentary focusing on a composite counterfeiting case cracked by the Treasury Department, and *Raw Deal* tells its story of prison breaks and criminal double-crosses courtesy of a distinctive, emotional voice-over read by co-star Claire Trevor—there is much the two films have in common.

Both are classic noirs, lean and efficient, rife with moral ambivalence and crackling, tough-talking performances from supporting performers such as psychotic crime boss Raymond Burr in *Raw Deal* and leading man Dennis O'Keefe, who stars in both. But truly uniting them is the cinematography of noir's great master, John Alton.

Though he eventually won an Oscar for his work on, of all things, *An American in Paris,* Alton is best known for his spectacular nobudget noir camera work. Even the most casual shots in these films show Alton's unsurpassed gift for light and shadow, and his bravura signature scenes, such as the opening of *T-Men,* and later, a murder set in a steam bath, are astonishing.

Mann brought something of this unnerving, claustrophobic tone with him when he started working on westerns. Unlike the region Hollywood usually presented, Mann's West was a callous, morally unstable world of continual menace, a place dark with pain and chaos that was home to anger, despair, and murderous, even hysterical rages.

The last person you'd expect to see at home in this world was James Stewart, but it was Mann's gift (which Alfred Hitchcock later built on) to see and utilize the potential for almost sadistic rage in an actor whose career at that point, critic Philip Kemp noted, "had been faltering, trapped in a prolonged adolescence."

Mann and Stewart made five westerns together, all of them featuring a Stewart who was especially terrifying to those who remembered his gee-whiz Frank Capra past. If you see enough of these films, you'll forget that other Stewart ever existed.

In the brutal *The Naked Spur,* Stewart played malevolent through and through, while in *Bend of the River* he was eager to reform. And as a stranger bent on avenging a brother in the gripping *The Man from Laramie,* Stewart managed to be both sweet and terrifying. His scenes taking tea with ingenue Cathy O'Donnell reveal a man who had probably been decent in some long-ago, distantly remembered past. But as always in the Mann westerns, Stewart in an instant becomes someone frighteningly eager to kill with his bare hands, a man who could convincingly say, as he moved in for the coup de grace, "I've waited a long time for this and I'm not going to rush it."

Winchester '73 is the crackling film that created the mold for these westerns. In it, Stewart plays for the first time a model of brusque, malevolent implacability, determined to track both the one-of-a-kind rifle the film is named after and bad guys Dutch Henry Brown (Stephen McNally) and Waco Johnny Dean (Dan Duryea) past the ends of the earth if necessary. Mann's direction adds a touch of the sinister to even the most innocent exchanges and leads to a tense climax that Britain's *Time Out* has called "one of the most neurotic shootouts in the history of the western."

That finale, set among dramatic rock formations, highlights an aspect of Mann that is unexpected given his theater background, and that is his exceptional use of real locations. Critic Andrew Sarris credits Mann and his cinematographers with turning out "some of the most brilliant photography of exteriors in the history of American cinema," and his western landscapes, especially, are models of how to use the outdoors not just as scenery but as an equal partner in dramatic development.

Passionate about shooting in the fresh air, Mann told one interviewer that "actors achieve far more truth on location. . . . When an actor has to play it on top of a mountain, by a river or in a forest, you've got the wind, the dust, the snow, the creaking of branches interrupting him, forcing him to give more; he becomes that much more alive."

Though Stewart and Mann worked impeccably together, one of Mann's best westerns, and one of his last, *Man of the West* (1958), starred Gary Cooper. Cooper plays Link Jones, a man so taciturn that sultry dance-hall singer Billie Ellis (Julie London) is half-serious when she asks, "Do you talk?"

Jones is a former outlaw struggling to stay straight whose circumstances force him to confront the leering and sadistic gang he left behind. His main nemesis, and one of Mann's most effective villains, is his uncle, the legendary half-mad bad man Dock Tobin, played with Shakespearean grandeur by Lee J. Cobb. A Lear-like monarch of darkness who rages against an indifferent universe, Dock Tobin roars lines such as "God forgive us, we painted those walls with blood that time." He inspired Jean-Luc Godard to write of the film that "each shot gives the impression that Anthony Mann is reinventing the western."

Besides the westerns, the noirs, and the epics, Mann also tried his hand at more offbeat subjects. Look for a radiant cameo by Ruby Dee in the tightly made *The Tall Target,* starring Dick Powell as a detective determined to stop an 1861 plot to assassinate Abraham Lincoln. And *Reign of Terror,* Mann's Alton-photographed look at the French Revolution, is famous for dialogue such as Robespierre's touchy "Don't call me Max!"

But perhaps the greatest surprise of Mann's career is the impeccably made, implacable 1957 *Men in War.* Set during the Korean War, it stars Robert Ryan as a lieutenant concerned about his men and Aldo Ray as a reckless loner who balances his complete amorality with peerless combat instincts. *Men in War* reduces Mann's themes and concerns to their most potent essence. Bleak and nihilistic as well as realistic and believable, it re-creates a combat situation so unnerving that only the most paranoid have even a fair chance to stay alive. Which pretty much says all you need to know about the unsettling world of Anthony Mann.

Jean-Pierre Melville

If French director Jean-Pierre Melville is known to American audiences at all, it is for his cameo role in Jean-Luc Godard's *Breathless,* playing the literary celebrity interviewed by Jean Seberg at Orly Airport. "What is your greatest ambition?" she asks. His reply: "To become immortal and then to die."

It has been more than two decades since Melville himself died of a heart attack at fifty-five, and like his *Breathless* character, he has achieved immortality—but of a particular kind.

Although domestic moviegoers may not be familiar with his haunting gangster films—fatalistic exercises in a minimalist style that are as enveloping as any drug—Melville is a pivotal modern director. He is often called the father of the French New Wave and credited with considerable influence on such diverse talents as Robert Bresson and John Woo, who says the director "has always been my spiritual idol."

And though Melville's thirteen features are difficult to see, he has increasingly become a secret pleasure to committed moviegoers, the cinematic equivalent of that knockout little restaurant you wish you knew about. Supercool and intrinsically cinematic, Melville's films not only tell wonderful stories but also, by implication, express the director's romantic, existential philosophy about the way life should be lived.

In many ways, the centerpiece of Melville's career is his dazzling *Le Samourai* (1967), an austere poem of crime as precisely cut as a diamond. As British critic Tom Milne wrote in a widely quoted essay, "The impossibility of love, of friendship, of communication, of self-respect, of life itself: All the themes from Melville's work are gathered up in one tight ball in *Le Samourai.*"

If Melville's influence and his lack of celebrity sound mutually exclusive, it should be said that the director seemed to enjoy being contradictory. A meticulous craftsman known for his careful, almost documentary-like re-creation of crimes, he claimed (in Rui Nogueira's excellent book-length interview, *Melville on Melville*): "I am careful never to be realistic. . . . What I do is false. Always." And though on the one hand he was proud to be considered the forerunner of the

New Wave style, on the other he said, "There's no such thing. The Nouvelle Vague was an inexpensive way of making films. That's all."

Melville's central contradiction, which fed all the others, concerned nationality. Though his films are quintessentially French, the director acknowledged that "the fantastic influence that American movies had on me made it impossible for me to make ordinary French films." The director, born Jean-Pierre Grumbach in 1917 and a fanatical film buff from his youth, was so passionate about things American that he changed his name to honor the author of *Moby-Dick* and *Pierre* and never went back.

When World War II ended, Melville (who had fought in the Resistance and made it the subject of his 1969 *L'Armee des Ombres*) wanted to make films himself. But he had no money and was unable to break into the closed French film industry. Undeterred, he decided to take the unusual step of working outside the system. Even more daunting, he decided to adapt a book, *La Silence de la Mer*. The author allowed the filming only if Melville promised to destroy the negative once it was finished if a jury of former Resistance fighters disapproved of it.

Silence is a strange and mesmerizing film, remarkably controlled and polished for a first-time work; it takes place almost entirely in a rural French house lived in by an older man (who tells the story via the film's extensive voice-over) and his young niece.

A German officer is billeted with the pair during the Occupation, but the woman and her uncle refuse to speak to him. Undeterred, the officer, who turns out to be a classical composer who admires France, delivers a series of philosophical monologues about love, war, and the persistence of culture. Gradually, as the film combines images and sounds but avoids conventional dialogue and action, the relations between these three people change in a way that is as dramatic as it is almost imperceptible.

This film—made on location in 1947 with a small crew and no stars (and marking the debut of the great cinematographer Henri Decae, who went on to shoot *The 400 Blows* and *Sundays and Cybele,* as well as much of Melville's work)—was a key inspiration for Godard, François Truffaut, and the rest of the New Wave gang. And since *Silence* predates Bresson's work in this precise, austere style, Melville is justified in claiming, as he did, that "it's Bresson who has always been Melvillian."

It was for the gangster genre that Melville eventually became best known. Seeing these films confirms the notion that Melville, in small ways and large, essentially made the same film over and over again. Once the director found a characteristic he liked, whether it was the big American cars his protagonists drive, the cloud of cigarette smoke they're always enveloped in, or the white editor's gloves they use while committing crimes, he used it repeatedly. In fact, you could almost swear that Melville's costume department had only one trench coat that was reused in film after film.

Yet seeing one Melville film is never enough. Because of the philosophical underpinnings that unite them, devotees insist on seeing them all. Who can resist a world where living by a code is critical but fate decides everything, where everyone has complicity in evil, and where a character comments on his rival on the other side of the law: "He is a danger to society, but he has preserved a sort of purity"? Melville, given to saying things such as "The only way I have found to avoid being betrayed is to live alone," often sounded like a character from one of his films, and his belief in what these people were saying gives them a rare integrity.

Melville's earliest experiment in this genre, *Bob Le Flambeur* (Bob the Gambler), released in 1955, is his first original script and remains one of his best works. The story of a professional gambler (Roger Duchesne) who wants to cap his career by robbing the casino at Deauville, it's a touch lighter in tone than the films that followed, but, drenched in the atmosphere of Montmartre during the wee hours, it offers a romantic view of a Paris that even then was disappearing from view.

Melville next passed the trench coat to Jean-Paul Belmondo, who'd played a priest for him in *Leon Morin, Pretre,* which examines an emotional relationship between a widow and a man of the cloth. Belmondo starred in *Le Doulos* (Doulos the Fingerman), a tale of underworld greed and revenge so crawling with double- and triple-crosses that Belmondo didn't know himself if he was a stoolie until he saw the finished film.

Italian actor Lino Ventura starred in Melville's most commercially successful thriller, *Le Deuxieme Souffle,* but the most permanent owner of the trench coat turned out to be Alain Delon. With his beautiful, blank face and the dead eyes of a killer angel, Delon was the perfect Melville actor. He appeared in three of the director's films, co-starring with the unlikely pair of Richard Crenna and Catherine Deneuve in *Un Flic,* Melville's last work, and sharing the honors with Gian Maria Volonte and Yves Montand in the rarely seen *Le Cercle Rouge,* an icy tale of jewel thievery, betrayal, and revenge.

The one Delon-Melville collaboration everyone remembers, however, is *Le Samourai.* Opening with an alleged quote from the Book of Bushido ("There is no greater solitude than the samurai's unless it be the tiger in the jungle") that Melville claimed to have made up himself, *Le Samourai* introduces Jef Costello, a Parisian hitman less emotional than a clock, whose life starts to unravel after he commits what seems to be the perfect crime.

Le Samourai's plot returns to one of Melville's favorite themes, the links between criminals and those who enforce the law, the intricate mechanics of their parallel operations. An attempt by the police to trap Jef on the Metro, a system he knows as intimately as the Phantom knows the catacombs under the Paris Opera, is one of the film's most bravura sequences.

Never an effusive director, Melville pared his style as far as it could go in *Le Samourai,* muting the colors to the point where he chose the bird that is Jef's only friend because of its black and white plumage and keeping the dialogue to terse exchanges: "Who are you?" "It doesn't matter." "What do you want?" "To kill you." Elegant, dazzling, and totally individual, it will, like all the best of Melville, end up leaving you breathless.

Max Ophuls

When you are dealing with the films of Max Ophuls, superlatives are unavoidable. Not just from critics, such as Andrew Sarris, who said that Ophuls "gave camera movement its finest hours in the history of cinema," but from humbled fellow directors such as Stanley Kubrick, who simply said, "His camera could pass through walls."

Born in Germany, Ophuls ended up making more than twenty films in five countries (France, Italy, Holland, the United States, and his homeland), and someone once wrote that he "could have made a film in Japanese without understanding a word of the language." For though we're used to the razzle-dazzle visuals that have become more standard than not in this MTV world, no one before or since has made the camera dance as sublimely as Ophuls, the acknowledged master of tracking and crane shots.

Co-workers might joke about "Max and his tracks," but to see an Ophuls film, especially one of the four he made in the 1950s (*La Ronde, Le Plaisir, The Earrings of Madame de . . .* , and *Lola Montes*) before he died prematurely in 1957 at the age of fifty-five, is to see something very special. For who could replicate the sensual, caressing nature of Ophuls' camera movements, or the unself-conscious ease with which they are executed? Unlike so many of today's baby auteurs, Ophuls was never showy for the sake of being showy, and his movements (done in collaboration with a variety of cinematographers) feel so natural, so intrinsic, that you're enjoying the shot before you even know it's happening.

Ophuls's masterpiece, at least for me, is the almost unbearably moving and beautiful *Earrings*. An elegant, visually opulent piece of work, it uses Ophuls's ravishing technique and a superb cast to turn the trifling story of the peregrinations of a pair of diamond earrings into an indelible French romance.

Danielle Darrieux stars as the beautiful and pampered Madame de, a countess whose last name we never learn. She is forced to secretly sell a pair of earrings, an expensive wedding present from her philandering husband (Charles Boyer), a prominent general. "We only sell to men because of women," the jeweler tells her. "Discretion is part of our profession."

But in the first of the film's series of betrayals, the jeweler confides in the general, and the earrings begin a journey that takes them first to

Constantinople and then back to Paris, where each change in owner-ship symbolizes the ebb and flow of love from one character to another.

Bringing the jewels back is an Italian diplomat and baron (Vittorio de Sica), a friend of the general. He is introduced to the notoriously fickle countess with the expectation that the two will engage in the usual superficial flirtations of the bored rich.

Instead, the countess and the baron find themselves in danger of committing the ultimate sin in their heartless world: genuinely caring for each other and allowing true feeling to penetrate their luxurious, suffocating lives.

Ophuls's lifelong fascination with camera movement bears excep-tional fruit in this film, especially in its visual centerpiece, a montage of gliding, gilded balls in which the countess and the baron realize they are falling in love, a sequence that has to be one of the most visu-ally sublime ever put on film. "The highest reaches of the actor's art begin, I believe," Ophuls famously said, "at the point where words cease to play a part," and those words are made flesh nowhere more eloquently than here.

Earrings is also noteworthy because it illustrates one of the direc-tor's recurrent themes: his empathy for women in distress owing to the callousness of unscrupulous men. Though his heroines were not timid, but rather strong women capable of taking things into their own hands, heedlessly ill-starred romance was very much the spe-cialty of the house in these films.

These themes spanned his career. A good example from his early works, which are almost unknown in this country, is the 1934 Italian *La Signora di Tutti,* translated as *Everybody's Lady,* the melancholy story of a movie star who is cursed by the ability to drive men wild, coupled with an inability to find someone with whom to share her private life.

In *The Reckless Moment* (1949), one of the most interesting of Ophuls's Hollywood films, the peril is more tangible than usual. Joan Bennett plays a Newport Beach Mother Courage who gets into major trouble protecting her headstrong teenage daughter from an odious gigolo. The film (which was remade as *The Deep End* in 2001) is notable for its subtly drawn characters and psychological acuity and for an almost perfect performance by that consummate film actor, James Mason, as a reluctant blackmailer.

Ophuls's other U.S. high spot is *Letter from an Unknown Woman* (1948). A classic romantic fantasy of the Hollywood-meets-Old-Vienna variety, it stars Joan Fontaine as a woman who spends her entire life paralyzingly in love with a thoughtless concert pianist (Louis Jourdan). She is, in the words of critic Molly Haskell, "a militarist of love."

The power of selfless passion is one of Ophuls's preoccupations—and his uncanny ability to capture this emotion, as much as his remarkable camera movement, inspired rhapsodies of admiration. As critic Philip Lopate wrote, "No other director in the history of movies wrung so much emotional resonance from cinematic technique." We're so used to seeing those qualities go their separate ways that watching them work together is close to inspirational.

Edgar G. Ulmer

It was French critics, always on the alert for American exotica, who first championed Edgar G. Ulmer and his work. Writing in *Cahiers du Cinema* in 1956, Luc Moullet called him *"les plus maudit des cineastes,"* the most cursed of filmmakers. American writers such as Peter Bogdanovich, Andrew Sarris, and Myron Meisel brought the gospel to this country, but Ulmer's work is still unknown to all but the most devoted buffs.

A wizard of low-budget filmmaking, the Austrian-born Ulmer claimed to have turned out 128 cheapie features in a career that lasted from the late 1920s to the mid-1960s. Shooting a film in six days for a $20,000 budget and moving through eighty camera setups a day were business as usual for this man, who cut his teeth as an assistant to two of the legends of the German film world: Max Reinhardt and F.W. Murnau. "Nobody ever made good pictures faster or for less money," says Bogdanovich, who interviewed Ulmer in 1970, two years before he died.

Ulmer spent much of his career with outfits so threadbare that when he began working for PRC, part of Hollywood's Poverty Row group of low-budget studios, it was the equivalent of moving to MGM. Yet if Ulmer couldn't have relished his often primitive working conditions, he did understand that they helped guarantee his artistic freedom. As he told Bogdanovich (in an extensive interview reprinted in *Who the Devil Made It*), "I did not want to be ground up in the Hollywood hash machine."

And he wasn't. Ulmer directed a vast body of provocative films, everything from *Damaged Lives,* a controversial anti-syphilis film sponsored by the American Social Hygiene Society, to the all-black *Moon over Harlem,* well ahead of its time in its naturalistic treatment of people of color but shot largely on short ends of film, which meant reloading the camera every few minutes.

And although he spoke neither language, Ulmer also made significant films in Ukrainian (*Natalka Poltavka, Cossacks in Exile*) and Yiddish (*Green Fields, The Light Ahead*). In fact, he told Bogdanovich that he once made pictures in both languages almost simultaneously on a pristine site in rural New Jersey owned by an open-minded Benedictine monastery.

It wasn't merely how economically Ulmer worked that made him significant—it was how well. The performers were often substandard. The dialogue featured lines such as "You're even more beautiful when you're angry" and "You're like your mother, a wanton." But Ulmer's sense of visual style, his talent for brooding lighting and smooth, elegant camera movements, made it clear—especially in his best work—that he was a gifted director.

One of his finest films, *The Black Cat* (1934), was one of his first in this country, his last for a major studio, and one of his few to star big-name actors. Vividly atmospheric and wonderfully disturbing, it featured Boris Karloff as Satan worshipper Hjalmar Poelzig and Bela Lugosi as his marginally less demented nemesis, Dr. Vitus Werdergast. A gloss on the horrors of World War I, it's one of the jewels of Universal's 1930s horror cycle and retains all its power to unnerve.

Ulmer's masterpiece, however, came a dozen years later, with the astonishing *Detour* (1946), probably the blackest, most doom-laden film noir ever made. In only 70 minutes, it relates the devastating tale of what happens to musician Al (Tom Neal) when he tries to hitch-hike across the country and runs into Vera, a fury incarnate. Ann Savage's sensational performance in that role, combined with the real-life mistakes of Neal, who ended up going to prison for murdering his wife, have made this the noir to end all noirs, what Sarris calls "this most despairing and most claustrophobic of all B pictures."

Ulmer could be as warm and empathetic as he was dark, most noticeably in his two Yiddish films. *Green Fields,* co-directed by the Yiddish Art Theater's Jacob Ben-Ami, is an elegy to the virtues of the simple rural life featuring a young scholar finding "the light of truth" among unsophisticated peasants. Made in five days for just $8,000, it stars Michael Goldstein, Helen Beverly, and a very young Herschel Bernardi.

Ulmer also used Beverly in *The Light Ahead,* in which she and David Opatoshu formed what's been described as the most beautiful couple in the history of Yiddish cinema. Based on Mendele Mocher Seforim's classic short stories and detailing the touching romance between a blind girl and a lame beggar, this is one of the most emotionally satisfying of all Yiddish films.

The other vintage Ulmers display further aspects of the director's multifaceted temperament. The vivid *Ruthless,* which stars Zachary Scott as an unapologetically heartless tycoon, shows Ulmer both remaking *Citizen Kane* and relishing the energy of pure melodrama.

The Man from Planet X, one of several Ulmer science-fiction items, showcases his ability to create arresting visuals on a shoestring. The Planet X spacecraft, its portholes flickering like the eyes of a malevolent Halloween pumpkin, and the blank face of the Planet X man are hard images to get out of your mind.

With a working life permanently assigned to non-prestige items, Ulmer is more appreciated now than he ever was while he was on the job. What one of the characters in *Detour* says applies as well to the career of its creator. "Those guys in Hollywood," the line goes, "don't know the real thing when it's right in front of them."

Chinese Martial Arts Films

When I think of Chinese martial arts films, my mind goes not to a director such as King Hu or a star such as Jackie Chan or Bruce Lee, or even to Ang Lee's breakthrough *Crouching Tiger, Hidden Dragon*, which gave the genre a worldwide presence. I think instead of a waiter whose name I never learned in a hotel restaurant in the Chinese city of Kaifeng, where I spent a few days in the early 1980s.

The waiter did not speak English and, as is often the case in places that deal with foreign tourists, did not seem especially pleased to be taking my order. But when I pointed to a beverage on the bilingual menu, his face broke into a wide smile of instinctive understanding and complicity. For what I'd selected as a kind of unspoken tribute to martial arts cinema was a drink called Shaolin Cola, named after the Chinese monastery that was a legendary repository of secret fighting knowledge.

"Ah, Shaolin," the waiter said, immediately dropping his pad and going into an elaborate comic burlesque of martial arts moves right in the middle of the restaurant, something that made me laugh and him laugh even harder. For the next few days, I ordered Shaolin Cola with every meal, each time eliciting the same moves and the same pleasure at an unexpected shared enthusiasm across a wide lingual and cultural divide.

The recent sale of classic films from the library of Shaw Brothers, the colossus of Hong Kong studios, to Celestial Pictures has made some of the best of Chinese martial arts cinema available in the West for the first time in decades. That provides a chance to do many things, not the least of which is to share the joy of these exhilarating films, which bring visual poetry, acrobatics, and athletic grace to a fighting world. Joining myth, drama, pageantry, ritual, and style to an exuberant physicality of action, they represent pure cinema in an irresistible form.

Seeing these films puts everything from *Crouching Tiger* to Hollywood's favorite martial arts choreographers into cultural and historical perspective. Even John Woo, now a big-budget studio action director of choice, got his start directing this kind of film, and as Hong Kong cinema expert David Chute reminds us, Woo "has often said that the self-sacrificing gangsters in *A Better Tomorrow* and *The Killer* were really wuxia in modern drag."

Wuxia, th,me Chinese name for this kind of film, is usually translated as "knight-errant" or "martial chivalry," a generic catchall phrase pressed into service because, as one authority puts it, it's "the least misleading of several possible translations." It refers to a hero, or paladin—think Richard Boone's Paladin in TV's *Have Gun Will Travel*—who combines exceptional fighting skill with a moral compass that insists that he, or she, always do the right thing.

In fact, it's been one of the characteristics of this world from the very beginning that women are just as likely as men to be possessed of exceptional combat moves. The central delight of these films, whether they feature realistic hand-to-hand kung fu fighting or more magical sword and sorcery duels, is watching individuals with jaw-dropping reflexes and astounding skills holding their own against a dozen attackers or facing off against each other.

Not only do these well-matched adversaries often compliment each other ("You're quite nimble"/"You're not so bad yourself"), they have so much control of their *qi,* or life force, that they've acquired powers on the order of flying and directing energy beams that seem to Western eyes to be next door to supernatural.

These paladins operate in a scruffy, hard-scrabble, anarchic universe that shares characteristics with everything from American westerns to Japanese samurai films of the 1960s, a cross-pollination that led to items such as *The One-Armed Swordsman,* a riff on the celebrated Japanese Zatoichi series.

If you see enough Chinese martial arts films, the genre's conventions start to take on the look of old friends. For instance:

- The protagonists, though they operate in a dusty, godforsaken world, invariably wear spotless, immaculately pressed clothing that looks as if it just came from the dry cleaner.
- If a weaving drunk enters the scene, it's as likely as not that he is

a martial arts master who either drinks as a disguise or because he is disgusted by the pressures engendered by the exercise of his great skill.

- Poisoned darts with names such as "the seven-star needle" are often the villain's weapon of last resort. Antidotes are invariably hard to come by, and sometimes the only intimacy hero and heroine are allowed to share is sucking the poison out of an otherwise fatal wound.

- Those villains, who are often foreign aggressors such as the Manchus or the Mongols or corrupt authority figures such as renegade abbots or degenerate eunuchs, are liable to have greater martial arts skill than the good guys, who have to use morality and strategic thinking to win the day.

The key thing to keep in mind about these wuxia tales is how deeply rooted they are in Chinese history and tradition. Similar heroes have been noted in Chinese literature from time immemorial; as scholar Sam Ho has written, the martial arts hero "is a figure deeply ingrained in the Chinese psyche. He is our Robin Hood, our knight-errant, our ronin samurai and our Westerner, all rolled into one. And he is over 2,000 years old."

Even if you didn't know this, it's virtually impossible to watch these films and not intuit the complexity and longevity of the universe in which they exist. The integrity of Chinese martial arts movies flows directly from the strength of the tradition in which they are rooted. Not surprisingly, the modern versions of the stories that became films were first published early in the twentieth century, when China was at its weakest point and desperate for heroes.

Though silent martial arts films were made in Shanghai as early as 1925, few of them survive because both westernizers and Communists considered them vulgar, anti-progressive crowd-pleasers. One of these, *Swordswoman of Huangjiang* (1930), features a battle with a monster bird that looks suspiciously like a refugee from *Sesame Street*. *Red Knight-Errant* has a heroine who flies through the air as well as a supporting cast that incongruously includes numerous women in abbreviated two-piece bathing costumes.

Also of historical interest is *The Story of Wong Fei-hung* (1949), an early postwar kung fu movie from Hong Kong based on the life of a celebrated herbalist and friend of the common people. The saga proved so popular that nearly 100 sequels followed in this film's wake.

Those interested in John Woo's early career can take a look at his 1979 *Last Hurrah for Chivalry*. More interesting is *Vengeance!*, a 1970 film for which Woo was an assistant director. Directed by Woo's mentor, Zhang Che, it's known for a bravura set piece intercutting an actor's death on stage with his real-life slow-motion murder in a tea house, a scene to which Woo himself paid homage in his later *Hard Boiled*. Incidentally, the film's scenes of a Beijing opera recital show how much that style of performance influenced the martial arts world.

One of the most interesting of the numerous Shaolin-themed films is *Executioners from Shaolin*. Directed by Lau Kar-leung, *Executioners* features a charming wedding-night sequence in which the hero finds out that his "Tiger" technique is no match for his bride's mastery of the "Crane." Trivia collectors will want to know that director Lau is a third-generation disciple of the real-life herbalist and friend of the common people Wong Fei-hung.

The 36th Chamber of Shaolin is also directed by Lau Kar-leung, who had a hand in directing the martial arts sequences in both films. *Chamber* devotes almost a third of its running time to the rigors that an apprentice monk must go through on the way to learning the secrets of Shaolin. Compared to this, Navy SEAL training is something for the Brownies.

King Hu's *A Touch of Zen* is probably the most celebrated and most widely seen of vintage martial arts films, but just as worthy are the director's terrific first two martial ventures, *Come Drink with Me* (1966) and *Dragon Inn* (1967).

Both films showcase the elegance, acrobatic vigor, and heightened sense of wide-screen choreography that King Hu brought to the genre. *Dragon Inn* has a marvelous villain, a eunuch of overwhelming powers; *Come Drink with Me* features the popular Zhang Peipei in a splendid role as a woman warrior who spends the first part of the film pretending to be a man. Those with sharp eyes will recognize Zhang as evil governess Jade Fox in *Crouching Tiger* thirty-five years later, or spot Jackie Chan in a group of young urchins.

Two of Hong Kong's most energetic and entertaining films were directed by Chu Yuan, a filmmaker little known in the West. *Killer Clans* is a marvel of treachery, intrigue, and atmosphere that features hidden chambers, secret weapons, and characters who introduce themselves by asking, "Are you swordsman Li, who shook nine states and killed 108 in a single night?" With martial arts choreography partially by Yuen Cheung-yan, who went on to choreograph *Charlie's Angels,* this 1976 film helped inspire Ang Lee in the making of *Crouching Tiger.*

Wild as *Killer Clans* is, *Intimate Confessions of a Chinese Courtesan* (1972) is crazier still. It's a delirious exercise in controlled hysteria as a newly enslaved prostitute learns both martial arts and sexual skills from the lesbian madam who loves her so much that she first has her caned and then licks the blood from her wounds.

Elaborate costumes share the screen with soft-core sensuality and a parade of dirty old men in this baroque fantasy version of an abused woman's revenge fantasy à la "Ms. 45." Would that waiter in Kaifeng have enjoyed it as much as I did? A cold bottle of Shaolin says the answer is yes.

Pre-Code Hollywood

Think of it as a tawdry and tarnished golden age, a five-year period, unique in Hollywood history, when studios turned out dozens of raffish films made with an exuberant frankness not seen before or since. It's an era that's become known as pre-code Hollywood, and its pleasures are as substantial as they are little seen.

Though they were produced only from 1930 to 1934 and usually lasted barely more than an hour on screen, the films turned out by Warner Bros. and other studios were considered such strong stuff that they led directly to the enforcement of an industry-wide censorship mechanism known as the Production Code that effectively snuffed out any kind of cinematic candor for the next thirty years. In fact, the code did its job so effectively that the existence of these pre-code movies, which cheerfully shattered taboos about sex, violence, and drug use, has been largely unknown except to devotees.

"Pre-Code Hollywood did not adhere to the strict regulations on matters of sex, vice, violence, and moral meaning forced upon the balance of Hollywood cinema," writes Thomas Doherty in his thoughtful history, *Pre-Code Hollywood.* "More unbridled, salacious, subversive, and just plain bizarre than what came afterwards, [these films] look like Hollywood cinema but the moral terrain is so off-kilter they seem imported from a parallel universe."

As befits any self-contained universe, these movies had a distinctive cast of characters. Some performers—such as Ruth Chatterton, Lyle Talbot, and the ever-smooth Warren William, a.k.a. "the king of pre-code"—did their best work in this period and are consequently little known today. Others—Bette Davis, Barbara Stanwyck, Edward G. Robinson, Humphrey Bogart, Clark Gable, and even John Wayne—were just getting started and are visible in fascinating roles as near-beginners.

And although some prominent pre-code directors, such as William Wellman, went on to major careers in later decades, others, such as Mervyn LeRoy, who directed a heroic twenty-six features during the period, and the underappreciated Roy del Ruth, who directed twenty-two, were not quite as successful outside its confines.

Hitting their stride just after the 1927 Al Jolson–starring *The Jazz Singer* thrust an unready and unwilling industry into the sound era, pre-code movies are characterized by the kind of verbal brashness we associate with precocious children, so excited to discover how well they have learned to talk that they refuse to stop.

Epitomized by Lee Tracy, who played rakish newspapermen who could have won Pulitzer Prizes for nonstop chatter in both *Blessed Event* and *Love Is a Racket,* pre-code movies are filled with torrents of snappy repartee. And their clever, sarcastic, and wised-up characters—given to saying things such as "You are the limit," "On the level, sister," and "What's the gag?"—are loaded with verbal attitude, and they don't care who knows it.

What everyone talked about as often as not was sex. In a manner that the Production Code would scrupulously stamp out, people in these films leered, flirted, and ostentatiously lusted after one another in the most carnal way. Married couples had affairs, single folks slept around, and no one was at a loss for a provocative line of chat.

In *Beauty and the Boss,* for instance, a banker chides his secretary with a "Don't squirm, I know you have hips," and she comes back with "When you dictate so fast, I never know where my skirt is." In other films, an innocent "You look familiar" would be answered with an eyebrow-raising "I'd like to be." And if a woman on the prowl could claim, "I'm all alone and going to waste, hanging over your head like a ripe peach," a man in a similar mood might say, "Must it always be the great love? No little detours?"

This kind of glib frankness extended to the visuals as well. In no period of American film was as much screen time given to backless gowns and elaborate, revealing negligees. Women were forever hopping in and out of tubs or changing their clothes, and when Barbara Stanwyck is caught in dishabille by a leering intern in *Night Nurse,* he cracks, "You can't show me a thing, I just came from the delivery room," and she responds with a blasé: "I guess everyone around here's seen more than I've got."

Other areas that the Production Code would make taboo were also fertile ground for pre-code films. Murderers could go scandalously unpunished in these films, heroes could turn bad (as in the Paul Muni–Mervyn LeRoy classic *I Am a Fugitive from a Chain Gang*), homosexuality was acknowledged, albeit in a clichéd way, and drug use was as well. In *Three on a Match,* for instance, Humphrey Bogart makes a hand-to-nose gesture indicating that another character is a woebegone user.

And if these films were not afraid of sex, they weren't timid about melodrama, either. Absurd, preposterous plots gave no one pause, and if things got slow, characters could be counted on to swallow poison, leap out of high windows, or even steal milk to feed starving children.

The Cheat, for instance, a startling remake of the silent Cecil B. De-Mille film, stars a convincing Tallulah Bankhead as a bored and fearless society wife who is also a compulsive gambler. After she loses $10,000 on a whim, she begins a flirtation with an impossibly wealthy and extremely oily seducer who has the habit, picked up from years in the Orient, of branding everything he possesses. Believe me, *Rawhide* was never like this.

But even this film has nothing on *The Story of Temple Drake,* starring Miriam Hopkins. Based on William Faulkner's novel *Sanctuary,* it is perhaps the most notorious of all pre-code films. "What is the function of the Hayes Office," thundered the *New York Daily News,* "if it doesn't keep projects like this off the screen?"

Hopkins plays a flirtatious daughter of the South with a wild streak that won't quit. On a dark and stormy night, she stumbles into a genuinely nightmarish situation and ends up being raped by a hypnotic gangster named Trigger (Jack La Rue). She then goes off with him. This dark, claustrophobic film is thick with menace, desire, compulsion, and despair as it traffics in areas of sexuality rarely explored on film.

Equally unusual is *Blood Money,* first on the list of films banned by the Catholic Church's Legion of Decency. It stars Frances Dee as a society type who is mad about crime and criminals. When someone tells her, "You would have been crazy about Al Capone," her reply is the brisk "You think you're kidding." As a side note, look for the future Dame Judith Anderson in her first screen role.

One of the most durable pre-code scenarios was that of white women driving men wild in the tropics. *Kongo,* based on a play that likely has not been recently revived, has a plot that's almost too lurid to recount. It stars Walter Huston as "King Deadlegs," introduced dragging those lifeless limbs across the floor to his wheelchair. His command of magic makes him the brutal law in his part of Africa, but he lives only to revenge himself on the rival who maimed him by kidnapping the man's convent-bred daughter and sending her to a brothel. Throw in a twitchy doctor addicted to, yes, the dread biyan root, and you're just getting started. When one character says, "The squalor, the humiliation, I can't take it anymore," you'll understand why.

White Woman is another tropical nightmare. It stars Carole Lombarde as a singer run out of town because men leer at her too much, but it is co-star Charles Laughton who owns the picture, body and soul.

Laughton plays Horace Prin, King of the River, the man who marries the singer, and it is a performance so skillfully over the top, such a masterful combination of wildly differing tones, that it's irresistible. Agreeing with that judgment is Laughton biographer Simon Callow, who wrote, "With his giggling and teasing and playacting, Laughton adds many layers of refinement to Prin's unpleasantness. . . . It's an original piece of acting, its preposterousness suggesting a real malevolence, a kind of absurd comic destructiveness which in a more credible setting . . . might have been very striking indeed."

Some pre-code efforts have an especially contemporary feeling. *Employee's Entrance,* directed by Roy del Ruth, stars Warren William in a remarkably abrasive and compelling performance as the heartless manager of a major department store who regularly lives up to his motto, "Smash or be smashed."

Given to ruining lives without a second thought, he casually forces a hungry Loretta Young to trade sex for a job and then tries to alienate her from her husband, Wallace Ford, by turning him into a workaholic. The ensuing battle for Ford's soul has a remarkably modern tone to it.

Even more notorious was the Barbara Stanwyck–starring *Baby Face,* one of the most outrageous of the pre-code films with a tag line of "She had IT and made IT pay." Forced to be a tramp by her father, who runs a speakeasy, Stanwyck decides to take revenge by turning her sexual attractiveness into a weapon to ruin every man in town. And New York is a very big town.

Stanwyck, whose role here prefigures her performance in *Double Indemnity,* can also be seen in *Night Nurse* as a sister of mercy going toe-to-toe with Clark Gable (without his mustache). Also getting a workout in sex-object parts was Bette Davis, cast as a society glamour-puss hooked on the thrill of crime in *Fog over Frisco* and a svelte working girl in *Three on a Match.*

And though she apparently hated the result ("A piece of junk; my shame was only exceeded by my fury"), Davis also had one of the most interesting women's roles of the era as an artist who loves her work and wants to live her own life in *Ex-Lady.* "I don't like the word 'right,'" she informs lover Gene Raymond. "No one has any rights about me but me."

Probably the most eye-opening of the pre-code independent-woman films was *Female*. It starred Ruth Chatterton as a decisive titan of industry who used the handsome men in her company as sexual toys, dismissing them with bonuses when she got bored. When a school chum asks, "Is it old-fashioned to want to be decent?" the unmoved Chatterton merely shrugs.

Though the pre-code films had a strong fantasy content, and liked to feature men in tuxedos and women in fancy gowns, they also tended to reflect the tenor of the times. Gangsters and bootleggers figured prominently, as did speakeasies, where booze was served in teacups, and taxi dance emporiums, where dime-a-dance veterans didn't ask too many questions. In fact, two of the best known of the pre-code films (both directed by William Wellman) unflinchingly reflected the killing desperation spawned by the Great Depression.

The best known of the pair is *Wild Boys of the Road,* starring Frankie Darrow as one of a small army of young hobos abandoned by impoverished parents. Basically good kids, they are overwhelmed by the pervasive joblessness and end up fighting anarchic pitched battles with unfeeling police. "Ain't you afraid?" Darrow asks a young lady riding the rails alone. "Wouldn't do me any good if I was," is her edgy reply.

Even tougher and grittier a film is Wellman's *Heroes for Sale.* It stars sad-eyed silent film hero Richard Barthelmess as a World War I veteran who gets a morphine addiction instead of the medals he deserves and then endures bread lines, labor unrest, and the scrutiny of the sour-faced Red Squad. An impressively honest if far-fetched film, *Heroes for Sale* actively explores the idea that Depression America was close to total collapse.

Especially suited to playing this end-of-the-Jazz-Age despair was Edward G. Robinson, who gave little-known but memorable performances, both in *Two Seconds,* where he plays a steelworker who marries the wrong kind of woman, and in Mervyn LeRoy's forceful *Five Star Final,* where he's a newspaper editor who callously trashes the lives of decent folks.

Though the movie industry's Production Code had nominally taken effect in 1930, it wasn't until 1934, after these films and their brethren had so outraged the Catholic Church that it threatened nationwide boycotts of movies and formed the Legion of Decency, that Hollywood acquiesced and finally put teeth into the document. Almost overnight, *Wild Boys of the Road* gave way to Andy Hardy, and realism began a thirty-year retreat from the screen.

Although in terms of nudity, profanity, and bloodshed, considerably more is allowed on today's screens than the pre-code films could have imagined, the freshness of these movies, their casual and unfettered sophistication, enables them to feel surprisingly more adult than Hollywood's current predilection for clumsy sex and violence. Breezy, inconsequential, and proud of it, these films knew better than to take themselves too seriously, and even seventy years after the fact, it's a pleasure to make their acquaintance.

Yiddish Film

From a language that its speakers often didn't take seriously came a cinema so precarious it had no business existing at all, a beleaguered cinema that barely had the strength to survive its numerous trials. Yet the world of Yiddish film turns out to be paradoxically vibrant and emotional, an endearing mixture of comedy, sentiment, and culture where mothers are venerated, children overfed, and everyone yearns not for riches and celebrity but "a normal life full of joy."

As J. Hoberman, author of the definitive *Bridge of Light: Yiddish Film Between Two Worlds,* points out, Yiddish movies had all the attributes of a national cinema without a nation to call its own. Though now often reduced to the joke-filled language of Las Vegas comics, Yiddish was once the lingua franca of a complex, sophisticated, transnational culture that thrived in prewar Europe and America before disappearing, like Atlantis, almost without a trace. Producer Joe Green, interviewed in the involving documentary *The Yiddish Cinema,* laconically explains: "Six million of my best customers perished."

In that brief window, some 100 Yiddish films were made on a scattershot basis, mostly in the United States, Poland, and Russia, by long-forgotten companies with names such as Sphinx and High Art.

To see these films is to immerse oneself in the *tam,* the taste of a world that is no more, to get just a hint of a destroyed culture that has left these films for us to ponder, weep over, and enjoy.

It was a world that was born of a division between religious and secular points of view, that echoed the stresses between the old civilization of Europe and the new one of America. Whom should you marry, how should you worship, what language should you speak, where should you live? Was it true, as a character in one film says, that it's better to be "a Jew without a beard than a beard without a Jew," or was that just a convenient rationalization?

One of the services these Yiddish films provides is an opportunity to see the physical world the Holocaust destroyed. Given when they were made, the European silents, especially films such as *Laughter Through Tears* and *Jewish Luck* (which featured intertitles by Isaac Babel and cinematography by Sergei Eisenstein's future director of photography, Eduard Tisse, and was the film debut of the celebrated comic actor Solomon Mikhoels), can't help but have a documentary feel.

Because these films were never intended to be shown to anyone who didn't speak the language, they are also the equivalent of the home movies of a culture, enabling us to share intimately in the emotional life of that long-gone audience and to worry, as they did, about questions of love, loss, and marriage.

And because Yiddish is, above all, a passionate, yeasty language, suited to conflict and confrontation, to scolding, pleading, finger-pointing, and haranguing, emotional minimalists seeking *Remains of the Day*-type restraint had best look elsewhere. It's the Yiddish cinema, after all, that gave us the story of a sweatshop girl jilted by the fiancé whom she has put through medical school and who's then struck by the car that is taking him to the synagogue where he will be married to someone else.

Though Yiddish had only fairly recently been established as a literary language when these films were made, an extensive literature existed that provided source material for numerous movie projects. It was a celebrated play by S. Ansky that produced what is generally considered to be the greatest of Yiddish films, *The Dybbuk,* praised by critic Parker Tyler in his *Classics of the Foreign Film* as "one of the most solemn attestations to the mystic powers of the spirit that imagination has ever purveyed to the film reel."

Made in Poland in 1937 in a stylized, Expressionistic manner that has been called "Hasidic Gothic," *The Dybbuk* is haunting and atmospheric, a chilling supernatural romance that functions as a privileged glimpse into the past, to a time when rabbis regularly performed prodigious miracles, when spirits of the dead wandered the Earth, and when tampering with the supernatural inevitably led to the most dire results.

When two disciples of a rabbi tempt fate by betrothing their unborn children, they hardly imagine that one of the fathers will die and the other will forget his vow. So when the poor orphan son Channon and the wealthy daughter Leah (Leon Liebgold and Lili Liliana, who later wed in real life) unknowingly meet and fall in love, Leah already is betrothed to someone else. On her wedding day, the bereft Channon feels he has no choice but to die and enter her body as a dybbuk, a wandering spirit that can find no rest in the other world.

The Yiddish theater produced more than plots, however. Its epicenter, New York's Second Avenue, was the breeding ground for stars who made the transition to films with their extensive international audiences securely in tow. And it had no greater idol than Maurice Schwartz, a towering performer with an ego to match, an actor who justifies his reputation with his appearances in two Yiddish film classics, *Uncle Moses* and *Tevye*.

Released in 1932 and trumpeted as the earliest Yiddish sound film, *Uncle Moses* reveals Schwartz as an actor of effortless presence, with a rich, textured voice and piercing eyes under heavy lids. Playing a flamboyant sweatshop owner who is shocked to find that money can't buy him love, Schwartz delights in his character's multiple contradictions. And to see Uncle Moses cutting his fingernails with an enormous pair of scissors is to watch an actor who knew how to milk the smallest moment as if it were Hamlet's soliloquy.

Tevye, which came out seven years later, was based, as were many Yiddish films, on the work of Sholem Aleichem, in this case the same group of stories that became *Fiddler on the Roof.* This is an older

Schwartz, still commanding but, in keeping with the part of the cele-brated philosophical diaryman, exuding wisdom and resignation. Singing, humming melodies, playing many of his best scenes to his horse, Schwartz's Tevye is, once again, a man torn, this time between his love for his daughter Khave and his agony at her marrying outside the faith to a brawny Ukrainian peasant (played, in a nice reversal, by *The Dybbuk*'s Leon Liebgold).

Molly Picon, "the Sweetheart of Second Avenue," was the Yiddish theater's ultimate ingenue, an irrepressible pixie who had liveliness and spunk to spare. In the silent *East and West* (1923), she was in her prime, lifting weights and practicing boxing as a Yiddish flapper.

By the time Picon made *Yiddle with His Fiddle* in 1936, she was thirty-seven, chronologically a bit old to play the gamin, but you'd never know it by her spitfire performance. Filmed in Poland, *Yiddle* featured Picon as a girl who masquerades as a boy so she can travel and play klezmer music with her father, stumbling into romance and stardom in the process.

With Picon singing her trademark "Oy mame, bin ikh farlibt" (Oh mama, am I in love), *Yiddle* was the first international Yiddish hit and led to a sequel, *Mamele,* where the always-game Picon reprised a role she'd done on stage a decade earlier.

Yiddish film also gave roles to stage luminaries less often remem-bered today. *His Wife's Lover* stars Ludwig Satz, an early sound ver-sion of Jerry Lewis. Satz plays a matinee idol who disguises himself as a rich old man to win a bet about women. "I'm going to the place from which one can never return," he says ominously at a key mo-ment. "I'm going to New Jersey."

American Matchmaker (*Amerikaner Shadkhn*) showcases Leo Fuchs, "the Yiddish Fred Astaire," as a wealthy, tuxedo-wearing Mr. Big in the garment trade who can't seem to find a wife. After his eighth engagement falls through, he decides to learn what makes a good marriage by becoming a matchmaker. The film is fascinating for its glimpse of nouveau-riche New Yorkers trying to assimilate. "They put sleighs on their feet," marvels a Yiddish-speaking butler about skiing lessons. "It's a wonderful America."

At the opposite end of the spectrum from these efforts is what was known as *shund,* or trash, and one can't leave Yiddish film without dealing with these take-no-prisoners schmaltzathons with preposterous plot twists that are exploited for all they're worth. Prime suspects include Moishe Oysher in *Overture to Glory,* a kind of Yiddish *Jazz Singer,* and the stately *Mirele Ephros,* known as "the Jewish Queen Lear," which matches an ambitious daughter-in-law against a regal mother "with the head of a cabinet minister," precisely the kind of woman who shouldn't be trifled with.

Two of the best of these soap operas involve either mothers or mothering behavior. *Letter to Mother,* the highest-grossing Yiddish film of its time, called "arguably the most artful and shameless of Yiddish weepies," tugs at the heartstrings with its story of lost children and found fame in the golden land of America.

Just as emotionally unrelenting is *Two Sisters,* starring Yiddish stage star Jennie Goldstein, an actress who knew how to suffer, in a story that the Center for Jewish Film calls a "Jewish General Hospital." Goldstein plays the oldest of two sisters, forced to be a parent by her mother's death, who sacrifices everything imaginable for her younger sibling. Eyes were not meant to be dry when she sobs, "I gave her my whole life, the best years of my life and just a moment ago, I gave her my soul."

Of all the still-surviving Yiddish films, none is more powerful, or more surprising, than *Long Is the Road* (1948). Shot just after the close of World War II in Landsberg, a camp for displaced persons in Bavaria, this somber drama telescoped the previous decade's experience of European Jews, who went from prosperity to Holocaust to the state of Israel, "our own land."

Because it was made so close to actual events, *Long Is the Road* (considered by the Center for Jewish Film to be "the first feature film to represent the Holocaust from a Jewish perspective") has a rawness and a pain that makes the line between drama and reality especially tenuous. It's also disquieting to realize that once the land of Israel was settled, those who came to live there embraced Hebrew and all but abandoned the language that had served them so grandly for a thousand years, a language that Yiddish film reveals in all its lively and irreplaceable glory.

COUNTRIES

FILMS

NAMES

PUBLICAFFAIRS is a publishing house founded in 1997. It is a tribute to the standards, values, and flair of three persons who have served as mentors to countless reporters, writers, editors, and book people of all kinds, including me.

I. F. STONE, proprietor of *I. F. Stone's Weekly,* combined a commitment to the First Amendment with entrepreneurial zeal and reporting skill and became one of the great independent journalists in American history. At the age of eighty, Izzy published *The Trial of Socrates,* which was a national bestseller. He wrote the book after he taught himself ancient Greek.

BENJAMIN C. BRADLEE was for nearly thirty years the charismatic editorial leader of *The Washington Post.* It was Ben who gave the *Post* the range and courage to pursue such historic issues as Watergate. He supported his reporters with a tenacity that made them fearless, and it is no accident that so many became authors of influential, best-selling books.

ROBERT L. BERNSTEIN, the chief executive of Random House for more than a quarter century, guided one of the nation's premier publishing houses. Bob was personally responsible for many books of political dissent and argument that challenged tyranny around the globe. He is also the founder and was the longtime chair of Human Rights Watch, one of the most respected human rights organizations in the world.

．　　　．　　　．

For fifty years, the banner of Public Affairs Press was carried by its owner, Morris B. Schnapper, who published Gandhi, Nasser, Toynbee, Truman, and about 1,500 other authors. In 1983 Schnapper was described by *The Washington Post* as "a redoubtable gadfly." His legacy will endure in the books to come.

Peter Osnos, *Publisher*